CARDINAL
OF SCOTLAND

CARDINAL
OF SCOTLAND

David Beaton, c. 1494–1546

MARGARET H. B. SANDERSON

Scottish Record Office, Edinburgh

JOHN DONALD PUBLISHERS LTD
EDINBURGH

To Rosalind

ISBN 0 85976 110 X

The publisher acknowledges the financial
assistance of the Scottish Arts Council in the
publication of this volume.

Exclusive distribution in the United States and
Canada by Humanities Press Inc., Atlantic
Highlands, NJ 07716, USA.

Phototypeset by Quorn Selective Repro Ltd.,
Loughborough.
Printed in Great Britain by Bell & Bain Ltd.,
Glasgow.

Preface

This book has been a long time in the making because research, although a prime interest, has perforce been a part-time occupation. I wish to thank Mr Robert N. Smart, Keeper of the Muniments and Manuscripts of the University of St Andrews, for his help in documenting the Cardinal's personnel in the records in his care and, more recently, for reading Chapter 7 in typescript and commenting on references in it to the University. I am also grateful to Professor Ian B. Cowan for help in using the Ross Trust microfilms of Scottish material from the Vatican archives, in the Department of Scottish History in the University of Glasgow, to the Earl of Airlie and the Earl of Dalhousie for permission to make use of documents in their family papers deposited in the Scottish Record Office and to the Earl of Southesk for allowing me, some years ago, to examine charters from Kinnaird castle. My thanks are also due to the Editor of the *Innes Review* and the Scottish Catholic Historical Association for permission to use the substance of my article, 'Kin, Freindis and Servandis', which appeared in Volume XXV of that journal. Quotations from public and legal records and from private archives gifted to the Scottish Record Office are published with the approval of the Keeper of the Records of Scotland, Dr Athol L. Murray. I am grateful to my friend, Miss M. M. Baird, for her help and advice when reading the proofs.

On a technical level, dates are given according to the new style, beginning the year on 1 January which, on the evidence of both English and Scottish documents of the period, is occasionally referred to as New Year's Day, money is in Scots unless otherwise stated, and in quotations from contemporary sources contractions have usually been extended and certain words modernised and punctuation inserted in the interest of clarity. While major sources such as the *Letters and Papers of Henry VIII* have been extensively consulted, references have been confined to the most important documents in order to avoid inflating the quantity of footnotes.

The jacket illustration, from a portrait in the collection of Blairs College, shows David Beaton, Cardinal, Archbishop of St Andrews, Bishop of Mirepoix, Commendator of Arbroath abbey, Legate *a latere* and Chancellor of Scotland, and is reproduced from the 'Scotland's Story Archive', courtesy of the Scottish National Portrait Gallery. The following note, based on research by the late Monsignor David McRoberts, may be of interest.

The Blairs College portrait of the Cardinal, which was brought to Scotland after 1829 by Abbé Macpherson, Rector of the Scots College, Rome, where it had hung from time immemorial, is believed to be a Catholic 'Martyr Portrait' painted after the Cardinal's death but based on an authentic contemporary likeness. It bears the inscription (not shown) along the lower edge of the canvas, 'David Betonius, S.R.E.Card., Archieps. S.Andreae in Scotia ab hostibus fidei barbare trucidatus':

'barbarously murdered by the enemies of the faith'. The belief that it is based on an authentic original is strengthened by its resemblance to the portrait in the collection at Balfour House which has strong claims to be a contemporary painting, although depicting a slightly younger man. The Blairs portrait may have been copied from a later portrait of the Cardinal, perhaps one that hung in his titular church in Rome, S.Stefano Rotondo on the Coelian Hill.

In the course of research and writing the book changed in emphasis, from the study of a great public figure to a contribution to Reformation history in which not only was the Cardinal himself important but also those whose lives were affected by him. It became worthwhile to consider not only what people are known to have done but what they may have thought and how they appear to have reacted to the changes and events of their time, and to investigate the significance of personal contacts and associations. I believe that these emphases are important in the study of Scottish Reformation history and that, together with continuing studies of regional patterns and of the writings of the period, they may help us to gain an all-round appreciation of the subject in all its complexity. More than twenty years ago, in an article on the cultural background to the Scottish Reformation, Dr John Durkan wrote, 'In any age there is nothing more difficult to pin down than a climate of thought, and nothing more necessary to reckon with than this particular intangible; historians who prefer tidiness to grappling with realities have an understandable impatience with what they feel is a flight from footnotes and factuality. The risks are great; it may be necessary to take them'. He may not agree with all my interpretations but it is in tribute to his scholarship, to which all students of the Reformation in Scotland and its contemporary background owe so much, that *Cardinal of Scotland* has been written in the spirit of his advice.

Margaret H. B. Sanderson

Contents

List of Abbreviations

A.A.N.H.S.	Ayrshire Archaeological and Natural History Society
A.D.C.	Acts of the Lords of Council (Acta Dominorum Concilii)
A.D.C.S.	Acts of the Lords of Council and Session (Acta Dominorum Concilii et Sessionis)
A.P.S.	Acts of the Parliaments of Scotland
B.L.	British Library
D.N.B.	Dictionary of National Biography
GD	Gifts and Deposits (private archives in the Scottish Record Office)
H.M.C.	Historic Manuscripts Commission
N.L.S.	National Library of Scotland
P.R.O.	Public Record Office (London)
R.M.S.	Register of the Great Seal (Registrum Magni Sigilli Regum Scottorum)
R.P.C.	Register of the Privy Council
R.S.C.H.S.	Records of the Scottish Church History Society
R.S.S.	Register of the Privy Seal (Registrum Secreti Sigilli Regum Scottorum)
S.B.R.S.	Scottish Burgh Record Society
S.H.R.	Scottish Historical Review
S.H.S.	Scottish History Society
S.R.O.	Scottish Record Office
S.R.S.	Scottish Record Society
S.T.S.	Scottish Text Society
T.A.	Treasurer's Accounts (Accounts of the Lord Treasurer of Scotland)

Prologue

David Beaton has not been forgotten by his countrymen. Just as contemporary records, formal and informal, Scottish and foreign, are full of references to him, so his name occupies more space than those of most of his contemporaries, the King apart, in the indexes to all sorts of books written since his death, from textbooks on general and church history to local histories and even guidebooks to many parts of Scotland, from East Lothian to Angus. Most Scots with a smattering of history have heard of him, although what they have heard will most likely be a few facts about the last months of his life: how he caused George Wishart, the Reformer, to be burnt to death and was himself murdered in revenge a few weeks later, his body slung over his castle's walls to let the citizens of St Andrews and others know that justice had at last caught up with him.

In spite of all this coverage, however, or because of it, there has been no recent attempt to take a critical look at him. It is sometimes more challenging to track the footsteps of an elusive individual than of one who turns up everywhere. It is as if the sheer quantity of source material has been accepted as an assessment in itself; one who has left behind so many traces must surely have played a prominent role, to verify which may seem unnecessary. But a man is not a great statesman simply because he throws his weight around in political circles any more than, in the sixteenth century, he was spiritually minded because he was a prince of the church.

Besides being too well-known the Cardinal has been the victim of typecasting, which may have discouraged historians from taking a second look at him. His only biographer so far, John Herkless, put him in 'the Wolsey and Mazarin class', immediately conjuring up a picture of power and intrigue. This is easy to believe in the case of David Beaton because of the many contemporary comments on his pride and ambition. Yet, all proud men are not alike and they achieve power in different ways. In a sense David Beaton was less self-made than Thomas Wolsey.

Historians are still using a working interpretation of the Scottish Cardinal created largely in the niheteenth and early twentieth centuries, when the writers were mainly ultra-Protestant constitutional historians for whom nothing was so damning as failure, who endorsed Froude's dictum that in the long run it is well with the good and ill with the bad. The generation which produced scholars such as David Hay Fleming was quite happy to transfer the concept of a nation's march towards liberty from constitutional to religious history. For them the Confession of Faith of 1560 was a natural corollary of the Declaration of Arbroath of 1320. They saw the Cardinal, one of the last leaders of the medieval church in Scotland, as the embodiment of an ecclesiastical tyranny that was doomed to destruction. 'He spent himself', John Herkless wrote, 'apart from his purely political interests, in continuing a spiritual system which was inadequate to the wants of the people,

1

and in supporting a Church which, to say nothing worse of it, was an anachronism.'[1] 'He promoted a policy which ran counter to the natural development of the country', wrote Peter Hume Brown.[2]

Today, the work of scholarly philanthropy is rehabilitating great men who have had a bad press. Occasionally there are passing attempts to mitigate the older verdict on the Cardinal by drawing attention to his statesmanship and to his patriotism in resisting the aggressions of Henry VIII of England. It would be a pity, however, if he were to make a kind of gratuitous comeback with no more examination of his case than lay behind the condemnation of earlier historians, without an attempt to answer some questions about him which have not hitherto been raised. Bearing in mind that only for the last two and a half years of his life was he really in control of the political situation, and although his supporters called him a wise man and the papal legate remarked that his talents were wasted on a backwater like Scotland, we are bound to ask how great his statesmanship really was. How far did circumstances play into his hands? Before labelling his enmity to Henry VIII 'patriotism' we must consider how far he was prepared to put Scotland at the disposal of the French King, in whose country he had personal interests. Although he is chiefly remembered as a prince of the church, we may still wish to ask questions about the nature of his churchmanship.

The traditional image of the Cardinal, which emerged in near-contemporary writing and has, with few exceptions, been reinforced ever since, is of an apocalyptic figure, typical and impersonal. There have been lost the outlines of the personality which leaps out of contemporary record. His proverbial vanity and arrogance were innate, given full rein in his ultimately exalted position but not altogether acquired with it. Yet, no man lives through thirty years of ordinary let alone public life without changing and, clearly, the debonair self-confidence of David Beaton's earlier years hardened into aggressiveness as he sought to control the shifting political situation and keep on top of all signs of opposition. His temperament made trouble for him for, like all unreflective activists, he used force as the first rather than last resort. Much of his power over men must have been due to sheer force of personality, an elusive element in written records but a vital one in real-life situations. In spite of long diplomatic experience he was quick-tempered, resorted to bullying when thwarted and got flustered when taken off his guard. His urbanity and open-handedness contrasted with his determination to win and the vindictiveness that was the weakness of his strength. He had a streak of gaiety, brought out in Sir David Lindsay's *Tragedie of the Cardinall*, and of impulsiveness, for all his astuteness, being credited once with dropping a remark that almost provoked a duel. His contemporaries, sensing the essential layman in him, treated him accordingly. While he seems to have known where to lay his hand on a rascal when he wanted one, those who were prepared to work with him included Robert Reid, bishop of Orkney, the best of the prelates on the eve of the Reformation, and the blind scholar of European standing, Robert Wauchope. His friends included the accomplished Lord Seton and Sir Adam Otterburn, advocate and ambassador, who knew him well enough to risk throwing a side-shaft into a letter.

In his lifetime, and since, the Cardinal was and has remained a figurehead, meaning different things to different people. At the time, reaction to him ranged from that of 'those who live under Monsieur D'Albrot [Arbroath] and love him wonderfully'[3] to that of the earl of Angus's servant, Sandy Jardine, who swore that he would cheerfully boil seven years in hell if only he could get the better of him. While the polemicists may have got the Cardinal's priorities wrong — for he was politician first and churchman afterwards — in one respect their assessment still holds good. David Beaton's story is inextricably bound up with that of the late medieval church in Scotland. Whether his attachment to it as a spiritual force was genuine, conventional or nominal, his career depended on its survival as the institution it had become, while the integrity of ecclesiastical authority was vital in the political and social order of the world to which he belonged.

NOTES

1. J. Herkless, *Cardinal Beaton, Priest and Politician*, 320 (Herkless, *Beaton*)

2. P. H. Brown, *History of Scotland* (1911), II, 19

3. *Letters and Papers, Foreign and Domestic, of the reign of Henry VIII*, XII, i, 647 (*L.P. Henry VIII*)

Part I

'Ane yong joly gentyll man'

'Quhen I was ane yong joly gentyll man,
Prencis to serve I sett my hole intent.
First, tyll ascende, at Arbroith I began, —
Ane Abasie of gret ryches and rent;
Off that estait, zit, was I nocht contente:
To get more ryches, Dignitie, and glore,
My hart was set: allace! allace! tharefore.'

Sir David Lindsay, *The Tragedie of the
Cardinall* (Scottish Text Society), lines 50–56

1

Master Davy

When David Beaton was born at the end of the fifteenth century, his home country of Fife was in many ways a dynamic community, lying almost at the centre of the heartland of Scotland which at that time swept crescent-wise from Dunbar to Aberdeen. In an age when travellers turned naturally to the seaways, Fife was linked to the Lothians in the south and Angus in the north by ferries on the Firths of Forth and Tay. It also had what by medieval standards might be called a reasonable network of roads, one of the busiest of which must have been that which passed through David Beaton's home parish of Markinch leading to the King's palace of Falkland, along which travelled courtiers, merchants and messengers and the beggars who haunted the tracks of richer folk.

Fife's southern and eastern coasts were studded with small, thriving trading communities in touch with the commercial life of northern Europe, the royal burghs of Inverkeithing, Kinghorn and Crail and the burghs created for Fife monasteries, Culross, Pittenweem, Burntisland, Kirkcaldy and Newburgh. St Andrews, the archbishop's burgh, and Dysart, in the shadow of Lord Sinclair's castle, were as prosperous as the royal burghs themselves; St Andrews had long been a *de facto* royal burgh, represented in the general council of the King since 1357 and in parliament from 1438, while Dysart, although Lord Sinclair's burgh of barony, was to be taxed as a royal burgh in 1535.[1] Inland lay good grain-growing country which had suffered less than that of the Lothians from the destructive tramp of invading armies. Travellers on the Firth of Forth ferries saw the passing coal boats with their grimy cargoes bound for the Baltic, from the coal heuchs around Pittenweem, Culross* and Dunfermline, and watched the clouds of steam that rose continually from the Culross saltpans.

Apart from the earldom of Rothes and the Lords Sinclair and Lindsay of the Byres, Fife was a country of small landholders many of whom were crown tenants and vassals. Many others were the inhabitants of the church's estates, on the lands of Balmerino, Lindores, Inchcolm, Pittenweem, Culross and Dunfermline abbeys and the archbishop and priory of St Andrews. There were many middling and smallish lairds, such as the Anstruthers of that ilk, the Lundies of Balgonie, the Boswells of Balmuto and the Ramsays of Clatto, all of whom were related to the Beaton family. Some of the church tenants were substantial and influential, like the Learmonths of Dairsie, vassals of the archbishop of St Andrews, and the Melvilles of Raith who held from Dunfermline abbey, but many others were simply tenant farmers whose families often enjoyed considerable continuity of tenure. Newcomers included Sir Andrew Wood, King James IV's sea captain from Leith, whose lease of the lands of Largo was converted to heritable

*Culross was then in the sheriffdom of Perth

6

possession by a crown charter in 1483. A rough equality of resources among the smaller people bred an assertive race of small lairds and freeholders. The lists of central government appointments for the fifteenth and early sixteenth centuries are peppered with Fife names: Sir Thomas Sibbald of Balgonie, Robert Lundie of Balgonie, James Beaton, abbot of Dunfermline, and Sir James Kirkcaldy of Grange as Treasurers, Alexander Nairn of Sandfurd, James Beaton, Sir James Colville of East Wemyss as Directors of Chancery, Lord Lindsay of the Byres as Justiciar, Nairn of Sandfurd and, later, Sir David Lindsay of the Mount as Lord Lyon by no means exhaust the list. About the turn of the century lairds like Scott of Balwearie, a frequent ambassador to England, Wemyss of Wemyss and Wardlaw of Torry were tapping commercial resources by having burghs of barony, with their market privileges, erected on their lands.

Three centres helped to widen the horizons of Fife society — Cupar, St Andrews and Falkland. Crown tenants great and small rubbed shoulders in the sheriff's court at Cupar where they followed the progress of their neighbours' endless court actions, discussed politics, grumbled at taxation and heard proclamations of all kinds including the ordinances of parliament, for the sheriff was a vital link in communication between the King's government and the localities, making official announcements and organising price-fixing, the valuation of land and military call-ups, as well as collecting all rents in money and kind due to the crown from land in the sheriffdom.

St Andrews was not only the ecclesiastical metropolis, with its magnificent cathedral-priory and other churches, but a prosperous burgh of wide streets and busy harbour. Set on a promontory, its boundaries were marked not in military fashion but with the functional features of the burgesses' 'back dykes', the ports (gateways) that controlled the passage of goods to and from the country, the episcopal fortifications and the impressive precinct wall of the ecclesiastical settlement at its eastern end. The city was also a centre of learning, the home of the country's oldest university, housed partly in the original foundation of Bishop Wardlaw, known as the Pedagogy, and partly in Bishop Kennedy's newer college of St Salvator the life of which revolved around its beautiful collegiate church. Here the sons of families from Fife and beyond enjoyed the comparative freedom of undergraduate life, and the more studious of them were put in touch with the scholarship of western Europe. Many lay folk brought their legal business to the ecclesiastical court of the Official of St Andrews and the archbishop's tenants to that of his bailie which met in the burgh tolbooth.

The attraction of the Renaissance court of King James IV, which often visited Falkland, must have been felt locally in many ways. It was stimulating simply to hang around its precincts and often easier to gain the King's ear in its relaxed atmosphere than in more formal Edinburgh. The palace, with its galleries, gardens and surrounding hunting grounds, was a sympathetic setting for the poets and musicians whose work the King patronised. The presence of the royal household brought appointments the way of some Fife families — David Beaton's uncles became keepers of the palace — while continual building operations attracted both skilled craftsmen and hired labour.

It is not surprising that this eminently accessible and outward-looking part of Scotland felt the full effects of developments at the heart of national life or that subjects in more remote regions, when they wished to shrug off the demands of royal authority, quipped about 'the king o' Fife'. This was the environment in which David Beaton grew to manhood and where, as it happened, he was to spend a great proportion of his adult, public life.

Although Beatons are to be found as witnesses of royal charters in the thirteenth century, the earliest certain ancestor of the Cardinal's family, the Beatons who settled in Angus, is Alexander Beaton whose son, Sir Robert, married the heiress of Balfour in Fife and settled there about 1360.[2] Sir Robert's son and grandson both married into families related to the royal house, the Stewarts of Rosyth and the Stewarts of Innermeath, so that in 1421 the Regent Murdoch, duke of Albany, cousin of the then captive James I, could refer to Archibald Beaton of Balfour as 'our dearest kinsman', because of the trickle of royal blood that had come through his mother and grandmother.[3] After that the lairds of Balfour chose wives from the daughters of other lairds, John Beaton, the Cardinal's grandfather, marrying Marjory Boswell of Balmuto and his father, another John, Elizabeth, or Isobel, Monypenny of Pitmilly whose family had held their lands from the priory of St Andrews since at least the thirteenth century.

David Beaton was born, probably about 1494 if we are to believe an allusion of his life-long acquaintance Sir David Lindsay,[4] into a large but closely-knit family. All his life family relationships were to be important to him, and his closest associates during his public years were his own brothers, his cousins, nephew and a handful of men from East Fife whom he had probably known since childhood. In an age when emphasis on blood and marriage relationships did not always prevent bitter family feuds the Beatons appear to have hung together, and it is difficult to find them at loggerheads in the many references to them in national and local records.

It is said that John Beaton and Isobel Monypenny had fourteen children and that David was their fifth son. Nine of his brothers and sisters can be identified with certainty. Of his sisters, Elizabeth, Janet, Margaret and Katherine, the first, being named after her mother, may have been the oldest. At least three brothers were older than him: John, heir to the barony of Balfour, who may have been considerably his senior, Walter, who went to university before him, and James, who married Janet Annand, heiress of Melgund in Angus. A second brother called James, probably David's junior, became laird of Balfarg and father of the last pre-Reformation archbishop of Glasgow. George, who may also have been younger than David, attended university about the same time. Katherine Beaton, a nun at Haddington, has been identified by some family historians as another sister and Thomas Beaton, a chaplain, as a sixth brother.

From what can be gathered about him, David's father, the laird of Balfour, would seem to have lived an unadventurous life. The tower of Balfour in which he reared his large family still stands, much altered, in a curve of the River Leven about two miles south-east of Markinch parish church. It may have been old-fashioned by the end of the fifteenth century, since John's great-grandson extensively rebuilt it. The barony itself was valued at less than £10 of old extent whereas that of the neighbours, the Lundies of Balgonie, with its coal heuchs, was valued at £20. John Beaton, although a regular attender at the sheriff court, rarely took turn on the assize, or jury, as did many of his neighbours.[5] He stayed away from the muster of the royal army at Ayton in 1509, paying afterwards for a remission for having done so,[6] escaped the fate of some of his acquaintances at Flodden in 1513 and, in 1515, when probably middle-aged, he and his brother Archibald asked for exemption from military service, on the not uncommon pretext of overweight.[7] In 1527, however, when his sons were old enough to abet him, he was accused, with James, elder, George and other local men of forcibly interrupting the proceedings of the sheriff court at Cupar. David, by then abbot of Arbroath, bound himself to repay any expenses incurred by their surety, Wardlaw of Torry.[8]

It was left to the laird of Balfour's younger brothers to distinguish themselves in the royal service and to bring home tales of the King's court to their nephews. Of these uncles the most colourful personality was probably Sir David Beaton of Creich who died when his namesake would be about ten years old, the King's 'familiar servant', treasurer of Scotland, chamberlain of Fife and keeper of Falkland palace. During Sir David's last illness King James IV paid the nurse who attended on him and offered fourteen shillings at his 'saule messe' in the chapel royal at Stirling when he died.[9] But it was to his younger uncle, James, that David was to owe the first important advancements in his career, even although their quarrel in later years over their respective shares of the revenues of Arbroath abbey turned out to be a serious exception to harmonious family relations. James completed his first degree at St Andrews university about two years before David was born and went on to take his master's degree. In the last year of Sir David Beaton's life James had been given responsibilities in connection with the royal finances, and on the former's death he slipped into his brother's other posts of chamberlain of Fife and keeper of Falkland palace. By the time his nephew went up to university James Beaton had been precentor of Caithness (more correctly, he had held the living without performing the duties), provost of Bothwell collegiate church, and was by then abbot of Dunfermline, one of the richest abbeys in Scotland, and a candidate for the vacant bishopric of Dunkeld. In March 1508 he was nominated to the pope by King James IV for the bishopric of Galloway but barely a year later was translated to the archbishopric of Glasgow.[10] In the reign of James V his was to be the classic career of an ecclesiastic-cum-statesman during which he showed unrelenting resistance to English attempts to dominate Scottish affairs, a policy fully endorsed in later years by David himself.

If it is true that a man often inherits his dominant characteristics from his mother it may have been from Isobel Monypenny that David Beaton got his forceful temperament. After her death her nephew, Archibald Hay, wrote of her that she had not been the kind of mother to shelter her sons under her wing if this meant depriving them of opportunities for advancement but that she cheerfully let them go to make their way in the world.[11] The allusion betrays something of the ambitious nature which she passed on to the son whom she lived to see reach the heights of ecclesiastical preferment and royal favour. There are glimpses of an affection between them which may have been strengthened by an affinity of temperament. On his mother's side of the family David inherited a tradition of diplomatic service and association with France, important ingredients in his own career. Isobel no doubt told her children tales of her kinsman, Sir William Monypenny, ambassador to Rome, France, Spain and Norway, whom King James IV created Lord Monypenny and to whom the French King granted the lands of Conquersault.[12] It is significant, however, that throughout his life David seems to have had few associations with his maternal relatives whereas he was continually surrounded by and entrusted his business to kinsmen of his father's family. In fact, towards the end of his life the Monypennys associated with his enemies and the laird of Pitmilly was involved in the plot to assassinate him.

Several careers offered themselves to a younger son in a laird's large family, but unless he turned merchant or became a landholder in his own right the problem of finding enough to live on most likely meant taking part in the general scramble for church livings whether he had a vocation for the church or not. A young man with a genuine spiritual calling who wished to engage in the practical exercise of religion might become a monk or a friar, very likely joining the Dominicans, with their emphasis on theological studies, or the Observant Franciscans, the reformed branch of the Grey Friars, or he might teach in the theology faculty of a university. Others who genuinely discharged religious duties ranged from the prebendaries of collegiate churches, privately endowed institutions where residence was sometimes enforced in the terms of the foundation, to the hundreds of chantry priests, attached to private foundations and altars in chapels and parish churches, and the poorly-paid deputising parish clergy, chaplains and curates, many of whom were removable and lived almost on the breadline.

The original provision of revenues for the parish priesthood — that is, the *teinds* and profits from lands attached to the parish church — had been relentlessly undermined over the centuries by the practice of appropriating these revenues to cathedrals, monasteries and collegiate churches until the hunt for 'livings' in these institutions turned the benefice system from being the provision for the parish service into a mass of property units in a market where the buyers exceeded the goods.[13] While the parish services were performed by paid deputies, many of the men who were presented to the livings, the nominal *parsons* and *vicars* who hardly, if ever, saw their parishes, leased their revenues to laymen for an annual payment (*tack-duty*) which was virtually a salary. Out of this salary the benefice-holder paid his deputy, the parish priest. If his benefice was a cathedral canonry, to which the parish had been appropriated, he would also pay the *staller*, or 'vicar-choral', who deputised for him in the cathedral choir so that he spent little more time in the cathedral than he did at the parish kirk. On top of absenteeism came pluralism, the holding of several benefices by one person, so that there were not enough livings to go round. Pluralists were often to be found among those whose salaries were notoriously ill-paid, such as royal officials. The practice of granting abbacies *in commendam*, a device that flourished by the second quarter of the sixteenth century, whereby the head of a religious house need not be a professed monk but the nominee of the crown or of an influential magnate, provided the income of ecclesiastics who were often royal officials or ambassadors and gave some landed families a grip on ecclesiastical revenues long before the Reformation.

The scramble for benefices was a matter not so much of 'job hunting', for the jobs were done by deputies, as of finding enough to live on while pursuing the career of one's choice. This emphasis comes out clearly in contemporary records. Crown officials were sometimes granted pensions until such times as they should be appointed to a benefice of stated annual value when the latter would replace the pension as the official's salary. Besides, it was common for benefice-holders to petition the Pope to be allowed to postpone full ordination, while retaining their benefices. It is not certain, for example, whether Patrick Paniter, King James IV's secretary, was ever in major orders although he held several benefices and the abbacy of Cambuskenneth.[14] It stood to reason that the more public and successful one's career, the greater the financial resources needed to sustain it, the greater the tendency to pluralism, and it need hardly be said that the amount of influence needed to secure a benefice in this competitive market was immense. As Professor Hale puts it, 'The church was coming to resemble a business which, secure from competition, ploughs its profits into directors' salaries and leaves its sales force slack or despairing'. David Beaton's contemporaries from his social background and upwards were groomed for the management class of this great ecclesiastical undertaking. Outwardly scarcely distinguishable from lay colleagues in their chosen careers, very many of them delegated the spiritual and administrative functions associated with their benefices and tended to regard the appointments which they, as they put it, 'purchased' from Rome, as title-deeds to the revenue deriving from their livings.

Nothing is known of David's early education. The nearest schools were the grammar school at Dunfermline, taught during his youth by Robert Henryson, the poet, and his successor, sir John Moffat, and the grammar and song school at St Andrews priory. He may simply have learned his Latin grammar at home or in some neighbouring household. When about fourteen years old he was incorporated as a student at St Andrews university, probably in the autumn of 1508. It is not certain whether he enrolled in the older Pedagogy or in St Salvator's College, some of the students whose names appear before and after his in the incorporations *determined* in the Pedagogy two years later. Among his fellow-students in the closely-knit university community were a handful who were to be associated with him in later life.[15] Incorporated with him were Thomas Annand, with whom he maintained contact while abbot of Arbroath, James Scrymgeour, like Annand from Angus, who became a canon of Lismore, received a pension from the revenues of Arbroath abbey and acted for David Beaton in the papal courts, John Roull, who was later prior of Pittenweem and a frequent witness of David's legal transactions as archbishop of St Andrews, Henry Lumsden from a Fife family and David Guynd (incorporated in 1510), both of whom were later to serve under him as archbishop. Among those who graduated masters of arts in 1509 and continued on the teaching staff was the forceful John Lauder, one day to become David Beaton's chief secretary and one of those closest to him in his public years. Rather different types were Gavin Logie and John Gaw. Logie later became principal of St Leonard's college and, like John Winram, subprior of the priory, was said to have encouraged the students of the college and younger canons to explore reformed ideas. John Gaw was to leave Scotland under threat of prosecution for heresy and to publish his book, *The Richt Way to the Kingdom of Hevine*, in Sweden in 1533.

David may have remained at St Andrews for little more than a year, moving to Glasgow soon after the translation of his uncle to that archbishopric in the winter of 1509. His name appears among those incorporated in that university in 1511 and it is likely that he completed his master's degree sometime during the following year.[16] Possibly, like his uncle James who is said to have graduated bachelor of arts seventh in order of merit, David's academic career was not spectacular. He was typical of the self-confident extrovert who passes examinations by dint of not taking them too seriously. There is no indication that he was bookish or reflective, but he was able, no doubt, to handle the set texts and commentaries of his lecturers in order to pass examinations. The medieval emphasis on public disputation in a student's training would bring out his gift as a natural spokesman and ability to hold the floor. It is tempting to believe that David Lindsay's pen-portrait of him in *The Tragedie of the Cardinall* as a 'yong joly gentyll man', putting his foot firmly on the ladder of ambition, playing cards and throwing money around him,[17] is nearer the truth than the paragon of academic attainment portrayed by his cousin Archibald Hay in the *Panegyric*, over which David, if he ever allowed himself moments of private honesty, must have smiled.[18]

It is Archibald Hay who states that he went to Paris on his uncle's advice to continue his studies before he was sixteen and that he remained there for ten years. He was probably nearer eighteen when he first went abroad and may have been in France for seven or eight years at this time. As the relevant records of Paris university are missing for this period, it is not possible to verify his attendance there.[19] On 16 October 1519, however, he was admitted to the university of Orléans, the great school of civil law.[20] A training in civil or canon law, or both, prepared many clerics for offices in ecclesiastical administration or royal service, and a civil law training was equipping more and more laymen for the career of a professional lawyer. The records of the Scottish *nation* at Orléans went back to the fourteenth century. Bishop William Elphinston of Aberdeen had been a professor of civil law in the 1480s. Mr James Foulis, the son of an Edinburgh skinner, returned from Orléans to become King's advocate and finally clerk register. Mr Thomas Marjoribanks (written 'Mgerbaulx' in the Orléans records), who became clerk register after Foulis, was procurator of the Scottish nation in 1517 and may still have been at the university when David Beaton arrived. It was perhaps here that their continuing friendship began. Walter Beaton, who was procurator in 1514, had preceded his brother to Orléans, while George Beaton, who was procurator in 1520, may have been there about the same time as David himself.

By this time the three Beaton brothers all held canonries of Glasgow cathedral, thanks to their uncle's patronage. David's first preferment is said to have been the canonry of Cambuslang to which was attached the office of sacrist of the cathedral, in the patronage of the earl of Arran, husband of his cousin Janet Beaton of Creich.[21] In 1518–19 a dispute dragged on before the lords of council over the archbishop's attempts to have David presented to the canonry of Kinkell in Aberdeen cathedral.[22] By the time he arrived at Orléans he held the chancellorship of Glasgow, one of the senior dignities of the cathedral. A proxy would have taken his oath to the dean of Glasgow cathedral in presence of the chapter and accepted installation in the cathedral choir in his name and institution, at the hands of the parish priest, in the parsonage of the kirk of Campsie in Dunbartonshire, the revenues of which formed the chancellor's living and were said in the middle of the sixteenth century to be worth over £260 a year.[23]

The effect on David Beaton's outlook of contact with the intellectual life of four universities and of his identification with the church through appointment to high office was probably slight. He is unlikely to have appreciated the tensions within the university of Paris between the schoolmen of the faculties of arts and theology and the modern textual critics and disciples of Erasmus, whose Greek translation of the new testament was published in Paris in 1516. Yet he must have been aware of the possible effects on the ecclesiastical structure of the shock sustained in 1517 with the first protest of Martin Luther. With the intellectual conservatism which so often characterises men of action he probably endorsed the reactionary attitude of the Paris doctors and the *parlement* in those years when the foundations of accepted religious belief and ecclesiastical authority were shaken. Whatever churchmanship he had at this stage would be coloured by that of his uncle in whose household he may have lived at Glasgow, of whom John Knox later commented that he 'was more careful for the world than he was to preach Christ, or yet to advance any religion but for the fashion only ... '[24] When the effect of Luther's revolt did reach Scotland, David Beaton was prepared to expend energy in defending the church's outer defences but was little inclined to lessen the impact of heretical attack by initiating substantial reform from within.

His late teens and early twenties were to be years of political apprenticeship. He was entirely at home in the world of power politics and diplomacy at the court of Francis I in the teeming, cosmopolitan city of Paris where, so his cousin Archibald Hay remarked, he might easily have been taken for a Frenchman. These were the years when the pattern of his career was set, his abilities channelled into the political field and the scale of his ambitions and style of living acquired, although he must have found it difficult to live extravagantly on the revenues of the chancellorship of Glasgow. As a young man he no doubt admired the autocratic, extravagant French monarch, Francis I, and his residence at the French court must have fulfilled his love of grandeur. Acquaintance with other rising clerical careerists around the royal court would make him aware of the need to build oneself into the secular, political system in order to survive, into royal service above all, since the independence of the French church had long been vitiated and the majority of her prelates were crown nominees, while ecclesiastical revenues were constantly subject to papally-sanctioned royal taxations, *tenths,* which became a regular feature of crown revenue. If at this time David Beaton contemplated a career abroad he must have learned that success did not come easily. Above all, these years in France gave to his political experience a European dimension lacking in that of many of his countrymen. They also taught him how to make the most of those elements in the diplomatic situation which gave his own small, remote home-country a part to play in international politics.

He undertook his first diplomatic responsibilities at a time when the affairs of Scotland were vitally affected by events in Europe and the Franco-Scottish alliance was under strain.[25] The death of James IV at Flodden in September 1513 left his English widow, Margaret Tudor, guardian of their infant son, James V, and nominal head of the Scottish government. The situation was, to say the least, something of an embarrassment since the Scots, far from regarding Flodden as the end of the world, were planning further military activity for the spring of 1514. An alternative to Margaret as head of state was found in a proposal to call from France John, duke of Albany, the French-born cousin of the late King and heir presumptive to the throne. This scheme, put forward at a general council meeting in November 1513, was supported by James Beaton, archbishop of Glasgow, and by James, first earl of Arran, next in line to the throne after Albany, who might have been expected to oppose it. It was hoped that a governor backed by French money and troops would help to strengthen the war-arm against England. In the autumn of 1514 the Queen Mother remarried, taking as her husband the young earl of Angus, thus forfeiting her position in the Scottish government in terms of the late King's will. This might have been expected to lessen English initiative in Scottish politics, leaving the way open for the acceptance of Albany as governor, backed by the French. The coming of Albany was delayed, however, by a change in the attitude of the French King, Louis XII, who, although he had secured a Scottish promise to renew the Franco-Scottish alliance, was now moving towards a truce with Henry VIII, and, in the month in which Margaret Tudor married Angus, a treaty was made between France and England by which Louis married Henry's younger sister, Mary. Scotland was now out of play in the political triangle. Besides, when Albany did eventually arrive in 1515 he brought the French King's request not to pursue the war with England and he had no French army or money with him.

However, he was warmly received, and for about two years he tried to work with the various Scottish factions. There was a certain amount of opposition, headed by Lord Home whose father had led the revolt against James III. Home was executed and Margaret Tudor and her husband were banished over the border, Albany keeping custody of the King. Eventually the new Governor tried to persuade the French government into promising support for a Scottish offensive against England, and in order to do so he returned to France in 1517 where he managed to conclude the treaty of Rouen by which France and Scotland reverted to the traditional position of mutual defence against attack from England. The treaty also included a tentative proposal for a marriage between the King of Scots and a daughter of the French King, now Francis I, a proposal which was to dominate Franco-Scottish diplomatic relations for the next twenty years.

The provisions of the treaty of Rouen were little more than parchment promises, however. The French King detained Albany in France for four years, largely at the request of Henry VIII who also managed to stall ratification of the treaty. In the Scotland which the Governor left behind him strife broke out between parties who were divided over the traditional reliance on France on the one hand and an increasing willingness to co-operate with England on the other. The council of regency which Albany had left in charge was divided between these two parties, consisting as it did of the two archbishops (James Beaton of Glasgow being chancellor) and the earls of Arran, Argyll, Huntly and Angus, the last-named pardoned and back in Scotland with his wife who had promised to be 'a good Scotswoman'. Open hostilities included the murder by the Homes of de la Bastie, the Frenchman whom Albany had appointed president of the council of regency, and the fracas known as 'Cleanse the Causeway' when the earl of Arran and the Hamiltons were chased out of Edinburgh by the Douglases led by the irresponsible Angus who had gained control of the capital. In the midst of this incident Archbishop James Beaton had to take refuge in the Black Friars' kirk, where at one point he had the rochet torn from his back and was only saved from further injury by the intervention of Gavin Douglas, the poet-bishop of Dunkeld, who had referred to his nephew, Angus, as 'a witless young fool'.

Albany came back to Scotland in 1521 as the result of another shift in international politics, as Henry VIII and the emperor Charles V agreed to unite against France. Even the expensive diplomatic masquerade of 'the Field of the Cloth of Gold', when Henry and Francis met, could not prevent the deterioration of their relations, and the French King increasingly felt the need of Scotland as the old threat at Henry's back. On his return to Scotland, however, Albany found many Scots reluctant to attack England at the French King's bidding without concrete proof of the latter's support in the form of men and money. As a result Albany crossed to France in 1522 and returned the following year with a considerable force as well as money and supplies. Even then it was clear that not all the Scottish lords were in favour of continuing the English war and some of them refused to cross the border. In disgust and frustration the Governor left Scotland for good in May 1524.

It was during the Albany experiment that David Beaton first appeared on the diplomatic scene when he returned with the Governor to Scotland in November 1521 and is said to have been presented by him to the King. Albany had taken notice of him while in Paris both on account of his own abilities and in return for his uncle's consistent support of the duke's governorship. While at home David was sent on diplomatic business to England in 1522, carrying letters of credence addressed by his uncle to Cardinal Wolsey. He was also chosen to attempt a reconciliation between the Governor and the Homes but without success.

During the summer of 1523 he was with his uncle at Dunfermline. They had much business to discuss at this time.[26] In the first place, James Beaton's translation from the archbishopric of Glasgow to that of St Andrews in 1521 became effective in June 1523, and the most urgent matter was to arrange for the archbishop's resignation of the abbacy of Arbroath in the papal court, under conditions agreed between them. Secondly, the French party thought it advisable at that point to press Francis I into clarifying the prospects of a French marriage for James V and also to send an account of Scottish affairs to France as Albany was having serious difficulty with the opposition party over his unsuccessful campaigns across the English border. David Beaton appeared to be the most suitable person to send as ambassador. Thirdly, the archbishop contemplated sending him to Rome to raise the troublesome question of the exemption of the archbishopric of Glasgow from the jurisdiction of the primatial see of St Andrews, something which as archbishop of Glasgow James Beaton had jealousy guarded but which, as the new archbishop of St Andrews, he was equally anxious to have defined and if possible limited.[27]

By the winter of 1523 plans were in the making for David's journey to the continent. On 29 November the earl of Surrey informed Wolsey of his forthcoming mission to France to negotiate a royal marriage, calling him the new abbot of Arbroath;[28] although not formally nominated by Albany to the pope until the following April,[29] his 'succession' to the abbey was no doubt long expected. In December letters were sent ahead of him to the pope and cardinals in the name of the King and from the archbishop himself, the latter explaining to the Cardinal of St Eusebius that he had thought it best to send his nephew to Rome on the business of Arbroath since it concerned him personally and saying that as far as the affairs of the realm were concerned, the Governor in full council had made David 'orator' to the pope and consistory.[30] In the official letter to the pope himself, Clement VII, David is designated *protonotary,* suggesting that he had already conducted business at the papal court.[31]

His instructions for his embassy to France, dated 18 January 1524,[32] made clear that he was sent to act in a subordinate capacity to Albany, the acting head of state, whom he was to accompany to France and on whose behalf he would undertake the actual negotiations. It would have been unusual, in the early stages of negotiating such an important matter as a marriage alliance, for an ambassador to be given power to reach final conclusions without reference to his principal. He was instructed to voice the Scottish hope that, on his return, Albany would take with him military assistance 'for the defence of the realm' of Scotland. Most important of all, he was to press for more definite provisions in the matter of the royal marriage than had been included in the treaty of Rouen, requesting that the bride be named, the articles of a marriage treaty be drawn up and the amount of the dowry stated, 'he doand the hale be advis of my lord duc of Albanye', who reserved the right to conclude any acceptable proposals that might be arrived at.

The council awarded David £1,250 Scots (2,500 francs) for his expenses. It was customary for governments to meet the initial expenditure of an embassy, the embarkation and travelling, and thereafter for the receiving government to bear the expense of the ambassador and his suite, although some home governments also paid their representatives a daily allowance. In practice, however, many diplomats met their expenses out of their own pockets and had to recover them from an unwilling treasury on their return, which explains why so many nobles and prelates were chosen for the job. Albany's departure was delayed well into the spring so that David's commission had to be renewed in May 1524, by which time the financial embarrassment of Albany's government resulted in a decision to split the burden of David's expenses between the Governor, who agreed to pay the cost of the resignation of Arbroath in the papal court, and the archbishop of St Andrews, who undertook to meet his nephew's initial outlay by advancing him £1,000 which the treasurer and comptroller were to refund from 'the rediest money that thai have or can gett'.[33] While David was abroad, his uncle wrote to him explaining that he was no longer able to meet his obligation for diplomatic expenses, which implies that either David was receiving these in instalments or had had to start without them. He travelled as a member of Albany's suite and seems to have been given only one clerk and one herald of his own, a somewhat parsimonious equipage.

His provision to the abbacy of Arbroath is dated 26 June 1524, altered to a *commendam* on 17 August, which was to last for two years, after which he was to hold it *in titulum* (as a proper abbot), and on 25 September he paid for the rochet of the monastery.[34] By mid-September Francis I, having heard the Scottish representations through David, had his replies ready, the latter being the bearer of the letter which the French king wrote to James V on 15 September.[35]

On the same day James Scrymgeour, David's one-time fellow-student at St Andrews university, wrote to him in some agitation telling him of the political revolution that had taken place in Scotland during the summer. Albany's departure had been the signal for a *coup* by the English party, who 'erected' the king, formally bringing the Albany government to an end, the Queen Mother now being associated with the earl of Arran in the government. Worst of all, the archbishop of St Andrews, who had refused to recognise the new régime, had had the office of chancellor and the great seal taken from him and was himself put into custody. He had formally demitted office on 1 August 1524 and his nephew, John Beaton of Creich, was deprived of his offices of steward and chamberlain of Fife on the 24th of that month. Scrymgeour urged David to use his influence at Paris and Rome for his uncle's release. He never received the letter, which was intercepted by English agents, but he would hear about the events it had described from Albany himself who heard the news at the end of August. Albany was formally deposed by the new Scottish régime on 14 November. Four days later ambassadors were sent to England to negotiate a marriage there for the king. The archbishop of St Andrews, by then released from Edinburgh castle, was present at that session of parliament but, although he must have realised that a revival of Albany's governorship was remote, he never wavered in his conviction that Scotland must adhere to the French alliance.

The new government was far from stable. No amount of effort on the part of Margaret Tudor, even though backed by her brother, Henry VIII, could wean the archbishop of St Andrews away from his adherence to France, so that Henry came to regard him as he was later to regard his nephew as the chief obstacle to his interests in Scotland. Arran's usefulness to the new government was qualified by the fact that he was the archbishop's nephew by marriage and might be influenced by him. Early in November 1524, therefore, Henry sent back to Scotland the earl of Angus whom he was told would be worth more to him than five earls of Arran.

Angus became the mainstay of the English party in Scotland, although the fact that by now he and his wife were hopelessly estranged helped to unsettle the new political situation. Angus's aim, which he achieved in less than three years, was to put himself at the head of the administration and in charge of the King.

When David Beaton slipped home from France at Christmas 1524 he was accompanied by Albany's secretary, treasurer and comptroller.[36] Anxious to make immediate contact with his uncle, he landed not at Leith but at Dunbar where the castle was still held for Albany. His arrival was noted by an English ambassador in Edinburgh, Magnus, who informed Wolsey on 22 December that two of Albany's galleys had put into Dunbar harbour with 'Mr Davy Betoun' and Albany's servants. He further noted that although he had been the King of Scots' ambassador to France, the archbishop's nephew had gone straight to his uncle at St Andrews and not to court. He and the Frenchmen spent Christmas with the archbishop. When asked what it all meant, James Beaton replied plausibly that he had known nothing of their coming until they hammered at the gate while he was at dinner.[37] By early January, however, the English ambassador had managed to get hold of a copy of Francis I's instructions to David Beaton which he forwarded to Wolsey with a covering letter: 'whereby the whole return of the said Mr Davy's business in France doth appear, unless he hath brought any other privy messages to any of the lords as yet not known or perceived.[38] In fact, David had brought home money provided by the French government at Albany's request, which was to be paid out as pensions among the Scottish lords to fortify their allegiance to France. In the following spring, however, the French government was asking what had become of it.[39] David did eventually make his way to court where he reported that Francis was willing to offer his daughter as a wife for James, but that the Scots must not count too much on his military support against Henry VIII at this point as he had other commitments which needed all his armed resources. In February 1525 the French King's campaign against the Emperor, Charles V, ended in the former's crushing defeat at Pavia and his own imprisonment in Spain.

The last phase of James V's minority, when Franco-Scottish negotiations were at a standstill and the King was under the control of the ascendant Angus and his Douglases, whom he grew to hate more and more each day, was a period of eclipse for the Beatons. The archbishop was still the key man of the Francophile party and the chief target of Angus's resentment. Communications were still maintained with Albany who continued to act as Scottish agent at the French court. Since diplomatic activity had diminished, David Beaton did not go abroad again until 1533, by which time James V was in effective control of his own affairs and was pressing once more for a conclusion of the French marriage arrangements.

David had had his first active experience of international politics — the power game played by England and France, Emperor and Pope. Attachment to the household of Albany strengthened his Francophile outlook which even at its most political was never without a personal element. But his later ability to reconcile rival parties, however temporarily, among the Scottish leaders may have been due more to sheer force of personality than to a genuine belief in a policy of appeasement such as he had had opportunity to observe in Albany, who seems to have had none of David's vindictiveness. Events at home bred in him a hatred of the Douglases, which matched that of James V himself, on account of Angus's potential as a channel of English influence. His years at home, in the 1520s and early 1530s, were to be spent partly in laying the basis of participation in the central government. Above all, he was now abbot of Arbroath, which meant keeping his hand on the running of extensive estates which were to be the main source of his livelihood and prestige for the next fifteen years. It was as 'Monsieur d'Albrot' that he was known when he next went to France.

NOTES

1. G. S. Pryde, *The Burghs of Scotland*, 32, 31
2. J. T. Clark, *MacFarlane's Genealogical Collections* (S.H.S.), I, 1–35
3. *Ibid*.
4. Sir David Lindsay, *The Tragedie of the Cardinall* (S.T.S.), 'semand ane man of two and fiftie yeir'. (*The Tragedie*)
5. W. C. Dickinson, *The Sheriff Court Book of Fife* (S.H.S.), *passim*
6. *RSS*, I, 1961
7. Manuscript minute book of Fife sheriff court (S.R.O.), SC20/2/1, fo 47v
8. Justiciary court minute book (S.R.O.), JC1/3, 8 October 1527
9. *Accounts of the Lord High Treasurer of Scotland*, I, 268 (*T.A.*)
10. D. E. R. Watt, *Fasti Ecclesiae Scoticanae Medii Aevi ad annum 1638* (S.R.S.), 149 (*Fasti*)
11. A. Hay, *Ad D. Davidem Betoun . . . Gratulatorius Panegyricus* (N.L.S.), 1540, fo xiii (*Panegyricus*)
12. *The Scots Peerage*, VI, 276
13. For a discussion of the subjects of appropriation and the benefice system see I. B. Cowan, *The Parishes of Medieval Scotland* (S.R.S.), Introduction, and I. B. Cowan, 'Patronage, Provision and Reservation: Pre-Reformation Appointments to Scottish Benefices', in I. B. Cowan and D. Shaw, eds., *The Renaissance and Reformation in Scotland, Essays in honour of Gordon Donaldson*, 75–92 (Cowan, 'Patronage, Provision and Reservation')
14. M. Mahoney, 'The Scottish Hierarchy, 1513–1565', in D. McRoberts, ed., *Essays on the Scottish Reformation, 1513–1625*, 56 (hereafter *Essays*) (Mahoney, 'The Scottish Hierarchy')
15. J. M. Anderson, ed., *Early Records of the University of St Andrews* (S.H.S.), 202–4 (*Early Records*); A. I. Dunlop, ed., *Acta Facultatis Artium Universitatis Sanctiandree* (S.H.S.), 293 (Dunlop, *Acta*)
16. *Munimenta Universitatis Glasguensis* (Maitland Club), II, 125 (*Glasgow University Muniments*)
17. *The Tragedie*
18. *Panegyricus*, fo viii
19. J. Durkan, 'The Cultural Background', in *Essays* 329
20. J. Kirkpatrick, 'Records of the Scottish Nation at Orleans', in *Miscellany* II (S.H.S.), 85 (*Orleans Records*)
21. R. Keith, *History of Church and State in Scotland* (Spottiswoode Society), I, 43n
22. Acts of the lords of council (S.R.O.) xxxii, fos 88v–9 (A.D.C.)

23. G. Donaldson, *Accounts of the Collectors of Thirds of Benefices, 1561–72* (S.H.S.), 20 (*Thirds*)

24. J. Knox, *History of the Reformation in Scotland* (ed. W. C. Dickinson), I, 11 (*Knox*)

25. For discussion of the political background to these years see G. Donaldson, *Scotland, James V to James VII*, Chapters 2–3, and J.Wormald, *Court, Kirk and Community*, Chapter 1

26. *L.P. Henry VIII*, III, ii, 3110

27. D. Hay, *The Letters of James V*, 96

28. *L.P. Henry VIII*, III, ii, 3576

29. *Theiner*, 952

30. *Letters of James V*, 96

31. *Ibid.*, 95

32. A.D.C., xxxiv, fo 41

33. *Ibid.*, fos 40v, 177v–178

34. Vatican archives, PRO 31/9–32, pp.25–6; Acta Misc., 17, fo 133v; Introitus et Exitus, 561, fo 93

35. *Letters of James V*, 105

36. *L.P. Henry VIII*, IV, 935

37. *Ibid.*, 943

38. *Ibid.*, 1004

39. *Letters of James V*, 123–4

2

Monsieur d'Albrot

The monastery of Arbroath stood on the Angus coast, dominating the few hundred houses of the community of farmers, fishermen, craftsmen and handful of merchants whose settlement had been granted to the abbey on its foundation in 1178 by its royal founder, King William I. The sound of horse and pedestrian traffic passing along the High Street and the distracting hum of business rising from the weekly market must have been heard in the cloister. The burgh merchants and the Angus lairds tramped into the church by the north door to do business with the local notaries, and on days when the *regality* court met in one of the great towers flanking the west entrance burgesses, landward tenants and their servants crowded the gateway and pend and the vaulted areas under the western towers that gave direct access into the great church. The abbot's house, extending from the south-west corner of the cloister, was fit to accommodate not only the household of the abbot but also, on occasion, the King himself.

The abbey was dedicated to St Thomas of Canterbury eight years after Becket's murder and only five after his canonisation. His assassination at the altar was depicted on the abbey's seal. The proportions of the church and its furnishings proclaimed it a royal foundation, and its revenues made it one of the richest monasteries in Scotland.[1] In addition to the *fruits* of forty-six parish churches, which provided the abbot with a tremendous reservoir of patronage, there were the money and grain rents — the *maills* and *fermes* — due from the tenants of lands that stretched diagonally from the coastal parishes of Kincardineshire through Angus to the Perthshire border, with the baronies of Torry, Tarves and Fyvie in Aberdeenshire, as well as fishings, forestry rights, the lucrative ferry at Montrose, saltworks at Stirling, the custom of the burghs of Arbroath and Torry and property in fourteen royal burghs. A rental for the year 1531 indicates that the money income alone amounted to about £2,500 Scots.[2] The market price of the grain rent in 1542 was about £1,900.[3] It seems safe to say, therefore, that the total income from the abbacy, on paper at least, was somewhere in the region of £4,000 Scots a year, or about £1,000 sterling according to the 4 to 1 rate of exchange in the early sixteenth century, almost comparable with some of the large English monasteries.[4]

The superior of Arbroath was officially a mitred abbot, entitled to wear mitre and ring, enjoying certain of the rights and privileges of a bishop: he was exempt from attendance at synods called by the archbishop of St Andrews, for instance, in whose archdiocese the abbey lay, and he might confer minor orders and consecrate the furniture of altars. As a great lord he rivalled his neighbour, the bishop of Brechin, whose diocese and temporal lands were on a comparatively small scale. His estate was a regality, excluding the jurisdiction of the King's sheriff and justiciar, which gave him wide powers over his tenants even in criminal cases. Should one of them be called before the royal judges he could be *repledged* to the abbot's own regality court for trial. His own bailie, justiciar and chamberlain administered the estates in his name. Even within the monastery itself he had the final word in some things: the prior of the cloister, who supervised the daily life of the monastery and the abbey's affairs in the superior's absence, and the subprior were both removable at his will. Although the master of the commons had charge of those funds held in common by the monks, the chief provision for the latter was their *portions*, including food allowance and habit-silver, paid to them by the abbot's chamberlain and graniter (the officer who was responsible for gathering in the grain rents) on whose goodwill they were therefore dependent. As lord of the regality the abbot had a powerful say in the affairs of the burgh of Arbroath which was administered by a council and two bailies, one of whom specially represented the abbey's interests.[5]

When he was about thirty years of age David Beaton became the thirtieth abbot of Arbroath. His correct designation was *commendator*, since he was not a professed monk or canonically elected by the community, but he is called both abbot and commendator in the contemporary records. Although taking virtually no part in the spiritual life of the monastery, he does seem to have kept his hand on the running of its temporal affairs to the extent of presiding personally in the regality court on occasion. His main concern in the early years was with the fact that in the terms of his appointment he was not entitled to all the revenues, a state of affairs that led to a prolonged quarrel with his uncle. In the first place, his income was burdened with an annual pension of £1,000 payable to James Stewart, earl of Moray, a natural son of James IV, who had resigned the abbacy to James Beaton in 1517.[6] On top of this, when the latter resigned it to David Beaton he reserved the right to half the revenues left after the deduction of Moray's pension. On 30 March 1525, three months after his return from France, David undertook to pay his uncle half the revenues for 1524 in two instalments of 1,000 merks,[7] but only a year later he had begun to whittle away some of the terms of their agreement for his own financial advantage. On 20 February 1526 the archbishop agreed to accept an alternative to the half revenues in the form of certain fruits from six named parish kirks.[8] What was envisaged was that the lairds and others who had *tacks* of the teinds of these kirks from the abbot should for the next three years pay their tack-duty to the archbishop. At the end of three years abbot and archbishop would revert to their earlier arrangement of direct payment. During these three years Moray's pension was to be paid off, and his rights to the pension were duly extinguished at Rome on 16 March 1527.[9] At the end of that year David managed to get his uncle to subscribe a cancellation of their initial agreement, in effect a receipt for no more than the half fruits of 1524.[10]

Trouble between the archbishop and his nephew really began when the latter failed to recommence payments on the expiry of the three-year interim arrangement. In February 1529 David witnessed a legal deed in the archbishop's Edinburgh lodging,[11] but by the summer of that year the breach in their relations had become open when the curate of Monimail, where the archbishop had his country residence, solemnly read letters of cursing, for non-payment, against David in the parish kirk of Monimail which were later read in Edinburgh.[12] The abbot, however, continued to lift his rents and to visit Arbroath from time to time. By the autumn of 1532 the matter had reached the civil courts, by which time James Beaton had had royal letters issued, demanding his share of the rents from the abbey tenants.[13] The case dragged on through the winter of 1532–3. John Beaton of Balfour died in November, when David excused his non-appearance in court by saying that he had had to attend the *erding* of his father.[14] If he and his uncle were both present at the burial, as seems likely, it may have been an uncomfortable family gathering. By February 1533 arrangements were being made for a new diplomatic mission to France, with David as ambassador, and when the archbishop complained that his case against his nephew was being hustled through the courts, he was told that he must produce his evidence quickly because the abbot of Arbroath 'is to depart furth of the realme for the materis concerning the commoun weill'.[15] In Scotland the matter lay dormant during the abbot's absence abroad but had by then reached Rome itself.[16] The weight of royal authority, however, was on David Beaton's side at this time when he was proving himself a useful servant in the King's efforts to conclude a marriage treaty with France, while James Beaton was currently out of favour.[17] The final settlement of the affair is difficult to disentangle but at the end of 1535 an agreement of a kind seems to have been reached which was definitely to David's advantage.[18] The archbishop probably never received more than his original 2,000 merks for 1524.

In spite of all this litigation over his income nothing seems to have disturbed the abbot's authority at local level. The first act in his name to be recorded in the abbey register — confirmation of an endowment by Robert Scott, burgess of Arbroath, to the altar in the Lady Chapel at the Bridgend of Arbroath — is dated 18 January 1525.[19] In 1528, a year in which the plague visited the burgh, the council paid one of the bailies and the town clerk 'to ryd togidder to my lord' in Edinburgh to ask for the remission of a fine laid on the town for the obstruction of one of the abbey's officers in the course of his duties.[20] In the same year they reached agreement with the abbey chamberlain about confining the market day to a Tuesday, except for the flesh market, and passed an act to the effect that the abbot had first claim on the use of the horses and carts hired by the burgesses. With a streak of independence, however, the council agreed amongst themselves to make this act only on condition that the abbey paid for their hires at current rates, 'and gyf thai [i.e. the council] gett nocht thankfull pament this act to be destroyit and depulsit and haf nane effect'.[21] On one occasion the abbot's graniter warned the smallholders of the Punderlaw and Disterland to pay their fermes promptly or lose their tacks.[22]

David Beaton visited Arbroath on several recorded occasions and presumably at other times of which there is no record. George Hay, whose *History of Arbroath* was published at the end of last century, was able to consult the court book of the regality which dated from the late fifteenth century but has since gone missing. According to the court book David 'occasionally presided in the regality court': in

1530, for instance, a burgess was admitted and new bailies were elected 'in presens of our derrest lorde David abbot of Arbroath'.[23] It was typical of David Beaton, who tended to make his presence felt whenever possible and to act personally in his own affairs, that he should have been in the court when the new bailies were admitted to office. On 2 June that same year he was at his mansion of Ethie further along the coast.[24] Among the Airlie family papers there is an eighteenth-century transcript from some pages of an abbey account book, now also lost, relating to about 1530 and giving details of provisions 'for the place of Arbroath'.[25] The large quantities mentioned suggest that at some time during that year the abbot and his household were in residence. It is unlikely that twenty to twenty-five monks and their servants would have consumed the 800 wedders, 180 marts, 11 barrels of salmon, 1,500 dried fish, 82 chalders of malt, 30 of wheat and 40 of meal in one year, over and above the abbey's considerable rents in kind. The mention of marts — salted carcases which had been killed off in late autumn — suggests a winter visit, possibly over the Christmas season. The anonymous transcriber of the account remarks that the amount spent on these provisions exceeded that for 1528, 'although in that year the King had been twice at Arbroath and the archbishop of St Andrews three times', as David entertained his uncle in the months before their relations broke down. According to the royal household books King James V also spent four days at Arbroath in 1529, from 12 to 15 July, when he was probably still in a mood to celebrate his escape from the Douglases and their banishment to England.[26] From all accounts David Beaton was a lavish host and a good companion. He and the King sometimes played a game of cards together, when it would probably be easier to sound the royal mind in the unguarded, desultory conversation accompanying the game than in a formal audience however private it might be.

The records kept by his chamberlain and clerks show how his estates were managed. On the one hand there was a fair amount of stability and security of possession among the abbey tenants. Of some 120 tacks granted in his name between 1525 and 1536 (when the surviving abbey register ends) fifteen were granted for life and the remainder for nineteen years.[27] Although some of these tacks went to his relatives, friends and servants and to influential people whose goodwill he sought to win, particularly in the royal household, the majority were granted to the small tenants and husbandmen who cultivated the settlements scattered over the abbey lands, many of whose families had lived on their holdings for several generations. Sometimes, however, tenants were replaced, not necessarily evicted but demoted to the rank of subtenant of a middleman. In January 1526, for instance, Andrew Gardin, whose family had held the lands of Dunbarrow since at least 1483, gave place to the abbot's brother, James Beaton of Melgund, as the principal tenant.[28]

The abbot was able to raise considerable sums of money by granting tacks, which required a down-payment, known as the grassum, and the payment of entry silver at the term when the tenant formally took up possession. The texts of some of these tacks actually state that the money paid for them was to be used to pay off Moray's pension. For £500 David Beaton made the provost of Aberdeen, Gilbert

Menzies, and William Rolland, an Aberdeen burgess, joint bailies of the barony of Torry.[29] A small tenant such as William Gray paid £40 for a tack of half the Kirktoun of Tarves.[30] It was possible to raise capital on those tacks granted to husbandmen and small tenants by breaking up large holdings into small ones, charging each tenant a grassum and entry silver. In 1525 the Punderlaw and Disterland, which had been held as a unit since 1485, were split up into thirty holdings.[31] Tacks of the teinds of annexed parish churches brought in ready cash and also saved the chamberlain and graniter the trouble of collecting or *riding* the teinds, thus cutting down on the 'office expenses' part of the chamberlain's accounts. Some people were prepared to pay enormous duty for a tack of teinds which, in a year of shortage and high market prices, they could sell for large sums: David Wood of Craig, the royal comptroller, paid £80 a year for those of Garvock in Kincardineshire[32] and the brother of the late Lord Glamis £1,000 for the teinds of the parish of Glamis itself.[33]

The abbot used his patronage over the annexed parish kirks to the full. The abbey register contains presentations to twenty-eight vicarages, to absentee vicars who were sometimes promised the benefice 'when it shall fall vacant' by the death or resignation of the existing holder. Benefices were granted to petitioners on the waiting list, exchanged and resigned under agreed conditions exactly as in the papal court, and a dispute over the abbot's presentation was sometimes the start of bitter litigation at Rome. It has been pointed out that 'resignation' often denoted the resignation of a rival claimant who would then expect to be compensated for stepping down.[34] The perpetual vicarage of Tarves in Aberdeenshire, in the abbot's patronage, changed hands four times in ten years, on each occasion the presentee gaining possession on resignation of the holder.[35] There was a fair amount of pluralism among the abbot's presentees, some of whom were his officers and servants; the grant of a benefice was one way of paying them, the business of screwing the actual income out of the tacksman of the vicarage revenues was thereafter the vicar's problem.

Although much business might be handled by the regular staff of clerks in the abbot's chancery and by those employed by his bailie and chamberlain, David Beaton himself kept in touch with what was afoot, and where a matter touched upon his own income or privileges would sometimes act on his own behalf. On a number of occasions he appeared personally in court in Edinburgh in cases affecting abbey property. He once appeared in the burgh court of Aberdeen for the same reason, when he took sasine, that is formal possession, of the property in question.[36] He ordered many medieval royal grants to be transcribed anew into the abbey register, including King David II's gift to the abbey of the right to the customs of Arbroath itself and exemption from tolls throughout Scotland.[37] In these early years he seems on the whole to have enjoyed good relations with his greater tenants, such as Lord Ogilvy, the abbey bailie, to whom on 18 July 1529 he granted a bond by which he promised that should he be made a bishop or be otherwise removed from the abbacy he would first renew Lord Ogilvy's charter of bailiary.[38] To Lord Innermeath he granted the use of the harbour of Ethie[39] and managed to keep on good terms with Lord Glamis and the influential Woods of

Boniton. A number of Angus noblemen and lairds were technically the abbot's men, holding land from him, but they could easily become overmighty subjects.

The abbot used a handful of widely differing individuals to act as his procurators, or spokesmen, in court actions: Robert Leslie of Innerpeffer, a layman trained in the civil law, who was given a pension of £10 a year in return for shouldering the task of acting for him against the archbishop in the King's court,[40] Mr George Beaton, his own brother, Mr James Scrymgeour, his old fellow-student at St Andrews, Mr Martin Balfour, the future Official of St Andrews, Gilbert Menzies, provost of Aberdeen, and Mr Henry Balnaves, a young lawyer who was privately attracted to Lutheranism.[41] While abbot of Arbroath he first gathered a household and staff about him, some of whom remained with him for the rest of his life, later merging with his greater household as archbishop of St Andrews. Apart from near relatives, his closest friend, to judge by the fact that he was constantly with him and was entrusted with personal and private business, was Mr Bernard Baillie, parson of his home parish kirk of Lamington in the upper ward of Lanarkshire. David and he were distantly related and their families were probably in touch in their earlier years, for Bernard's father, Mr Cuthbert Baillie, brother of the laird of Lamington, parson of Sanquhar and commendator of Glenluce abbey, followed archbishop James Beaton as treasurer of the realm and sat with him as an auditor of the exchequer in 1511.[42] Bernard's younger brother, Richard, also became one of the abbot of Arbroath's servants.[43] There are no contemporary comments on Bernard Baillie but he seems to have been entirely in David Beaton's confidence and a regular member of his staff and household. He was chamberlain of Arbroath by 1528 and held the office for ten years. He never went abroad with the abbot but was one of those who received crown letters of protection in his absence, and looked after his affairs at home.[44]

David Beaton must have grown up with his cousins, Archibald Beaton, son of the laird of Pitlochie, and Robert, Andrew and George Durie, sons of his aunt, Janet Beaton, and her husband, John Durie of Durie, whose castle lay only a few miles from Balfour. He continued to keep in close touch with them, especially with George Durie whom he made *conservator* of the privileges of Arbroath.[45] Andrew Durie, who may have been at Glasgow university and in the archbishop's household there with David, had a reputation for riotous living and, according to an aside of John Knox, for versifying.[46] The Duries, like their Beaton cousins, benefited from their uncle's patronage. The archbishop resigned his title of abbot of Dunfermline in favour of George, but kept a grip of the abbey revenues and administration during his own lifetime. In 1526, after much string-pulling, Andrew was admitted to the abbacy of Melrose, another rich monastic house, in succession to his late uncle, Robert Beaton.[47]

David's own brother, George, who appears to have been closest to him in the Arbroath days, embarked on a career as procurator in the courts after his return from Orléans university and appeared on David's behalf on several occasions, not only in church courts but in those of the royal justiciar at Perth and Dundee, in cases involving the abbey.[48] In 1532 George was called one of the abbot's servants.

In the following year, when he was involved in a dispute over the parsonage of Glasgow, David, then abroad, attended to the business at Rome for him and when George died, in April 1536, received a *grace of provision* to the parsonage.[49] Walter Beaton, although he is recorded once or twice as having been with David at Arbroath, spent more time with his brother after the latter became archbishop of St Andrews. Indeed, Walter spent a commendable amount of time at Glasgow cathedral of which he was canon of Govan.[50] James Beaton, with his wife, Janet Annand of Melgund, received several tacks of abbey property from his brother and attended to personal business for him, even although it appears that James was unable to write.[51]

Next to his relatives the abbot entrusted his business to a group of men from east Fife whom he may have known since his youth. George Ramsay of Clatto, who stood surety for the 2,000 merks payable by David to his uncle, fell heir to the barony of Clatto in 1516 when he was about twenty-one years of age, making him an almost exact contemporary. They were related through George's paternal grandmother, Elizabeth Monypenny, the second woman of her family to marry a laird of Clatto. George was occasionally with David at Arbroath and was sufficiently familiar with the Beaton family to take part in their disruption of the Fife sheriff court proceedings in 1527.[52] James Auchmowty, a non-graduate priest who served David Beaton for over sixteen years, probably belonged to the family of Auchmowty of that ilk in Markinch parish, perhaps a son of the laird who was killed at Flodden. From 1530 onwards he handled the fees derived from David Beaton's keepership of the privy seal and acted periodically as chamberlain of Arbroath.[53] David presented him to the vicarage of Arbroath in 1535, a living which he held until his death.[54] Sir David Christison, who was given much responsibility, also came from east Fife, possibly from Dysart.[55] For some time he was a member of the royal household but was presented to several vicarages in the abbot's gift, including Lunan (traditionally associated with Walter Mill, the priest whom David Beaton is said to have early suspected of heresy), and was not the only royal clerk to go over to the abbot's service. In April 1536 he was still a steward in the royal household,[56] but in the autumn of that year he acted as the abbot's procurator and was soon afterwards numbered among his servants.[57] Sir William Pettilock[58] (or Pettillo), born at the East Ferry of Portincraig in 1500, admitted notary in 1524, was resident in Arbroath throughout the 1520s and transacted much abbey business. A chaplain in the Lady Chapel of Arbroath, he frequently represented David Beaton's interests in other courts and made extracts from the abbey register at his request.[59] In 1533 he was the abbey graniter.[60] Sir William Blantyre, another notary whose services David Beaton used regularly, was probably a native of Angus. In 1527 he was presented to the vicarage of Fyvie in Aberdeenshire by way of payment for his services.[61]

Like the abbot himself, the men to whom he entrusted his affairs were mainly from families of small lairds and proprietors. Lacking the patronage and influence that had put him where he was, they were grateful for his. As in his own case, the association of a number of them with the church as a religious institution was largely nominal.

NOTES

1. *Letters of James V*, 54; *Theiner*, 524; *Thirds*, 9

2. Dalhousie muniments (S.R.O.), GD 45/13/300

3. R. K. Hannay, *Rentale Sancti Andree, 1538–46* (S.H.S.), 120 (*Rentale*)

4. G. W. O. Woodward, *The Dissolution of the Monasteries*, 5

5. G. Hay, *History of Arbroath*, 115 (Hay, *Arbroath*)

6. *L.P. Henry VIII*, II, ii, 3630; Vatican archives, PRO 31/10/Reel 15

7. A.D.C., xxxv, fos 20r–v

8. *Ibid.*, fos 218–20

9. Vatican archives, PRO/31/9/Reel 5

10. A.D.C., xxxviii, fo 63v

11. Protocol book of Thomas Kene (S.R.O.), NP 1/2a, fo 15v

12. Acts of the lords of council and session (S.R.O.), i, fo 120 (A.D.C.S.)

13. *Ibid.*, i, fos 117v–118, 119v–120, 133v; ii, fos 4v–5, 7

14. *Ibid.*, ii, fo 7v

15. *Ibid.*, ii, fos 85, 93

16. Vatican archives, PRO 31/9/Reel 3

17. A.D.C.S., ii, 157r–v; Cunningham of Caprington muniments (S.R.O.), Royal Letter Book, GD 149/Additional, 1/1, fos 28, 47 (Caprington letter book)

18. Vatican archives, Reg.Supp., 2192, fos 133v–134

19. *Liber S. Thome de Aberbrothoc* (Bannatyne Club), II, 583 (*Arbroath Liber*)

20. Hay, *Arbroath*, 121

21 *Ibid.*, 119, 123

22. *Ibid.*, 123

23. *Ibid.*, 115–16

24. Arlie muniments (S.R.O.), GD 16/42/6; 47/2

25. *Ibid.*, GD 16/25/127

26. *Liber Domicilii James V* (Bannatyne Club), App., 22; *RSS* II, 210

27. For an examination of the pattern of leases at Arbroath see M. H. B. Sanderson, *Scottish rural society in the sixteenth century*, 48–9

28. *Arbroath Liber*, II, 219, 612

29. *Ibid.*, II, 646

30. *Ibid.*, II, 676

31. *Ibid.*, II, 282, 557, 596

32. *Ibid.*, II, 774

33. *Ibid.*, II, 713

34. Cowan, 'Patronage, Provision and Reservation', 87

35. *Arbroath Liber*, II, 584, 589, 789, 798

36. British Library, Additional MSS, 33245, fo 75v

37. *Arbroath Liber*, II, 738

38. Airlie muniments, GD 16/41/6; 46/8

39. Northesk muniments (S.R.O.), GD 130/1/1

40. *Arbroath Liber*, II, 675

41. *Ibid.*, II, 758

42. *Exchequer rolls*, XIII, 448; *Transactions of the Dumfries and Galloway Natural History and Antiquarian Society*, 3rd series, XII, 72

43. *RSS*, II, 2166; *Rentale*, 140, 197

44. Hay, *Arbroath*, 119; *RSS*, II, 1512; as witness, Yester writs (S.R.O.), GD 28/446;

Dalhousie muniments, GD 45/13/300, fo 20; *RMS* III, 1328; procurator, *Arbroath Liber*, II, 746; A.D.C., ii, fo 403

45. British Library Additional MSS, 33245, fo 105

46. *Knox*, I, 129

47. *Letters of James V*, 127; Vatican archives, PRO 31/9/Reel 2; *RSS* I, 3584

48. *Orleans Records*, 86; *Arbroath Liber*, II, 588, 643; Burnet Stuart Collection (S.R.O.), GD 115/4

49. Caprington letter book, fo 6; Vatican archives, Reg. Supp., 2217, fos 123v–124; G.Donaldson, *The St Andrews Formulare* (Stair Society), II, 376 (*Formulare*)

50. *Orleans Records*, 84; Airlie muniments, GD16/14/15; Protocol book of Cuthbert Simon (S.R.O.), NP 1/195, fos 4v, 195; W. Fraser, *The Stirlings of Keir*, 318–19; *Registrum episcopatus Glasguensis* (Bannatyne Club), II, 541

51. *Arbroath Liber*, II, 612, 776, 778; *RMS* III, 337, 897; A.D.C., xxxviii, fo 22v, xlii, fos 142v, 161; *RSS*, II, 1492; Dalhousie muniments, GD 45/16 575

52. Manuscript minute book of Fife sheriff court, SC 20/2/1, fo 18; A.D.C., xxxv, fos 20r–v; *Arbroath Liber*, II, 633, 638; Justiciary court minute book, JC 1/3, 8 October 1527

53. *RSS*, II, 766–7; 768, 770; A.D.C.S.i, fos 109v–110, ix, fo 91v; *Arbroath Liber*, II, 836; *Rentale*, 120, 135

54. *Arbroath Liber*, II, 830

55. *Notices of the local records of Dysart* (Bannatyne Club), 24; *Rentale*, 126; Dickinson, *Sheriff Court Book of Fife*, 220

56. Exchequer records (S.R.O.), E 32/8, fo 130v

57. *RSS*, II, 2166

58. Biographical details in Register of admission of notaries (S.R.O.), NP 2/1, fo 61

59.. *Arbroath Liber*, II, 588, 641, 643; Airlie muniments, GD 16/1/96; Hay, *Arbroath*, 126–7, 131; his protocol book (S.R.O. microfilm), RH 4/96

60. Airlie muniments, GD 16/47/2

61. *RMS* III, 573; *Arbroath Liber*, II, 588, 641, 643, 678

3

Marion Ogilvy

No all-round consideration of David Beaton's career would be complete without taking account of the woman whom for over twenty years he treated almost as a wife. In this as in so many other respects he was so much a product of his times and circumstances that to introduce Marion Ogilvy is to raise the subject of the contemporary attitude to the rule of clerical celibacy. Contemporaries who were in any way concerned with the matter did not pretend that the prohibition of clerical marriage was anything higher than a rule of the church. Mr William Hay, professor of theology at Aberdeen, in his lectures on the law of marriage delivered to his students at King's College in 1530 stated, 'Although it is [not] laid down [i.e. in scripture] that no one in sacred orders should marry a wife, nevertheless this was observed from the beginning of the Church of Christ', and, later, 'The Church makes a man in sacred orders altogether incapable of marriage, and so this is not something essential to the vow [of chastity] but due to the Church's institution. For a solemn vow [i.e. followed by sacred orders] has no greater force in God's eyes than a simple vow [i.e. taken voluntarily]. Yet a solemn vow invalidates a marriage later contracted and a simple vow does not. This is due to the Church's institution and also because breaking a solemn vow is more serious than breaking a simple vow'.[1]

The rule of celibacy, that is the non-marriage of the clergy, which became a characteristic of the western church, having failed to become general in the earlier centuries of Christianity although practised voluntarily by many clergy and other Christians, was imposed on the secular clergy by Pope Gregory VII (Hildebrand) in the late eleventh century, thus extending to the seculars the standard adopted by the religious orders. This coincided with a period of increasing clericalisation of the church and a deepening separation in outward respects between the clergy, or *spirituales*, and the laity, or *carnales*, the latter immersed in their family ties and material possessions. Gregory saw the non-married state as being not only nearer to the ideal of Christian perfection but also as essential to the supremacy in society of the spiritual, detached yet privileged part of the Christian community — the clergy. The rule was long and at times strongly resisted by the secular clergy and, indeed, was never consistently practised. Until the eleventh century marriage of the clergy had been common: as late as 1107 Pope Pascal II, writing to Archbishop Anselm of Canterbury, said that he understood the majority of the English clergy to be married and accordingly gave permission for their sons to be ordained.[2] The repetition of decrees against clerical marriage thereafter only serves to show that it persisted. Finally, the first and second Lateran councils of 1123 and 1139 made the reception of orders, from that of subdeacon upwards, an impediment to marriage.

By the thirteenth century, when the earliest statutes of the provincial council of the Scottish church begin to survive, clerical marriage had, so to speak, gone underground, transmuted into mere concubinage — more or less perpetual or long-term associations of clerics and women.

Of the cohabitation of clerics and women: Although the rulers of the church have always sought to drive away from the homes of churchmen that filthy contagion of lustful naughtiness whereby the good fame of the church is shamefully discredited, yet that vice exists and in such wantonness that it always shamefully reintroduces itself ... we [the prelates] ordain and by our decree direct that clerics, and specially those in holy orders, who publicly in their own or other houses keep concubines shall be suspended from office and benefice, unless they utterly put them away from them within a month, promising in no wise to keep them or other hereafter ... [3]

In the fourteenth and fifteenth centuries there were renewed suggestions for a relaxation of the rule on the lines of the practice of the eastern church, where clergy who were married before taking orders were permitted to remain so (except for bishops), but all attempts to bring the matter before various church councils of the period, supported at times by secular rulers, failed. The practice of concubinage had increased by the sixteenth century and continued to do so until the Reformation when the rule of celibacy was denounced by Martin Luther and other reformers, Luther himself marrying in 1525. At the same time moral laxity in general among clerics seems to have become more blatant, largely due to the debasement of the benefice system which filled their ranks with many unspiritual men, frequently in the highest offices in the church.

The statutes of the provincial councils of the Scottish church of 1549 and 1558–9 are unfailingly quoted to illustrate the low moral state of many of the clergy and, indeed, the council of 1549 blamed the increase in heresy and the indifference of the laity on two principal causes, 'the corruption of morals and profane lewdness of life in churchmen of almost all ranks, together with crass ignorance of literature and all the liberal arts'.[4] However, with regard to the first of these shortcomings the assembled fathers were simply quoting from the decrees of the general council of Basel against concubinaries, which as a provincial council was all they were empowered to do, demonstrating at the same time that in this respect Scotland's problem was no different from that of the rest of Europe. It is doubtful if the Scottish prelates present intended to do more that pay lip-service to these fervent expressions of the need to reform clerical morals. Nevertheless, it is worth taking a closer look at the Basel decrees, which at least some of the original framers had intended should be taken seriously.

The weight of censure falls on the practice of concubinage, not on actual sexual immorality; there is less concern with lust than with lawbreaking, breaking the rule of non-marriage. Every sort of irregularity in this connection, whether habitual, casual or only suspected, is to be treated as concubinage in the fullest sense:

Now, by open keepers of concubines are to be understood not only those whose concubinage is notorious [i.e. known] by sentence passed or by confession made in a court of law or by evidence of the fact which no subterfuge can conceal; but he is a public concubinary who keeps a woman suspected of and ill-famed for incontinence, and when admonished by his superior does not utterly put her away.[5]

The Scottish council made provision for discretionary penalties against unbeneficed but fully ordained clergy according to the degree of their offence and persistence in the irregularity — a rider aimed at the unbeneficed parish curate.[6]

Thus, lust was for the confessional, concubinage for the courts. This distinction is clearly made by Mr William Hay in his lectures on vows:

A vow of chastity which is solemn by reason of the church's institution, that is as the church has instituted it, is concerned with refraining from marriage, and not from fornication ... The church can dispense from this vow. But the church cannot dispense from fornication. Therefore, a priest having carnal copula outside of marriage is ... not breaking his vow although he is a transgressor of the divine law.[7]

If the breaking of the rule of non-marriage, rather than disregard of the divine law forbidding fornication, was the primary concern of the decrees with regard to clerical morals, then the Scottish provincial councils who endorsed them were unlikely to start a reforming operation on their authority. Spiritually-minded churchmen in 1549 and 1558–9, however, were doubtless concerned that priests should live chaste lives according to divine commandment since the rule denied marriage to them, obeying the spirit as well as the letter of the law, just as spiritually-minded ordinands would keep both rule and divine law out of personal commitment and integrity.

What was disturbing to the authorities about persistent clerical concubinage was that it helped to blur the distinction in everyday life between clergy and laity. It might be popularly supposed to constitute a *de facto* marriage. These words were used by Mr William Hay in his comments on clerical 'bigamy':

... when a man in sacred orders contracts a *de facto* marriage with a woman and has intercourse with her. We say *de facto* because he cannot contract a lawful marriage. Bigamy, because although there is no question of marriages, either true or presumptive, there are two equivalent acts. A professed religious has contracted a sort of marriage by taking a vow of chastity, and so has a man in sacred orders, for these vow to keep their bodies chaste for God and the most blessed Virgin, and this can be said to be equivalent to marriage ... Thus they have equivalently contracted two marriages.[8]

The 'open' and 'notorious' elements in these relationships echo the element of 'habit and repute' in at least one kind of situation where in Scotland a man and a woman might be regarded as married. Cohabitation and treating each other as man and wife was taken as implying mutual consent to the partnership. The element of *consent* in marriage was regarded as vital by the canon law of the church. 'Common report', or *fama*, was equally important. Therefore the situation in which a man and woman cohabited, treated each other as man and wife and were commonly known to do so was regarded as a valid if irregular marriage.[9] Lay folk who were familiar with examples of this phenomenon in a community must often have regarded the cohabitation of their clerical relatives and their womenfolk as little different in practice. One wonders if John Forman, the careerist abbot of Kilwinning, who was pursued at law in 1514 for the alleged abduction of one Sybil Galloway, was making a test case of their circumstances by submitting a supplication to the lords of council in which he claimed that Sybil 'come to me of hir awin frie will and motive, as scho that promittit of befor, the quhilk Sibell, in the tyme, was nother madene, mannis wyfe nor wedow, bot ane anelape [single] weman, quhilk wes als frie to me as ony uthir man'.[10] Were more background information available it might put a more involved construction on the affair, which for David Hay Fleming simply won Forman the accolade for effrontery. If concubinage made it easier for the clergy to merge with the laity, especially those clerics who postponed the taking of major orders for much of their careers, it was characteristic of the times that they should make use of the secular court to assist them.

The detailed prohibitions contained in the decrees against concubinaries only serve to show how many clergy, in resisting the rule of celibacy in practice, were identifying themselves with the lay community, to whom they were closely related and among whom they lived, in matters of family provision, the possession of property, gainful occupations and, in the case of the richest of them, style of living. As John M. Todd has reminded us in his biography of Martin Luther:

> The step from layman to priest was not the same size as it is today. Biographers have emphasised the great divide between priest and laity in the medieval system but have failed to guard their readers against thinking in terms of modern priests, turned out all very much in the same mould, after many years of training which, coming at the end of adolescence, have a radical effect. The medieval priest was in some ways much nearer to the people than the twentieth century priest. Indeed, part of the claims of those who wished to reform the church, and finally succeeded at the Council of Trent, was that the priest was much too near to the people, too liable to live just as they did, treating his priesthood as a sort of incidental increment or accretion, a mere office, a sacramental (and in this sense very nearly a magical) power.[11]

Concubinaries were forbidden to maintain their children in their own houses; there was to be no recognisable 'family unit' in the manse or curate's house. In 1557, George Dunbar, canon of Fortrose, granted as parson of Kilmure and vicar of Rosemarkie, the parson's manse in the canonry of Ross and the vicar's croft in the burgh of Rosemarkie to Janet Thomson, in liferent, and to their eldest son, George, in feu-ferm, entailing the property to George's younger brothers Patrick and John, with the proviso that they should receive him, the parson, in the manse when he so wished.[12] In effect, the canon was obtaining for himself and his family heritable possession of the house in Rosemarkie, with plot of land, which they already occupied. The ordinance forbidding churchmen to grant ecclesiastical property to their children born in concubinage was a dead letter in this decade in which the feuing of church land was at its height. In 1552, George Durie, abbot of Dunfermline, the Cardinal's cousin, feued the Nether Grange of Kinghorn-Western with the 'fortalice built thereon' (now known as Rossend) to Peter Durie, a son of himself and, probably, Katherine Sibbald. Peter renovated the castle and placed his coat of arms on it (now above the modern porch).[13] Mr Gavin Hamilton of Raploch, firstly dean of Glasgow and then, by exchange, commendator of Kilwinning, feued to his son Gavin, later of Raploch, the abbot's lodging near the cross of Irvine, reserving the liferent to Margaret Hamilton of Broomhill, the mother of his family.[14] Thus a piece of property which was meant to be reserved for the use of the head of the monastery passed into the hands of the young laird of Raploch, a secular estate in Lanarkshire which the commendator himself had earlier inherited from one of his brothers.[15] The acquisition of secular property was also forbidden, either acquired for sons or by marrying daughters into the landed classes, both of which David Beaton was to do. Daughters were not to be dowered 'out of the patrimony of Christ' when they married landed men having more than £100 yearly rental; in effect, clergy should only ally with the less wealthy landed classes because their betters would expect larger tochers in the form of church property.

Bishops were warned not to collate priests' sons to what had been their fathers' benefices, to avoid the possibility of the living becoming hereditary *de facto*. This in fact, however, happened. Mr Alexander Dunbar succeeded his father as dean of Moray in 1559 and was himself succeeded in the benefice after the Reformation by his second son, Thomas; three generations of Dunbars lived in the dean's manse in Elgin.[16] Succession from father to son also took place lower down the benefice scale: at Stewarton in Ayrshire the vicarage passed through the hands of five generations of Montgomeries in the sixteenth century, two of these before the Reformation.[17]

Like so many other legal edicts, those of the provincial councils of the church, so far as clerical concubinage was concerned, were trying to control rather than prohibit. The documents betray elements of compromise dictated by a situation which had become so well established that the possibility of removing it completely was remote. Bribes/fines were evidently being passed to ecclesiastical superiors in return for turning a blind eye to the circumstances, superiors who were probably in the same boat themselves.[18] Churchmen who were deprived for the first offence were to be reinstated once the appropriate dispensation enabling them to retain their benefices had been obtained. The existence of a body of opinion, ecclesiastical and lay, calling for internal reform of the church and for a spiritually-responsible ministry in the hierarchy and at parish level may have caused the Scottish prelates to issue what are often referred to as 'reforming statutes', but it is doubtful whether they intended, or even hoped, to overturn the practice of clerical concubinage or eradicate its effects by this means alone. It is probable, in an increasingly secular although still essentially Christian age, that many people regarded clerical concubinage as acceptable provided the association was habitual and constant, something which was probably true of the humbler parish clergy who lived and served in the communities to which many of them belonged. It is also fair to say that the genuinely celibate priest, living a personally chaste life, would earn the greater respect of his parishioners.

At least two earlier Scottish historians suggested an element of acceptance in society, John Hill Burton and Bishop John Dowden. Hill Burton discussed it in the third volume of his *History of Scotland*, published in 1905, two years before

David Hay Fleming gave his Stone Lectures which became the basis of his book on *The Reformation in Scotland* in which the subject of clerical concubinage got the most superficial treatment it has ever received. While Hill Burton's prose borders at times on the idyllic, what he is saying makes sense in the historical context:

> For many of the clergy who lived in concubinage according to the letter of the law, there was doubtless the plea that morally they led a life of married domesticity. They were dissenters or schismatics, rather than sinners. They repudiated the doctrine of clerical celibacy; ... and took to their homes women who held the same view, and lived with them in soberness and constancy, regretting that perverse laws denied them the legal privileges of wedlock, but with consciences void of offence, doing what seemed to them right amid the difficulties by which they were surrounded ... At the best, however, it was a lax and dangerous system. Every man who practised it was a law unto himself. There was no distinct sanction drawing, as the law of marriage draws, an obvious line between domesticity and profligacy.[19]

Bishop Dowden wrote in 1910:

> In spite of many statutes it is a fact that clergy of England and Scotland (in considerable numbers) were living with women either in a relationship scarcely distinguishable from marriage, or (less frequently) associated with them in looser or more temporary connections ... the priest's concubine and the priest's children must have been familiar figures in many parishes.[20]

There must have been fairly widespread sympathy with the predicament of those whose way of life was a silent protest against the rule of celibacy — it had to be silent, however, for to voice such an opinion openly was to run the risk of being accused of heretical opinions, while to take the belief to its logical conclusion and marry might be punishable. Lay opinion was more shocked at the hypocrisy of ecclesiastical judges who passed sentence on priests who married while they themselves lived in a *de facto* married state or, worse still, with a reputation for promiscuity, than it was by concubinage itself. Lindsay of Pitscottie, recording the death of Norman Gourlay, wrote, 'They wald thoill no preistis to marrie bot they wald punische and burne him to the deid, bot gif he had ussit ten thowsand huris he wald nocht have been brunt'.[21] George Wishart, when accused during his trial of having taught that priests should marry, replied bluntly, 'But as many as have not the gift of chastity nor yet for the Evangel have not overcome the concupiscence of the flesh, and yet have vowed chastity, ye have experience, although I should hold my tongue, to what inconvenience they have vowed themselves',[22] no doubt glancing along the bench of his accusers as he said so.

The double standard was applied on a wider scale by the papacy itself. In spite of decrees aimed at preventing the clergy from living like laymen, the Roman curia operated a system whose venality was deplored by protestant and catholic reformers alike. The appointments to benefices, including the highest offices, had become a market in which livings were bought and haggled over. The misuse of the power of dispensation turned this from being an opportunity to use fairness and discretion into a means of selling licences to set aside some rule of the church. In

Scotland, due to the bargain between Pope and King in the late fifteenth century, prelates were the nominees of the crown or of influential families, only a minority of whom had spiritual priorities.[23] The practice of granting commendatorships of religious houses to royal and baronial nominees removed the effective control of the 'patrimony of Christ' from ecclesiastical to secular hands, since many commendators were operating in the dynastic interests of their families. In this situation the sons of priests were dispensed at Rome by the hundred to hold benefices in spite of the impediment of illegitimacy, and absentee parsons and vicars put paid deputies in their parish kirks and went off to live in centres of political and social life where the atmosphere was decidedly secular. The Pope, through his commissioners, confirmed the granting of scores of ecclesiastical feu charters which, besides conveying the use of church land into the hands of laymen great and small, enabled some clerics to establish their children in property which would subsequently be inherited. All this must have had the effect of inculcating cynicism and lowering the standard of moral responsibility in private life. Yet, in spite of prevailing anti-clericalism, itself a time-honoured phenomenon, clerics who lived flagrantly immoral lives were probably a minority, and it seems realistic to say that the rule of clerical celibacy was commonly set aside rather than flouted deliberately. It is also arguable that, as Hill Burton infers, a good many clergy silently dissented from the rule, especially when one considers how many married clergy there were in the first decade following the Reformation settlement and that large numbers of them had served in the pre-Reformation church.

What was particularly denounced, and pilloried in literary and popular satire, was a life of profligacy supported by a rich living and high ecclesiastical office. Professor Cowan remarks in his recent book on *The Scottish Reformation*, 'If there had been any moral outrage it related to the bishops and commendators with their many mistresses rather than to the humble parish priest with his loyal housekeeper who also shared his bed and bore his children'.[24] The Abbot in *Ane Satyre of the Thrie Estaitis* is a caricature of the worst type of abuse:

> My paramours is baith fat and fair
> As ony wench into the toun of Ayr.
> I send my sons to Paris to the schools,
> I traist in God that they sal be na fools!
> And al my dochteris I have weill providit.
> Now judge ye if my office be weill guidit.[25]

This, after all, could only be afforded by the greater prelates who as a result came in for the most biting ridicule. The fault, however, of some contemporaries and of many writers since has been to assume that promiscuity necessarily accompanied a luxurious standard of living, or was necessarily implied by a number of children. Both Hill Burton and Bishop Dowden endorsed the belief that the less respectable forms of the association of clergy and women were mostly to be found among the higher clergy, and both writers, in what has become traditional fashion, cite David Beaton as the most notorious example.

Does the available evidence put him in the same category as Patrick Hepburn, prior of St Andrews and, later, bishop of Moray and commendator of Scone, whose associates ranged from the daughters of Moray lairds to that of a wright in the village of Scone, two charters of entail, one to his sons and one to his daughters, listing their mothers' names,[26] or John Hamilton, abbot of Paisley and, after David Beaton, archbishop of St Andrews, who, as Knox correctly states, 'stole his kinsman's wife'?[27]

It is interesting that a charge of profligacy, which is now so much a part of the folk-history that has gathered around his name, was not the main contemporary charge against him. Sir David Lindsay, who put his condemnation into his own mouth in *The Tragedie of the Cardinall*, attributed Beaton's downfall to pride and listed his vices as gambling, simony and sedition without suggesting that the 'yong joly gentyll man' of his Paris days had been a womaniser as well.[28] Admittedly, Lindsay need not have put all he thought or knew of David Beaton into the poem, but notoriety of this kind would surely have been relevant to the theme. *The Thrie Estaitis*, in which the Abbot boasts of the education of his sons and the provision for his daughters, was first performed in January 1540, two years before two of the Cardinal's sons, described as 'scholars', left for France and six years before his oldest daughter, the only one to wed during his lifetime, was married. George Buchanan and David Beaton knew and hated each other, Buchanan including a retrospective pen-portrait of the latter in his *History*, written as a disillusioned old man. His description of how David Beaton at home 'wallows in lust with his Minions' and when abroad 'ravages to destroy the Innocent' is the kind of prose born out of hatred.[29] At its most factual it may be a denigration of Marion Ogilvy and the partners of other men in David Beaton's circle, such as George Durie and Bernard Bailie, although in the gatherings of a large household and retinue, which was often open to access, disreputable individuals might be found who need not have had any personal association with the master of the household. The innuendo of John Knox,[30] like that in passing by Sadler,[31] suggesting over-familiarity between the Cardinal and Mary of Guise is unlikely on the grounds of Mary's known character. It is from Knox, of course, that we learn that David Beaton spent his last night with 'Mistress Marion Ogilvy', a grudging use of the title of a gentlewoman who was, presumably, too well known to need further identification.[32] It was largely as a persecutor of reformers that David Beaton was hated at the time. 'It proved the very rock on which he and all his fortunes perished,' wrote John Spottiswoode, whose father had known him.[33] This, together with personal resentment, was why his assassins killed him, or so they told him.

It took post-contemporary writers a little while to warm to the theme of the Cardinal's sexual depravity, although it is by now customary to give it at least passing mention while paying some kind of tribute to his abilities. Calderwood repeated Knox's words almost *verbatim*. Bishop John Leslie, predictably, gave the Cardinal a good press.[34] Surprisingly, the worst said of him by that embroiderer, Lindsay of Pitscottie, is that 'the cursed Cardinal ... could nevir consider his dewtie towards God, nor the commoun weill of the countrie'.[35] Principal William Robertson, writing in mid-eighteenth century, said, 'by nature of an immoderate ambition; by long experience he had acquired address and refinement; and

insolence grew upon him from continued success ... an avowed enemy to the
doctrine of the reformers. Political motives alone determined him to support the
one [the church of Rome] and oppose the other [reformed beliefs]'.[36] Robertson
got the Cardinal's priorities right, but these were speedily lost sight of by the
predominantly ultra-protestant historians of the nineteenth century. As David
Beaton became more and more identified with the 'doomed' medieval church, so
he became the personification of those vices to which its downfall was attributed.
This was the posthumous reward for his success in becoming the leader of the
ecclesiastical establishment: remembered by many, while the name of Patrick
Hepburn, who it could be argued merited more of the opprobrium, is known only
to students of the period. Robert Chambers, in his *Biographical Dictionary of
Eminent Scotsmen*, echoes the tone of historians of the nineteenth century: 'zealous
churchman and the hired tool of France ... It is probable, as his enemies alone
have been his historians, that the traits of his character and even the tone of his
actions are greatly misrepresented; yet there seems abundant proof of his
sensuality, his cruelty and his total disregard of principle in his exertions for the
preservation of the Catholic faith'.[37] The denunciations of David Beaton's private
life thereafter became consistent and stereotyped, culminating in those of David
Hay Fleming, armed with his painstakingly compiled dossier of clerical
legitimations, who could at least denounce in the grand manner, his ferocity
reminding us of that of John Knox himself.

David Beaton's masterful personality, laced with vanity, was of the kind found
attractive by some women, of whom there were doubtless those at the court of
James V and, even more likely, the court of Francis I, who may have been prepared
to waylay him, churchman though he was. At the same time, with his love of
worldly power and material comfort, he was not the kind of man cut out to lead a
celibate life. Apart from whatever unrecorded lapses he may have had, however,
Marion Ogilvy's is the only woman's name reliably associated with him. There is
the shadowy suggestion of one other, that of Isobel Ogilvy, wife of John Guthrie of
Colliston whose family had long been tenants of Arbroath abbey and to whom
David Beaton feued the lands of Colliston in 1545.[38] There is nothing to
substantiate a modern allegation that Guthrie received the lands as a sop because
the Cardinal had seduced his wife, a story put about by David Hay Fleming on the
basis of second-hand information about Guthrie's charter itself, communicated to
him by a man whose father had had connections with the management of the
Colliston estate at the end of the nineteenth century.[39] The Arbroath gentleman
gave Fleming to understand that the Colliston charter bore, in its initial letters, a
caricature of the Cardinal in the arms of the cuckolded Guthrie's wife, the
information having been passed on by the writer's father who had actually seen the
charter. The document was by then unfortunately 'lost', suppressed, so Fleming
believed, by some 'medievalist' who was anxious to cover up this vital evidence of
the Cardinal's immorality. At one point in their correspondence the good man
from Arbroath, regretting having associated the memory of his respected father
with a piece of muckraking, tried to back out of the whole business but the
historian, bent on getting at the truth, continued to bombard him with questions

about the fateful charter. The fact that their correspondence eventually died off did not deter Fleming from publishing the information he had received in a characteristic piece of sustained vituperation.[40]

It so happens that the Colliston charter is in the Scottish Record Office in Edinburgh, where all interested may see it. It is one of the finest surviving writs issued from the Arbroath chancery, measuring 22″ by 21″, written in an imitation of the papal chancery style by an anonymous clerk who had by then been working for David Beaton in Arbroath business for many years. In the initial letters of the first three important words lie the grains of truth behind the legend, not, as Fleming was given to believe and as he stated in his pamphlet, a picture of the Cardinal in a compromising situation, but tiny drawings, in lighter ink than that in which the charter is written, of three heads, a male head on each side and a female one in the middle, no doubt representing the grantor and grantees: John Guthrie, if it is he, looks rather disgruntled and the lady somewhat coy. A close examination of the document shows that it was signed by the Cardinal as commendator of Arbroath *before* it was taken to the abbey for signature by the monks, a procedure that applies to a number of Arbroath writs. The drawings could have been added at any time after the Cardinal saw the charter — much later, perhaps. If John Guthrie *did* receive his feu 'in compensation', he would hardly be grateful to have a pictorial record of it put in his charter chest. It is perhaps most likely that someone reading the charter confused Isobel's with Marion Ogilvy's name and decorated the document to illustrate a story which the personalities suggested to him.

It has sometimes been suggested that David Beaton and Marion had contracted some kind of marriage before he entered the church. One divine who wrote the history of her family and tied himself in knots trying to dispose of various black sheep made a valiant attempt to reduce Marion to respectability by putting her name in the index to his book as 'Betoun, Marion, *née* Ogilvy'.[41] It is not quite as simple as that. One fact is almost certain, however: that David Beaton was not in major orders for more than half their life together.[42] Lord Herries was correct when he said of their oldest daughter, Margaret, that she 'was gotten and born when the cardinal was young and before he was a priest'.[43] In fact, all eight children were born before he was fully ordained, which probably took place about the time he was consecrated to the French see of Mirepoix in July or August 1538. This means, however, that they were born out of wedlock, for with Beaton's career prospects there could never have been any question of marriage, unless to a woman who was later prepared to renounce her wife's status. But, in common with many other churchmen, as we have seen, he lived in circumstances which in everyday terms scarcely differed from the married state.

It is the recorded identities of his eight children that have largely won the Cardinal much of his notoriety in private life. It is rarely explained that they were all the children of Marion Ogilvy:[44] Margaret, Elizabeth, David, George, James, Alexander, John and Agnes, born between *c*.1525 and *c*.1534–5. Margaret was certainly the oldest child; Elizabeth completed her 18th year by 18 September 1545 (born in 1527); George was legitimated with his older sisters on 5 March 1531 but must have died young as this is his one and only appearance on record; and

David, the oldest surviving son, was dispensed to hold clerical character, with his next brother, James, in September 1542,[45] two months after they had left for France under the charge of sir David Christison.[46] Alexander, a little younger, was being tutored by Mr Adam Mure in 1544[47] and was resident in France in the 1550s.[48] John does not seem to have been destined for an academic career but, in any case, like the youngest child, Agnes, could only have been in his early teens at the time of the Cardinal's death in 1546.

The fact that Alexander, James and John were twice legitimated, on the second occasion with their older brother, David, has raised the question as to whether there were three other sons with these names. Inconsistencies in the ages assigned to the Cardinal's sons in the documents of the papal curia regarding their dispensations and benefices raise similar questions. However, in the cases of David and James different papal documents which plainly refer to the same individuals nevertheless give irreconcilable ages,[49] so that complete reliance cannot be placed in the matter of ages in papers issued by the Roman court. The Cardinal's children are very well documented in public, private and legal records. Of the several hundred references to them throughout their lives which have been collected, none appears to refer to any individuals other than the eight just named who, according to documentary evidence, are demonstrably brothers and sisters german. If the Cardinal did have other offspring in Scotland, they were uncharacteristically unprovided for. Numerous legends have grown up over the years in secondary sources about the castles which he is said to have built or acquired for his supposed mistresses. These were the homes of his daughters, who settled in Angus: Margaret at Finavon, as countess of Crawford; Elizabeth at Vayne, as the wife of Alexander Lindsay of Vayne; and Agnes at Kellie, as wife of her first husband, Ochterlonie of Kellie. Melgund castle was acquired, with the barony of North Melgund, in 1543 and was the home of Marion Ogilvy until her death there in 1575.[50] She and her younger son, John, had an interest in the property of Hospitalfield near Arbroath.[51]

Marion is of interest on her own account. She was the younger daughter of the fourth marriage of Sir James Ogilvy of Lintrathen, created Lord Ogilvy in 1491 on the eve of his departure as ambassador to Denmark.[52] Her mother, Janet Lyle, was possibly a daughter of Robert, second Lord Lyle, who held large tracts of land in Renfrewshire and was ambassador to Spain, also in 1491.[53] Marion probably grew up at Airlie castle, on the Angus-Perthshire border, built by her grandfather in the 1430s. If she remembered her father at all it must have been as an old man, for he was about sixty when he married her mother. Her oldest half-brother, John, who became second Lord Ogilvy, was almost forty years older than her and even the children of her father's second marriage were very much her seniors. There were no surviving children of his third marriage. Her nearest contemporary, apart from her full-sister, Janet, was John, fourth Lord Ogilvy, bailie of Arbroath abbey for David Beaton, who was actually her great-nephew.

At the time of his death the first Lord Ogilvy had made only partial provision for his two youngest daughters, an indenture made in 1503 with Sir Alexander Gordon of Midmar by which Janet (then aged thirteen) was to marry one of

Gordon's kinsmen, with her younger sister Marion named as an alternative bride in the event of Janet's death.[54] So far as is known this was the only provision made for Marion by her father who died in 1504. Janet Lyle remained a widow for the rest of her life — about twenty-one years — and brought up her two daughters at Airlie castle of which she would enjoy the liferent. Marion, therefore, was trained by a woman who had learned to manage her own affairs, an experience which stood her in good stead in later years. When her mother died, probably in 1525, she was left with few near relatives of her own age-group, an unmarried woman of about thirty, poorly provided for. The fact that she was the sole executrix of both her parents suggests that her sister had already died but that there had been no attempt to implement the indenture of 1503.[55] Her oldest half-brother, John, second Lord Ogilvy, had died in 1505, a year after their father. The third Lord was killed at Flodden in 1513. The head of the family in 1525 was Marion's great-nephew already mentioned, John, fourth Lord Ogilvy. His youngish great-aunt was well above the normal marriageable age. While she may have represented a problem for him, it is perhaps unjustified to suggest that he turned to David Beaton, whom he knew well, to get him out of his difficulty, but it is possible. On the other hand, Marion herself may have seen a way out of becoming a dependent member of her great-nephew's household.

She and David Beaton had an overlapping circle of acquaintances among whom they may have met. Both came from families with a tradition of royal and diplomatic service. In 1503 Marion's oldest half-brother had sat on the King's council with David's uncle James, long before the latter became archbishop of Glasgow. In 1512, by which time James Beaton had been promoted to that see, he received a crown gift of the ward and marriage of John, the young Lord Lyle, who was possibly Marion's cousin, whom he eventually married off to his niece, Grizel Beaton of Creich. David Beaton may have met Marion in the household of Lord Ogilvy, perhaps in the family's lodging in Arbroath, and their association may date from about the end of 1524 when he returned from France after the collapse of the Albany régime, the year in which Lord Ogilvy was served heir to his estates. In the 1520s John Beaton of Balfour and Isobel Monypenny were marrying off their large family: James, elder, to Janet Annand, heiress of Melgund; Janet to David Cockburn of Treton, a near neighbour; Katherine to William Graham of Fintry; Elizabeth to John Wardlaw of Torry; and Margaret to John Graham of Claverhouse. David's association with Marion Ogilvy was just as likely to have been mutual as arranged; the fact that they were about the same age and were still together when over fifty suggests that this was the case. Marion was a good and resourceful, if occasionally unscrupulous, manager of her affairs,[56] the kind of character able to cope with a personality such as David Beaton's. Like him she seems to have had a strong, not to say indomitable, nature; she leaned heavily enough when signing her name to split the quill on more than one occasion. She bore her large family in quick succession when she was over thirty, and once appeared in the law courts — she was incorrigibly litigious — when carrying her second daughter, Elizabeth, although whether this denotes stamina or effrontery is a matter of opinion; on that occasion she employed a *forespeaker*.[57] On 6 April

1525 she was at Airlie winding up her mother's affairs, but by February 1526 she was with David Beaton in Edinburgh.[58] Although often in the capital on legal business, she seems to have spent most of her time at Arbroath, probably at the abbot's manor of Ethie which seems to have been granted to her in liferent. Unlike some women from her social background whom marriage removed from their home country, she spent her life in her native Angus and must have been a well-known figure in Arbroath itself where the notaries who worked for the abbey did business for her, where she once *redeemed* a piece of wadset land at the altar of the Lady chapel at the Bridgend and, on another occasion, deposited redemption money, unclaimed by her creditor, with the custodians of the abbey treasury.[59]

Whatever money she received directly from the abbot, she was granted various pieces of abbey property from which she was able to build up a living for herself: a life-lease of the Bruntoun and Easter green of Ethie, with the brewland, meadowland and teinds,[60] parts of the Kirktoun of St Vigeans (Arbroath),[61] an eighth of the lands of the village of Auchmithie[62] and a piece of ground against the abbey precinct wall on which to build a kiln for drying grain.[63] In practice she would draw the rents of subtenants. Judging from the many times she either wadset or redeemed land, she both borrowed and lent money. There are no indications that she frequented the royal court, or that she ever went to France with David Beaton; there is documentary evidence that she was at Arbroath during at least one of his longer visits abroad. She kept a firm grasp of her family's affairs throughout her life, taking charge of their business and legal papers and, at times, those of David Beaton himself, including papers relating to money which he had borrowed from the King.[64] Apart from John Knox's passing reference to her there are no contemporary comments on her, but one imagines that the woman who once got herself into the exceptional position of being a member of a panel of arbiters in a legal dispute was a character to be reckoned with.[65]

NOTES

1. W. Hay, *Lectures on the law of marriage* (Stair Society), 293 (Hay *Lectures*)

2. J. Dowden, *The Medieval Church in Scotland*, 308 (*Dowden*)

3. D. Patrick, *Statutes of the Scottish Church, 1225–1559* (S.H.S.), 14–15 (*Statutes*)

4. *Ibid.*, 84

5. *Ibid.*, 90

6. *Ibid.*, 90–1

7. Hay, *Lectures*, 295, 299

8. *Ibid.*, 255

9. *Ibid.*, 17, 23, xxxviii

10. A.D.C., xxvi, ii, fo 37, quoted in D. H. Fleming, *The Reformation in Scotland*, 570–7

11. J. M. Todd, *Martin Luther*, 33

12. Register of Abbreviates of feu charters of kirklands (S.R.O.), E14/2, fo 278

13. *Registrum de Dunfermelyn* (Bannatyne Club), 554; *Royal Commission on the Ancient and Historical Monuments (Scotland), Report on Fife, Kinross and Clackmannan*, 72

14. Eglinton muniments (S.R.O.), GD 3/2/91/1
15. British Library, Additional MSS, 32005
16. Sanderson, *Scottish rural society*, 147
17. C. H. Haws, *Scottish Parish Clergy at the Reformation, 1540–1574* (S.R.S.), 224
18. *Statutes*, 91
19. J. H. Burton, *History of Scotland*, III, 308–9
20. *Dowden*, Chapter 19, especially 309–10
21. R. Lindsay of Pitscottie, *Historie and Cronicles of Scotland* (S.T.S.), I, 351 (*Pitscottie*)
22. *Knox*, II, 242
23. Mahoney, 'The Scottish Hierarchy', 43–61
24. I. B. Cowan, *The Scottish Reformation*, 70
25. Sir David Lindsay, *Ane Satyre of the Thrie Estaitis* (S.T.S.), lines 3421–6
26. Register of Abbreviates of feu charters of kirklands, E 14/2, fo 322; *R.M.S.*, V, 681
27. *Knox*, I, 59
28. *The Tragedie*
29. G. Buchanan, *Rerum Scoticarum Historia*, trans. J.Aikman, II, 212
30. *Knox*, I, 40
31. *Hamilton papers*, II, 55
32. *Knox*, I, 76
33. J. Spottiswoode, *History of the Church of Scotland*, I, 162 (*Spottiswoode*)
34. J. Leslie, *De Origine, moribus et rebus gestis Scotorum* (S.T.S.), 245 (*Leslie*)
35. *Pitscottie*, 418
36. W. Robertson, *Complete Works*, ed. D.Stewart (1840), *History of Scotland*, 27
37. R. Chambers, *Biographical Dictionary of Eminent Scotsmen*, I, 180–1
38. Register House charters (S.R.O.), Supplementary, 25 July 1545; text printed in *R.M.S.*, V, 1104
39. D. Hay Fleming papers in the Hay Fleming Reference Library, St Andrews
40. D. H. Fleming, *Were Cardinal Beaton and Archbishop Hamilton not Libertines?* reprinted from *The Bulwark*. Copy in the Beveridge Papers (S.R.O.), GD 215/1906
41. W. Wilson, *The House of Airlie*, I, 75
42. Vatican archives, Reg. Supp., 2020, fos 173r–v
43. Lord Herries, *Historical Memoirs of the Reign of Mary, Queen of Scots* (Abbotsford Club), 15–16
44. Documents associating the children with Marion Ogilvy include (Margaret) Forfar diligence records (S.R.O.), DI 57/1, fos 42–4, (Elizabeth) Dalhousie muniments, GD45/16/575, (David, Alexander and John) *RMS* III, 3150, (David and James) *RSS* II, 2467, (Agnes, David and Alexander) Agnes's testament, Miscellaneous collections (S.R.O.), GD1/311/2. George is associated with Margaret and Elizabeth in the legitimation, *RSS* II, 843
45. Vatican archives, Reg. Supp., 2466, fos 272r–v
46. *Rentale*, 139
47. *Ibid.*, 199
48. Register of deeds, old series (S.R.O.), ii, fo 347; Register of acts and decreets (S.R.O.), xviii, fo 81
49. Vatican archives, Reg. Supp., 2466, fos 272r–v, 2486, fo 259v and 2466, fos 271v–2; Reg. Lat., 1778, fos 49–51
50. Edinburgh commissariot records, register of testaments (S.R.O.), CC8/8/3, fo 260 (Edinburgh testaments)
51. *RSS* IV, 1285

52. *Peerage*, I, 114; *Acts of the parliaments of Scotland*, II, 228 (*A.P.S.*); *T.A.*, I, 200
53. *Peerage*, V, 553–4
54. *Records of Aboyne* (Spalding Club), 220
55. Airlie muniments, GD 16/42/5; A.D.C., xxxv, fo 208v
56. Accused of 'interlining' the text of royal letters of horning, *T.A.*, IX, 362, 390
57. *A.D.C.*, xxxvii, fo 43
58. *Ibid.*, xxxv, fo 208v
59. Register of acts and decreets, vi, fo 227
60. *Arbroath Liber*, II, 697
61. *Ibid.*, II, 747
62. *Ibid.*, II, 797
63. *Ibid.*, II, 804
64. Register of acts and decreets, vii, fo 1
65. Register of deeds, old series, i, fo 292v

4

The King's Servant

During his years at home, from his return to Scotland at Christmas 1524 until his next visit to France in the spring of 1533, David Beaton set about making a place for himself in the central administration and became involved in developments of national significance. The contrast between the intensive documentation of his last few years and the more dispersed evidence of his part in politics during the lifetime of King James V is apt to give the impression that in this earlier period his involvement was marginal and spasmodic. This cannot have been the case, for it was in this period, when he was in his thirties, that he built up his career in Scotland, as he had done in France in his twenties for which there is even less documentation; then it had been with the patronage of Albany, now that of the King himself was vital.

There were some obstacles in the way of his progress, the first of which was the ascendancy of Angus, rallying point of the English party, which lasted from the winter of 1524–5 until the summer of 1528 when the King escaped from the Douglases and was placed at the head of the government by a representative group of influential men. The rise of the Douglases meant the eclipse of the French party's political programme, to which the Beatons gave consistent support, and the possibility of Henry VIII's gaining a foothold in Scottish affairs. Angus seized control in 1526 by simply refusing to hand over the person of the King to the councillors who were his next guardians by rotation. He tightened his grip on the administration by putting his kinsmen and dependants into key government posts and into those in the royal household nearest to the King: his uncle, Archibald Douglas of Kilspindie became treasurer and, for the second time, provost of Edinburgh, his brother, George Douglas, became master of the household, James Douglas of Drumlanrig, master of the wine cellar, and James Douglas of Parkhead, master of the larder. He alienated some of the nobles by whose help he had come to power. In addition, Lennox, Argyll, Cassillis and Glencairn disappeared from the council in August 1526; Arran was hardly ever present after October of that year and Archbishop James Beaton had ceased to attend after 17 March.

There was growing cohesion among the opposition to the Douglases, which took two main forms: surreptitious support for the French alliance led by Archbishop James Beaton who still kept in touch with Albany, and outright attempts to rescue the King from Angus's custody led by the earl of Lennox, supported by Argyll, Cassillis and Glencairn, during one of which Lennox was killed in a trial of strength with the Douglases at Linlithgow in 1526. When parliament met in June of that year the King, now fourteen years old, was declared head of the government and a council was named which excluded the archbishop of St Andrews, from whom Angus took the great seal a month later. Until Christmas 1526, when he gained Angus's consent to his spending that season with the King and Queen Mother at Holyrood, James Beaton kept away from the capital, even resorting to disguise, so it was said, in order to avoid Angus's spies.

In spite of the Douglas régime David Beaton stayed in Edinburgh for as long as possible, no doubt watching the way the wind was blowing. Between February 1525 and March 1526 he attended five sessions of parliament as abbot of Arbroath, on several occasions as a lord of the articles, the committee that initiated legislation, presenting it to the full parliament for acceptance, which in its composition formed a personal link with the King's council. On 17 July 1525 those lords to be charged with the safekeeping of the King's person were named, to act in rotation. The first rota, to take charge from then until Allhallowmas (1 November), were Angus himself and the King's tutor, Gavin Dunbar, archbishop of Glasgow, in association with the bishop of Orkney, the abbots of Holyrood and Arbroath and Lord Seton. The same session of parliament passed an act aimed at curbing the interest in Lutheran literature in Scotland.[1]

The abbot of Arbroath was even more regular in his attendance at the council where he first appears on record on 27 March 1525, three months after his return from France.[2] He took part both in business relating to public affairs and in hearing legal cases brought before the lords of council in their judicial capacity, rather more often in the latter than the former. He attended on 30 March 1525 and, thereafter, once in May, throughout July, once in August, once in September and frequently from mid-October until the end of the year. He attended regularly in January and February 1526, but his appearance on 14 March, when he also attended parliament, was his last until the end of that year.[3] When in June Angus had refused to hand over the King to the next set of lords David Beaton was in Dunfermline with his uncle, who at one time used him as his spokesman with the earl of Arran and his friends.[4] In 1527 David came back but did not appear in council until 18 April.[5] However, as Marion Ogilvy compeared personally before the lords in pursuing a legal action in March and early April, it is likely that he too was in Edinburgh at that time. He attended again on 11 and 13 May 1527, on 6 August, 4 October and regularly throughout the last week in November and first two weeks of December, even although Angus was at that time at the height of his control.[6] He did not attend again, however, until 14 July 1528 when the King, having assumed control of the government on the downfall of Angus, was himself present in council.[7] Evidently, towards the end of the Douglas régime it became more difficult for David Beaton to participate in public affairs and legal business, or he may have chosen to stay away. If during the first half of 1528 he was actually among those excluded by Angus from participation in the administration, it not only prevented his taking part in public policy-making but threatened to put an end to the legal career for which he had been trained.

Even after the downfall of Angus in the autumn of 1528 and the forfeiture and banishment of him and his Douglas kinsmen, all was not straightforward. There were rivals for royal favour. The Beaton interest was dealt a serious blow when the chancellorship, on the departure of Angus, was not returned to the archbishop of

St Andrews but given to Gavin Dunbar, who had been promoted to Glasgow on James Beaton's translation to St Andrews, on whom the King greatly depended in the early years of his reign. To an ambitious family this meant a serious loss of patronage, political initiative and royal confidence. The Beatons' resentment was aggravated by the animosity between the two archbishops over the question of Glasgow's claim to exemption from the jurisdiction of the primatial see, a question which later led to bitter relations between David Beaton and Gavin Dunbar. The growing influence of the archbishop of Glasgow was bound to be disturbing for the abbot of Arbroath, whose ambition to succeed his uncle in St Andrews was probably even by then clear-cut. He could not hope to step into his uncle's shoes, however, without crown nomination, and his family's influence seemed to be diminishing. It was possible that with royal favour Gavin Dunbar might one day be translated from Glasgow to St Andrews, thus blocking David Beaton's expected line of advance. There was even the danger that other powers which James Beaton had hoped might come his way, namely those of legate *a latere* which would make him papal representative in his own country, might with the King's influence go to Dunbar. Although it seems as if James V's letter to Pope Clement VII in 1530, urging the need for a Scottish cardinal with legatine powers and suggesting the archbishop of Glasgow in preference to that of St Andrews,[8] was unknown at the time to the Scottish prelates, David Beaton knew that his uncle's plea for these powers for himself had received no encouragement from the King, and the possibility of Dunbar's receiving the honour instead must have preyed on his mind. The grant of such full powers to the archbishop of Glasgow would mean a curb on the authority of David Beaton even should he one day succeed his uncle in the primatial see; after all, England's cardinal legate, Wolsey, was only archbishop of York.

Royal confidence had to be worked for. Since in 1528 Archbishop James Beaton was only partially restored to favour, it may have looked to his nephew as if further advancement might mean shelving the uncle through whom he had gained his earliest advantages. It is significant that, just as during the Angus régime David Beaton had clung whenever possible to his place in the central administration while his uncle withdrew, so now he remained in James V's favour and won his support in a quarrel with the archbishop over the Arbroath revenues while the latter was under a cloud. There is no doubt that taking care of his own interests was his priority whatever that might do to family relations. It is even more remarkable that he continued in the King's favour in spite of the fact that, with his uncle and other ecclesiastics, he resisted James's fiscal policies of the early 1530s. It is the measure of his astuteness that he could regulate, or at least conceal, his opposition so that it did not prevent his becoming a trusted royal servant, especially in the diplomatic field, and it is an indication of his ability and experience in that field that James chose him as his ambassador when more co-operative individuals were available.

Since the King's main problem on assuming the government was his lack of money, any policy which he worked out, domestic or foreign, was bound to be concerned with refilling the royal coffers which the Queen, Albany and Angus among them had emptied. There were two important potential sources of the much-needed money, if only they could be successfully tapped: the revenues of the church and the dowry that would come with a European marriage. Taxation of the church for public purposes was not new, but a levy of the order envisaged by the King needed a convincing pretext.[9] It was easy in those days of growing heresy to play on the fears of Pope and clergy, yet the latter were reluctant to dig further into their pockets unless for a good reason. In the spring of 1531 the King's secretary, Thomas Erskine, travelled to Rome and among other business may have presented a royal letter to the Pope, to which the latter replied with the request that the prelates give their opinion on a proposal that they contribute £10,000 Scots a year to the crown for what was loosely described as 'the protection and defence of the realm'. The Pope followed this shortly afterwards with the imposition on the Scottish church of a *tenth*, for three years, calling on the prelates to regard it, unwelcome though it was, as a duty in the light of Scotland's vulnerability to attack, both of a military and spiritual kind, from the powers around her, chiefly from England.

On 13 September, before the prelates had had time to voice their reaction in a formal assembly, another papal bull was issued repeating the demand for £10,000 but substituting for 'the protection and defence of the realm' a much more concrete proposal. The bull narrated how the duke of Albany, also recently in Rome on James's behalf, had explained the King's desire to set up a college of judges for decisions in civil causes, half of whom were to be churchmen. Since the King was unable to do so on his own expenses the Pope had been asked to impose the subsidy on the prelates. Those commissioned to levy the tax were the chancellor, Gavin Dunbar, Alexander Stewart, Albany's half-brother, and Henry Wemyss, bishop of Galloway. Whatever the petition that resulted in the Pope's bull, perhaps a revised version of that originally presented by Thomas Erskine, it may well have been known to the secretary and those prelates named as commissioners, all of whom stood high in the King's confidence at this time.

The practice of periodically setting aside a group of lords to dispense civil justice had a long history, going back to the reign of James I. James IV's attempts to regularise the practice had died with him at Flodden. Neither Albany nor Angus had tried to revive them, although occasional efforts to enforce regular holding of and attendance at 'the sessions' as they were known, as well as to formalise procedure, were made by those sympathetic to the idea of a permanent, professional civil court, who included, notably, Archbishop Gavin Dunbar. But the sessions were seen by many of those who attended them as simply one of the functions of the King's council, the same personnel often sitting on both, including untrained but experienced laymen such as feudal magnates whose function was to represent the King's council on the sessions. What *was* new was the proposal to set apart permanently those lords who handled the purely legal business of the sessions, as distinct from the administrative and public business of the council, and, above all, to *endow* them with regular salaries. It should be stressed that while the papal bull of 1531 authorised the endowment of a body of judges, it did not establish the college of justice — another bull from another Pope did that four years later. The idea of endowing such a body probably owed much to the inspiration of the chancellor, Gavin Dunbar, and to Thomas Erskine, the secretary, a Pavia-trained lawyer, who may have suggested the title 'college of justice' as a term familiar in Italy.

The move was bound to be unpopular with conservatives generally, with the unqualified feudal magnates who looked down on the sometimes humbly-born professional lawyers, and with the prelates who were asked to provide the large sum for the endowment. The amount demanded was staggering. The three *tenths* were to be uplifted from all benefices worth more than £20 a year on their own estimated worth. The 'great tax' of £10,000 alone meant a permanent contribution from the prelates of about one sixth of their valued revenue. During the three years in which both contributions were to be paid the prelates would be handing over to the crown more than a quarter of their incomes. Whereas there was no marked objection to the three *tenths*, the great tax provoked instant opposition. This was almost inevitably led by Archbishop James Beaton, partly because he had not been consulted in the negotiations and partly because the whole scheme owed much to the chancellor. Whether or not David Beaton made his opposition apparent at the time, events were to show that he entirely shared his uncle's reluctance to co-operate. So great was the clerical opposition that the Pope sent Silvester Darius, an apostolic auditor of causes, to Scotland to see that James remained a faithful son of the holy see in any compromise worked out between King and clergy. When parliament met in May 1532 no decisive action was taken on the Pope's bull.[10] There were some measures aimed at regularising procedure in the sessions: it was laid down that the King should set aside fourteen judges, with a president who would be a churchman, and that he should also nominate three or four lords to sit on the session as representatives of the council. It was the old pattern, with the royal role in the nominations strongly emphasised. The customary statutes confirming the liberties of the church were more elaborate than usual, to impress the envoy, and special mention was made of the generosity of the present Pope to the Scottish church. The papal ambassador took home a certified copy of these enactments to reassure the Pope of James's loyalty.

A rule that the chancellor when present in the session should occupy the presidential chair and have a hand in the formulation of procedural rules did nothing to cool the Beatons' resentment at the whole affair. David Beaton must have been angered at the prospect of an additional burden on the Arbroath revenues over which he was then haggling with his uncle. But the spiritual estate was in a cleft stick, unwilling to forfeit the fifty per cent representation on the session and clerical monopoly of the presidency and at the same time in need of an efficient, professional civil court of appeal in days of growing disregard of ecclesiastical censures and resentment at the length of their procedures. The solution, therefore, lay in a compromise acceptable to the King. In the end the prelates compounded for a lump sum payment of £72,000 to be paid over four years and a perpetual contribution towards the judges' salaries of £1,400 a year, to be supplemented by the crown. The £1,400 was to come, not directly from the prelates' pockets, but from the fruits of benefices in their patronage to be earmarked for the purpose, the deduction to be postponed during the lifetimes of the then incumbents. It was a poor lookout for the judges' salaries which, as it turned out, were irregularly paid. In 1532 the King tried to supplement his share of the salaries by ordaining that the profits and fees from the privy and great seals and the signet should be set aside for that purpose. The order was abortive, however; it is difficult to see how the then keepers of these seals, Gavin Dunbar, David Beaton and Thomas Erskine, would have agreed to a diversion of their incomes without compensation.

The bull of Pope Paul III erecting the college of justice was issued on 10 March 1535. In its terms we see signs that James V had been out to protect his own interests in the whole business. The £1,400 was named as the sum modified from £10,000 set aside for the college, with no mention of the £72,000 which with the three *tenths* appears to have been spent later on the royal palaces. As Professor Hannay has said, 'The actual effect of the bull was to free the King from the need to supplement the annual £1,400 and to leave the college with a poor endowment'. It is no wonder that the controversy between King and prelates became bitter. When parliament met in 1535 Archbishop James Beaton did not attend, but his silent protest did not daunt the King who, in the following year, when the last instalment of the £72,000 fell due, hit on the idea of a provincial council of the Scottish church at which he might force the prelates to ratify the papal bull of erection and, in so doing, acknowledge their liability for the first payment of £1,400 towards the judges' salaries. The idea of a council was startling, for none had been held since 1470 and, since the erection of the archbishoprics, first of St Andrews in 1472 and then Glasgow in 1492, such a council had been impossible to convene because of the jealousy between the two metropolitans and Glasgow's unwillingness to obey a summons to a council at the bidding of the primate.

On this occasion James Beaton appeared reluctant to convoke a council at the King's request, but after a persuasive-cum-admonitory letter from James V he gave in. Dunbar formally protested that his attendance should in no way prejudice the see of Glasgow. At the council, which met in the church of the Dominicans in Edinburgh from 11 to 16 March 1536, the recalcitrant prelates were made aware that the King's determination to gain their complete submission carried more serious threats. In a second-hand account of the council which he sent to his brother, Sir George Douglas, on 24 March Angus claimed that the King had threatened to make the church abolish mortuaries and to feu church land without increasing the rentals, adding that the Scottish churchmen had never been more discontented.[11] Already the preambles to some feu charters carried clauses to the effect that the grantees' down-payments were being used to recoup contributions to 'the great tax'.[12] Another report of the council even claimed that the prelates agreed to pay the judges' salaries themselves until such times as the earmarked benefices fell vacant,[13] paper promises if made at all. The fiscal tussle between King and kirkmen in Scotland ran concurrently with an important stage in the relations between Henry VIII and the church in England. The Scottish provincial council met during the final session of the English so-called 'reformation parliament' which, before it rose on 14 April, approved the Act for dissolving the lesser monasteries. This followed on the royal commissions to examine clerical incomes, in the spring and summer of 1535, and the visitations of the English monasteries in the autumn and winter of 1535–6. Although the Scottish prelates knew that through papal concessions James was able to manipulate the appointments to the greater benefices and fill the royal coffers with the revenues of monasteries held *in commendam* by his infant sons, they never could rest content that he would not succumb to pressure from his uncle to make a more direct attack on church property.

James's tone was dictatorial and the clerics gave in. Yet, not until 1541 did parliament ratify the erection of the college of justice,[14] when nothing was said about the prelates' personal liability for a contribution, and the judges' salaries continued to be irregularly paid. From an action raised in court just after the 1541 parliament rose, we learn that neither David Beaton, as abbot of Arbroath, nor his uncle, as archbishop of St Andrews, had paid a penny towards the tax since 1536; their combined debt, for which David, by then both abbot and archbishop, was sued by the King's advocate, amounted to £770.[15] It is clear that the whole idea of the great tax was for the King's personal convenience. The pretext of a college of justice was arrived at suddenly. There is a flavour of cynicism in the episode: the King, having got his £72,000 to spend on his building programmes, could afford to wait five years to see the erection of the college ratified.[16] It was really the lawyers who were concerned to have the situation regularised, some of whom may have been behind the later test-case against David Beaton for non-payment, although they had to wait until after the King's death to complain seriously about the arrears of their salaries. It should be mentioned that Gavin Dunbar, one of those most concerned to achieve the endowment of a professional court, was himself considerably in arrears of payment with his own contribution to the tax; with substantial revenues behind him he could afford to take his place on the bench unpaid, as hitherto, unlike the less wealthy but professionally-trained laymen who hoped to embark on a legal career, the increase in whose numbers was resented by some churchmen.

On 3 January 1529 David Beaton had been made keeper of the privy seal for life, an appointment which carried with it a considerable amount of patronage.[17] From mid-fifteenth century onwards the keeper was a high-ranking official, taking precedence over the King's secretary who was keeper of the signet. Documents passing under the privy seal were either warrants to the chancellor to issue writs under the great seal, such as grants of land and major offices, or documents which required the attachment of the privy seal only, including grants of minor offices, commissions, pensions, gifts of escheat, pardons, remissions and letters of legitimation and naturalisation. The keeper could often use his patronage for the benefit of friends: less than a month after David Beaton's appointment his brother, James Beaton of Melgund, received the gift of an escheat *gratis*.[18] Grantees normally paid two sums, or a sum consisting of two parts, one of these representing the composition to the King's treasury and the other the fees for writing and sealing the document which went to the keeper as his salary. The fact that business arrived in the privy seal office from that of the secretary and that a good deal of it passed on to that of the chancellor called for a reasonably good working relationship between the keeper and these other officials. David Beaton worked fairly well with the royal secretary, Thomas Erskine — they were joint ambassadors to France in 1534[19] — but not so well with the chancellor, Gavin Dunbar.

Memoranda scribbled in the margins of the register of the privy seal by the clerks throw light on his keepership.[20] There are many references to him, including notes of days when he left Edinburgh. Quite large sums were gathered from the fees, such as the £70 16s 8d taken at the justice ayre, the criminal court on circuit, at Aberdeen in July 1531. Since the privy seal was taken around by the clerks to wherever the court was held in order that they might authenticate documents with it, the keeper's servants, including sir James Auchmowty, sir John Arnot, graniter of Arbroath, and two probable kinsmen, John and Thomas Beaton, travelled about collecting the fees in places as far apart as Aberdeen, Dumbarton and Kirkcudbright. David Beaton was sometimes present at the justice ayres himself: on 8 July 1531 at Aberdeen, when he witnessed Fraser of Philorth's payment of £10 as satisfaction for killing one David Scott, the money to be used to found a mass for the soul of the victim;[21] or at Dumfries on 21 November 1535 where he was one of the compositors along with his uncle the earl of Montrose, the treasurer and comptroller.[22] In December 1529 Robert Leslie of Innerpeffer, his 'man of law' in Arbroath affairs, was made custodian of the privy seal itself; a note in the register mentions his taking delivery of it 'after the return of my lord from the justice ayres'.[23]

Sums from the fees were often handed over to individuals 'at my lordis command': £30 to Patrick Fleming, burgess of Edinburgh, £15 to the treasurer 'at my lordis command for the yong lard of Torreis compositioun' (David Beaton's nephew), sums to Mr Thomas Kincraigy, who was later his procurator fiscal in Lothian, and Mr John Gledstanes, advocates. At other times the proportion of the fees handed over to the keeper is noted: £18 out of the £23 from the ayres of the south-west in 1529, £42 out of the £70 16s 8d collected at Aberdeen in 1531. Clearly, after certain authorised deductions had been made, he still realised a fairly regular income from the emoluments of the office. Mr George Cook, who held the prebend of Crieff in Dunkeld cathedral, took over the post of chief clerk to the privy seal in May 1535.[24] From an Edinburgh burgess family, Cook also continued to work in the chancery of Archbishop James Beaton and ultimately in that of David Beaton himself after he was promoted to St Andrews in 1539. In July 1537, while the keeper of the privy seal was out of Scotland, Mr Bernard Bailie annoyed Cook by walking into the privy seal office on one occasion and personally sealing a document the contents of which he refused to divulge.[25] At other times David Beaton might hold up procedure himself: in August 1532 Lord Maxwell complained that the keeper had refused to allow the privy seal to be appended to royal instructions for him about peace-keeping on the borders, when David Beaton 'took instruments' that he had refused merely 'for the sake of the commoun weal', and 'until the lordis had been advisit'.[26]

As keeper of the privy seal his name appears among the official witnesses of royal charters, although, as in the case of other officials, this does not necessarily imply that he personally witnessed every document in question. He did witness some royal charters granted to his friends, however, including some to Sir James Hamilton of Finnart between 1531 and 1536.[27] More importantly, he frequently acted as an auditor of the treasurer's accounts.[28] In August 1531 he was one of the lords who gave a decree to enforce payment to the exchequer clerks of fees due by the late treasurer.[29] He was also among those chosen to draw up arrangements for the expedition to the borders in May 1530.[30] He himself appears as a supplicant in the courts from time to time. Letters of *lawbŭrrows* raised against him by some Arbroath tenants were annulled in August 1532.[31] Slightly earlier he won his case to obtain custody of the young Alexander Bannerman of Watterton, whose ward and marriage had been granted to him by the crown, when his procurator proved that Alexander was over seven years of age and could be taken from his mother.[32] With the laird of Boniton, one of his Arbroath tenants, he got exemption from the effect of a gift to John, Lord Innermeath, of all the profits from the baronies of Innermeath and Inverkeillour.[33] All of these rights and privileges affected his income.

By the mid-1530s he had clearly become the most influential and probably the most prosperous member of a wide circle of family and friends who depended on his patronage and protection: lending 200 merks to a distant relative, Lord Hay of Yester, to pay an Edinburgh merchant, Nicholas Cairncross, handing over the money to Hay in the collegiate church of Kirk o' Field;[34] keeping custody of legal papers, including those relating to the unfortunate mental incapacity of his brother-in-law, the laird of Torry;[35] and paying his own man of law, Robert Leslie of Innerpeffer, and his advocate friend, Mr Thomas Marjoribanks, to act in the civil court on behalf of his mother, the widowed lady of Balfour.[36] When he went to France as ambassador in 1536, those granted protection from legal actions during his absence included over fifty named persons, with their dependants, in addition to the tenantry of Arbroath abbey — some indication of the extent of his patronage and financial interests.[37]

At court, tensions between parties must have been felt in personal terms in council and session. Yet David Beaton appears to have remained on fairly good terms with a number of councillors: the earl of Moray, the King's natural brother, with whom he reached agreement about the Arbroath pension and who remained his ally until Moray's death in 1544; William Gibson, lawyer and scholar, dean of the collegiate church of Restalrig and lord of session from 1533, who much later was chosen as his suffragan bishop; Adam Otterburn, son of an Edinburgh burgess, lawyer and diplomat, who remained one of his closest friends in the critical years after the King's death. Above all, in this busy but often frustrating period he was able to maintain himself in the King's favour, even when his family's fortunes as represented by the archbishop of St Andrews appeared to be under threat. During James V's visit to France in 1536–7 an observer referred to 'the abbot who directs him [the King]', and 'the abbot whom one might call the King himself'.[38] It was in his support for the King's plans for a French marriage, strengthened by his own diplomatic gifts and experience of the French court, that his advantage lay.

NOTES

1. *A.P.S.* II, 295
2. A.D.C., xxxv, fo 12
3. *Ibid.*, xxxvi, fo 8v
4. Burnet Stuart collection, (S.R.O.) GD 115/4
5. A.D.C., xxxvii, fo 112v
6. See Itinerary, Appendix 2
7. A.D.C., xxxviii, fo 131v
8. *Letters of James V*, 183–4
9. For background to and narrative of events leading up to the endowment of and ratification of the college of justice I have relied extensively on R. K. Hannay, *The College of Justice*
10. *A.P.S.*, II, 334–6
11. W. Fraser, *The Douglas Book*, IV, 143
12. *RMS*, III, 1330, 1885, 2332, 2624, 2657
13. A.D.C.S., xv, fos 102r–v
14. *A.P.S.*, ii, 371
15. A.D.C.S., fos 102r–v
16. Hannay, *College of Justice*, 67
17. *R.S.S.*, I, 4019
18. *Ibid.*, I, 4050
19. *L.P. Henry VIII*, VII, 205–8, 210
20. *R.S.S.*, II, Appendix
21. *Antiquities of Aberdeen and Banff* (Spalding Club), IV, 97
22. *R.S.S.*, II, Appendix
23. *Ibid.*
24. *Ibid.*
25. *Ibid.*
26. A.D.C.S., i, fo 103v
27. Hamilton muniments, S.R.O. Survey, Box 7/102/9, 19; Box 8/103/3
28. *Exchequer rolls*, XVI, 402, 447, XVII, 70; *T.A.*, VI, 239
29. A.D.C. xliii, fos 30v
30. *Ibid.* xli, fo 78v
31. A.D.C.S., i, fos 109v–10
32. *Ibid.*, i, fos 72v, 95v
33. *R.S.S.*, II, 1987
34. Yester writs (S.R.O.), GD 28/446
35. A.D.C.S., ix, fos 105v–6
36. *Ibid.*, vii, fos 150r–v, viii, fo 63
37. *R.S.S.*, II, 2166
38. J. Herkless and R. K. Hannay, *The Archbishops of St Andrews*, IV, 22 (Herkless and Hannay, *Archbishops*)

Part II

'One Prince abufe all preistis'

'I maid sic servyce tyll our Soverane kyng,
He did Promove me tyll more hie estait, —
One Prince, abufe all preistis for tyll ryng,
Archibyschope of Sanct androus consecrat.
Till that honour quhen I wes Elevate,
My prydefull hart was nocht content, at all,
Tyll that I create wes ane Cardinall.'

Sir David Lindsay, *The Tragedie of the Cardinall* (Scottish Text Society), lines 57–63

5

The French Marriage

In 1532 the Franco-Scottish alliance pledged by Louis XII and James IV became due for renewal at a time when France and England were drawn together against the Emperor. In the spring of 1533 James V sent David Beaton, his 'very intimate, familiar and confidential counsellor', to France with letters to the King and parlement of Paris pointing out the dangers of France's desertion of her old ally. 'Not only is the relationship broken by a common enemy as it should not have been', ran the letters which the abbot of Arbroath carried, 'but the age-old friendship has given place to a temporary one, to the grave peril of both realms'.

For the next decade David Beaton's public life was largely lived in the arena of international politics, where the circumstances created by the power-struggle of Hapsburg, Valois and Tudor gave his own small home-country the chance to play a rôle out of all proportion to her actual consequence. It was not so much a question of Scotland's being able to put pressure on any of the great powers as of being able to take advantage of those moments in the diplomatic game in which one of them played Scotland off against another as a threat. In this respect James V was exceptionally lucky. When the Emperor tried to divide France and Scotland by offering a marriage alliance to the latter, James appeared to consider the proposal in order to remind Francis I that the 'auld alliance' must be kept in good repair. The King of Scots quite genuinely played the role of champion of Catholic orthodoxy on the fringe of Europe while calling for papal approval and realistic French support for his military activities on the Anglo-Scottish border.

Just as James was able to make capital out of the uneasiness of the papacy and the King of France, so David Beaton used the opportunities created by the international situation for his own advantage. Since the success of his career in Scotland depended on his retaining James's trust, he consistently supported the King's unalterable ambition to win a French wife and a substantial dowry with her, making him an indispensable servant, familiar with the personalities and shifts of the diplomatic scene, able to distinguish between the long-term aims of politicians and their temporary expedients. At the same time Francis I, who had known him in his early days at court as Albany's protégé, recognised that French interests in Scotland were safe in his hands and secured his continued services with nomination to a French bishopric, Mirepoix, in 1537 and personal privileges in France, the right to hold benefices and personal property and to pass the latter on to his heirs.[1] Virtually no records survive concerning his administration of the see of Mirepoix and its temporalities. Snippets of information show that he granted certain revenues to his sons, from which they later supported their studies in Paris, and that he regained possession of the episcopal castle from Philip de Levis, lord of Mirepoix, nephew and heir of his predecessor in the bishopric.[2] It was equally apparent to the papal diplomats who met him at the French court that 'Monsieur d'Albrot' was likely to succeed to his uncle's leadership of the church in Scotland, able to keep the King of Scots free of the contagion of Henry VIII's apostasy and handle firmly the matter of heresy should it become a problem — although both he and his master assured them that this was unlikely. Combined papal confidence and French influence led to the grant of a cardinalate in the winter of 1538, making him protector of papal interests in an outpost of Christendom.

In promoting the interests of his own country in France, therefore, he was protecting his own interests. With a long experience of the French court, speaking French fluently, and doubtless with personal friends in the country acquired over the years, he probably thought of himself very much as a French subject, eventually prelate, during his extensive spells of residence — the equivalent of about four and a half out of the next ten years. The French King probably thought of him as such as well. In January 1539 James V wrote to let Francis know that the new cardinal would shortly be on his way 'vers vous', at the latter's command, although in the event he did not leave Scotland until March.[3] About the same time, when there was some diplomatic bickering about the number of new cardinals created from different countries, Cardinal Farnese remarked in a letter to the papal diplomats in France, 'as for the Scottish cardinal, everyone considers him as one of the French'.[4] David Beaton took part in public ceremonies in France: at the requiem for the Empress in June 1539, at which the Cardinal du Bellay officiated, he was one of seven other French cardinals assisting at the service, being referred to on this occasion as 'the Cardinal of Mirepoix'.[5] Besides, he was astute enough to realise that within the context of the Franco-Scottish alliance itself the initiative lay with France. Public opinion in this respect must sometimes have been humiliating: 'Nothing can be done against England without Scotland', Ferrerio the papal nuncio wrote to Cardinal Farnese in March 1539, 'but the latter has no money'.[6] Another nuncio explained in 1542, again to Farnese, 'There is a treaty ... by which if Scotland is attacked by England France should go to her aid ... usually it is the other way round'.[7] Only complete self-confidence and opportunism could help a Scottish ambassador keep his end up in that climate of opinion.

During the next ten years he made seven separate journeys to France, spending varying lengths of time abroad each year except for 1535 and 1540. In 1533 he was sole ambassador but the following year he was associated with the King's secretary, Sir Thomas Erskine; the latter gave the report of their mission to James V towards the end of 1534, the abbot of Arbroath having taken ill on their return.[8] In the autumn of 1536, although it was originally planned that he should go alone, he accompanied James V who decided to go personally to France to woo his bride, the abbot of Arbroath conducting the formal negotiations. Having returned to Scotland in mid-May 1537 with James and his new Queen, Madeleine, he returned to France about two months later, after the Queen's sudden death, to arrange the King's marriage with Mary of Guise whom he escorted home to Scotland in June 1538. He crossed to France again in the autumn of the same year for a brief visit during which he was in all probability consecrated to the see of

Mirepoix.[9] On his last two residences abroad he acted as sole ambassador: in the summer of 1539, by which time he was Cardinal and Archbishop of St Andrews, and from July 1541 until August of the following year, his longest spell abroad, when he travelled in considerable state with part of his household.[10]

The crossings to France, which might take anything from five to nine days, were usually made in vessels belonging to one or other of the merchant-shipmasters of Leith, notably those of the wealthy John Barton. The number of persons in his entourage varied. In 1533 when he travelled home through England, a passport was issued for himself and twelve servants, with horses and baggage.[11] In the autumn of 1537 when he again travelled through England, this time on his way to negotiate the marriage with Mary of Guise, he had twenty-four persons with him some of whom were the French servants of the late Queen Madeleine returning to France.[12] In 1541 some of the household went abroad with him, but at all times his most trusted servants remained at home to look after his interests. On the eve of his departure royal letters of protection, issued free under the privy seal of which he was keeper, were granted to his near relatives and dependants and to all the administrative staff and tenants of the abbey of Arbroath, suspending all court actions against them until forty days after his return. In February 1533, for example, about the time that his own diplomatic credentials were issued, protection was granted to all his 'propir men', tenants, familiars, servants, factors, etc., to John Beaton, his oldest brother, the new laird of Balfour, the latter's son John, James Beaton of Melgund, his brother, and the lairds of Fintry, Torry and Claverhouse, his brothers-in-law. Also included were Robert Maule of Panmure, with whose son, Thomas, he was already planning a marriage for his second daughter, Elizabeth, and Alexander Ochterlonie of Kellie, an Arbroath tenant, whose son, James, was eventually to marry his third daughter, Agnes.[13] Separate letters of protection were granted to Mr Bernard Bailie and to the abbot's recently widowed mother, Isobel Monypenny,[14] while the new laird of Balfour was granted exemption from military service in the expedition then being planned against England under the earl of Moray.[15]

Whatever the theory, ambassadors often found themselves bearing much of the expense of their journey. As Professor Mattingly remarks, 'it was sometimes hard to disabuse the treasury officials of the idea that individuals entrusted with diplomatic missions ought to pay for the honour conferred'.[16] On 23 March 1539, on arrival at Dieppe, David Beaton paid James Coutts, his skipper, £100. The freight of his horses alone cost £66 13s 4d in 1541. While it was usual for the receiving government to bear the expense of a visiting embassy, the home government often allocated a certain amount to cover the ambassador's daily expenses. The latter amount was not usually advanced, however, but reimbursed on return.[17] In 1542 David Beaton was refunded 2,000 crowns 'for his expenses in France in recent years, especially in treating of the King's marriage and bringing home the queen'. Sometimes he borrowed money in advance: £1,000 in 1539 from his friend Mr Thomas Marjoribanks,[18] £500 and £100 respectively from two wealthy Edinburgh merchants who lent money on a large scale, Gilbert Lauder and Patrick Tennant.[19] Money was occasionally sent on to him in France: £100 through John Meldrum, a Scot resident in Dieppe, and on another occasion 500 francs, supplied by William Fisher, an Edinburgh money-changer.[20] Once he borrowed £200 directly from William Todrick, citizen of Paris, and did business through Richard Dalvene, a Florentine banker there.[21] That he was largely expected to foot his own bills is clear from an entry in his chamberlain's accounts which states that on his departure for France in 1541 he *borrowed* 3,000 crowns of the sum from the treasurer out of the King's coffers;[22] at least he thus managed to reverse the usual financial procedure.

Normally he arrived at the port of Dieppe with its colony of Scottish merchants, where one could find a countryman able to lend money or a bearer to take a letter back to Scotland, but in 1537, having travelled south through England, he landed at Boulogne from Dover.[23] Once arrived, he and his entourage lived the itinerant life of an embassy, following the royal court from place to place, waiting for an audience, picking up news to be sent home in dispatches and sounding the envoys of other courts and rulers. Among the places that occur in his letters are Paris itself, Blois, Fontainebleau, Rouen, Compiègne, St Germains, Senlis, Dijon, Lyons, Mascon, Crepy, Amiens, Cambouy and Chateau-Dun. He was constantly in discussion with other diplomats: Charles de Marillac and Claude de Annebault, both of whom were ambassadors to England at one time or another, the Cardinal du Bellay, brother of the French poet, in whose house he dined with Paget, the English ambassador, the Cardinal de Tournon who had earlier been president of the council of Bourges which took a firm line against the growth of heresy, and the bishop of Faenza, the papal nuncio in France, whose influence helped his promotion to the cardinalate. Beaton offered hospitality in his turn; dining at his house in Paris in 1542 the nuncio, Capodiferro, presented to him Horace Farnese, to whom the Scottish cardinal gave 'a fine little hackney, well equipped'.[24]

The job in hand, the conclusion of business amicably yet advantageously, involved an ambassador in many situations, from the formal ceremonial entry into the presence of the prince to whom he was accredited and the presentation of his credentials, an occasion which David Beaton must have loved, to discussion with his fellow-negotiators, cultivating the friendship of whoever was in royal favour, talking to those passing through the court to and from other centres of power, listening and spying. Success depended not only on the ability to strike while the iron was hot but to make the best of the time spent waiting, either for an audience or for fresh instructions from home, and demanded gifts of being able to think and act quickly and, at the same time, of tremendous persistence.

Clearly, 'Monsieur d'Albrot', later 'the Scottish cardinal', impressed those who met him with his executive ability and grasp of international matters. Other diplomats, notably the papal nuncios, put a good deal of dependence on his reading of affairs, particularly with regard to events in England on which he seems to have had an effective line of communication.[25] Developments were always reported to him: Aquilar wrote to the Emperor in April 1539, at a time when the best means of executing the papal bull against Henry VIII was being discussed, that matters were at a standstill in Paris 'as they are expecting the early arrival of the Scottish cardinal to whom all this English business is to be communicated'.[26]

David Beaton had offered to have the bull published in Scotland. He was expected to keep the other diplomats and the French government posted as to all military operations on the Anglo-Scottish border. He was usually amenable to the requests of the French authorities, whose favour was vital to him: when he was anxious to leave for home in the late summer of 1539 the French King and the Constable prevailed on him to wait for replies from Rome, Spain and England to approaches from France.[27] He showed more independence of the papal representatives: 'Cardinal Beaton shows no sign of going to Rome meantime', the nuncio told Farnese in September 1541, 'perhaps a brieve might be sent to encourage him'.[28] Six months later when he was handed the brieve, the Scottish cardinal replied that he could be of greater assistance to the Holy Father where he was than in Rome[29] — in the event he never went. Letters were sent on after him to Scotland on occasion, and delays in his replies had the papal diplomats worried about whether he was having 'difficulties on the seas', until the arrival in France of one of his servants would set their minds at rest and bring them news of Anglo-Scottish relations.[30] Their comments on his abilities must have been based largely on their own observations, even although he was out to create an impression of authority, especially in those months during which he was working for the grant of a cardinalate. The bishop of Faenza, with whom he often discussed affairs, advised the papal secretary to gratify him, referring to him as 'one of his [James's] *prelati* who conducts everything and is a man of good wit'. It was in an interview with Faenza that David Beaton acted as interpreter for King James, assuring the bishop of Scotland's perpetual loyalty to the Pope, while James beamed at the bishop, inarticulately indicating his goodwill.[31] Only a month or two later, when David was on his way back to France *via* England, Margaret Tudor wrote to her brother, 'I beg the abbot be well treated for he is great with the king your nephew'.[32] Francis I never seems to have found fault with him and commended him on more than one occasion. His political affiliations were clear-cut, governed by his vested interests, family tradition and personal experience and, while he might shift his position a little to gain an advantage, there was never the slightest sign that he would change sides; his aims if not always his methods were predictable.

Only a little of his correspondence has survived, thirty-two letters bearing his signature, of which the extant originals show his strong, swiftly-written, small handwriting. Five letters to King James, in Scots, are all that remain of his diplomatic dispatches.[33] These date from the time of the negotiations for the King's marriage to Mary of Guise, in 1537–8, and from his last visit to France in 1541–2. The year-date is never given, only the day and month. The letters begin abruptly; 'Sire, pleise yor grace to onderstand', 'Schir, I resavit yor gracis writting', 'Schir, eftir the writtingis of my last'. They usually end with a flourish, however; 'I pray the creator preserve the samyn [your grace] eternally', ' ... and sanct Andro preserve yor grace eternally', They are all briefly addressed, 'to the Kingis grace'. There is an absence of verbal deference to principalities and powers; ' ... the king yor gracis fader [Francis I]', 'the king of Ingland', 'Schir, I have written to the pape ... '. There is very little 'padding'. The impression is of a quick-thinking, quick-acting energetic person who minced no words.

Map of Western Europe showing major places mentioned in the text.

Sometimes he had to wait a long time for an audience; 'I have evir differit to writ to yor grace sene my cummyne to this court . . . because the king yor gracis fader was evir removand and I culd nevir gett him and his counsal togiddir quharthrou I myt have resolutioun of sic thingis I thot was necessar to advertise yor grace'.[34] At times matters were discussed with Francis I in presence of his council, as when the ambassador outlined Henry VIII's military preparations on the Scottish border in 1541 and urged the need for realistic help from France.[35] Other matters may have been put before the King and council separately. When he asked for an exemption for Scottish merchants from commercial impositions in France, the council objected 'that it is tane of all the kingis awin subjectis and thinkis strange to mak strangearis freare nor his awin subjectis'. 'But', he reassured James, 'I beleiff to gett it done be the kingis speciall command in favouris of yor grace', adding, 'I sall do gud will to gett it maire ample nor it wes of befor', and he was as good as his word.[36] Francis sent for him to explain the rumour of a meeting between James and Henry at York in 1541 and, in return, David Beaton asked for an audience at which he questioned the French King about the proposed marriage of Henry's daughter Mary to the duke of Orléans.[37] Letters intended for Francis were sent to the ambassador first and passed on by him with full verbal explanations.

The shopping-list which James regularly included in his letters gave his ambassador considerable trouble. 'Yor gracis harnes is at the making. As for the gyire falconis yor grace wrait for, thair is nane cummyne heire as yit . . . ' 'The king yor gracis fader . . . send to me . . . viii fair gyire falconis quhilkis salbe at yor grace the sonest that is possible . . . wyt ane falconer that can mak and handill thame.' James, while in France in 1536–7, had seen and coveted Casso, one of the court fools, and had asked David Beaton to make enquiries about him in 1541: 'as for Casso the fule he is cummyne ane sely seikly body and is not worth to be spokin for nor may not travel'. Having received the King's rents from Guyenne, due to him in terms of Madeleine's marriage contract, David arranged to spend them 'upoun wyne and sic uthir necessaire thingis as I sall think for yor grace, and as it plesis yor grace to advertise me'. When the same revenues were collected in 1541 and had arrived in Paris, the ambassador pocketed 4,000 francs towards his own expenses.[38]

The letters are sprinkled with gossip. In September 1541 he passed on the request of the Dauphin and Dauphine that the King of Scots might help to find a second husband for the widowed duchesse d'Aubigny, 'quhilk wer grete honor to yor grace to do the samin . . . Scho giddis [guides] hirself mervellous weill, and the house and persoune scho hes maist ee to is the maister of Grahame. And quhay evir gettis hire will gett xij thousand frankis . . . As to it wes said betuix hir and the schiref of Air, thair is na thing ther of'. The following day he reported that Patrick, earl of Bothwell, banished by James for corresponding with Henry VIII, was now in France offering his services to the French King: 'I schew the king at length the gret offence and falt he maid to yor grace and how graciouse yor grace wes agane to him. And fra that time he [Francis] herd the verite he said he wald have na ado with him . . . ' According to the gossips Bothwell 'is furnist as I am advertisit be ane gentilwoman quhilk come with him fra Birges [?Bruges] in Flanderis, and kepis ane tryne [train] of xx horses and may [more]'.[39] More important was the job of keeping abreast of who were in and out of royal favour and of making use of the influence of the former: 'My Lord Constable is clane out of credit heir and ay the langer the mair ... Howbeit yor grace want [lack] the constable heire, yor grace may beleif weill that thair is na thing yor grace has ado bot the king ... will caus it to be done'.[40] Telling the King that he had presented hawks to the Cardinal de Tournon, he explained that the latter 'at this houre is in als grete credit wyth his maister as ony man in this cuntre. I traist yor grace wariit [spent] nevir halkis bettir nor thai ar'.[41]

The aim of all Scottish diplomacy was the final implementation of the treaty of Rouen, drawn up during James's childhood, by the terms of which he had been promised a French bride. In order to bring pressure to bear on the King of France, James was prepared to cultivate the friendship of the Emperor to the extent of negotiating a marriage with the latter's sister, Mary, widow of the King of Hungary. Francis's official reply until 1534 was that his daughter Madeleine was too young and delicate to be sent to Scotland, which proved tragically true in the end, and in 1534 he put forward an alternative bride in the person of Mary, daughter of the duke of Vendôme, offering to pay her dowry of 100,000 crowns. James, after seeing Mary's unprepossessing portrait, asked for an additional pension, the Order of St Michael, the surrender of Dunbar castle and extended commercial rights for Scots merchants in France. In July 1535 a Scottish embassy, led this time by Robert Reid, abbot of Kinloss, set out to finalise the marriage settlement which was drawn up on 29 March 1536. A month later James received the Order of St Michael and by the autumn was planning a personal visit to France for his marriage.

He finally set sail from Kirkcaldy on Saturday 1 September with several ships, provisions for a long stay abroad and, according to one English report, about 500 people in his company, prominent among whom were the earls of Argyll, Arran and Rothes, Lord Fleming, the laird of Drumlanrig, the prior of Pittenweem and the abbot of Arbroath, all, presumably, with their own servants.[42] Also in the entourage, with some of whom David Beaton would be in close contact during the voyage and ensuing visit, were David Lindsay, a royal herald, who took his wife with him, Oliver Sinclair, already high in the King's favour, who later proved useful to the Cardinal but whose incompetence led to the rout at Solway Moss six years later, David Rutherford, who may be identified with the master of the horse to the Cardinal in subsequent years, Mr George Hay, whose mother was a Beaton and who negotiated the business of the cardinalate at Rome, Sir James Kirkcaldy of Grange, then treasurer, and Sir John Borthwick whose orthodoxy was soon to be called in question. In addition, James took with him many household servants including embroiderers, who must have worked overtime if the catalogue of richly-trimmed clothes made for the King's state appearances are anything to judge by, the keepers of the hounds and even his organist.[43]

On 10 September 1536 the King's ship was piloted into the New Haven of Dieppe where the baggage was taken off and send downriver to Rouen. King James himself, so it is said, went in disguise to the home of the duke of Vendôme to

catch a glimpse of his bride. Poor Mary turned out to be not only plain but
hunchbacked and James hurriedly withdrew his suit. Determined to marry the
often-refused Princess Madeleine, he arranged to meet the French King and have
the terms of the marriage treaty altered. The combination of the breakdown of the
Anglo-French alliance and the outbreak of war between France and the Emperor
swayed Francis towards a closer marriage alliance with the King of Scots. The
marriage contract between James and Madeleine, whom he met at Amboise, was
drawn up at Blois on 6 November 1536, David Beaton being authorised to give
Buchel, the French King's secretary, 200 crowns for writing it.[44] The religious
ceremony of betrothal took place on 26 November after which the court left for
Fontainebleau. The mood of the whole visit was one of fête and constant
travelling, involving James's ambassador as much as himself, for the abbot of
Arbroath was not only on hand to supervise expenditure, including large sums to
the royal pursemaster, but acted as interpreter for James. Like the King, who was
then making Renaissance-inspired additions to his residences at Falkland and
Stirling, David Beaton must have looked covetously on the French King's
magnificent homes which he already knew well, including the gallery at
Fontainebleau which was then blossoming under the hands of Rosso and
Primaticcio, and may perhaps have wondered what he might do with the interior
of St Andrews castle when it should be his. Like King James, honours came his
way that winter in France, honours with satisfyingly tangible benefits. In
November, about the time the King's marriage contract was drawn up, he was
granted French nationality with the right to hold benefices and property as if he
had been a native-born Frenchman. Meanwhile, crowns from the King's coffers
flowed like water, spent not only on necessities such as food, lodging and travel,
but on a host of luxuries. On the afternoon of 31 December James rode in
procession into Paris and was married to Madeleine in Notre Dame on New Year's
Day.

It must have been to the satisfaction of David Beaton and the orthodox, pro-
French party in Scotland that James was thus firmly tied to the interests of his
father-in-law the King of France. A few weeks later at a ceremony in Compiègne
James was invested with the cap and sword blessed by the Pope on Christmas Eve
and sent to him as a token of papal confidence in his orthodoxy and willingness to
defend the faith and the authority of the church.[45] Sir John Borthwick, a member
of the entourage who had for some time held Lutheran opinions, wrote
disparagingly to Thomas Cromwell of the Pope's gift, remarking of the cap that it
was meant to 'covar and hald downe all the fals simulation and wikit ypocrisy that
ringis [reigns] in papists; but it is to litil to hydd all . . . ' On 13 March, as he and his
Queen were preparing to leave for Scotland, James promised the bishop of Faenza
to punish the Lutherans in his kingdom.

Queen Madeleine, in confirmation of her father's worst fears, died a few weeks
after her arrival in Scotland. With almost indecent haste the broken link in
Franco–Scottish relations was reforged as the abbot of Arbroath led an embassy to
negotiate a second French marriage for the King of Scots. An important prelude to
the French mission was David Beaton's journey through England in August 1537

for the purpose of allaying English fears about the outcome of Franco–Scottish co-operation and Scottish activity on the borders. The ambassador's movements were reported by the English warden's informant, the prioress of Coldstream, and forwarded to Cromwell by Norfolk who at the same time complained huffily about not being recalled south to be present during discussions with the Scottish ambassador. On 9 August, having left Stamford, David Beaton wrote to Cromwell asking for an audience, which was granted within a week at Grafton, Henry's Northamptonshire residence which he had recently rebuilt and where he had previously received other ambassadors.[46] Not many details survive of this one and only meeting between David Beaton and Henry VIII, each taking the measure of the other on the eve of their political confrontation. On 16 August Henry wrote a non-committal letter to the King of Scots acknowledging receipt of his letters from the ambassador and answering them 'in a manner that [James] will accept as agreeable to his desire and ... to the perfect amity' between them.[47] Norfolk confided to Cromwell that he feared the Scottish ambassador had not 'written so frankly to his master as at Grafton he promised' concerning the mutual promise to punish rebels on both sides of the border.[48] In fact, the administration of the frontier had just had a period of comparative success and peace as the Scottish regents who were left in charge during the King's visit to France had been careful that nothing should happen to give offence to the English. Henry's refusal to allow James to travel home through England, however, had given rise to rumours of war. David Beaton, now waiting at Dover for a ship to Boulogne, put it succinctly to his master: 'the King of Ingland wes nathing contentit that yor grace schew yow sa affectit to the king yor gracis fader, quhowbeit I ken perfitly that bath he and his counsale sall haif yow in greter estimatioun quhill thai leif [if they live long enough]'.[49]

King James's second choice of a wife, Mary, daughter of Claud, duke of Guise, whose first husband, the duke of Longueville, had died a month before Queen Madeleine, could scarcely have been made on the spur of the moment. It is possible that she and the King of Scots had met while he was in France the previous winter. He was certainly entertained by her kinsmen at that time, giving ten crowns to the Cardinal of Lorraine's varlets and twelve crowns to the minstrels of her father, the duke of Guise.[50] Even if the abbot of Arbroath did not actually recommend her to James, he must have been pleased with the King's choice which promised to link the latter with one of the most orthodox and influential families at the French court whose head, the duke of Guise, was for good measure a first-class soldier, a reassuring thought should the question of French military help arise. The ambassador was commissioned to express James's choice for Francis's approval and thereafter to conclude all necessary negotiations. Writing from Lyons on 22 October 1537, he was able to inform the King that Francis had agreed,[51] offering to 'accept hir as his dochtir and gife hir for the samin', and that the French King had spoken highly of her wisdom and conduct. At the same time her uncle, the Cardinal of Lorraine, showed his pleasure at the match, saying that 'he and thaire house was perpetuallie oblist to remane yor guid servandis and that yor grace suld fynd thame als reddy as ony subject youre grace had in the world'.

Francis sent for the duke of Guise who met the ambassador cordially: 'quhome I find mervellous desirous of the expeditioun and haistie end of the mater'. The French King's war preparations on the Italian border postponed the marriage negotiations for some time, during which King James was assured of his ambassador's continual efforts to conclude the business: 'Schire, sene all thir materis gais sa weill and na apperand difficulte bot all sall cum sone and weill to gud effect, for the luf of god and weill of yor gracis successioun, realme and subjectis, have pacience for ane litill tyme for in guid fayth the tyme is landsummer to me nor to ony other levand quhill I se yor grace ... ' Mary herself waited with her mother in Champagne. 'Loving to god scho is stark [strong] and weill complexionit and may indure travel', wrote David Beaton appraisingly, who was used to women would could give a good account of themselves, to reassure the King who had recently lost a delicate wife.

Negotiations slowed down during the winter and were not without their moments of suspense. In January 1538, Henry VIII, at that point a widower, asked for the hand of the duchess of Longueville. Castillon, the French ambassador in London, remonstrated in an audience with Henry and at the same time remarked in a letter home that the abbot of Arbroath had better speak up for his King.[52] At one time the house of Guise seems to have been tempted to consider Mary as Queen of England, but by the end of January Cardinal Carpi told a colleague that 'the abbot raised his voice so boldly that it appears they will decide for Scotland'.[53] Perhaps their minds were partly made up for them by the French King; better to retain the loyalty of his Scottish ally than hope that a Guise wife would keep Henry VIII perpetually friendly towards France. The marriage contract was drawn up in which the King of France promised to pay the dowry of 100,000 francs and an annuity of 20,000 francs to be partly collected from the rents of Guyenne. In the total amount was calculated the original dowry which he had given the duchess on her first marriage.[54] The marriage, by proxy — Lord Maxwell taking the place of the King of Scots — eventually took place at Château-Dun on 4 May 1538. James paid 150 crowns for the writing of the contract, 200 crowns for the papal dispensation, as his bride and he were within the forbidden degrees of relationship through the house of Gueldres, and 300 crowns for the Queen's 'spousing ring'.[55] He settled on her a jointure equal to Madeleine's, which included the royal residences of Falkland and Stirling, income from the lands of the earldoms of Strathearn, Ross, Orkney and Fife and the Lordships of Galloway and the Isles.

The long delay had at least given the King of Scots and his court time to prepare a fitting reception for the Queen. David Lindsay directed the preparation of pageants with which to celebrate her entry into St Andrews, where the King had taken up residence in the new royal palace in the priory precincts, and later in Edinburgh. Lindsay of Pitscottie relates how David Beaton came home in a bad temper, offended at having been asked to travel in a separate ship from the Queen and Lord Maxwell, having quarrelled with Maxwell over the business before leaving France. Relations between the two were never good and the slight on this occasion, coming after his diplomatic successes, must have been particularly resented by David Beaton. The Queen arrived in Scotland on 10 June, and a few days later the royal marriage was confirmed in a ceremony in the cathedral of St Andrews. The little city, which had just staged its own processions on Trinity Sunday in honour of the dedication of its parish church, must have been overflowing with the concourse of notables and their followers gathered for the royal marriage.

'Bringing home the Queen' took place at a watershed in David Beaton's career, about the time he became a genuine churchman. During 1537 he had been made *coadjutor*, administrator, of the metropolitan see for his ageing uncle,[56] as near as an ecclesiastic could get to being recognised 'heir' to a living he hoped to 'inherit'. On 5 December of that year, while negotiations for the King's marriage to Mary of Guise were hanging fire, Pope Paul III provided him, on the French King's nomination, to the bishopric of Mirepoix in the Languedoc, a suffragan see of Toulouse said to be worth 10,000 livres a year, a welcome addition to his income from Arbroath and his keepership of the privy seal.[57] On 13 January 1538 the Pope dispensed him from being consecrated and seeking the episcopal *pallium* in the canonical time,[58] and on 8 February he took the oath of allegiance to Francis I.[59] He was reaching the end of his predominantly secular career. Consecrated to Mirepoix sometime between 26 July and 13 August 1538, during his brief visit to France, and described by the King of Scots in August as 'soon to be primate of Scotland',[60] he was about to be more closely associated with the ecclesiastical establishment than ever before.

On 20 December 1538 the Pope created five new cardinals, one of whom was the bishop of Mirepoix. On the same day Cardinal Carpi, who had special charge of Scottish affairs at Rome, wrote to King James V saying that the Pope had testified to the King's character and services, 'almost more gratifying than the promotion itself'.[61] A batch of congratulatory letters arrived from Rome for the King and new Cardinal in the New Year's post to which James replied fulsomely on 8 March.[62] Civilities count for little, however, in trying to detect real attitudes behind the diplomatic correspondence. It is as well to remember that while these letters from the cardinals at Rome were congratulating the loyal King of Scots, one of his well-wishers, Cardinal Farnese, was soon to make his remark to a colleague that all the world knew that the Cardinal of Scotland was regarded as one of the French appointees. It is difficult to escape the impression that it was the influence of the French King on behalf of the bishop of Mirepoix that had really counted in obtaining the appointment. For his part, James hardly ever wrote to the Pope protesting his willingness to maintain papal authority in his kingdom without begging for some concession, often of a substantial nature. Yet it is significant that while the grant of the cardinalate came reasonably quickly after pressure was first put on the Pope, with French influence, the grant of the faculty of legate *a latere*, a devolution of papal jurisdiction, begged for just as long but largely by Scotland itself, was not given to David Beaton until after the death of the King of Scots and after a papal legate had been in Scotland to assess the need at first hand.

On 6 January 1539 Francesco Casale, with unrivalled inaccuracy over the new cardinal's many designations, informed Thomas Cromwell of the elevation of 'the grand chancellor of the king of Scots here called the abbot of St Andrews'.[63] The news was intimated to the Emperor by Aquilar, who described 'the abbot of Embrot' as 'a person of much learning and example'.[64] Papal instructions to the exiled English cardinal, Reginald Pole, encouraged him with the reminder that in his efforts to bring his own country back to the fold he now had the help of the King of Scots and 'this new Scots cardinal who is a man of great power and authority in those parts'. Pole wrote enthusiastically to David Beaton from Rome saying that he had heartily supported his promotion.[65] He treated his colleague to a homily: 'we should be prepared to follow the Lord and shed our blood in this cause — cardinals especially, the colour of whose robes is symbolic of their duty', a symbolism unlikely to have occurred to David Beaton in connection with these distinguished outward signs of his new ecclesiastical superiority. Sir Ralph Sadler, at his master's bidding, wrote King James a letter of less pious sentiments once Beaton was safely overseas, to the effect that cardinals were a perfect pest, as both King Henry and his father had discovered, and if James was wise he would not allow a subject to take upon him 'the red hat of pride'.[66]

Ever since the first papal censures against him the English King had kept an eye on his nephew's relations with the powers calling themselves the Catholic League and sent several embassies north to encourage James to follow his example in breaking with Rome and dissolving monastic property. But, having steadily mulcted the church through the system of commendation, taxation and his right to nominate to prelacies, James was unco-operative, especially as he was anxious for a marriage alliance with The Most Christian King. As early as the winter of 1536, just before the first mention of his cardinal's status, David Beaton had offered to help implement the Pope's sanctions against Henry.[67] Again, in discussions with the bishop of Faenza in 1537 the bishop 'made bold to let the abbot know that I have censures in hand from the pope and he himself has offered to get them published in England at this time'.[68] In the same year, while the King of Scots was still in France, Sir Ralph Sadler was sent north to sound Scottish opinion but found the Scottish council of regency orthodox and unwilling to co-operate. In the spring of 1538 the abbot of Arbroath told the bishop of Faenza that 'censures had already arrived in England and that upon his arrival in Scotland he would send a man in post to inform me of how they had been published'.[69] A little later the bishop of Verona spoke of copies of the censures having been given 'to that Scotsman who has undertaken to publish them'.[70] The marriage with Mary of Guise came at a time when Francis I and the Emperor, having made peace in June 1538, were inclined to listen to the Pope's request for a joint crusade against the infidel, the Lutherans and the King of England. When David Beaton slipped over to France for his brief visit in late July/August 1538, English spies watched his movements closely. Not only might he be going to commit his sovereign to collaboration with the Catholic League, but he himself was a threat to Henry's peace of mind in that it was about then that the campaign for his promotion to the cardinalate was stepped up at Rome. The appointment would mean that Henry had a determined papal representative on his northern border.

For some time it looked as if the plans of the European powers were taking shape against England. English ships were arrested in Flanders early in 1539, the Spanish ambassador was recalled from London and a considerable fleet, whose destination was unknown, assembled at Antwerp.[71] At the end of January Henry heard of the arrival of a French envoy at the Scottish court,[72] and in the spring the Cardinal crossed to France where he remained until the autumn. Henry's agents watched closely; on 3 April Norfolk asked Cromwell to find out the cause of 'the false bishop of St Andrews' going to France, remarking that he was the worst enemy the King of England had.[73] Apart from whatever instructions he carried about Scotland's part in the crusade against Henry, he went to receive his red hat from the papal representative, Latino Juvenale, who had been dispatched with it to France as early as January, the Scottish cardinal having been exempt from travelling to Rome for it, a concession only rarely granted. Significantly, Antwerp was named as one of the places where it might be handed over, at a time when that port was a centre of the Catholic League's mobilisation.[74] He may have received the hat about Easter, possibly at Chantilly, in the presence of the constable of France. By April, however, the military preparations and the fleet at Antwerp had broken up and Scottish manoeuvres on the border came to nothing at this time. The Cardinal was making preparations to leave France by late August, when he and the papal nuncio, Ferrerio, agreed on a cipher in which to communicate with each other.[75] 'No news yet of the coming of the abbot of Arbroath out of France',[76] Wharton reported to Cromwell on 5 September, using either by habit or intentionally the title by which David Beaton had been known in international circles for fifteen years, and when he returned towards the end of the month his ship had to be escorted from Dieppe by three well-armed vessels for fear of attack by the English shipping which had been sighted off the Scottish coast.[77]

NOTES

1. *Fasti*, 298; *L.P. Henry VIII*, XIV, i, 1185

2. *Archives du château de Léran: inventaire historique et généalogique des documents de la branche Lévis-Mirepoix*, edd. S. Olive and F. Pasquier (1927), V, 314; *Inventaire des registres des règnes de François 1er et de Henri II: Insinuations du Châtelet de Paris (1906–)*, No 4169 — I am grateful to Dr John Durkan for drawing my attention to these references. A. Ciaconius, *Vitae . . . pontificum Romanorum et S.R.E. Cardinalium* (1677), B.L.2011.g.468. e.l. — Mr Peter Murray kindly drew my attention to this early printed work and the summary of David Beaton's career which it contains.

3. *L.P. Henry VIII*, XIV, i, 179

4. J. Lestocquoy, *Correspondence des Nonces en France*, I, 443–4 (*Correspondence des Nonces*) — I am grateful to Professor Ian Cowan for drawing my attention to this source.

5. *Ibid.*, I, 460–1

6. *Ibid.*, I, 447–8

7. *Ibid.*, III, 159–61, 186

8. *Letters of James V*, 280–1

9. J. Dowden, *The Bishops of Scotland*, 210 (Dowden, *Bishops*)

10. *T.A.*, VIII, 91; *Hamilton Papers*, I, 73; *Rentale*, 113

11. *L.P. Henry VIII*, VI, 929 (35)

12. *Ibid.*, XII, ii, 430

13. *R.S.S.*, II, 1508

14. *Ibid.*, II, 1512–13

15. *Ibid.*, II, 1490, 1492

16. G. Mattingly, *Renaissance Diplomacy*, 33

17. *Ibid.*

18. *Rentale*, 93

19. *Ibid.*, 93–4

20. *Ibid.*, 94–5

21. *Ibid.*, 108; Register of acts and decreets, xvi, fo 240

22. *Rentale*, 126

23. *L.P. Henry VIII*, XII, ii, 566

24. *Correspondence des Nonces*, III, 112

25. *Ibid.*, I, 251, 479, 599

26. *L.P. Henry VIII*, XIV, i, 787

27. *Correspondence des Nonces*, I, 462

28. *Ibid.*, III, 79–80

29. *Ibid.*, III, 115

30. *Ibid.*, I, 234, 503, 508, 572

31. *L.P. Henry VIII*, XI, 1173

32. *Ibid.*, XII, ii, 55

33. The texts of these letters were printed by Andrew Lang in *Scottish Historical Review*, VI, 150–8 (*S.H.R.* 'Beaton letters'). Originals, British Library, Additional mss, 19401, fos 34–42

34. *Ibid.*, 152

35. *Ibid.*

36. *Ibid.*, 158; *Extracts from the burgh records of Edinburgh*, II, 108

37. *S.H.R.*, 'Beaton letters', 153, 157

38. *Ibid.*, 158

39. *Ibid.*, 154–5

40. *Ibid.*, 153

41. *Ibid.*, 155

42. *L.P. Henry VIII*, XI, 400

43. Accounts of David Beaton during the King's visit to France are printed in *T.A.* VII, 1–46

44. *Ibid.*, VII, 18

45. *L.P. Henry VIII*, XII, i, 414

46. *Ibid.*, XII, ii, 491

47. *Ibid.*, XII, ii, 525

48. *Ibid.*, XII, ii, 588

49. *Ibid.*, XII, ii, 566

50. *T.A.*, VII, 15, 17

51. *S.H.R.*, 'Beaton letters', 155–6

52. *L.P. Henry VIII*, XIII, i, 118

53. *Ibid.*, XIII, i, 180

54. A. Teulet, ed., *Papiers d'état* ... relatifs à l'histoire de l'Ecosse du XVIème siècle (Bannatyne Club), i, 115 (*Teulet*)

55. *T.A.*, VII, 56

56. *Fasti*, 298
57. *Ibid; L.P. Henry VIII*, XII, ii, 1176
58. Dowden, *Bishops*, 41
59. Archives de France, P556² n° CLXXIX
60. *Letters of James V*, 349–50
61. *L.P. Henry VIII*, XLLL, ii, 1109
62. *Ibid.*, XIV, i, 471–6
63. *Ibid.*, XIV, i, 27
64. *Ibid.*, XIV, i, 14
65. *Ibid.*, XIV, i, 8; *Letters of James V*, 362
66. *L.P. Henry VIII*, XIV, i, 773
67. *Ibid.*, XII, i, 414
68. *Ibid.*, XII, i, 463
69. *Ibid.*, XII, i, 923
70. *Ibid.*, XII, i, 987
71. Herkless, *Beaton*, 171
72. *Ibid.*, 172
73. *L.P. Henry VIII*, XIV, i, 687
74. *Ibid.*, XIV, i, 36
75. *Correspondence des Nonces*, I, 479
76. *L.P. Henry VIII*, XIV, ii, 131
77. *Correspondence des Nonces*, I, 481

6

This New Scots Cardinal

The country to which the Cardinal returned had already felt the effects of his new ecclesiastical authority. Archbishop James Beaton had died on 14 February 1539, and one chronicler remarked that the new primate was scarcely 'well warmed in his seat' before at least one aim of his future policy became clear, the maintenance of ecclesiastical authority in the face of religious dissent in all its forms, from the politico-religious sympathy with Henry VIII's 'reformation' to be found among some of the landed classes, to signs of Lutheranism among the common folk. In the second half of the very month in which he became archbishop there was a round-up of offenders, five of whom were burnt to death.[1] Whether or not his plans for this particular campaign had been laid for some time, David Beaton's attitude to heresy had had almost twenty years to harden from what he had seen of it at home and abroad.

He had first encountered religious criticism and dissent in his early years in France, as a student and while learning his political skills. When he was probably a student in Paris the university must have been humming with discussion over Erasmus's Greek new testament. In 1521, during his earliest days at the French court, the theologians of the Sorbonne condemned Luther's doctrines as heretical and tried to stem the flow of Lutheran literature into the country, just as the Scottish parliament was to do four years later. The worldly French church establishment, with its benefice system permeated with venality and aristocratic dynasticism and manipulated by the crown with papal connivance, attracted a good deal of anti-clerical abuse.[2] In quite different circles scholarly piety such as that of the biblical scholar, Jacques Lefèvre d'Etaples, and his more radical associate, Guillaume Farel, created cells of reforming studies which shared some of Luther's priorities, such as that the bible should be made available to all who wished to read it. Lefèvre, under the patronage of the bishop of Meaux, led a reforming movement in that diocese, some of whose members preached against the selling of masses, purgatory and the cult of the saints. The movement at Meaux appears to have had adherents from all social classes, from academics to the humbler sort of craftsmen. This social cross-section characteristic of early French dissent was also to be seen in Scottish Lutheranism in the 1530s and 1540s: craftsmen were among those tried for heresy in the Cardinal's presence at Perth in 1544.[3] In both France and Scotland the Augustinian canons, Luther's own order, provided a number of early protestants: the earliest French Lutheran martyrs were an Augustinian and a wool-carder from Meaux, while in Scotland in the 1530s the Augustinian communities at St Andrews and Cambuskenneth were power-houses in the spread of reforming opinions within the church. The Dominican Friars of Scotland, who were cultivated by David Beaton, were, like those of France, on the whole bulwarks of orthodoxy, although the handful of notable protestants who emerged from their ranks hints at the tensions that existed within the order, particularly among the younger men.

Almost from the time of his first return from France, late in 1524, David Beaton had been associated with attempts to contain the activities of such heretics as there were in Scotland. As abbot of Arbroath he sat in the parliament of July 1525 which passed an act threatening with imprisonment and escheat those who brought Lutheran literature into the country through the seaports.[4] As a lord of the articles he would have taken part in the discussions which gave shape to the legislation.[5] The act claimed that there had been no indigenous heresy in Scotland until then. Certainly, James Reseby, an English Wycliffite, and Paul Craw, a Hussite from Bohemia, burnt as heretics in 1407 and 1433 respectively, had brought heretical teaching from outside. There is some evidence, however, that between these two executions the Scottish authorities were on the look-out for the infiltration of Wycliffe's teaching, either directly from England or through the Hussites. Winton wrote of Robert, duke of Albany, regent of Scotland, who died in 1420,

> He was a constant Catholic,
> All Lollard he hated and heretic.[6]

The trial of Reseby had been presided over by Laurence of Lindores, designated 'inquisitor of heretical pravity', showing that formal steps had been taken to deal with the threat, even if the inquisitor was not called upon to do much business thereafter. As one of the first teachers in the new university of St Andrews, however, Laurence may have been influential in imposing the oath on the masters of arts, from 1417, by which they swore to defend the church against Lollards and other heretics.[7] Both Dietrich von Nieme, writing from Constance in 1414, and Jean d'Achery, envoy of Paris university to the Pope in the following year, spoke of Wycliffite doctrines reaching Bohemia, Moravia and Scotland; it is unlikely that they would have mentioned this small country on the fringe of Christendom without some justification. Hector Boece claimed that Craw admitted to having been sent from Bohemia to preach to the Scots.[8] Even before his arrival, however, the first parliament of King James I after his return from captivity in England, held in March 1425, passed an act setting up episcopal inquisitions for the discovery of heretics, with power to the bishops to call on the secular authority to assist them if need be.[9] John Ireland in *The Merroure of Wisdome*, written in the vernacular towards the end of the century for the instruction of the faithful, claimed that 'many errouris agane the faith and haly doctrine of Jhesu and the kyrk ar writtin in this tounge [vernacular] and in Inglis, at a part of the pepil of the realme are infekit with'.[10] The 1494 so-called 'Lollards of Kyle' who were summoned before James IV by the archbishop of Glasgow, by a procedure envisaged in the 1425 act of Parliament, were a group of closely-associated families living near the south-west communication routes with England, including the sea-route to Bristol which was a centre of Lollardy, whose activities show that religious dissent could take root in Scottish soil even if in a restricted area. A persistent, if small, native readership of the bible in that area is suggested by reference to

F

Murdoch Nisbet's manuscript rendering into Scots of Purvey's revision of Wycliffe's new testament which, around 1520, Nisbet and his friends were secretly reading.[11]

In some ways Lollardy, or such of its tenets as were transmitted to the next generation of those families who had been affected by it, may have prepared the ground for the reception of Lutheranism. It is known that in England the latter was welcome in surviving Lollard enclaves and that some Lollards sold copies of Tyndale's new testament and certain Lutheran literature.[12] The Wycliffite emphasis on the authority of scripture and the importance of preaching, its denunciation of clerical celibacy, confession and masses for the dead and its tendency to undermine papal authority and the mediatory role of both the priesthood and the saints, were echoed in Luther's teaching even if it was less preoccupied with Luther's central concern with man's justification before God. It is not surprising that the Lollards of Kyle created a local religious tradition which accepted each phase of Scottish protestantism as it came, alongside conventional forms of piety, through the preaching of Wishart and Knox and on into the seventeenth century. Claims that this could happen in other parts of the country through the influence of individuals may not be without foundation; John Andrew Duncan of Airdrie, having spent a number of years after his capture at Flodden with Alexander Burnet, a 'Wycliffite', in Yorkshire, to whom he was related through his mother, returned to Scotland in the 1520s where he became a friend of Patrick Hamilton and his family, taking part in the abortive attempt to rescue Patrick which was led by Sir James Hamilton of Kincavil. Duncan's house was said to have been the resort of Lutherans and their adherents.[13]

The act of parliament anent heresy of 1525 came in the wake of the rapid spread of Luther's influence outside Germany largely through the vehicle of the printing press. It is not surprising, then, that the Scottish authorities took steps to curb the infiltration of 'ony opunyeounis contrare the Christin fayth'.[14] As is often the case with such enactments, however, that of 1525 was probably an attempt to stop rather than prevent the practice. The penalties of the act covered not only the introduction of Lutheran books but any attempt to discuss Luther's doctrines publicly unless in order to refute him. No sixteenth-century merchant risked his precious capital on either exporting or importing a cargo for which there was not a fairly certain market, so it must be supposed that Lutheran literature, whatever it consisted of, had a readership in Scotland. That the act of 1525 failed to some extent in its purpose is suggested by an extension of its scope in 1527,[15] its ratification in 1535[16] and its amplification in 1541.[17] These dates mark not so much isolated patches of heretical activity as the intervals at which the authorities for particular reasons felt that the current level of activity warranted a clamp-down; 1527 saw the anxiety of the ecclesiastical establishment over the effects of Patrick Hamilton's presence as a preacher and disputant in the Lothians and at St Andrews, the confirmation of 1535 followed a series of prosecutions in 1533–34, and the more detailed legislation early in 1541 came not so very long after David Beaton's prosecutions of 1539 and after he had spent the year 1540 in Scotland when he was in a position to hear and take note of what was afoot among suspects, during which he made a public example of the Lutheran layman, Sir John Borthwick.[18]

The 1527 additions to the act anent heresy extended its penalties to include native Scots, 'the kingis lieges assistaris to ony sic opunyeounis', and at the same time restricted discussion in order to refute Lutheran teaching to 'clerkis in the sculis allanerlie', hinting at a widening extra-academic interest in Lutheranism. The discussion of radical reform in the church, or at least the need for it, and the ability to question its teaching had recently been facilitated in academic and literate lay circles by the availability of Tyndale's English new testament, copies of which are believed to have been reaching Scotland in considerable numbers in 1526-7. One of Wolsey's agents reported that they were being imported not only into Leith and Edinburgh, but mostly into St Andrews itself. Here, in the ecclesiastical capital, the church was confronted with the first heresy case to involve a native Scot[19] and it was the first such trial in which David Beaton as abbot of Arbroath took part. Patrick Hamilton, Paris graduate and later a student at Louvain, had since his return to Scotland in 1523 become increasingly open about his unorthodox views, engaging in discussion with those who were prepared to take part in the university of St Andrews where he was incorporated in 1523. Hamilton's emergence as a heretic was something of an embarrassment for Archbishop James Beaton. To begin with they were related: the reformer's father, Sir Patrick Hamilton of Kincavil, although illegitimate, was the half-brother of the 1st earl of Arran, husband of the archbishop's niece, Janet Beaton of Creich. Apart from the possibility of his receiving protection from the powerful house of Hamilton, heirs-presumptive to the throne, Patrick was a distant kinsman of the King himself, and although James V was then young and in the hands of Angus, it might be thought dangerous to bring the law to bear on one who shared the blood royal. The fact that Hamilton could preach and dispute openly for about three years and that, according to Alexander Allan, a canon of St Andrews priory, James Beaton gave him the hint to make his escape at the eleventh hour, suggests a hesitation in dealing with him. Perhaps, as some contemporaries remarked, the archbishop was not an over-zealous prosecutor.

There were others who were differently inclined, however, including David Beaton who had had fairly recent experience of the world that had made Patrick Hamilton what he was, the cosmopolitan world of Paris and its university. It is just possible, if David Beaton were at Paris before 1520, that their periods of study may have briefly overlapped and that being kinsmen, as the sixteenth century counted kinship, they may then have known each other. At Paris, neither the reactionary attitude of the older teachers nor the vigilance of the Sorbonne doctors who were on the look-out for signs of anything that smacked of heresy could dampen the enthusiasm of many students for the writings of Erasmus long after he had left the university, or their appreciation of his satire at the expense of clerical corruption and hypocrisy. Not long after Hamilton had taken his master's degree and gone on to Louvain to study the ancient languages of the bible, the Spaniard Vives wrote to Erasmus, then himself at Louvain, 'anyone who presents himself . . . with a cargo of the old subtleties, which used to be such wonderful favourites with our callow scholastics, is driven off now-a-days with a storm of shouts and hissings and clappings'. Since 1519–20 Luther's works had been pouring into France. It is not known when or how Patrick Hamilton moved intellectually and spiritually from the Christian humanism of Erasmus to the evangelical protestantism of Luther, but by the time he returned to Scotland in 1523 to study theology he would be fully aware of the latter's claims and the ground of his debate with orthodoxy. In France, too, he would have experienced the excitement that accompanied not only the announcement of the Sorbonne's condemnation of Luther's doctrines but the arrival soon afterwards of the retaliatory *Defence of Martin Luther against the Furibund Decree of the Parisian Theologasts*, written by the young professor of Greek at Wittenberg, Philip Melanchthon, which sold in its hundreds before the French authorities could put a stop to its distribution. With fellow-Scottish students Patrick may have felt embarrassed by Melanchthon's sideshaft in which he held up to ridicule the respected Scots doctor, John Major, as a particularly telling example of scholastic obscurantism.

In short, Hamilton had known an intellectual environment in which religious alignments were known and where discussion and debate between adherents of the old and the new learning and for and against the doctrines of Luther took place openly, or informally among friends, in a period before the French King took the offensive against heresy. It was still a time when, in France at least, the writings of men of Erasmus's calibre and social acceptability, however critical of the church they might be, changed hands and were discussed in academic circles and among laymen and where a wider readership was devouring what has been called the 'corrosive journalism' pouring from the printing presses, in which the graphic woodcuts carried an unmistakably subversive message to those who could not read the texts for themselves. For some time after his return home Patrick Hamilton followed this pattern in his personal contacts and more formal addresses, discovering here and there some who shared his own growing acceptance of Lutheranism. He seems to have moved with most freedom in St Leonard's college, St Andrews, among the younger canons of the priory, some of whom taught or studied there, being encouraged to discuss the bible and available Lutheran texts by such individuals as Gavin Logie, the principal of the college, whose commitment to reform in the church was shortly to carry him over the bounds of orthodoxy, John Winram, subprior of the priory, still keeping his thoughts to himself but prepared to discuss the new ideas, and John Duncanson and Alexander Allan, canons, then orthodox but sufficiently receptive to new ideas to go over to protestantism shortly after Hamilton's death. Even John Major, in spite of Melanchthon's aspersions, was sufficiently liberal to encourage his students to think for themselves, saying that Luther had done a good thing in recalling theologians to the scriptures and vigorously advocating conciliar methods in church government.[20] As it happened, Major was called to St Andrews from Glasgow university in the same year as Hamilton was incorporated.

Patrick Hamilton made a favourable impression on most people who met him, intellectually keen and personally agreeable, if argumentative, sufficiently intimate with the life of the priory to employ his musical talent in composing a modern nine-part mass 'in honour of the angels' which was performed in the cathedral with himself as precentor. By 1527, however, his influence in university circles and among friends of his family led to a summons from Archbishop James Beaton on a charge of heresy and to Hamilton's sudden departure for the continent. Here he offered for disputation, at the new protestant university of Marburg, a thesis on the subject of faith and good works and gained the friendship of the reformers Francis Lambert, John Frith and William Tyndale. The thesis, later known as 'Patrick's Places', is clearly indebted to several of Luther's writings.[21] Hamilton returned to Scotland a second time, in the autumn of 1527, preaching openly and emulating Luther by marrying. His visit to Marburg and his association with notable Lutherans in Europe sealed his fate, however, and the freedom he was allowed and even encouraged to use just before his arrest was permitted in order to gather evidence against him. He was arrested early in 1528 and on 29 February he became the first Scottish subject to be burnt for heresy. It used to be suggested that David Beaton may have forced his uncle's hand, which is possible.

During his frequent visits to France as Scottish ambassador in the decade following Patrick Hamilton's death David Beaton was in a position to observe the growth of religious dissent in the two countries and to watch the changing attitude of the French King to heresy. As long as French reform bore the colour of Christian humanism, as exemplified in Lefèvre, Francis I was prepared to tolerate it, even to the extent of protecting some individuals from the persecuting zeal of the parlement of Paris, the most notable of whom was the noble, Louis de Berquin, who translated the works of Erasmus and Luther into French, whom the parlement finally managed to arrest and execute in 1529 while the King was away from Paris. There were allegations of heresy against some in the royal circle including the liberal-minded Jean du Bellay, bishop of Bayonne, and the King's sister, Marguerite d'Angoulême.[22] Later, the presence of those with protestant sympathies in the household of James V of Scotland was to frustrate the Cardinal in his attempts to remove heretics from positions of influence. The years 1533–4 which saw a number of executions for heresy in Scotland were also a watershed in the attitude of the French King to dissent. Matters came to a head in France in October 1534 when radicals posted placards against the mass not only in the towns of northern France but on the very door of the King's chamber at Amboise.[23] This attack on a fundamental tenet of Catholicism, as well as the insult to the King, united Francis, the Sorbonne and the parlement against the Lutherans, and in January 1535 the publication of new books was prohibited until further notice.[24] Another reason for repression was probably the recent outbreak of iconoclasm which suggested that French heresy had reached a radical stage, less characteristic of Lutheranism than of the Swiss reformers.[25] Impressions must have been made on David Beaton who was in France, in all likelihood at court, when the Affair of the Placards took place.[26] He sat in the Scottish parliament of June 1535 which ratified the 1525 act against importation of Lutheran books and the discussion of Luther's doctrines, six months after the French ban on new publications. Indifferent to theology though he was, he no doubt appreciated the potentially subversive element in the more radical Swiss reform movement. What turned out to be his own final effort against heresy, the trial and execution of George Wishart in 1546, came at a point when Scottish dissent was beginning to feel the influence of Switzerland as represented in Wishart.

It suited David Beaton's temperament perfectly that during his lifetime the church was on the offensive against heresy. A watchful, vigorous authority could still hope to contain its activities. Repression was the appropriate weapon. The recorded opinions of those accused of doctrinal heresy reflect Lutheranism, occasionally with lingering overtones of Lollardy or suggestions of Zwinglianism, but mainly centred on the doctrine of justification by faith alone, and on the supreme authority of the bible in matters of faith and practice. Since the church had no official reply to these propositions until the theological pronouncements of the council of Trent in 1547, there was never any question of formal public debate, although academics like Patrick Hamilton and educated laymen like Sir John Borthwick might make known their views in discussion or by writing. No official statement of orthodoxy was issued in Scotland at this time and no popular explanation of the faith for the people. This was left to Archbishop John Hamilton in the 1550s when the church was on the defensive in face of an increasingly articulate protestant party.

Repression or not, there were few protestant martyrs in Scotland in the 1520s, '30s and '40s.[27] Between the death of Patrick Hamilton in 1528 and that of the Cardinal in 1546 nineteen persons are so far known to have been put to death for heresy. A greater number formally recanted, 'burnt their bills'. Many were in effect fined, by their or their families' buying their escheats on recantation or remission. Not only is the number put to death small compared with that in some other countries, including England, but it is even small when set against the number of those now known to have been actively protestant in sympathy throughout the period, or whose religious views were sufficiently radical to be construed as heresy. Besides, it is remarkable that with the notable exception of Patrick Hamilton those who were executed were of fairly humble social standing: a few gentlemen, craftsmen, lesser clergy and a handful of friars and canons regular.

It would be unrealistic, however, to regard these facts as a guide to the amount of heretical views around in one form or another. The uneven and scattered documentary evidence does not necessarily reflect a low level of incipient protestantism. Heretics may have occurred more often in some communities than they do in surviving records, which include few of those of the relevant church courts. Not all advocates of reform were the stuff of which martyrs are made, as Erasmus once said of himself, and many must have loved life sufficiently to express their thoughts in private to trusted friends and colleagues only. We shall never know how many times a discussion led to an argument and to near-betrayal; one chaplain in Haddington parish church publicly asked forgiveness for having accused another chaplain of saying that 'the Virgin Mary had no more power than any other woman to do anything for men'.[28] Even formal recantation need not mean that the accused inwardly abandoned his or her convictions, as some case-histories show.[29] This may simply mean that in some instances the authorities were content with a fine, which is what buying one's escheat meant in effect. As has recently been pointed out, we know about the 'diers' and a number of the 'flyers' but 'we can only guess at the number of 'liars' who were successful in concealing their views'.[30] We must not make the mistake of regarding the number of recorded martyrdoms, or even of prosecutions, as an indication of the amount of heretical opinion in Scotland before 1560. The extent of commitment to 'Lutheranism', as it was usually designated by contemporaries, is simply not quantifiable from the surviving evidence but its strength is sometimes implicit rather than explicit in the records we do have.

For one thing, the kind of activities of which people were accused were not the sort of thing one did on one's own. Walter Stewart, son of Lord Ochiltree, who was accused in 1531 of decapitating a statue of the Virgin Mary in the Observantine friary at Ayr, appears to have been acting with other local men.[31] Offences likely to have involved groups included hanging the image of St Francis, being in possession of Lutheran literature and reading the new testament in English or, more likely, hearing it read as David Strachan had it read to him by his kinsman, the laird of Lauriston, or James Hunter, 'a simple man', and his craftsmen friends in Perth who heard it read and discussed, interrupting sermons and demanding to be given the sacrament while under sentence of excommunication. John Ranaldson, the Perth skinner, who with his wife, Helen Stirk, was condemned to death in January 1544 after David Beaton had taken the carving on his forestair to be 'in mockage of his cardinal's hat', belonged to a circle who were so committed to Lutheranism, however untheological in character, that they were bold enough to let it show. Friends of Ranaldson may have stood with him on his forestair watching the entry into Perth of the Cardinal and the Governor on that January day when the mood was so tense that it is said they feared a riot.[32] Of course, David Beaton could never weather a personal insult, however trivial, even in the interest of public quiet, but the significance of this incident is the evocation of the atmosphere of confrontation in which Ranaldson dared to provoke him. The skinner's wife's refusal to call on the Virgin Mary in her recent childbirth or to recant when accused with her husband, even though it meant leaving an orphaned family behind them, could only have been the outcome of fairly well-established protestant attitudes shared with a circle of acquaintances from their own craft background.

There is also the possibility, in trying to assess the strength of adherence to Lutheranism, that the seriousness of some people's commitment may be belied by the seemingly trivial grounds on which they are said to have been accused. When the authorities crack down on people for eating a goose on Friday, if they ever did pounce on them for that alone, it is either because the authorities' nerves are on edge or because they suspect the fire beneath the smoke. By the 1530s even the more familiar offences, such as outbursts of anti-clericalism, could lead to deeper investigation and to the confession of Lutheran beliefs. The force of the orthodox Friar William Arth's sermon at Dundee against the abuse of 'cursing' and 'miracles' provoked the bishop of Brechin to call him 'heretic' and required the opinion of Mr John Major to clear him.[33] In those days a heretic could as easily be hanged for a lamb as a sheep, and to be guilty of the least article of heresy, including denial of those tenets which had arrived comparatively late in the church's canon, such as private masses, clerical celibacy and the duty to pay customary kirk dues, might lead to the imputation of Lutheranism. The marriage of sir John Cocklaw, parish priest of Tullibody, and the defiant refusal of David Strachan to pay his teinds, the latter an endemic offence, were the respective occasions of their apprehension, leading to the revelation of fundamentally heretical opinion, shared in each case by a circle of colleagues, friends and relatives.[34]

The significant feature of dissent in the 1530s and '40s was not that it was spectacular but that, without leadership, it persisted and that protestantism seems to have made an appeal to people of very different backgrounds and outlook: some from the younger generations of academics and members of religious orders, particularly the friars, influenced by Christian humanism with its historical concept of the church and attention to the written sources of Christianity in the original languages; a few sons of noblemen, who had had a European education; professional laymen, especially lawyers, with a lay outlook, resenting clerical dominance of their chosen career; lairds, increasingly literate and socially mobile; merchants and shipmasters with English and European contacts through trading partners and expatriate relatives; members of the close-knit craft incorporations, with their common interests and opportunities for communicating ideas and grievances; the lower clergy, whose rôle calls out for greater study, carrying the burden of the parish service and relations with the laity in the kind of top-heavy organisation in which an unequal distribution of work and wealth creates alienation between management and workforce. The period was one of increasing lay initiative in government and the professions — more lay royal councillors and officials, advocates and notaries public. The lay presence that had long been felt in parish life was now fully developed, giving lay folk the opportunity to benefit from the offices of religion to some extent on their own terms: through municipal rules laid down for the clergy of burgh churches, especially chaplainries, the foundation of collegiate churches in landward areas, lay patronage of endowed altarages, the formation of confraternities for mutual spiritual and material support, the privilege of having private chapels and portable altars and a choice of confessor. Many noble and other landed families were already exploiting the wealth of the church, with the connivance of their ecclesiastical relatives, through the system of commendation; these transactions and the general trade in benefices did nothing to endear the church as an institution to those who failed to get a share of the spoils, or earn the respect of those who did benefit but watched the church do business in the common marketplace. Although protestantism was to be a mainly urban phenomenon in its early stages, there may have been something about Lutheranism, as they received and apprehended it, which also encouraged landward men and women, lairds, freeholders and even tenant-farmers, to read into it, especially into the doctrine of the priesthood of all believers, a do-it-yourself element that appealed to them. It is possible that some of these people, accustomed as they were to solving many of their secular problems without recourse to officialdom — the landed classes rendering local society more stable through their network of bonds of manrent and the farmers ensuring their families' continued possession of their holdings by making full use of customary inheritance practices — welcomed the apparent suggestion implicit in much protestant teaching to help themselves to the means of salvation, especially in districts where parochial provision was meagre and local lay influence strong and sympathetic to reform, a description that applies, for instance, to the Kyle district of Ayrshire.[35]

Posing the greatest problem for the ecclesiastical authorities may have been the friars, of whom about a dozen accused were Dominicans, with a few Franciscans and members of other orders. By preaching to both learned and popular audiences, and able to move around the country, they were eminently suited to spreading heretical views and provoking discussion and may have been links in the chain of communication between protestants in the different burghs and among different classes. Public preaching, especially if topical and controversial in tone, would be attended not only by the local burgesses but by landward folk who were in town for various reasons. In 1534 John Grierson, provincial of the Dominicans, and the Franciscan, John Bothwell, each with a friar of his order, sat with the King's council to deal with the spread of heresy through books and preaching, each undertaking to see that there was 'no rehers of opinionable materis' in the preaching of their brethren.[36] The Franciscan, Alexander Dick, having abandoned his profession and the Aberdeen Observantine convent about 1532, moved for reasons of secrecy to Dundee whence two burgesses were summoned before the lords of council for breaking their promise to hand him over to the authorities should he be formally accused of heresy.[37] James Hewat, at one time sub-prior of the Perth Dominicans, also moved to Dundee where he is said to have confirmed the Wedderburn brothers in protestantism.[38] Alexander Seton, the King's confessor, prior of the St Andrews Dominicans, after his Lenten sermons of 1531 had been condemned in his absence, justified himself by preaching publicly in Dundee.[39] Friar John Roger, before his imprisonment and death in St Andrews castle in 1544, was said to have 'fruitfully preached Christ Jesus to the comfort of many in Angus and Mearns', and held a brief appointment as a preacher in Aberdeen during Arran's reformation-experiment of 1543. He was arrested after ignoring the Cardinal's monition against his preaching in the parish church of Glamis.[40] Friar Kyllour, a Dominican burnt in February 1539, four years after performing an outspoken passion play in Stirling in the presence of the King, had received support from two Aberdeen men who were imprisoned for having assisted him.[41] Thomas Guillaume, who bore an East Lothian name and was said to have had an early influence on John Knox, was one of Arran's Edinburgh preachers in 1543 but may be identified with the prior of the Inverness Dominicans in 1525.[42] John Rough, threatened by a conservative congregation in Edinburgh when he preached there for Arran in 1543, went to Ayrshire after the protestant preachers were discharged on the Cardinal's release from detention.[43] The Franciscan James Melville, after a confrontation with the bishop of Moray in 1526 and a temporary flight from Scotland, preached to such effect 'among the ignorant people' on his return that nine years later the King appealed to the Pope, on behalf of the Observants, not to restore him to the order.[44]

A number of friars are known to have left their houses in the 1530s as the tensions caused by their commitment to Lutheranism made their continued residence difficult, tensions which can only be guessed at from the extreme case of Alexander Campbell, prior of the St Andrews Dominicans, whose private discussions with Patrick Hamilton followed by his public role of accuser and witness of Hamilton's death seem to have brought on a mental breakdown from which he never recovered.[45] Some of these men went to England, including Alexander Seton, Thomas Guillaume and John Willock, the Ayr Dominican, who became a preacher in London but eventually returned to Scotland to help establish the reformed church.[46] Others went to Europe where they followed careers in protestant churches and universities: John McDowall, prior of the Wigtown Dominicans, who left England for Germany about 1540, John McAlpine, Dominican prior of Perth, who fled on being accused of heresy and remained in England until 1540, becoming a canon of Salisbury but who subsequently took a doctorate of theology at Wittenberg and became professor of theology at Copenhagen from where he maintained Scottish contacts, Andrew Charteris, Perth Carthusian, who went to England in 1538, thence to Wittenberg and then Zeeland and Italy, John Lyne, a Franciscan, who 'left his hypocritical habit', a friend of Melanchthon at Wittenberg, and John Craig, Dominican, who came near to being executed for heresy in both Scotland and Italy but lived to become the colleague of John Knox in St Giles church in 1562. The effect of the departure of these men from their houses within a decade of the death of Patrick Hamilton, especially of those who were priors, must have been traumatic and have given rise to much talking and thinking among their younger colleagues. It was to the effects of their actions that the council referred in 1534 when it decided to 'put remeid to the freris at ar tholit to pas furth of the realme in apostacy . . . '[47]

Another group of Lutherans with lines of communication among them and, through their practice of serving parish churches, the means of spreading their ideas beyond academic circles, were the Augustinian canons regular. We are familiar with the names of those whose opinions were publicly expressed through their own writings, accusations of heresy or the texts of their escheats, but as with the friars the defection of these canons regular must have caused heartsearching among colleagues, not to mention the questions raised in the minds of their lay relatives and friends. There was clearly a good deal of discussion of Luther's teaching in St Andrews during and following the residence of Patrick Hamilton, both at the priory itself and in St Leonard's college where the canons had considerable influence. Alexander Allan, or Aleysius, as he Latinised his name, traced his change of mind and heart in his own account of his career.[48] Escaping from the vendetta of Prior Patrick Hepburn in 1530 he subsequently spent time in Malmo, then in England where in 1535 he was welcomed by Cranmer and Latimer and lectured in Cambridge, moving on to Wittenberg in 1540 where he became a friend of Melanchthon, Frankfurt-on-Oder where he became professor of divinity and, finally, Leipzig where he died in 1565. It became customary to remark of those known to be sympathetic to Lutheranism that they had been drinking 'at St Leonard's well'. It is unlikely, however, that formal teaching in St Leonard's college openly supported Luther's propositions but rather that teachers such as the principal, Gavin Logie, and John Winram, the subprior of the priory, permitted freedom of discussion as a result of which students became familiar with protestant belief to the extent that some adopted it, as is alleged of canons John Duncanson and James Wilkie. Logie and Winram themselves, whatever their private views, operated within the confines of the ecclesiastical establishment, taking part in heresy trials, for example. Winram's ambivalent attitude, however, did not protect him from the Cardinal's suspicions as early as the latter's succession to the primacy in 1539.[49] A probable relative, Gilbert Winram, who was a student at St Leonard's college and the owner of a copy of Erasmus's Greek new testament among other books, joined the reformers in 1527 and accompanied Patrick Hamilton to Marburg.[50]

Family connections and friendships dating from university days formed the links between some of those whose names appear baldly in the meagre records of heresy trials and escheats.[51] Gavin Logie's brother Robert, canon of Cambuskenneth and teacher of the novices there, was a friend of other convicted Lutherans including Thomas Forret, canon of Inchcolm and vicar of Dollar, Thomas Cocklaw or Gibson, vicar of Tullibody, and Robert Richardson, who is said to have gone over to Lutheranism soon after writing his commentary on the rule of St Augustine. Richardson and his brother John, also a canon at Cambuskenneth, who was exiled for his beliefs in 1538–9, were closely related on their mother's side to Alexander Allan. Robert Logie and Thomas Cocklaw had been in Paris together, probably with Robert Richardson; the first two after being preachers in London became naturalised French citizens in 1544. Thomas Forret, the lawyer Henry Balnaves, the friars John McAlpine, John McDowall and, probably, James Hewat, were graduates of Cologne. When Robert Logie made his escape from Scotland a search was made for him in Forret's house, while Cocklaw left him a cache of money for his voyage from Dundee. Through the Augustinian practice of serving parish churches annexed to their abbeys, Forret and Cocklaw found, may indeed have established, fellow-Lutherans among the parishioners of Dollar and Tullibody. Thomas Forret, whose name is preserved in 'the vicar's bridge' which he erected for his parishioners, is known to have systematically taught them each Sunday from the English bible. In spite of an altercation with the bishop of Dunblane over his preaching activities Forret escaped punishment 'until the cruel cardinal David Beaton got the upper hand'; there can be no doubt that the arrival of the Cardinal in the primatial seat early in 1539 marked a more repressive attitude to suspects and known heretics, Forret being among those burnt in February that year. Thomas Cocklaw's commitment to protestantism extended to his marriage to a widow, Margaret Jameson; even living according to the letter of the law in separate houses did not save them from conviction. Their wedding was said to have been attended by sympathisers and friends who included Dominican friars Beveridge and Kyllour, sir Duncan Simpson, a chaplain, Robert Forrester, 'gentleman', probably from the family of Arngibbon in Kippen parish and a relative of William Forrester who was convicted at the same time but escaped with an escheat and, so it is said, by George Buchanan from the same part of the country. Beveridge, Kyllour, Simpson and Robert Forrester were among those burnt in February 1539. Cocklaw, condemned to be immured, was helped by his friends to escape to England. His wife was escheated in April 1539 for 'certane crymes of heresy'.[52]

Fragmentary information about some secular priests accused of heresy reveals not only the personal contacts that introduced them to Lutheran beliefs but occasionally the circumstances that led to their detection. Mr Norman Gourlay, said to have been a married priest, 'a man of reasonable erudition . . . albeit joined with weakness', who stood firm enough by his convictions to be burnt with others at the Greenside of Edinburgh in August 1534, had connections with the family of the earl of Rothes,[53] one of several Fife families inclined towards heresy. Sir Henry Elder, chaplain, from Perth was one of the circle of Lutherans in the burgh who were accused of meeting to hear the bible read and discussed, thus 'breaking the acts of parliament anent heresy'. Some of the accused in this period moved in circles about whom the Cardinal was in a position to receive information: it is significant that the escheat of sir David Hutchison, provost of Roslin collegiate church, went to Oliver Sinclair who was not only a member of the patron's family but a client of the Cardinal.[54] David Lindsay and John Wigton, priests, were both tried as a result of the inquisition mounted against heresy in Angus and the Mearns in 1544. To secure his release, Wigton became the Cardinal's agent and in 1546 attempted to kill George Wishart.[55]

It was claimed that prominent young laymen stood by Alexander Allan in his confrontation with Prior Patrick Hepburn in the early 1530s, possibly including students who identified with their open-minded and outspoken mentor. There can be no doubt that the influence of tutors and the exchange of ideas with fellow-students at university led laymen as well as clerics towards protestantism:[56] Sir John Borthwick, who may have been influenced by his kinsman, Nicholas Borthwick who was a student at Wittenberg in 1528, John Sandilands, younger, of Calder, a Paris student, later a supporter of Wishart, Mr David Borthwick and Mr William Johnston, both advocates, who had studied at St Leonard's in the 1520s, Mr Henry Balnaves, the example *par excellence* in this period of a lay lawyer, able to express his protestant beliefs in writing, who had studied at Cologne, the young 3rd earl of Cassillis, tutored by George Buchanan in the 1530s. Cells of Lutheran adherence in certain families multiplied through a variety of contacts. The most influential on record is probably that of John Erskine of Dun, who was said to have been committed to Lutheranism from the early 1530s and was himself to be an important link between pre- and post-Reformation protestantism in Angus. Lutherans who resorted to Erskine's house included the laird of Brigton, denounced with Friar John Roger in 1544, Andrew Stratoun of Lauriston and his kinsman, David Stratoun, the latter said to be the first layman to be burnt for heresy in Scotland, and George Wishart, the laird of Pittarrow's kinsman. The laird of Dun's role was paralleled in Ayrshire by the influence of families such as the Cunninghams of Glencairn and the Stewarts of Ochiltree. It would be interesting to know how Lutheranism percolated to lay folk further down the social scale. So far no light has been shed on the connection, if there was one, between the family of Henry Balnaves, who is said to have belonged to Fife, and that of 'Walter Piper alias Balnavis', burgess of Perth, who was among those banished for heresy and was related to another Perth Lutheran, the merchant Robert Lamb.[57]

Whatever the extent of protestantism in Scotland before 1550, the churchmen of the period appear to have taken it seriously enough, with legislation passed in their interest, periodic inquisitions and a sufficient number of prosecutions to serve as a warning to others. Anti-clericalism of the abusive sort, although liable to provoke increasing reaction, was something that the clergy, particularly the higher clergy, had learned to live with. Those of them who had attended the performance of David Lindsay's *Thrie Estaitis* or were present at the farcical trial of Sandy Furrour, who cavorted into the court like an entertainer demanding compensation for having been cuckolded by a priest, so that the company had a 'whip-round' in order to get rid of him, doubtless laughed it off with the best of them.[58] Perhaps King James's warning, after seeing Lindsay's play, that if they did not mend their ways he would pack off 'the proudest of them' to his uncle of England, was delivered in a more jocular tone than is conveyed by protestant annalists. His own standards of behaviour were not such as to encourage the prelates to take him seriously. But anti-clerical gestures took on a more threatening aspect in a period of increasing lay resentment of clerical privilege, soft living and exemption from the secular law courts accompanied by long and expensive ecclesiastical legal procedures for the laity, the exaction of customary kirk dues, especially on the death of relatives, and the harassment of clerical sanctions such as 'cursing' for non-payments, including arrears of teinds, all of which demands tended to fall on people already under stress.

It is probably also true, although more difficult to demonstrate from surviving Scottish evidence, that the alienation of the laity became more dangerous still when protestant preachers, or tracts, put over a message which appeared to undermine the theological basis of clerical control and when the vernacular bible was found to contain descriptions of the pastors of the early church whose character and commitment were far removed from what people saw in many contemporary churchmen. To radical would-be reformers of the church there were less flattering parallels to be found in scripture; 'If Christ himself were in Scotland,' wrote the exiled Carthusian, Andrew Charteris, to his brother in Dundee, 'he should be made more ignominious by our spiritual fathers than he was of old of the Jews'.[59] When Friar Kyllour put over his Good Friday message in the form of a play on Christ's passion, using a traditional vehicle for a radical statement which, Knox asserted, later cost him his life, 'the very simple people understood and confessed that as the priests and obstinate pharisees persuaded the people to refuse Christ Jesus, and caused Pilate to condemn him, so did the bishops and men called religious blind the people and persuade princes and judges to persecute such as profess Jesus Christ his blessed evangel'.[60] James Wedderburn who 'had a good gift of poesie' made several plays on biblical themes, such as the fate of John the Baptist, in order to provoke criticism of the religious establishment, the dramas being performed in the public playfields.[61] When the doctrine of justification by faith alone was grasped by many people it appeared to knock the bottom out of the doctrines of purgatory, private masses, indulgences and the intercession of the saints. This could only alarm the late medieval church which largely used these beliefs and associated practices, including the confessional, if manuals for clerical guidance are to be taken seriously, to maintain intact not only the fabric of religious life but its own authority over the lives of the laity. Lay resentment which sometimes broke out in acts of iconoclasm grew not simply because people felt themselves 'fleeced' but spiritually cheated in the process. We have to remind ourselves that in the sixteenth century people took these matters seriously, that lay piety of which there was much in pre-Reformation Scotland was genuinely trying to find salvation from a sense of guilt and did not take kindly to finding itself misled. There must have been Scottish equivalents of the farmer in Nicholas Manuel's *Die Totenfresser* who, having spent the family's egg-money on an indulgence only to be told by his enlightened neighbours that it was worthless, put the piece of paper to the most insulting of domestic uses, saying that he was 'still sick to my stomach about it':[62]

> Since laymen knew the verity,
> Pardoners gets na charity
>   Without that they debate it.[63]

It did not allay churchmen's apprehensions that the attachment to Lutheranism which they were trying to break was scarcely organised, lacked leadership and put forward no positive alternative at this time to the system that it criticised. In the first place, it was sufficiently disquieting to have the church's image impaired at a time when it was trying to defend its integrity and resources in the face of the King's material assaults. James V made it clear on more than one occasion that it was at his mercy. Even the Cardinal was aware of the danger, warning his agent at Rome to avoid doing anything that would in any way irritate the King 'incontrare the liberty of holy kirk, considering the time is perilous'.[64] It was never entirely certain that the King of Scots would not emulate his uncle by making a direct attack on church property or detaching the Scottish church from Rome. The lesson learned in the early 1530s during the battle between King and prelates over 'the great tax' and the endowment of the college of justice, in which James had been the victor, remained applicable throughout his reign. In a number of individual instances the tension between royal and ecclesiastical authority can be detected: in the same letter to his agent the Cardinal discussed ways and means of setting free two clerics imprisoned by the King for barratry — 'in order to preserve the liberty of the church' — and in 1541 he found himself having to enforce a papal decision in favour of the reformist provincial of the Carmelites on the latter's recalcitrant rival who appears at one point to have appealed to the King for support.[65]

Secondly, although the Scottish Reformation may have crystallised late, by textbook standards, churchmen in the pre-1550 period could see for themselves how far things had gone in other countries, particularly in the German and Swiss towns and in Scandinavia where even the most evolutionary protestant settlements had taken place by 1540, many of them by 1530.[66] David Beaton, with his personal European contacts, knew perfectly well what could and did happen elsewhere when it suited a ruler or municipal government to decide for protestantism. It is significant that he made a bid to control the council of Perth about the same time as he launched an attack on that burgh's enclave of Lutherans. Some Scots who were exiled in European cities remained in touch with their countrymen; in April 1544 a group of Scots visited Alexander Allan at Frankfurt-on-Oder where they complained to him about the Cardinal's treatment of the Perth heretics three months before.[67]

Thirdly, clerical apprehensions must also have been due to the fact that the prelates and their officials possessed more information than has survived for our enlightenment on the activities and associations of known and suspect heretics. Indeed, the whole phenomenon must have been much more in the open, so to speak, than our meagre information on sporadic prosecutions conveys. It must have been a source of frustration to the Cardinal that he rubbed shoulders daily at the royal court and in the law courts with those whose favour with the King and their public office made it difficult to accuse them but whose presence in public life gave protestantism a measure of *de facto* acceptability. The parallel with the earlier situation in France must surely have occurred to him. It was said of the treasurer, Sir James Kirkcaldy of Grange, that he 'always had a new testament in his poutche'. The treasurer's clerk, the lawyer Henry Balnaves, practised in the consistorial court of St Andrews in the 1530s, occasionally even acting as procurator for David Beaton as abbot of Arbroath, while at the same time frequenting the households of the heretically-inclined laird of Raith, who was the treasurer's father-in-law, and the earl of Rothes. Balnaves became an advocate in the court of session in 1537, a judge in 1538 and a commissioner to parliament. Mr David Borthwick, a prominent advocate of Lutheran persuasion, had studied at St Leonard's college in the 1520s. Sir John Borthwick, a trusted member of the King's circle, had made Lutheran contacts in Paris. In touch with Thomas Cromwell in the 1530s, Borthwick made free with his opinions which were chiefly concerned with the practical implications of protestantism, a priority which he shared with other laymen. At the same time his library contained the works of Oecolampadius, Melanchthon and Erasmus as well as a copy of the new testament in English.[68] When Cromwell's aide, Ralph Sadler, arrived in Edinburgh as ambassador early in 1540, James V delegated Borthwick to attend him. Lord Maxwell, whose Lutheran views were to extend to support for the distribution of the bible in English, was at various times master of the household and captain of the King's guard. His personal relations with the Cardinal were never good. In the case of George Buchanan, the scholarly tutor of the King's natural sons, personal animosity as well as objections to his alleged religious views may have fuelled David Beaton's vendetta against him. Both had spent their early years in Paris, were associated with Albany in the 1520s and became naturalised French citizens. David Lindsay is a more enigmatic figure. There is no doubt that, like his contemporaries, he saw the need for reformation in the broadest terms, affecting King, church and people and that his early works were just as concerned with this theme as his more famous *Satyre of the Thrie Estaitis*. There is equally no doubt that the failings of the church — secularised through its preoccupation with property and the abuse of the benefice system, failing in its duty to the people — came in for the sharpest edge of his tongue. Although remaining orthodox on essential points, such as the mass and justification, some of his views, including those on confession and the intercession of the saints, came close to heresy.[69] Intimate with the King since the latter's troubled childhood, he was allowed a freedom of speech that few others would have dared to use. Probably acquainted with David Beaton since their early days, Lindsay identified the essential layman in him, and their relations can have been little more than an exchange of uneasy resentment, on the part of the Cardinal, and amused disdain on the part of the Lord Lyon.

Beyond the royal court heresy was also a kind of 'open secret' ever since the death of Patrick Hamilton had let loose speculation about the Lutheran doctrines. From 1534, the very year in which Archbishop James Beaton consigned a group of heretics to the flames, the customary feast of the faculty of arts at St Andrews had had to be abandoned in an acrimonious atmosphere partly due, so it is believed, to divergent sympathies in religious matters.[70] John Winram, subprior of the St Andrews Augustinians, while he maintained an ambivalent aspect, was nevertheless credited by Knox and others with having encouraged the younger canons who were drawn to Lutheranism. By the time David Beaton became archbishop he must have been aware that there were those among the teaching staff of the university, of which he was chancellor, and among the canons of the priory, who formed his chapter, who were suspect in religious matters.

Still further afield, some parishioners of Dollar and Tullibody presumably identified with the reforming stance of their respective parish priests in the 1530s, while those who did not must have talked about it. The Lutheran circle in Perth, which included merchants, craftsmen, chaplains, friars and a schoolmaster, were not suddenly discovered, only suddenly prosecuted, for good reasons. It may be that the short roll-call of martyrs is simply due to the fact that Lutherans were not actively pursued during the régime of Archbishop James Beaton, and only if the King allowed it — after all his sanction was necessary for the actual executions whatever the ecclesiastical verdict. It has been suggested that the King encouraged heresy hunts only when it suited his own purpose, very largely when he wished to impress the Pope with his orthodoxy in order to gain some concession: in 1533–4 when he was waiting for papal confirmation of the endowment of the college of justice, in 1539 when he was begging for the faculty of legate *a latere* for the Cardinal, which would give the Scottish church a measure of freedom of action without recourse to Rome, and in 1541 when he again wanted papal sanction for a clerical tax.[71]

As for the Cardinal himself, perhaps his reputation as a persecutor rests more on his known intentions than on his successes. But he may have had less cause for complacency about his control of heresy than he liked to convey in letters to papal representatives; after all he wanted Rome to think that his authority in Scotland was absolute. It is true that he got off to an energetic start. In 1538, while he was still only coadjutor of St Andrews, an attack was launched against Lutherans in Dundee, some of whom were merchants defying the ban on the importation of Lutheran books. Fourteen burgesses abjured and bought their own escheats, their fines going into the office of the privy seal of which David Beaton was keeper and would receive his share of the proceeds.[72] As we saw, a handful of more serious cases were tried early in 1539, five of whom were burnt. At much the same time, in order that the church might show a united front against heresy the Cardinal brought his primatial powers to bear on Gavin Dunbar to take strong action against offenders in the archdiocese of Glasgow, sending Friar Maltman with the two secretaries, John Lauder and Andrew Oliphant, to conduct the trial. They overrode Dunbar's inclination towards a lenient verdict and Jerome Russell, a Cordelier friar, and a young man from Ayrshire, named Kennedy, were sent to the stake.[73] Other inquisitions in the west at this time brought to light the case of Donald McCartnay, monk of Glenluce, and three unnamed Paisley monks, against whom John Wallace, a novice at the abbey, appears to have testified.[74]

This forceful beginning by the Cardinal, however, was scarcely followed up. Although he prosecuted more heretics than any other churchman before the Reformation, they are few compared to the number of those whom he might justifiably have accused. The fact is that he went as far as he could go without antagonising influential families, some of whom were his own vassals and tenants. If heretics were to be found anywhere it was in Fife, Angus and the Mearns, but as lord of the archbishopric's temporal lands he was torn between prosecuting heresy and maintaining the political support of his tenants. He did try to bribe a number of them with grants of church land, including Henry Balnaves, at a time when he was also courting the King's officials with feu charters.[75] As a result, his inquisitions throughout the province, in Angus, the Mearns and Aberdeenshire, in 1544, like his attacks on the Lutherans in the burghs, such as Dundee and Perth, resulted in the prosecution of fairly humble folk. Where more substantial persons were accused, such as the earl Marischal, Fraser of Philorth and Meldrum of Fyvie in the Aberdeenshire inquisition in which Huntly had a hand, they were usually offered the chance to abjure after which they paid for a remission or bought their escheats.[76] The humbler victims served as a lesson to others — the usual pattern in sixteenth-century Scotland when someone had to be made an example of. The fate of people like the tragic Helen Stirk of Perth or the faithful vicar of Dollar earned the Cardinal his reputation of persecutor and, as in the case of Patrick Hamilton's death, provoked a good deal of questioning and discussion as to what the victims had stood for, but he caught very few of the big fish. Persecution, as often happens, probably sent many of the earlier heretics underground to emerge a decade later in the 'privy kirks' and ultimately the congregations of the reformed church.

Ironically, those who were to prove the greatest threat and who took the initiative when political circumstances favoured an active stage in the reform movement, that is those landed families and individuals who combined their Lutheranism with Anglophile politics, remained relatively unharmed. Ever since the pro-English administration of Angus in the 1520s there had been those who believed that Scotland's future lay in greater amity with 'the auld enemy'. With the infiltration of protestantism and growing support for some kind of reform, the English solution became increasingly attractive to a number of Scots, the viewpoints of some of whom would nevertheless have horrified the theologically orthodox King Henry VIII. Their views were strengthened in the last years of James V's reign as his inclination to invade England took on the appearance of a crusade in the interests of France and the papacy, a crusade which the Cardinal undertook to further. When relations between the leading 'crusaders', France and the Empire, broke down and hostilities were reduced to an Anglo-Scottish war, a number of Scottish magnates became less and less inclined to take part. When James V, abetted so it was claimed by the prelates, finally mustered his army in 1542 many did not attend the hosting. It is surely not simply coincidence that many of the absentees came from those parts of the country most affected by Lutheranism,[77] or were men whose personal commitment to it was known; Lord Maxwell was blamed for sabotaging the raid from the western marches and so contributing to the rout of Solway Moss. Even before the 1542 campaign, however, some Scots were interested in a Cromwellian solution to the need for reform. The English commissioner on the border had reported to Thomas Cromwell the results of 'divers communings' between himself and Thomas Bellenden of Auchnoule and Henry Balnaves at Coldstream, 'especially touching the stay of the spiritualitie in Scotland, and gathering him [Bellenden] to be a man inclined to the sort used in our sovereign's realm of England I did largely break with him in those behalves, as to know of him what mind the King and Council of Scotland was inclined unto concerning the bishop of Rome'. Bellenden asked Eure, the English commissioner, for copies of acts of the English parliament and other measures concerning the dissolution of the monasteries and 'the reformation of the misdemeanors of the clergy'.[78] The link between Lutheranism and amity towards England remained the focus of David Beaton's vigilance: 'the whole pollution and plague of Anglican impiety', as he described it in a letter to the Pope.[79] England was a refuge for the Scottish heretic 'flyers' and the source of supply of much subversive literature, including English bibles, sent not so much in answer to actual demand as to maximise the disaffection that existed. The English 'reformation' was the clearest possible demonstration of the church's vulnerability at the hands of a monarch. Dangerous as the Anglophile protestants were, however, they were the Cardinal's most elusive victims.

His task may have been made more difficult in his early years as archbishop by a perceptible change in his relations with the King. It is just possible that having passed the zenith of his diplomatic usefulness, the negotiation of the King's French marriages, he found himself a little less in the King's confidence. In the atmosphere of tension which James's opportunism must have created no one knew better than he that royal confidence could never be taken for granted. He was now leader of the ecclesiastical estate but the major secular office, that of chancellor, was held by his rival Gavin Dunbar of Glasgow. The year 1540, which began prestigiously with the Queen's coronation at which he officiated, was a difficult one. Early in the year the English ambassador made an attempt to discredit him with James V by confronting the King with the intercepted correspondence between the Cardinal and his agent at Rome, Mr Andrew Oliphant, in which the former expressed his fears about the King's policy towards the church. Sadler also passed on information to James about the Cardinal's action in releasing some prisoners, apparently on his own initiative. James enjoyed the revelation of the clergy's fears but snubbed Sadler's suggestion of the Cardinal's disloyalty by saying that the matter of the prisoners, who were unimportant, had been delegated to Beaton by himself. The King's reaction was probably less a defence of his servant than a reminder to Sadler that he himself could decide who to trust and that he was able to control their activities. 'I assure your Majesty', Sadler wrote to Henry, who never took the envoy's defeats easily, 'he excused the Cardinal in everything, and seemed wondrous loath to hear anything that should sound as an untruth in him, but rather give great praise.'[80] Sadler, not always the most shrewd of diplomats, was perceptive enough to identify the Cardinal, who took him affably by the arm as they went in to dinner, as his master's chief enemy north of the border.

His relations with the King may have become strained at this time through the failure of a proposed attack on heresy, in connection with which the King's attitude was important. Early in the year the Cardinal and other prelates are said to have presented James with a long list of names of laymen, nobles and gentry, whom he might justifiably forfeit for breaking the acts of parliament against heresy.[81] If this was an attempt to shift the problem of the Anglophile heretics on to the King's shoulders, the plan failed. It may have been the reference to possible forfeitures that nettled the King into throwing the list back at the clergy with the warning not to come between him and his nobles and servants. At the same time it was said that Sir James Kirkcaldy of Grange, the treasurer, whose name was presumably on the list, advised the King to ignore the accusation. Even if the alleged number of 300 suspects was an exaggeration, the scale does indicate the intention of the prelates, led by the Cardinal, to undertake a thorough round-up of offenders, albeit from the shelter of the King's authority, and suggests widespread gathering of information. It may also have been that the heavily-taxed churchmen hoped that the forfeitures might provide James with an alternative source of revenue, or at least shift part of the burden of the King's avariciousness on to the laity. The rebuff provoked a characteristic reaction in David Beaton who, in the spring of the same year, staged a more overt attack on heresy by citing Sir John Borthwick, the King's familiar servant, for trial.[82]

The Borthwick episode has the look of having been stage-managed, by the Cardinal as a warning to Lutherans in high places and by the King in order to let David Beaton have his way without doing any real damage. Sir John Borthwick, made aware of what was in store for him, made his escape to England so that he was tried and condemned *in absentia* and his effigy burnt in the market place of St Andrews. The King himself was in residence in his palace within the priory precincts while his servant's 'trial' took place 'in the cloister' and the Cardinal pronounced the sentence in the cathedral. In fact, King and Cardinal met later

that same day in the royal lodging, first at the baptism of the week-old Prince
James, to whom David Beaton was a godfather,[83] and later when the laird of
Allardyce resigned lands in the King's hands, the Cardinal witnessing the
transaction in company with Sir Thomas Erskine of Brechin, the royal secretary,
and Henry Kemp of Thomastoun.[84] It is possible, however, that the Cardinal was
able to make some capital out of the Borthwick trial. In order that judgement
might be seen to fall he walked in procession from the castle to the cathedral with
those whom he is said to have summoned to St Andrews. Before pronouncing the
sentence he addressed the assembly from an appropriately raised chair,
emphasising the urgent need to take action against heresy among those who were
bold enough to voice their opinions in the royal circle. The membership of the
company who listened to him is interesting, especially if, as is claimed, they had
come at his request. In addition to those theologians, canonists, representatives of
orders of friars, bishops and abbots whose presence was to be expected there were
four earls, five lords and two knights, together with the clerk register and the
justice-clerk. The support of some of them for the Cardinal, however, was more
likely to have been a political gesture against the King, from whose counsels they
were said to be excluded at that time, than an endorsement of the clerical campaign
against heresy. So far as their attitudes to protestantism can be detected, the
laymen were fairly evenly divided.

Sir John Borthwick's mixture of protestantism and Anglophile politics was the
most dangerous thing about him. The accusations against him reveal a
recognisably Cromwellian programme for the effective dissolution of ecclesiastical
authority in Scotland as David Beaton understood it: the pope's authority is equal
to any bishop's, the pope is a simoniac, indulgences have no force, priests should
marry, churchmen, not only the religious, should have no temporal possessions,
King James should do as King Henry did and get back what his forefathers had
granted, the canon law is not binding, the religious orders should be dissolved, as
in England. It was no wonder that the prelates, led by David Beaton, saw this
programme as undermining their position in the Christian commonwealth:
detachment from Rome, loss of property and revenue, eradication of the social
distinction between clergy and laity, the weakening of lay dependence on the
religious offices of the church, removal of the laity from the scope of her legal
sanctions, the unequal and unnatural division of society into King, second and
third estates on the one hand and the embattled first estate on the other through
the redistribution of church property. To tamper with the balance of society by
attacking any one of its parts was to 'shake loose the commonweal'. Besides,
whatever the lay leaders of society thought and acted upon could filter down to the
commons sooner or later. They may not have fully understood what was being put
about but they followed from long habits of interdependence and mutual support.
A 'simple man' such as James Hunter of Perth, or a 'faithful brother' like James
Watson in Innergowrie may not have posed much of a threat on their own, but
their practice of meeting with others to read (or hear read) and discuss the new
testament betrayed the influence of their social superiors. If these leaders could
channel the inarticulate but real grievances and perplexities of the so-called

'simple people', there was no saying where it might end. George Wishart when he came was equally at ease in the homes of lairds, burgesses and countrymen like James Watson because all shared his aspirations according to the measure of their understanding.

In the minds of the Cardinal and his colleagues the threat of Anglophile reform was not necessarily detached from that of the half-understood Lutheranism of the common folk, in that the one could easily make use of the other to strengthen its impact; as the Lords of the Congregation were to find a decade later, it was difficult to restrain the 'rascal multitude' once it had got its head. The more open the leaders of society were allowed to be about their views, the more it would embolden lesser people. How that influence was felt, how it filtered down, may be difficult to tell now but we may be sure that in the days when society was seen as a whole, contained within the traditional framework of church and state, the silent majority was led by the articulate minority. What contemporaries could plainly see happening we have now to reconstruct from the fragments of the picture that are left; surviving records of heretical activity are mere fragments, but at the time they fitted into a more complete pattern of life. If the commonweal was in danger of shaking loose, this only strengthened the determination of the Cardinal to make use of all the power and means of patronage at his disposal to hold it together.

NOTES

1. D. Calderwood, *The History of the Kirk of Scotland*, I, 124–9 (*Calderwood*)

2. J. H. M. Salmon, *Society in Crisis, France in the Sixteenth century*, 79–84

3. *Calderwood*, I, 171–5; biographical details of individuals associated with heresy and named in this chapter will be found in Appendix 3

4. *A.P.S.*, II, 295

5. *Ibid.*, II, 291–2

6. Wyntoun, *Originale Cronykil*, ed. D. Laing, II, 100

7. Dunlop, *Acta*, 11–12

8. D. Laing, *Works of John Knox*, I, Appendix II (Laing, *Knox*)

9. *A.P.S.*, II, 7

10. Quoted in J. H. Burns, 'John Ireland and the Meroure of Wyssdome', in *Innes Review*, VI, 77–98

11. T. G. Law, *The New Testament in Scots, Purvey's Revision of Wycliffe's Version turned into Scots by Murdoch Nisbet, c. 1520* (S.T.S)

12. C. Cross, *Church and People, 1450–1660*, Chapter 2; M. Aston, *Lollards and Reformers, Images and Literacy in Late Medieval Religion*, Chapter 7; A. G. Dickens, *The English Reformation*, 56–62

13. *Lorimer*, 209

14. *A.P.S.*, II, 295

15. *Ibid.*, marginal note; see *Source Book of Scottish History*, ed. W. Dickinson, G. Donaldson and I. Milne, Vol. II, 108

16. *A.P.S.*, II, 342

17. *Ibid.*, II, 368

18. D. H. Fleming, *St Andrews Kirk Session Register* (S.H.S.), 89–104

19. P. Lorimer, *Patrick Hamilton*; Knox, I, 13–34, II, 219–29 for text of 'Patrick's Places'; A. R. McEwen, *History of the Church in Scotland*, I, 417–24

20. Durkan, 'The Cultural Background', 282–4

21. Printed in *Knox*, II, 219–29

22. Salmon, *Society in Crisis*, 85–6; R. J. Knecht, *French Renaissance Monarchy: Francis I and Henry II*, 57–9

23. Salmon, *Society in Crisis*, 86; Knecht, *French Renaissance Monarchy*, 60–2, 91–2

24. *Ibid.*, 60

25. *Ibid.*, 62

26. See Appendix 2

27. See Appendix 3

28. *Transactions of the East Lothian Field Naturalists' and Antiquarian Society*, X, 57, quoting from the protocol book of A. Symson

29. George Wishart went through a repeated ceremony of abjuration in Bristol in 1539. J. Durkan, 'Scottish "Evangelicals" in the Patronage of Thomas Cromwell', in *Records of the Scottish Church History Society*, XXI, ii, 144 (Durkan, 'Scottish "Evangelicals"')

30. G. Donaldson, *All the Queen's Men*, 14

31. Cowan, *The Scottish Reformation*, 92

32. See page 000, below, for a fuller discussion of the Perth heresy trials

33. *Knox*, I, 15

34. *Calderwood*, I, 123–4; *Knox*, I, 24

35. M. H. B. Sanderson, 'Some Aspects of the Church in Society in the Era of the Reformation, illustrated from the sheriffdom of Ayr', in *Records of the Scottish Church History Society*, XVII

36. A. Ross, 'Some Notes on the Religious Orders in Pre-Reformation Scotland', in *Essays*, 204n (Ross, 'Notes on the Religious Orders')

37. Appendix 3

38. *Ibid.*

39. *Ibid.*

40. *Ibid.*

41. *Ibid.*

42. *Ibid.*

43. *Ibid.*

44. *Ibid.*

45. Ross, 'Notes on the Religious Orders', 200

46. Durkan, 'Scottish "Evangelicals"', 153–5

47. Ross, 'Notes on the Religious Orders', 204n

48. Durkan, 'Scottish "Evangelicals"', 137–9, 150–1

49. J. Spottiswoode, *History of the Church of Scotland . . . to the end of the reign of James VI* (Spottiswoode Society), I, 159–60 (*Spottiswoode*); *Pitscottie*, II, 77

50. Durkan, 'Cultural Background', 282; J. Durkan and A. Ross, *Early Scottish Libraries*, 160

51. Appendix 3

52. *RSS*, II, 2987

53. St Andrews University Muniments, SS 'B', fo 84v

54. *RSS*, II, 3612

55. *Knox*, I, 63–4

56. Appendix 3

57. *RMS*, III, 1275 (1533); *RSS*, III, 1437; Appendix 3

58. *Knox*, I, 18–19

59. *Calderwood*, I, 114

60. *Knox*, I, 26

61. *Calderwood*, I, 141–3

62. S. E. Ozment, *The Reformation in the Cities*, 45

63. Sir David Lindsay, *Ane Satyre of the Thrie Estaitis* (S.T.S.)

64. A. Clifford, *State Papers of Sir Ralph Sadler*, I, 14 (*Sadler*)

65. A.D.C.S., xiv, fos 190–4, xv, fo 2

66. A. G. Dickens, *Reformation and Society in Sixteenth-Century Europe*, 74–9, 87–90; Ozment, *The Reformation in the Cities*, 121–31

67. Durkan, 'Scottish "Evangelicals"', 150

68. *Ibid.*, 132–3

69. A. Ross, 'Notes on the Religious Orders', 204; M. Taylor, 'The Conflicting Doctrines of the Scottish Reformation', in *Essays*, 251n (Taylor, 'Conflicting Doctrines')

70. Dunlop, *Acta*, lvii

71. M. Mahoney, 'The Scottish Hierarchy', 68–70

72. *RSS*, II, 2648

73. *Knox*, I, 27–8; about this time the Cardinal gave Friar Simon Maltman 'or Hepburn', £3 to buy a cloak, *Rentale*, 95

74. J. Durkan, 'Some Local Heretics', in *Transactions of the Dumfries and Galloway Natural History and Antiquarian Society*, XXXVI, 71–2; same author, 'Paisley Abbey in the Sixteenth Century', in *Innes Review*, XXVII, ii, 121–2

75. Leven and Melville muniments (S.R.O.), GD 26/3/1194 (Balnaves); *Rentale*, 165 (James Stewart, son of James V); *ibid*, 127 (Sir Thomas Erskine, royal secretary), *Ibid.* (Oliver Sinclair); *Ibid.* (Sir James Learmonth of Dairsie, master of the King's household); *Ibid.*, 165 (Henry Kemp of Thomastoun, gentleman of the bedchamber)

76. Cowan, *The Scottish Reformation*, 100

77. Donaldson, *All the Queen's Men*, 14

78. Lorimer, *Patrick Hamilton*, 215

79. *L. P. Henry VIII*, XVIII, i, 494

80. *Sadler*, I, 41–4

81. *Knox*, I, 34

82. *St Andrews Kirk Session Register*, 89–104

83. Laing, *Knox*, I, 34

84. *Historic MSS Commission Report V* (Allardyce), 631

7

A Prince Above All Priests

To be archbishop of St Andrews was to rule a kingdom within a kingdom, which stretched from the Mearns to the Lothians. Writs might be addressed to 'our subjects' and the King's capital referred to as 'the toun of Edinburgh within our diocese of St Andrews'. The archbishop had power over the spiritual and material aspects of many lives, and most of his representatives, professionally trained and non-hereditary, were more readily answerable to him than were some royal officers to the King. He was at the head of two administrative systems, the one temporal, through which he administered those lands that had accrued to the see over the centuries, the other ecclesiastical, operating through the diocesan machinery to bring his spiritual authority to bear on the clergy and lay inhabitants of a large part of eastern Scotland.

The analogy of a ruler is not without substance. Preoccupied with public affairs, the archbishop exercised his powers as *ordinary* through a system of delegation which by the time of David Beaton's incumbency was fully developed. Even in matters which were nominally reserved to his personal jurisdiction he was accustomed to appoint special commissioners to act on his behalf, in everything from disputes over benefices to the granting of degrees to the graduands of St Andrews university of which he was chancellor. Like the King of Scots he acted through his officers and their deputies whose activities were his everyday contacts with clergy and laity at local level. The archbishop had acquired a princely image at odds with the pastoral character of his office. It was certainly the impression of him likely to be gained by ordinary parishioners who chanced to see him on his travels, while his tenants and vassals, who owed him a dual obedience, probably thought of him as landlord first and spiritual superior afterwards.

Delegation of duties did not end with the archbishop. From as early as the fourteenth century the chief administrative officer, the *archdeacon*, had become an increasingly detached figure whose concerns lay elsewhere than in the daily business of the diocese.[1] By the sixteenth century the two archdeacons, St Andrews principal, north of Forth, and Lothian, south of Forth, were characteristically non-resident appointees whose duties had largely devolved upon the *deans of Christianity* of the rural deaneries into which the archdeaconries were divided. It is no surprise to find the archdeaconries used by the Beaton archbishops as pieces of family patronage. David Beaton's cousin, George Durie, when already abbot of Dunfermline, had a ten-year tussle over the archdeaconry of St Andrews principal with John Cantuly who eventually gave up the contest in 1535 in return for a pension out of the benefice.[2] Four years later the King failed to stop a family deal whereby, with the necessary papers from Rome, Durie passed the archdeaconry on to his nephew, Robert Pitcairn, effectively retaining the liferent.[3] Thus Durie was already archdeacon of St Andrews when his cousin became archbishop in 1539. They had previously worked closely together, with Durie as conservator of the privileges of Arbroath abbey, once sharing the distinction of being cursed by their uncle, Archbishop James Beaton, for failure to pay him dues from their respective abbacies to which they had been appointed through his classic nepotism.[4] George Durie became one of the most frequent witnesses of the Cardinal's writs, constantly in his company and in his political counsels, a recognised member of 'the French party'. Mr Walter Beaton, the Cardinal's brother, who became archdeacon of Lothian in 1546 within a year of the death of the previous holder, Mr Patrick Stewart, has been overshadowed by his younger, more famous brother but had an early career of ecclesiastical preferment, having preceded David to the university of Orléans.[5] Walter was canon of Govan in the cathedral of Glasgow, but also enjoyed an annual pension of £100 from the archbishopric of St Andrews, granted to him in 1541 just before the Cardinal left for France.[6] He became effectively archdeacon of Lothian only a few months before the Cardinal's death, and his appearance as a witness bearing that designation occurs only in a few family transactions, including a charter to David Beaton of Melgund, the Cardinal's oldest son, and one to the master of Crawford, then about to be married to his oldest daughter.[7] In 1548 an arrangement was made whereby, like the archdeaconry of St Andrews, that of Lothian passed to the next generation, in this case the Cardinal's son, Alexander, who held it until 1584.[8]

Administrative responsibility in diocesan affairs largely fell upon the deans of Christianity of the eight rural deaneries. During David Beaton's six years as archbishop the dean, whose responsibilities included the moral oversight of the clergy and laity, the confirmation of lesser testaments and the collection of other ecclesiastical dues, changed quite frequently. A notable exception was Mr Hugh Lindsay, dean of the Mearns from 1525 to 1544 and, concurrently, of Angus from 1533 to 1555.[9] Mr John Somerville, dean of the Merse, died during a brief term of office in Lent 1543.[10] Sir Simon Young, dean of Gowrie from 1517, concurrently commissary of Tillilum for the bishop of Dunkeld, in which cathedral he was a canon, had long and close associations with the burgh of Perth in which he is said to have been born and where he acted as a schoolmaster prior to March 1545. In 1543 he ended his connection with the archdiocese of St Andrews, resigning as dean of Christianity for Gowrie and becoming *official* of Dunkeld.[11] While it is difficult to say whether the archbishop influenced any of the other changes, he sometimes filled a vacancy with his own man. When the rural deanery of Linlithgow, which held the rich *mensal* church and episcopal barony of Kirkliston, was resigned in 1539 by Mr John Williamson who had held it since 1523, it was successively held by the archbishop's two secretaries, Mr George Cook and Mr Andrew Oliphant. In fact, Cook held the deaneries of Linlithgow and Haddington concurrently from 1541 to 1543. Linlithgow may have been a case of deliberate replacement.[12] So may Fothrif which Oliphant held from 1539 to 1544, but lack of records makes it impossible to say exactly when and from whom he took it over.[13] The appointment of such preoccupied servants as Cook and Oliphant to posts involving supervision and visitation implies that they operated through deputies.

It suggests that visitations, meetings of local clergy and the watchful oversight of moral standards may have declined in regularity while the more easily-organised collection of the archbishop's revenue may have been the deputies' main concern, although even this was often in arrears. The appointment of a largely absentee dean of Christianity may have encouraged a resort to the fines which the provincial council of 1549 was to interpret partly as bribes and attribute to collusion between the deans and clerical offenders.[14] Financial commutation in place of the appropriate discipline would appeal to David Beaton who was more concerned with the regular revenue which he so badly needed for public purposes than with clerical reform.

The appointment of senior members of his central staff to posts of local authority reflects a policy of centralisation which can be detected elsewhere in his administration. Mr George Cook, who in addition to his secretarial duties had been chief clerk of the privy seal under David Beaton's keepership since 1535, accounted in his own name for the *synodals, procurations* and other dues from his deaneries.[15] Mr Andrew Oliphant, however, who as a senior secretary in diocesan business, involved in heresy trials and an occasional agent at Rome, must have been even more of an absentee dean than Cook, accounted through his deputy, sir Andrew Syme, vicar pensioner of Ballingry, between 1539 and 1542.[16]

Occasionally a dean would be given some *ad hoc* responsibility which called for a deputy to handle his normal business: sir Andrew Mill, who became dean of Haddington after Cook and is referred to as actively engaged in clerical oversight, made returns on behalf of Mr Thomas Wemyss, dean of Fife, from December 1543 when Wemyss was detailed to confirm the 'greater testaments' in the Cardinal's name in Edinburgh.[17] Whatever their main responsibilities, in the end the Cardinal, like the King, might deploy his servants as and where he needed them. The deans are found accounting not only for strictly ecclesiastical revenue including the teinds, but also for rents and custom payments from the archbishopric lands, an activity which brought them into contact with the laity as did the confirmation of lesser testaments and the collection of offerings for special purposes. They might even find themselves employed in ways that underlined their character as the archbishop's servants, as when sir Andrew Mill, dean of Haddington, was refunded his expenses incurred in accompanying the Cardinal's tapestries by boat from Edinburgh to St Andrews.[18] His very princeliness caused David Beaton to look on all service as his personal service; there is a good deal of perception in John Knox's comment that 'whosoever would not play to him the good valet was reputed amongst his enemies'.[19] Lairds might resent and react to this implicit demand in their association with him but officials and representatives could not.

The archbishop's judicial officers, the *officials* of St Andrews principal and Lothian, differed in character from the archdeacons in being more actively involved in the discharge of their duties, professionally qualified church lawyers who presided over their respective courts, in St Andrews and Edinburgh, whose jurisdiction affected the lives of both clergy and laity. Their deputies, the *commissaries*, were equally qualified to hear and judge causes, as they frequently did in the absence of the officials. In 1540 both officialates required to be filled. Both appointees, Mr Martin Balfour, who became official of St Andrews principal, and Mr Abraham Crichton, who became official of Lothian, had not only a long legal apprenticeship behind them and in Balfour's case a distinguished academic career, but also connections with David Beaton and his family. Balfour, who had been a student at St Andrews in the 1490s, witnessed acts of the then official of St Andrews in the 1520s[20] and served as commissary of St Andrews from 1528 to 1530 and in 1533.[21] A nephew of Mr Hugh Spens, official of St Andrews from 1506 to 1516, he held a number of benefices in Fife including the vicarage of Monimail in the patronage of Archbishop James Beaton. Having appeared as a procurator in Fife sheriff court in 1518,[22] Balfour's association with David Beaton began when between 1527 and 1535 he repeatedly acted as procurator on his behalf as abbot of Arbroath, once in partnership with the young lay lawyer, Henry Balnaves.[23] In 1526 he witnessed a charter by the abbot's brother, James Beaton, and his wife, Janet Annand, heiress of Melgund in Angus,[24] and sixteen years later he witnessed the charter by which Janet, then widowed, conveyed that barony to the Cardinal himself.[25] In 1540 he appears in company with a group of men who were permanent members of the archbishop's staff, witnessing the latter's charter to the son of the earl of Rothes.[26] Balfour was official of St Andrews from 1540 to 1545 and during David Beaton's chancellorship of the university was dean of the faculty of arts, a canon of St Salvator's collegiate church and a reliably orthodox member of the teaching staff of the college.[27] He appears as a commissioner for the archbishop in cases relating to heresy, witchcraft and disputed presentations to benefices.

Like his colleague of St Andrews, Mr Abraham Crichton, from the Angus family of Crichton of Ruthven, had had long experience as a procurator in both church and secular courts before his appointment as official of Lothian in 1540.[28] He had sufficiently close associations with the Beaton family to be made joint curator with the abbot of Arbroath and others of the latter's brother-in-law, John Wardlaw of Torry, who in 1532 was declared *non compos mentis*.[29] Although in the same year Crichton appeared in the civil court on behalf of Archbishop James Beaton in his case against his nephew over the Arbroath revenues, and was at that time attached to the archbishop's household,[30] he seems to have worked well enough with David Beaton after the latter's promotion, appearing as a witness to his writs both at Edinburgh, where the official of Lothian held his court in the consistorial aisle of St Giles' church, and at St Andrews,[31] and in 1545 he was an auditor of the archbishopric accounts.[32] His long tenure of office as official of Lothian ran from 1540 to 1553.

The church courts did not operate in specialist isolation. There were close personal and professional links between the courts of the officials and other major institutions: the university of St Andrews in the case of the official principal and the court of session in the case of the official of Lothian.[33] There was a two-way exchange of ideas and expertise between the personnel of the official's court at St Andrews and the university where there was an increasing interest in contemporary legal studies. Walter Fethy, James Rolland and Patrick Scott, who were distinguished in academic circles for their knowledge of canon and civil law, served as commissaries in the 1540s and 1550s.[34] Fethy, who is found as commissary of St Andrews early in 1542 and occasionally acted as notary for the Cardinal,[35] had been appointed to the staff of St Mary's college in 1539 by Archbishop James Beaton.[36] Above all, Martin Balfour while official of St Andrews acted as dean of the faculty of arts during a period of tension in the university. At Edinburgh some of the sixteenth-century officials of Lothian, notably John Weddel, Abraham Crichton and William Cranston, became judges in the court of session which drew its early expertise from among the church lawyers. Many procurators who practised in the Lothian court appeared regularly in the court of session.[37] The Cardinal's procurator-fiscal in the official's court of Lothian, Mr Thomas Kincraigie, who had previously served James Beaton, is found practising in the official's court as early as 1531.[38] The following year he was one of the original 'procurators of the counsale' when the court of session was endowed and thereafter followed a distinguished career in the secular court, dividing his time between ecclesiastical and lay clients. As the Cardinal's procurator-fiscal before the official of Lothian he was empowered to prosecute and demand the execution of sentences on both civil and criminal offenders.[39] The archbishop's procurator-fiscal at St Andrews, Mr Hugh Wishart, appeared not only in the official's court but also in the secular courts where he repledged the archbishop's tenants to his regality court.[40]

Not only had the archbishop's judges and procurators a mixed secular and ecclesiastical expertise but the courts of the officials provided the widest area of involvement with the laity — even wider than that covered by the regality court which applied only to the archbishop's own tenants and freeholders. The courts of the officials received business from the entire archdiocese, and in addition that of St Andrews principal heard appeals from the officials' courts throughout the province. Laymen, therefore, from many parts of Scotland turned to the courts of the archbishop of St Andrews for decisions on a whole range of matters closely associated with their everyday concerns, but chiefly in connection with testamentary business, marriage, the rights of widows and young children and the settlement of disputes arising from many kinds of contracts and business transactions. It has been estimated that 70% of all sentences passed in the Lothian court during the 1540s and almost half of those coming before that of St Andrews principal in the same period were concerned with business involving the lay community.[41] It has also been remarked that those who had most cause to resent the 'cursit consistorie' and its lengthy and expensive procedures were the lairds and 'middling' folk who used it most and who were at the same time the core of anti-clerical feeling in this period. It is just as likely that the many who resorted to the church courts simply regarded these as part of the nationwide system of justice to which they might have recourse: in other words that the church's courts like the church's sacraments existed to serve them. The interaction of courts spiritual and temporal, the all-round legal experience of the archbishop's judges, the service which their courts provided for the laity, not without complaints from the latter, demonstrate the inseparable character of the religious and secular in sixteenth-century life. To David Beaton himself, the administration of his archdiocese and the authority of his courts throughout his province represented both the material resources and the mechanism by which he maintained his own status and the stability of the establishment over which he had control.

His direct influence was felt in the activities of those whom he appointed in matters within his personal jurisdiction, such as his 'greater commissaries', or commissaries of the 'greater excesses', as they were called, and his special commissioners. Archbishop Forman's appointment of three greater commissaries empowered them to cite, admonish and accuse those who had been discovered by the deans of Christianity during their visitations, fines being put towards the fabric of the cathedral. It is not known what precisely the 'greater excesses' were, but they are likely to have been cases of clerical indiscipline which attracted the most severe penalties which it was beyond the power of the rural deans to enforce. The £17 2s 7d from the synod of 1543 which was handed to the Cardinal's chamberlain by sir Robert Marshall, clerk to the greater commissaries, was not a very large sum and does not suggest a vigorous campaign of correction;[42] Marshall himself was to become rural dean of Fife by 1551 in succession to Mr Andrew Oliphant for whom he had previously deputised. More is known, from documents in the *Formulare* compiled by the secretary, Mr John Lauder, and elsewhere, of the powers of the archbishop's commissioners. These were chosen according to the nature of the work to be done. Where the matter on hand was a legal case the commission was always headed by the official: those in the *Formulare* name the officials of Lothian, John Weddel and Abraham Crichton.[43] Where a benefice was involved (but not necessarily a legal dispute) the commissioner was a bishop: 'W. bishop of D', probably William, bishop of Dunblane, was commissioned to receive the resignation of two benefices.[44] In a case of witchcraft the official of St Andrews principal, Martin Balfour, was associated with theologians John Major and Peter Chaplain of St Salvator's and John Winram, subprior of St Andrews priory.[45]

David Beaton's vicars-general, first empowered to act on his behalf in 1539 at the start of his primacy and formally re-appointed in July 1541 before he left for France, were Alexander Milne, abbot of Cambuskenneth, and Robert Reid, abbot of Kinloss and, from 1541, also bishop of Orkney.[46] Associated with them in the appointment of July 1541 were Robert Cairncross, bishop of Ross, and William Gibson who at the same time became the Cardinal's suffragan. Gibson continued to act in the latter capacity until his death a year later but no documents have survived running in the name of the bishop of Ross as a vicar-general. In Milne and Reid, two extremely competent and respected figures, the Cardinal could hardly have chosen representatives whose characters and preoccupations differed more widely from his own. Both had early careers in diocesan administration. Milne, who was a student at St Salvator's about the time that David Beaton was born, had become clerk to the bishop and chapter of Dunkeld by 1500 and, later, master of works there. He was rural dean of Angus (Dunkeld diocese) from 1505 to 1514 and official of Dunkeld from 1513 to about 1519. At the same time he held the canonry of Philorth in Aberdeen cathedral and in 1519 was provided to the abbey of Cambuskenneth. His public career in civil law brought him the presidency of the newly-endowed college of justice in 1532. In 1540 he was entrusted with the administration of the abbacy of Holyrood and the priory of St Andrews on behalf of the young commendators, the King's sons.[47] Robert Reid, who took his master's degree at St Andrews in 1515 and later studied at Paris, was subdean of Moray from 1524 to 1529 and official of that diocese from 1527 to 1530. Having been provided to the abbey of Kinloss in 1528, he became a professed monk the following year. As abbot of Kinloss he had a supervisory role in connection with the abbeys of Deer and Culross and was commendator of Beauly priory. He was provided to the bishopric of Orkney in the spring of 1541.[48]

Both Milne and Reid, in spite of the plurality of their benefices, indeed prelacies, were supporters of contemporary reform movements in the educational standards and spiritual commitment of both regular and secular clergy. Milne had contacts with a circle inspired by such reformers as the Netherlander, Jean Standonck, and wrote admiringly of John Adamson's programme of reform among the Scottish Dominicans.[49] In his *Lives of the Bishops of Dunkeld* he commended the pastoral activities of Bishop George Brown as the episcopal ideal. How much he worried over the fact that some of his canons at Cambuskenneth pushed their reforming zeal as far as acceptance of Lutheranism and a certain amount of protestant practice in the 1530s is difficult to say. Robert Reid's patronage of scholars is well known, especially of the Italian, Giovanni Ferrerio, whom his predecessor at Kinloss, Abbot Thomas Chrystal, had employed to teach the humanities there. Much of Reid's own library has survived and he is perhaps best remembered for the endowment he left for a college which was to become in the event the post-Reformation university of Edinburgh.[50]

Doubtless David Beaton chose these men as vicars-general because of their pre-eminence in the central law courts — who better to take care of his interests in his absence? The name of the abbot of Kinloss, later bishop of Orkney, consistently appears behind that of the president, Milne, in the sederunts of the lords of council and session throughout the 1530s and 1540s, Reid taking over as president after Milne's death in 1548. The new primate put his trust in the civil lawyers, thinking as he did of all he possessed in terms of real property. He may not have shared the ideals of his vicars-general, but Milne was a supremely practical man with much experience in the law and administration, while the scholarly Reid, with his motto 'Moderate', possibly hoped that the new primate's drive if it could only be channelled properly might bring about an increase of ecclesiastical prestige which Archbishop James Beaton's confrontations with the King had to some extent diminished. The enactment of one of the church councils which the Cardinal convened, which laid down that prelates should assign benefices for the support of professors of theology and preachers, is more likely to have been inspired by men like Reid and Milne than by the Cardinal himself.[51] He was no doubt prepared to let them have their preachers — by all means necessary in these days of slipping standards of orthodoxy — so long as they voted the money for his anti-English guns.

Relations between David Beaton and such colleagues must at best have depended on establishing a *modus vivendi* which they rather than he sustained in the interests of clerical solidarity. Milne's name is associated with the Cardinal's authority entirely in formal documents, such as granting letters of provision and collation, confirming charters, collecting taxes and holding the annual synod, with the suffragan, in 1542 while the Cardinal was in France.[52] Robert Reid, however, in addition to the proper business of a vicar-general, was employed by the Cardinal as a negotiator, for which Reid's temperament no doubt suited him, such as in discussions with the Governor's party in the summer of 1543.[53] Reid was capable of independent action, however, and with other episcopal colleagues he was one of the group who formally suspended the Governor from power in June 1544 in an attempt, possibly motivated by the Queen Dowager, to wean him away from the Cardinal whose personal initiative in public policy was arousing resentment at this time.[54] Later, however, the bishop of Orkney was back in the Cardinal's company. In fact, like lesser servants he was occasionally called upon to lend countenance to the Cardinal's personal dealings: he witnessed land transactions between David Beaton and his brother-in-law and nephew, the Grahams of Fintry, in 1541, and the earl of Crawford, at Dundee, in 1545.[55] It may have been this tendency to treat him almost as a member of staff and even personal associate that caused the bishop to chafe a little at times at the Cardinal's domination of affairs.

The archbishop's suffragan, whose term of office was short-lived as it happened, was Mr William Gibson, son of Gibson of Durie of Scoonie parish, Fife, an academic with experience of the civil law.[56] A graduate of Glasgow university, Gibson was elected bursar and joined the university staff just before David Beaton moved to Glasgow from the university of St Andrews in 1511. By 1526 Gibson was dean of Restalrig collegiate church near Leith and as such received a joint dedication with his colleague in the faculty of arts at Glasgow, John Sproull, from John Major in his *Octo Libri Physicorum*.[57] From 1533 he was a senator of the college of justice but had not held any diocesan responsibility before 1540 when James V petitioned the pope for his appointment as the Cardinal's suffragan-bishop.[58] He was provided to the titular see of Libaria on 16 July 1540 and consecrated in August 1541 soon after the Cardinal had left for France. He died slightly less than a year later. David Beaton employed the suffragan-elect's services before 1541, appointing him joint-commissioner with the official of Lothian in the case of a disputed parish clerkship[59] and on another occasion to conduct a visitation of the collegiate church of Corstorphine at the request of the patrons.[60] In the Cardinal's absence Gibson is found summoning those clergy who were in arrears of their share of the royal tax, appointing a president for the collegiate church of Haddington, granting collation, hearing appeals and giving sentence.[61] The short-lived suffragan appointment suggests that the Cardinal, increasingly preoccupied though he was, must have personally carried out such episcopal duties as ordination. He himself heard cases and passed sentence, but all of these were cases of heresy, where he wanted the maximum effect of his authority to be felt. He presided personally over the trial of those who were burnt at the Greenside of Edinburgh at the start of his régime. He passed sentence on Sir John Borthwick whose ideas were dangerously representative of the connection between religious dissent and Anglophile politics and of the presence of heretics at

the royal court. He stage-managed the trial and execution of the Perth heretics
early in 1544, whose craft background demonstrated how heresy might filter down
the social scale from more influential circles, and he sentenced and probably
witnessed the death of Mr George Wishart, the protestant preacher who had
gained the widest support and most public results.

Behind the scenes the archbishop's writing office was under the direction of his
chief secretary, Mr John Lauder, an industrious and dominating personality.[62]
The pages of the great account book of the archbishopric, of the book of styles
which he compiled during a busy working life, now known as the *St Andrews
Formulare*, and an impressive pile of extant charters and other writs are in his bold
handwriting. A graduate of St Andrews, Lauder gained his early experience in
various parts of the country: in the diocese of Moray where he was a notary, in that
of St Andrews where he was secretary to Archbishop Andrew Forman and at
Glasgow where he first of all served Robert Forman, dean of Glasgow, and then
Archbishop Gavin Dunbar. He was made archdeacon of Teviotdale in 1534 and
five years later returned to St Andrews as David Beaton's secretary, having had
considerable experience in diocesan business.

Lauder and the Cardinal appear to have got on well together, for two such
positive characters, although the secretary had not seen eye to eye with
Archbishop James Beaton. He was entrusted with much important business
throughout his master's lifetime. In addition to his duties as secretary and notary
he was empowered during the Cardinal's absence to confer benefices, according to
a list held by the lay chamberlain of the regality, the laird of Capildrae,[63] and to
make diocesan appointments when necessary. He was also clerk to the
chamberlain and graniter of the regality, writing up the accounts, of all but one of
which he was an auditor,[64] and witnessed many writs issued from the archbishop's
chancery. Of the 615 documents which he collected in his style book, about one
third belong to the period of his service with David Beaton. In 1542 Lauder was
made chief clerk of the court of the official of St Andrews principal, with custody
of the court registers and the official's seal.[65] Not only was responsibility for both
the judicial and administrative records of the see thus placed in the hands of the
archbishop's personal secretary, but the latter's appointment displaced Mr John
Brown, the previous clerk to the official, who now became deputy-clerk under
Lauder. If Brown can be identified with the commissary of St Andrews in 1545, he
may have gained promotion in the long run.[66] Lauder's application to his work
atoned for pluralism if ever anything could, for he had as many jobs as he had
benefices. In April 1543 he was party to a transaction at Rome whereby he
resigned the archdeaconry of Teviotdale to John Hepburn, parson of Dalry,
keeping a pension, the title of archdeacon and a stall in the choir of Glasgow
cathedral — in effect, he kept the dignity and part of the income. Energetic, loud-
voiced and proud of being the representative of a master of many titles, he
conducted several heresy trials at which he was a thorough interrogator, if
somewhat inclined to go beyond his terms of reference and argue with the accused,
something for which he was reprimanded at the trial of George Wishart.[68]

Lauder's senior colleague was Mr Andrew Oliphant, another Fife man; his sister Grizel, of whose testament he was made oversman in 1550, made her will at Kellie mills, parish of Carnbee, suggesting that they were connected to the Oliphants of Kellie.[69] A probable graduate of St Andrews, Oliphant had previously served Archbishop James Beaton. In the 1520s he witnessed documents relating to Crail collegiate church and several charters by James Beaton, as his secretary, in the 1530s;[70] the copy of the sentence against Sir James Hamilton of Kincavil, of 1534, which is among the state papers of Henry VIII, is in Oliphant's hand.[71] In 1538 he was the archbishop's procurator at Rome in the latter's case against his nephew George Durie,[72] and early in 1539, a few days before James Beaton's death, his notarial sign appeared on letters of procuratory by the new college of St Andrews.[73]

As the new archbishop's 'weel belovit clerk' he was secretary and notary in mainly diocesan rather than regality affairs and his representative at Rome over the thorny question of the Glasgow exemption.[74] He was rural dean of Fothrif (1539–40) and Linlithgow (1544–5) and was a considerable pluralist, holding the vicarages of Fowlis, Ballantrae in Ayrshire and Carnbee in Fife, probably his own home parish, as well as chaplainries in St Salvator's and St Andrews parish church.[75] He took part in the proceedings at several heresy trials. In the 1540s he is found as a regular witness to the Cardinal's transactions, official and personal, including charters to Lord Seton (1543), Lord Borthwick (1544) and Oliver Sinclair (1546).[76] The Italian, Alessandro Thealdini, wrote to him as go-between when asking about the Cardinal's offer of employment early in 1546.[77] Compared with his rumbustious colleague, Lauder, Oliphant appears as an efficient, professional, curial official, writing in a neat, almost impersonal notarial hand. He could keep his temper, something that even long diplomatic experience had failed to teach his master. Even at the farcical trial of Sandy Furrour he refused to be provoked beyond giving the accused a terse initial warning — 'It shall be no play to you, Sir, before that ye depart'.[78] When serving under his third archbishop he was described by the English ambassador, Randolph, as 'a faithful chaplain and a paynefull . . . '[79]

Mr George Hay who at one time acted for both King and archbishop at Rome was distantly related to the Cardinal: his mother was Janet Beaton and his father was Mr George Hay of Minzean, second son of John, 1st Lord Hay of Yester.[80] In March 1539 Hay received a pension of £100 from David Beaton as the new archbishop and was sent to Rome in the following year.[81] He obtained the Aberdeen canonry of Rathven and the Glasgow one of Eddleston on the resignation of his brother, Mr Thomas Hay, who had been a royal secretary in the 1520s during the Albany régime.[82] He wrote some of the formal documents issued by the episcopal chancery and witnessed many others. He was later to conform at the Reformation, becoming minister of Eddleston where he was reprimanded for falling into old habits of non-residence, and he eventually married.[83] Mr George Cook, who was also a rural dean and clerk of the privy seal under David Beaton, had served Archbishop James Beaton until the end of his life. Six days before James Beaton's death Cook subscribed the charter to the new college at St

Andrews on behalf of the sick primate. He also wrote the earliest extant document running in the Cardinal's name as archbishop, letters of collation to a prebend in Bothans collegiate church for the brother of Cook's colleague, Mr George Hay, on 16 February 1539 just two days after James Beaton's death.[84] He witnessed many of the Cardinal's transactions in the 1540s, travelled on his business and occasionally paid his servants.[85] Cook was still alive in 1570[86] and, with Mr George Hay, was probably among the younger men in the Cardinal's service.

Sir Thomas Knox, 'writer to the cardinal', was an acquisition from the archdiocese of Glasgow in which he had been ordained and to which he was to return after the Cardinal's death. He may have belonged to the family of Knox of Ranfurly in Renfrewshire. Thomas Knox's beautifully-controlled handwriting was a gift to any chancery and is mainly to be found on the large prestige documents issued under the Cardinal's authority as legate *a latere*, although an early example is a decreet by the suffragan dated 15 June 1542, in which Knox is designated 'clerk of the city of Glasgow and notary public'.[87] Later that year, after the Cardinal's return from France, he was paid £5 for writing some of the archbishopric accounts,[88] and by 1544 he was full-time on the chancery staff. The Cardinal's French secretary, simply called 'Peter' in the accounts, may perhaps be identified with Francis Petrus, Frenchman, who was 'writer of letters and provisions' to Archbishop John Hamilton in the 1550s and used the italic hand.[89] No examples of the secretary 'Peter's' handwriting have survived from David Beaton's time. A handful of notaries are known to have worked for the Cardinal, including Mr John Ballantyne, Mr John Chapman, Mr John Brown and Mr Henry Methven, the last being a layman and bailie of St Andrews who lived in South Street and was clerk of the regality court.[90] The sprinkling of chaplains in the archbishop's household included Mr John Methven and Mr William Young, who had charge of the private chapel in St Andrews castle,[91] the two almoners, sir Michael Hogg and sir Gilbert McMath, the latter a priest of Glasgow archdiocese,[92] sir Walter Mar, son of a St Andrews baxter, who was master of work at the new college as well as at the kirk of the Holy Trinity,[93] and sir John Simpson, who acted as graniter of the archbishopric lands.[94]

A very large number of documents issued in the Cardinal's name have survived on record, either in the original or referred to in contemporary sources such as Lauder's *Formulare* or the accounts of the archbishopric. The writing office was a busy one and the archbishop's secretaries and clerks must have been accustomed to working against a background of the coming and going of men about their worldly business in Edinburgh, St Andrews, Arbroath, Linlithgow, Stirling Glasgow or wherever their master happened to be, sometimes in the midst of a political crisis. As time went on business increased; the feuing and profitable management of the estates had progressed so far by the spring of 1545 that a completely new rental had to be drawn up just at the time when the senior secretaries were going over to writing the much larger, more prestigious documents which followed the appointment of the Cardinal as legate *a latere*. Thomas Knox and John Lauder wrote all the extant writs running in his name as legate, which were then endorsed by Knox and entered by him in the relevant register. In most cases George Cook signed as *datarius*, dating and authenticating them, but on one extant example authentication was done by Andrew Oliphant. The margins of these documents, the earliest of which is dated 10 February 1545,[95] are generous and the initial word is ornamented in imitation of the papal chancery style, a refinement used, rather better, by one of David Beaton's writers at Arbroath as early as 1529 when the whole document was treated in this way.[96] This ornamental style continued at Arbroath, occurring in documents of 1533, 1543 and 1545; the 1543 example is particularly ornate although a piece of routine business, the replegiation of a tenant to the archbishop's court.[97] The gifted Arbroath penman was not transferred to St Andrews — he may have been one of the monks — but on the other hand some Arbroath charters dating from 1539 onwards were written in the episcopal chancery by Lauder and Knox and sent on to the monastery to be subscribed by the convent, sometimes *before* and sometimes *after* subscription by the Cardinal as commendator. Another element of centralisation lay in the fact that Mr Bernard Bailie and sir James Auchmowty, who alternated as abbey chamberlain, were regular members of the archbishop's household although the graniter and sacrist of the abbey, sir John Arnot and sir William Ford, the latter having charge of 'the great barn', seem to have been based at Arbroath.[98] It is most unfortunate that the abbey accounts have not survived to complete the picture both of the administration and finance.

Examination of a sample of 53 original documents, relating to both St Andrews and Arbroath, from family papers deposited in the Scottish Record Office, showed a considerable number of different writers at work. John Lauder wrote 11 of those examined, Thomas Knox 7, George Cook 3, Andrew Oliphant 2 (he may have been employed more in correspondence), William Meldrum is identified as the writer of one writ and John Bannatyne of another. Three anonymous but distinct hands account for 9 other documents (5 from Arbroath and 4 from St Andrews). This leaves 19 writs in which the hands are not readily identifiable with others in the group, suggesting a pool of scribes in the chancery who may have changed from time to time. From the spring of 1545 documents begin to get noticeably larger and more carefully set out, in keeping with the Cardinal's enhanced authority as legate but also to be found in documents of a routine nature. Clearly, everything was being done on a grander scale. The Cardinal's designations multiplied over the years. On Arbroath documents before his promotion to St Andrews he was styled abbot, although he was never a professed member of the Benedictine order, and he signed 'David de Aberbrothok'. After 1539 he was styled commendator and signed as such. Thereafter, his signature was either 'David Sancti Andree' or 'David Cardinalis Sancti Andree', eventually adding 'Legatus'. His style also included, of course, 'Bishop of Mirepoix' or 'Administrator of the bishopric of Mirepoix'. Occasionally he used only the initial of his christian name. His signature naturally covered more and more of the parchment, making a problem for the monks of Arbroath on those occasions when he signed the document before they did. In a tack of 17 September 1544 the document was not only signed first by him but also had his round seal attached to it before it was sent from St Andrews, where it had been written by John Lauder, to

Arbroath where it was formally dated; lack of space caused the signature of one of the monks to run on to the fold made to take the tags of the seals.[99] The business was even more complicated when another tack was drawn up and signed by the monks at Arbroath and sent to Glasgow, where the Cardinal was, in June 1545 with the date and place of granting left blank. The clause (inserted at Glasgow) beginning 'our seal and that of the chapter has been appended ... ' has been amended to read, 'the common seal is appended in express consent of the convent of the monastery'.[100] Was this recast in more emphatic terms because the convent had quibbled about some point? This is only an isolated case which has accidentally survived, and we should not read too much into it, but it is tempting to detect possible signs of friction brought about by a trend towards centralisation and remote control in the administration. The circle of those appearing as witnesses widened with the extension of the Cardinal's powers, from the regular appearance of those on his closest staff, such as the secretaries, chamberlain and friends such as George Durie and Bernard Bailie, to the suffragan bishops of his province and even some from outside it whose names appear as the witnesses to his legatine writs, such as confirmations of feu charters of church land and dispensation for the marriage of parties within the forbidden degrees of consanguinity. Also, from the winter of 1543 onwards, by which time he had regained control of the political situation and the government machinery, following the struggle for power after the King's death, his lay supporters appear as witnesses to his transactions from time to time, including Lord Home, Lord Seton, and Robert Douglas of Lochleven.

Documents in the *Formulare* and elsewhere illustrate the scope of the archbishop's powers with regard to ecclesiastical appointments, diocesan administration and the use of his ecclesiastical sanctions. In the all-important matter of appointments David Beaton received wide powers when on 4 February 1539, just ten days before he took over as archbishop, Pope Paul III granted him an indult empowering him to confer benefices, otherwise reserved to the Pope, which were at his disposition as bishop of Mirepoix, coadjutor of St Andrews and commendator of Arbroath.[101] So long as his presentations were uncontested the indult gave him the opportunity to place his men in benefices over a wide area — the kirks appropriated to Arbroath alone were to be found in the dioceses of Moray, Aberdeen, Brechin, Dunkeld and Dunblane in addition to those in the archdiocese of St Andrews itself. He must also have hoped that the concession would give him more freedom of action as a patron in an era when the rights of both ecclesiastical and lay patrons were threatened by the unregulated papal powers of reservation and encroaching royal claims.[102] Like the King, who used the indult granted to the crown in 1487 to the full, the Cardinal was in a position to use the revenues of benefices both for his dynastic schemes and in order to support the careers of his servants. In one instance, the rival of his brother, Mr Walter Beaton, for the parsonage of Inverarity — a benefice in the alternate patronage of Arbroath abbey and the earl of Crawford — having been refused collation by the Cardinal after the earl's presentation, took his case to Rome in the spring of 1544 but eventually renounced his rights.[103] Mr Adam Mure, the Cardinal's servant and probable tutor of his sons, was presented to the vicarage of Kinerny, Aberdeenshire, in the patronage of Arbroath and received due letters of collation from Bishop William Gordon of Aberdeen early in 1541. After Mure had accompanied the Cardinal to France in the summer of that year, however, the bishop rescinded the collation in favour of Mr Alexander Kyd, subchanter of Aberdeen, who in the meantime had obtained papal provision. Mure took his case to Rome and also raised an action before the lords of council and session early in 1542 against Kyd over his right to the fruits of the vicarage, winning his case in both courts. In the summer of 1544, by which time he was subdean of Trinity collegiate church in Edinburgh, he ceded his rights to the vicarage of Kinerny.[104] The *Formulare* contains the Cardinal's letters of *provision* to a vicarage by reason of his indult, which permitted the living to be adjudged to his candidate although the previous incumbent had died in the month of August, one of the months in which the death of the benefice-holder meant that the provision was reserved to the Pope.[105] A few other letters of provision survive including one in favour of Mr Robert Erskine of the house of Dun to the parsonage of Glenbervie in September 1539,[106] issued in the Cardinal's name by his vicars-general sitting 'in vestario' of Trinity collegiate church, Edinburgh, and another in favour of James Hamilton to the deanery of Brechin, running in his name as legate in October 1544.[107]

Letters of *collation*, following on provision, entitled the presentee to receive institution in his benefice. Examples of these writs also illustrate the Cardinal's use of his wide powers in the matter of appointments, both as holder of the indult and as metropolitan and therefore court of appeal. In 1539 he issued letters of collation in favour of John Wilson, canon of Holyrood, to the vicarage of Kinneil, a benefice usually held by a canon and in the patronage of the abbot of Holyrood. Once more the previous incumbent had died in the month of August so that the presentation which would otherwise have been reserved to the Pope fell to the Cardinal's disposition.[108] In 1541 and 1542 the suffragan, Mr William Gibson, hearing an appeal on his behalf, found in favour of Alexander Udwart, royal presentee to the sacristanry of Tain collegiate church, overturning the later provision of two rivals by the bishop of Ross who had also refused to give Udwart collation. The bishop's actions were judged to have caused collation to devolve to the metropolitan.[109]

Institution in a benefice was granted to corporate as well as to individual presentees: on 25 February 1539, at the start of his régime, the Cardinal authorised the institution of the new college of St Andrews in the fruits of the parish kirk of Tynninghame, when sir Walter Mar and Mr Walter Fethy received institution on behalf of the college; the actual document was dated at Edinburgh, 'in the first year of our consecration'. The *admission* of the somewhat humbler parish curate after his examination by the archbishop's commissioners was not formal entry to the material benefits of the living but a signal to get on with the job — 'the rule and government of the parish church and cure of souls of the parishioners'.[110] The parishioners themselves came into the picture in the election of the parish clerk, the parish priest's assistant. The parish clerk was nominated by the patron — a right which sometimes lay with the parishioners themselves — after which they voted as to whether they accepted the nominee, an election in which both men and women participated. The names of those who voted went forward to the archbishop, or *ordinary*, in a notarial instrument so that he could see that the 'greater and sounder part' of the parishioners had accepted the nominee. To the instrument the archbishop attached a writ ordering the clerk's induction. There were frequent disagreements about nomination, for although in the burgh churches the parish clerk was usually in holy orders, in landward parts a member of an influential family might get hold of the emoluments of the office of clerk and appoint a deputy to act in his place,[111] and the acting clerk was sometimes a married clerk in minor orders. Here, at the only point where the lay community had a voice in the choosing of a minister of the church, the line between cleric and layman was at its thinnest. It is possible that the line was sometimes ignored: in a letter of gift recorded in the *Formulare* the Cardinal granted the parish clerkship to a tonsured clerk (that is, in minor orders), disqualifying an elected layman who had not received the tonsure at the time of his election and had not had himself admitted within the canonical time.[112] There are examples of appointments which did not carry the cure of souls, such as that of president of the choir of the collegiate church of Haddinton and of the Holy Rude at Stirling.[113] The archbishop also appointed his official and the clerk of the official's court, in this case his secretary, Mr John Lauder, who wrote the text of his own appointment into his style book.[114]

The archbishop *confirmed* the appointments of individuals presented by other authorities: a parish clerkship to one of three claimants after two of them had renounced their rights,[115] the assignation of a monk's pension made by the priory of Coldingham[116] and the gift of a chaplainry granted by the King himself.[117] He endorsed the widespread practice of burdening benefices with pensions; one of these reservations was in favour of that prince of pluralists, Mr John Thornton, who himself resigned three benefices in favour of his nephews, reserving a pension to his natural son.[118] The Cardinal himself, about 1545, appointed procurators to resign his commendatorship of Arbroath in favour of his nephew, James Beaton, reserving the fruits of the churches of Monifieth and Abernethy to his son Alexander.[119] On the credit side he authorised the erection of a new parish church on petition from the parishioners who found it difficult and dangerous to walk to the existing one, a state of affairs that must have applied in many extensive rural parishes.

As ordinary, metropolitan and eventually legate *a latere* there were many ways in which the Cardinal could enforce his spiritual authority on both clergy and laity. He could prevent secular officers, including the King's representatives, from operating within his own sphere of jurisdiction. For example, he *inhibited* the sheriff of Kincardine from proceeding in a case pending before the court of the official of St Andrews, between the family of Stratoun of Lauriston, who at times showed scant respect for ecclesiastical authority, and Mr James Strachan, parson of Fettercairn, over the use by their respective tenants of land belonging to the chapel of St Martin at Fettercairn;[120] the most formal legal confrontations often involved the basic business of everyday living in the last analysis. The archbishop's process of *anathema*, implemented by the rural deans with their local information, threatened the laity with a procedure which could culminate in excommunication with its consequent threat to material and social support. The example in the *Formulare* denounced those who bought and ate meat in Lent, who were to be regarded as heretics in order to preserve 'the unity of the catholic faith and church'.[121] Church and secular rulers alike feared the potential for sedition inherent in nonconformity.

Mr John Lauder's style book contains several documents relating to the spiritual crime of heresy itself, in the prosecution of which he himself was actively involved. Of the documents relating to the punishment of heretics a few date from before David Beaton's time. Two of them relate to the west of Scotland where Lauder had served Archbishop Gavin Dunbar. One of these is a *summons* to those Ayr parishioners who in 1533 were accused of holding Lutheran ideas of the eucharist, reading the new testament in English and of damaging a statue on the Observantine friary at Ayr.[122] The other is the summons to the vicar of a parish in the archdiocese of Glasgow on charges of reading and disputing on Lutheran literature.[123] The *process of purgation* of a layman accused of heresy, dating from the time of Archbishop James Beaton at St Andrews, contains a brief catalogue of the accused's views, summing up what was probably the attitude of many discontented laymen who were drawn to Lutheranism — increasingly anti-clerical as their material tribute to the ecclesiastical establishment brought in decreasing spiritual returns causing them to question the mediatory role of churchmen.[124] The accused was said to have carried a book called 'Querella Pauperum', which he was in the habit of calling his prayer book and which no doubt echoed the sentiments of the English anticlerical pamphleteer, Simon Fish, in his *Supplication of the Beggars*.

Into this climate David Beaton launched his prosecutions. One of the earliest documents in his name to be transcribed by Lauder is a commission to examine heretics, the first part of which is almost identical with a monition of Archbishop Gavin Dunbar to the same purpose.[125] It details the procedures by which information was gathered, depositions taken, the accused examined, handed over to the secular authority for punishment, and all incriminating literature confiscated from the heretic, including copies of the old and new testaments, torn and burnt. The written record of depositions had it survived might have told us a lot about the nature and extent of heretical beliefs and activity in the 1540s. The *Formulare* contains the form of accusation of a heretic, in the vernacular, which Lauder himself delivered in his 'hoggish voice' on more than one occasion, the text referring to both personal opinions and shared beliefs, 'being at syndry conventiclis aganis the sammin [apostolic faith]';[126] the form of abjuration, also in the vernacular, spoken by a heretic on recantation, in which he or she became obliged to underlie the penalties of the common law on being accused a second time, since having been tried already they could be handed over to the secular authority for immediate punishment;[127] a commission to Henry Adamson of the Edinburgh Dominicans, the Cardinal's greater penitentiary of Lothian, to grant dispensation or commutation of penance to an abjured heretic, probably Walter Cousland, burgess of Stirling, who also bought his own escheat from the crown in March 1539;[128] and the text of the sentence pronounced by the Cardinal against

Sir John Borthwick *in absentia* in 1540, which was to be overturned twenty years later by the court of the superintendent of Fife, John Winram, who had been present on the earlier occasion.[129] The urgency of the campaign against heresy is reflected in the *licence* granted to the bishop of Ross, who was also one of the Cardinal's vicars-general, empowering him to prosecute and punish heretics who belonged to his own diocese wherever they might be found in the archdiocese of St Andrews and to try and punish them there if need be.[130]

The closest involvement with ecclesiastical authority likely to be experienced by an ordinary family was at the time when one of its members died, especially the head of the household. The initial solace gained from the church's ministers at deathbed and burial was closely followed by a period of payment-making and possible litigation, the payments including the customary *corspresent* and *umaist claith* lifted by the parochial clergy as a customary death-duty, which was bitterly resented, and the tax or *quot*, charged on the value of the departed relative's free estate and rendered to the diocesan authorities on confirmation of the testament. Parishioner and archbishop were thus at each end of a fiscal chain. The variable but continuous flow of quots reaching the coffers of the archbishop's chamberlain was an important part of his revenue. Confirmation was done by the rural deans where the net estate was valued at less than £40 Scots and directly by the archbishop's commissaries, sometimes by his vicars-general or secretary where it exceeded that amount. David Beaton's accounts from 1540 to 1546 show receipts of over £3,000 from the quots of 'the greater testaments' alone. In the bereaved family an inventory of moveable goods in house, farm or booth had to be drawn up within nine days of death so that the amount of the quote might be determined — usually reckoned at a twentieth of the free goods after debts had been deducted. The diocesan procurator-fiscal might be involved in the drawing up of an inventory which gave rise to dispute. Where the person had died intestate, an executor was nominated by the official's court, usually on petition from the nearest of kin but allowing an interval for objections to be lodged. The executor was given a year in which to administer the estate and render account of the intromissions to the official's court. During that time many families found themselves caught up in litigation, over the office of executry itself or by pursuing for debt or by being themselves pursued by creditors. Testamentary matters accounted for a very large proportion of business coming before the courts of the officials.

Through a variety of procedures the clergy themselves were reminded of their responsibilities, punished for their shortcomings and, like the laity, made to pay their contributions. *Licences* were granted to those wishing to act outwith their normal sphere: to a claimant to the parish clerkship of Kelso to take his appeal to judges within the archdiocese of St Andrews,[131] or to a canon of Holyrood to leave his monastery in order to study at a university overseas.[132] The clergy might find themselves before the archbishop's judges for a variety of reasons: for non-payment of the tax granted to the crown, for obstructing a royal officer in the course of his duties, even on an occasional charge of homicide.[133] The archbishop's vicars-general heard appeals from those of the suffragan bishops — examples of appeals from those of Caithness and Aberdeen involved overruling the bishop's refusal to grant collation,[134] one from Dunkeld concerned a disputed benefice.[135] The St Andrews court also pronounced in favour of the Cardinal's suffragan bishop, Mr William Gibson, whose own prebendaries at Restalrig had accused him of tampering with the text of a papal bull.[136] At the request of the lay patron, the Cardinal authorised a visitation of the collegiate church of Corstorphine to examine charges of non-residence and neglect of the fabric of the prebendal manses.[137] The burden of financial contributions fell somewhat unequally on the diocesan clergy: the freewill subsidy which the Cardinal obtained permission to levy for the expenses of his promotion fell more heavily on parochial benefices than on higher livings and, in fact, carried exemptions in the cases of certain prelacies, such as those monasteries held *in commendam* by the Cardinal himself, his relatives, such as George Durie of Dunfermline, and the King's sons.[138] *Monitions* were issued to convoke synods and general councils, to pay clerical taxation and to those charged with enforcing its payment, as well as to individual clergy for specific purposes, such as the monition to a rural dean to warn a vicar–pensioner to pay his curate's salary, at least £10 a year.[139] This last reminds us that in spite of the archbishop's exalted station legal procedures kept open a line of communication between him and the working parish priest, along which the latter's complaint might travel.

As archbishop of St Andrews the Cardinal seems to have had a fairly good working relationship with the eight suffragan bishops of his province: Aberdeen, Brechin, Caithness, Dunblane, Dunkeld, Moray, Orkney and Ross. Conditions in the 1530s and 1540s — strained relations with the King, the increasing heresy problem, political instability after the King's death and the threat of English intervention — may have thrown the prelates in on themselves as a party, creating a cohesion they might not have had in more settled times. When David Beaton succeeded to St Andrews in 1539 the longest-serving members of the hierarchy were John Hepburn of Brechin (1516), Andrew Stewart of Caithness (1517) and George Crichton of Dunkeld, William Chisholm I of Dunblane and Robert Maxwell of Orkney (all 1526). William Stewart had been bishop of Aberdeen since 1532. Patrick Hepburn of Moray and Robert Cairncross of Ross were working their way in, so to speak, having been appointed in March and November 1538 respectively.[140] The bishops' experience of the political changes of the past two decades had been varied, but probably none of them had learned to sail as close to the wind as the Cardinal-Archbishop himself. George Crichton, distantly related to the Cardinal, had been 'a good Englishman' in the 1520s, being nominated to Dunkeld in 1526 during Angus's ascendancy.[141] In the same year William Chisholm's brother and predecessor at Dunblane, James Chisholm, had thought it prudent to resign the bishopric in his favour, reserving the fruits, the right of collation and the right of regress; in these unsettled times the bishop's tactics resembled those of a laird resigning his barony in favour of his son in order to make sure of the safe transfer of the property.[142] The same device was used in the same year by David Arnot, bishop of Galloway in the province of Glasgow, in favour of his nephew, Henry Wemyss.[143] William Stewart, who as treasurer had supported

James V's policy of clerical taxation, was appointed to Aberdeen in 1532, the year in which the King's college of justice was formally endowed.[144] Others had been appointed to suit the King's interests: Patrick Hepburn to Moray and Robert Cairncross to Ross in order to free the priory of St Andrews and the abbey of Holyrood for the young commendators, James's illegitimate sons.[145]

Five of the suffragan sees fell vacant during David Beaton's primacy. When it becomes possible to make a thorough examination of all the evidence from the Vatican records, signs of the Cardinal's influence in the making of these appointments may emerge. It can at least be said that the results suited him very well. Aberdeen went (1545) to the uncle of his ally Huntly, and Caithness (1541) to the brother of the earl of Lennox who for a time he drew into his schemes. After the death of George Crichton of Dunkeld and litigation with his nephew, Robert Crichton, that see came into the hands of the Governor's natural brother, John Hamilton (1544), while that of Ross was given (1545) to Arran's secretary, David Paniter, giving the Cardinal important footholds in the Governor's circle. It was rumoured that John Hamilton had abandoned an earlier flirtation with protestantism when the Cardinal promised him support in his nomination to Dunkeld. Substantial pensions, charged on the see of Dunkeld, were awarded to the theologian, Robert Wauchope, who enjoyed David Beaton's favour, and Alexander Campbell, brother of Argyll, from a family whose support the Cardinal continually retained with material gifts. Orkney, of course, went to Robert Reid whose association with the Cardinal has already been discussed. Reid's appointment was almost exceptional in being one in which the appointee possessed personal merit and suitability for the job, in spite of his pluralism. In his hardline policy against heretics the Cardinal could count on the support of the reactionary William Chisholm of Dunblane, who presided with him at the trial of those heretics burnt in February 1539, John Hepburn of Brechin, who had dubbed Friar Arth's biting sermon on certain abuses 'heresy', George Crichton of Dunkeld, who boasted of never having read the new testament, and the dissolute Patrick Hepburn, the bishop of Brechin's nephew, whom many years previously David Beaton had had personally to restrain from assaulting the outspoken canon of St Andrews, Alexander Allan.

At the end of January 1544 the Pope granted the Cardinal the widest possible delegation of papal powers over ecclesiastical affairs in Scotland, the office of legate *a latere*, the rare device by which he, like Wolsey in England, became resident papal representative in his native country. Like Wolsey he was also chancellor of the realm when he received the grant of supreme spiritual powers, but he scored over the English Cardinal in that he was also primate, archbishop of St Andrews, whereas Wolsey had been only archbishop of York. However, just as Archbishop Warham's longevity had prevented Wolsey from adding Canterbury to York and thus completing the official basis of his secular and ecclesiastical domination, so Archbishop Gavin Dunbar's determination to maintain his independence, coupled with the clash of their personalities and difference of opinion about some aspects of public religious policy, prevented David Beaton from gaining the obedience of the province of Glasgow which would have unified his control over the church in Scotland, although he came nearer to doing this than any Scottish churchman before him.

He must have watched the early preferment of Gavin Dunbar with some apprehension and resentment. Their competition for the King's favour in the early 1530s, during which Dunbar's position was probably the more secure of the two, had been preceded by a period of dependence on the patronage of Albany when both had been in the Governor's circle in France and Scotland.[146] Like the Beatons, Dunbar was rewarded for his support of the French party when Albany secured his promotion to the see of Glasgow in 1523, after James Beaton's translation to St Andrews; a substantial pension was reserved from the Glasgow revenues to Thomas Hay, Albany's secretary. As archbishop of Glasgow Dunbar jealously guarded the exemption from the jurisdiction of the primatial see, granted to Glasgow on the creation of the archbishopric but through the instrumentality of the autocratic Andrew Forman limited to the lifetime of the archbishop for the time. In spite of renewed petition to Rome by James Beaton soon after his translation to St Andrews, Dunbar obtained papal confirmation of the exemption in July 1524, a few days before his own promotion to Glasgow was officially granted and about the time that David Beaton was provided to Arbroath. The first open confrontation between the prelates was in the winter of 1535 when during a visit to Dumfries James Beaton had his primatial cross publicly borne before him and blessed the people. On 22 November, Dunbar's official of Dumfries, John Turner, protested and took an instrument that the archbishop of St Andrews' public action was in violation of the papal indult granting exemption and that it should in no way prejudice his own authority within the province of Glasgow.[147] It is worth noting that a royal justice ayre was then taking place in Dumfries, a fact which is recorded in the register of the privy seal of which David Beaton was keeper.[148] He personally attended the justice ayre as a compositor and may have encouraged his uncle to make a public demonstration of superiority; it may not have been the first troubled occasion on which his presence was felt as the power behind the episcopal throne. A few months later James Beaton's summons to Gavin Dunbar to attend the provincial council of March 1536, although resented by Dunbar, did not lead to an open quarrel. James Beaton himself was less than willing to convoke the gathering and the archbishops may have come to an agreement at this time.[149]

David Beaton's head-on tactics, however, caused friction with Glasgow from the start. In the spring of 1539 he sent his own personnel to conduct a heresy trial in Glasgow over which Dunbar presided, with whom his representatives did not hesitate to disagree publicly when the archbishop of Glasgow appeared to favour a lenient sentence, reminding him that it behoved him to fall in with the Cardinal's policy in these matters. On 14 May, on the grounds of an alleged agreement with Dunbar, the Cardinal obtained a papal bull limiting the exemption to the duration of the former's term of office.[150] The next step was to reduce this piece of parchment to mere theory by requesting papal sanction to have his cross borne before him in the archdiocese of Glasgow. Three times in the early winter of 1539 he wrote to Andrew Oliphant at Rome urging him to speed the bulls about the exemption.[151] His impatience was no doubt aggravated by the failure of his attempt to take the matter into his own hands when on 27 November during a visit to the borders, four years almost to the day since his uncle's demonstration and in the same place, the burgh of Dumfries, he had his cross publicly carried, only to be countered by another protest from the Glasgow diocesan authorities.[152]

Difficult relations with the King for the remainder of the reign, including the rebuff over the list of heretics, and the temporary appearance of episcopal solidarity at the time of Sir John Borthwick's trial, may have sent the contention over the exemption underground. The Cardinal did not give up, however, for only a month after his return from France in August 1542 he sent Andrew Oliphant to Dunkeld for a transumpt of the bull of May 1539, a piece of business which suggests that his efforts to gain papal backing were long drawn-out and not entirely successful.[153] His relations with Dunbar continued to have their ups and downs. Dunbar's triumph over the Cardinal's initial failure to seize power after the King's death was tempered by his reaction to the Governor Arran's reformation-experiment, which may have produced a certain cohesion among the episcopate after the Cardinal's comeback to power in the autumn of 1543. David Beaton's replacement of Dunbar as chancellor at the end of that year, however, and his attempts to maintain control of public policy in 1544 caused Dunbar to side with those who suspended Arran from the governorship that summer in an attempt to deprive the Cardinal of a tool in building up his supremacy. The year 1544 was also an ecclesiastical turning-point, bringing with it the Cardinal's papal grant of the powers of legate *a latere* which Dunbar must have feared as David Beaton's opportunity to completely dominate ecclesiastical policy.[154] It is certainly significant that thereafter the Cardinal carried the battle for acknowledgement of his authority into the city of Glasgow itself, on at least one occasion into the cathedral. His first attempt to have his cross carried publicly in Glasgow was on Palm Sunday, 5 April 1544, which resulted in the usual 'instruments' of protest being taken.[155] The fracas in the summer of 1545, which is probably that reported in Knox's *History*, may have been a second personal attempt to forestall the archbishop of Glasgow publicly, or perhaps the crucifers and young clerics in the respective processions, entering into the spirit of the long-running feud, simply took matters into their own hands:

> Coming forth (or going in, all is one) at the choir door of Glasgow kirk, begins striving for state betwixt the two cross-bearers, so that from glowming they come to shouldering; from shouldering they go to buffets and from dry blows, by neffs [fists] and neffeling; and then for charity's sake they cry, *Dispersit dedit pauperibus*, and essays which of the crosses was finest metal, which staff was strongest, and which bearer could best defend his master's pre-eminence; and that there should be no superiority in that behalf, to the ground go both crosses. And then began no little fray, but yet a merry game; for rochets were rent, tippets were torn, crowns were knapped, and side gowns might have been seen wantonly to wag from one wall to the other ... But the sanctuary, we suppose, saved the lives of many. How merrily that ever this be written, it was bitter bourding [jesting] to the Cardinal and his court ... ; and yet the other [Dunbar] in his folly, as proud as a peacock, would let the Cardinal know that he was a bishop when the other was but Beaton, before he got Arbroath.[156]

Dunbar's taunt, delivered in the heat of sorting things out, has a ring of authenticity about it, full of frustration and pent-up personal animosity. Not long after the episode the Cardinal had the last word by dispatching to Dunbar, on his authority as papal legate 'throughout the whole realm', a sternly-worded intimation of a provincial council, threatening the archbishop of Glasgow with eternal penalties if he failed to attend. John Lauder must have enjoyed writing it.[157] Apart from their outward confrontations it must have irritated Dunbar that the Cardinal had pockets of personal influence within the province of Glasgow. His brother Walter Beaton, as canon of Govan, attended a fair number of chapter meetings at the cathedral and no doubt kept him well-informed of what transpired there.[158] His chief secretary, John Lauder, was archdeacon of Teviotdale, with connections in theory at least with the clergy of that detached but extensive portion of the archdiocese of Glasgow. In 1541 the Cardinal's cousin, Andrew Durie, previously abbot of Melrose, became bishop of Galloway, the most important suffragan see of Glasgow, spreading his personal contacts right across country. In November 1544 during the involved litigation over the vacancy in the bishopric of the Isles, another of Glasgow's suffragans, the Cardinal reinforced the Governor's letters of nomination by writing himself to the Cardinal of Carpi on behalf of the crown nominee, Roderick MacLean.[159] If, as Knox remarks, the animosity between the two archbishops was irreconcilable, it may also be true that the arrival of George Wishart and his preaching activities in both the east and west of Scotland brought about a truce between them in the last year of the Cardinal's life.

An absence of relevant records prevents our knowing to what extent David Beaton may have used his powers as legate *a latere* to interfere with the authority of other episcopal courts as Wolsey had done in England.[160] He was certainly the kind of man to consider the possibility, intent as he was on engrossing all spiritual and temporal power. Perhaps it was a tendency to sharpen his new weapon that caused some prelates to side with those who in the summer of 1544 reacted to his ascendancy. They may later have resented his plans for another clerical subsidy which seems to have been the main reason for the provincial council which he called in his own name as legate early in 1546, just as they, and he himself, had resented the fiscal demands of James V over a decade earlier. The papal grant of the legateship of January 1544 — the original commission fell into English hands — came during the visit to Scotland of a specially appointed legate *a latere*, Marco Grimani, patriarch of Aquilea, who had arrived at Dumbarton in October 1543 with instructions to assess the situation in Scotland, try to bring about the Cardinal's release if he was still detained and arrange for the collection of the tax sanctioned just before the death of the King.[161] In December 1543, in conversation with Grimani, the Cardinal urged him to use his influence with the pope to grant him the faculty of legate which was so badly needed in Scotland in the current unsettled conditions, which Grimani himself commented upon in a letter to Cardinal Farnese on his arrival.[162] Grimani left Scotland early in April 1544, although documents running in his name continued to emerge from official channels after that date. One, a confirmation of a feu charter of church land to

Swinton of that ilk, is dated as late as 28 February 1545.[163] An earlier document, confirming an excambion of land for the new college of St Andrews, dated 2 April 1544, was issued at 'the dwelling house of the papal legate' in Edinburgh.[164] It ran in the name of Grimani's secretary, Alessandro Thealdini, whom the Cardinal, always ready to wring the most out of an opportunity, retained in his service the following year, making use of the secretary's experience in legatine affairs. Thealdini is mentioned in the archbishopric accounts as being with the Cardinal at Castle Campbell early in May 1544, just after Hertford's invasion, whence he was conducted to Lindores.[165] The following year he was captured by the English on a return journey to France when the Cardinal wrote to the Pope on his behalf. On leaving Scotland he had been offered the post of vicar-general for the Cardinal in his diocese of Mirepoix but had declined at the time. On 8 January 1546, freed from his English prison but penniless, he wrote to Andrew Oliphant as to a friend with whom he had worked in the Cardinal's service asking him to find out if the Cardinal's previous offer of a post and salary still held good.[166] No clear evidence has come to light of his connection with David Beaton in subsequent months but he is known to have worked at Rome for Scottish patrons in later years. During his brief stay in Scotland he formed part of the foreign element in the Cardinal's entourage and must have been of assistance in international matters.

Only a handful of writs and letters survive to illustrate the Cardinal's use of his legatine authority. Some of these relate to benefices: he was empowered to confer these 'howsoever vacant', even if generally reserved to the Pope or even if in lay patronage, and to provide to monasteries under the value of 2000 ducats, a considerable expansion of the authority he had received under the indult of 1539. Royal nominations addressed to him, all dating from 1545, have survived in connection with the provision of John Campbell to the priory of Ardchattan, 'as the priory situated among wild people requires a native ruler', James Nasmyth to the deanery of Brechin, although within six months it was resigned in favour of James Hamilton, the Governor's natural brother, James Johnston to the abbey of Saulseat, and his own kinsman, Archibald Beaton, to the precentorship of Aberdeen, a benefice which he held until his death in 1582.[167] No doubt the Cardinal hoped to gain the Governor's co-operation in conferring benefices on those of his own choice in return for which Arran would expect a number of Hamilton appointments. Even a glance through the *Fasti* of those appointed to diocesan and other senior offices in 1544–6 reveals Archibald Beaton as precentor of Aberdeen, Mungo Monypenny as dean of Ross, Walter Beaton as archdeacon of Lothian, David Hamilton as provost of Dumbarton collegiate church, then treasurer of Dunkeld, and James Hamilton as dean of Brechin. In the case of the greater prelacies, to which he was not empowered by his legacy to provide, the Cardinal asked the Pope to listen only to the petitions of the Governor in providing to them, hoping to influence the nominations. Disputes arose, inevitably, from his presentations. The repercussions from one of them at least were heard long after his death, when in 1568 it was claimed in the court of session that his gift of a pension from the vicarage fruits of Longley, Aberdeenshire to the resigning vicar, Mr Gilbert Keith, had not been in his power to give, being 'against the common law', provision and reservation of fruits lying with 'the general council'.[168]

There are three legatine dispensations for marriage granted to couples within the forbidden degrees of consanguinity: Andrew Toscheach and Janet Murray, addressed to the bishop of Dunblane for implementation, Patrick, son of Lord Lindsay of the Byres, and Euphemia, daughter of Robert Douglas of Lochleven, addressed to the official of St Andrews, who ratified it in the consistorial aisle of St Andrews cathedral with Sir David Lindsay of the Mount as one of the witnesses, and William Meldrum, son of the laird of Fyvie, and Elizabeth Abernethy, directed to Mr William Hay, canon and commissary of Aberdeen.[169] The Cardinal arranged the marriage of Janet Beaton, daughter of his cousin, John Beaton of Creich, widow of Crichton of Cranstonriddell and divorced wife of Preston of Craigmillar, to Walter Scott of Buccleuch, 'his other wife being yet on life', as it was asserted. It would make political alliances easier to fix if the legatine faculty to grant dispensations could be used; the Cardinal was once accused, with some exaggeration, of making and ending marriages when it suited him. Equally welcome was his legatine faculty to confirm charters of church property without recourse to Rome. The texts of a number of such confirmations survive, as do confirmations of some ecclesiastical foundations, some of them by laymen, such as that of the collegiate church at Biggar founded by Lord Fleming in 1546.[170] Laymen and churchmen are thus found petitioning the Cardinal for ratification of their initiatives. At the same time in obedience to his apostolic letters senior clerics in both provinces of the church in Scotland were called upon to implement his legatine acts. In February 1545 the abbot of Glenluce, in a dispute with the earl of Cassillis, agreed ultimately to accept the decree of the Cardinal as legate in name of the Pope. Thus his presence was felt nationwide at the highest level of spiritual authority.[171]

Within the university of St Andrews during his chancellorship the atmosphere was not at its most harmonious. Between the colleges and within the faculty of arts relations among the staff appear to have been strained, while student numbers were low.[172] The cryptic minutes of the faculty of arts, written in his own hand by the dean, Martin Balfour, while they hint at discords, give little detail about the cause of the dissensions. On the face of things Balfour's long term of office as dean, from 1522 to about 1542, suggests a measure of continuity, yet there was opposition to him which made itself felt. Before his election in 1540 no fewer than four regents of his own college of St Salvator's and three of St Leonard's intimated that they would not support him and in the event walked out of the congregation when things did not go their way; two of them, David Garden and John Sheill, had previously transferred from St Salvator's to St Leonard's, perhaps because they were at variance with him.[173] In 1541 he was again elected, 'but from mixed motives', as it was expressed.[174] The election of 1542 after being postponed was a perfunctory affair, and in 1543 the machinery of election seems to have broken down.[175] It is likely that tensions were due not only to animosity and specific grievances, such as that over the choice of examiners, but also to an underlying difference of outlook between conservatives and progressives in the world of religious attitudes. From 1540 Balfour's role of official of St Andrews may have helped to identify him with the legalistic face of the religious establishment in the eyes of those who were in sympathy with the tendency towards speculation and debate in religious matters. He himself had long personal associations with David Beaton since the latter's Arbroath days.

It is St Leonard's college which furnishes the weather-vane by which the changing academic climate can best be noted in this period, entering a mood which could only cause friction with the chancellor-archbishop. Following the death of Patrick Hamilton, when Martin Balfour was continued in office as dean of the faculty of arts only after 'various altercations',[176] the discussion of new ideas was reasonably open, led by those who sided with the canon regular, Alexander Allan, but opinions must have come to be less openly expressed and eventually have gone underground in the face of Archbishop James Beaton's periodic prosecutions for heresy and especially after the Cardinal's repressive policy took shape early in 1539. Personal attitudes, however, were probably tacit rather than secret, and the fact that people were watched for signs of unorthodoxy is demonstrated in the absolution from a charge of heresy granted to Mr David Guild in 1541, over his definition of the persons of the trinity made during the *quodlibet* exercises.[177] There seems to be no reason to doubt those post-Reformation accounts which claim that in the 1530s and 1540s protestant ideas were discussed and even encouraged in the overlapping intellectual circles of St Leonard's college and the priory under the influence of Gavin Logie and John Winram.

Both these men, as it happened, enjoyed slightly wider areas of influence than their posts might have been expected to afford them. Logie, who was transferred from the Pedagogy between 1516 and 1519, was not a canon regular, thus owing no personal obedience to the priory.[178] He was among those who in the 1520s worked to gain recognition for the college's separate identity within the faculty of arts in the face of the authority of the older colleges on the one hand and that of the priory on the other. His request, made about the time he joined St Leonard's as a regent, that the college be represented among the examiners, was realised in 1523 at the request of the prior himself.[179] Logie is found as 'acting' principal at St Leonard's at a time when Alexander Young, a canon regular whose time was divided between his monastic and academic duties, was principal in the legal sense. Logie enjoyed this measure of executive authority with the approval of the prior who had acquired him from the Pedagogy on account of his teaching abilities. He had connections, through his brother Robert, with the Lutheran circle of Augustinians at Cambuskenneth. Another relative, George Logie, a student of St Leonard's, shared his books with John Winram. Winram, himself a student of St Leonard's, became subprior of the priory about the time that Gavin Logie reached the end of his teaching career and may have taken his place as the focus of unorthodox thinking. Outwardly orthodox, however, Winram never demurred at undertaking responsibility on behalf of the establishment and, indeed, his ability to take care of his own skin and welfare later gave rise to criticism among his post-Reformation colleagues.[180] In the later 1530s, due to the fact that the prior of the monastery was the King's son and that his administrator, Abbot Alexander Milne of

Cambuskenneth, was too preoccupied to spend much time at St Andrews, Winram was acting head of the priory's affairs, able to set his stamp on its religious and intellectual life.

Besides infecting the students with heretical ideas, including a growing trickle of students who were not destined for the church and who sometimes boarded outwith the college, the staff of St Leonard's had the opportunity to contact the laity outside through the function of the curate of the college's attached parish. The risk may have been a small one, considering that the holders of this office were occasionally accused of failing to attend to their duties,[181] but it did exist. When in 1525 an endowment was left for the curate, it was entrusted to Gavin Logie who bestowed it on Mr Thomas Fyfe, whose kinsman and successor, Mr John Fyfe, was unwilling in 1550 to say his masses or live 'in the chamber by the front gate' where the parishioners might easily contact him.[182] A breakdown in discipline, which included reluctance on the part of some holders of altarages to say private masses for the college's founders, is part of the background to the visitation and revision of the college's statutes in 1545.

This state of affairs was not lost on David Beaton, preoccupied though he was; on the day of George Wishart's execution he is reported to have told John Winram in an angry outburst that he had known for some time what he was up to. The apostolic confirmation of the St Leonard's statutes by the Cardinal as legate in 1545 was not only a recognition of its separate collegiate status but part of an attempt to recover discipline. The first step had been the appointment of a more determined principal, found in the conservative John Annand, canon regular, in Knox's venomous phrase 'a rotten papist'. His appointment in 1544 may have been on the suggestion of the priory administrator, Alexander Milne, and must have met with the chancellor's approval. The new principal and the subprior may not have seen eye to eye and it is not certain that Winram was even consulted in making the initial approach to the Cardinal for the confirmation, although no doubt he would approve of the step.[183] The formal role of petitioning the chancellor was given to the somewhat unworthy provost of the Kirkheuch, James Learmonth. The Cardinal's charter granted the college the right to gather 'in chapter' for the first time. The fact that after 1545 the college seal was attached to writs first and that of the priory second, 'in consent', denotes the reversed order in the relationship of the two institutions. One concrete benefit from the new status was the college's right to handle the disposal of its own property. But the overtones of the charter reflect the desire to restore discipline. The Cardinal's delegates who were instructed to oversee the application of the statutes were addressed not as conservators but judges. The charter, in fact, brought the college into direct contact with the Cardinal's authority, a significant precaution in the case of an academic community which had gradually changed from a training school in arts and theology to one which emphasised the liberal arts, which had also edged away from its direct answerability to the monastic community, and whose orthodoxy was being undermined from within. There is no knowing how much tighter the chancellor's control might have become had he lived longer.

On the whole he was too preoccupied to take an active part in the daily life of the university, even appointing prominent academics to preside on his behalf on formal occasions such as the granting of degrees.[184] From time to time, however, he did interfere in procedure: on 26 February 1540 a *determinant*, David Chapman, was dispensed to proceed to the master's grade along with the *intrants* of that year on petition from the Cardinal and on payment of the requisite 'fine',[185] while in 1545 he ordered the re-election of the rector of previous years, James Strachan, canon of Aberdeen and provost of Guthrie collegiate church, a disciplinarian who was a royal secretary and the King's representative at Rome in 1538.[186] That great things were expected of the new chancellor is suggested by the petitions he received from members of the university begging him to remedy its decayed state, as they saw it. Early in 1546, probably at the provincial council of the church held that spring, he received such a memorial headed by the rector James Strachan, just two months after he had confirmed the status of St Leonard's college.[187] In 1540 his cousin Archibald Hay, then in Paris, had dedicated to him the second edition of his *Panegyric*, first offered two years before to their uncle, James Beaton, in which Hay advocated a new foundation planned along humanistic lines, to include the teaching of Latin, Greek and Hebrew.[188]

David Beaton's only response to these academic pleadings was his continuation of his uncle's plans for a college which was originally intended to improve the recruitment of the clergy (as St Leonard's had been intended for the regulars), primarily through the study of theology and canon law, and which was planned to replace the older Pedagogy. Archbishop James Beaton had made certain appointments to St Mary's, or 'the new college', as it was commonly called, shortly before his death on 14 February 1539,[189] including Mr Robert Bannerman as principal, who held the post for the rest of David Beaton's lifetime, Mr David Guthynd, the rural dean of Fife as subprincipal, Mr Thomas Kincraigie, who became the Cardinal's procurator-fiscal, as canonist and Mr John Gledstanes as civilist. It is generally regretted that the Cardinal did so little to set the new college on its feet but, considering the other calls upon his attention, it is remarkable that he did anything at all. After all, his uncle had first tried to secure papal approval for his educational scheme as early as 1525 but had been similarly deflected from pursuing his plans.[190] It is likely that it was the Cardinal himself who, at the end of his life, invited his cousin Archibald Hay over from Paris to take part in the development of the college, and who became its second principal in 1546. The archbishopric accounts record that sums totalling over £860 were spent on the building of the new college under the Cardinal's direction, a little more than the recorded expenditure on fortifying the castle of St Andrews. Marble was brought from France for the altar of the college church and French masons came from the royal works at Falkland to advise on the building. Seven days before Archbishop James Beaton's death sir Walter Mar was authorised by the newly appointed college staff to take possession of the fruits of the parish kirk of Tynninghame, resigned to them by the archbishop's nephew, John Hay, and before the end of February the Cardinal granted Mar institution.[191] Sir Walter Mar was concurrently master of work at the new college, the parish kirk of the Holy Trinity and the archbishop's castle. On 7 March 1539 the King confirmed the foundation and the Cardinal's right to continue the work.[192] The following July the latter petitioned the Pope about those parochial revenues to be annexed to the college.[193] In the spring of 1541 an excambion of tenements in South Street was carried out in order to facilitate building operations.[194]

The Cardinal's few personal associations with the university were with St Salvator's college. One friend was Dr William Manderston, one of the 'maisteris and actuall lectoureris' in the university in the 1530s, former student of John Major at Paris and himself a teacher of Patrick Hamilton there, philosopher and doctor of medicine.[195] Manderston, who was rector of the university in 1530 and deputy-rector early in 1545,[196] also held the prebend of Gogar in Trinity collegiate church, Edinburgh, and was associated with the foundation of St Mary's college. In addition to witnessing the Cardinal's legal transactions from time to time, he gave both Archbishop James Beaton and the Cardinal the benefit of his medical advice, receiving an annual fee of £40 and frequent travelling expenses which suggest regular attendance: in the late autumn of 1542 he and the apothecary rode to Arbroath accompanied by John Beaton of Balfour presumably to attend the Cardinal after his return from France.[197] In January 1540 Manderston and John Major founded a bursary in theology in St Salvator's college, the holder to recite three masses or more for the souls of the founders and their families, the King and Queen and the Cardinal, 'because continual prayers mitigate the pains of purgatory'.[198] In September 1545 further revenues were assigned to the then bursar, John Forrous, the document being drawn up 'in the chamber of Mr William Manderston in the college of St Salvator's'.[199]

From January 1540 to March 1543 the Cardinal gave refuge in St Salvator's college to Dr Richard Hilliard, the distinguished preacher from Yorkshire and chaplain to the bishop of Durham, who had been an outspoken critic of Henry VIII's dissolution of the monasteries.[200] Hilliard was not unfamiliar with Scotland through the presence of Scottish clerics, both seculars and friars, in the north of England from time to time, including some in Bishop Tunstall's own household. At St Andrews Hilliard was among those who formally absolved Mr David Guild from a charge of heresy in December 1541. His presence in the university, and that of other English priests such as Henry Bretton and Richard Smith and the Dominican Richard Marshall, for shorter periods, provided the Cardinal with welcome orthodox anti-Henrician propagandists and he generously provided for their maintenance.[201] On more strictly theological grounds, Hilliard and Marshall were experienced controversialists against Zwinglian 'sacramentarianism' which had characterised some Scottish heretics of the 1530s, including Thomas Forret, and was alluded to in the anti-heresy legislation of 1543. In the summer of 1542 King James advised Hilliard's removal to the Cardinal's manor of Monimail during the latter's absence in France, and the English doctor left Scotland in March 1543 during the Cardinal's detention and the reformation-experiment of Arran and his party, although he and David Beaton continued to be in touch through the international correspondence network between England, Scotland, France and Rome.

The Cardinal's relations with the canons regular of St Andrews priory, who formed his episcopal chapter, are more difficult to determine and can only be inferred from the evidence of formal documents. Even so, there can be detected the mixture of affability and pressure which must have made personal relations with him such a tense experience: the gift of £20 to the subprior John Winram when he took his doctorate in theology in 1540,[202] and the £22 given to David Guthrie, third prior of the monastery, to distribute to the convent for their consent to the sealing of a charter of the lands of Carsbank to the Cardinal's son, David Beaton of Melgund, in November 1543.[203] It was not unusual for a consenting chapter to receive payment but someone may have voiced disapproval on this occasion. Similarly, we cannot tell now what discords lay behind the formal statement by Winram and Guthrie, before a notary, that the Cardinal's charter to his henchman, Oliver Sinclair, in March 1541 had been sealed with the bishop's and chapter seals before being handed over to Sinclair's representative. The canons were associated with every area of the Cardinal's responsibilities: appearing on heresy trials, acting as principals of St Leonard's college, as penitentiary north of Forth, an office held by James Wemyss who thus had a measure of delegated authority over the secular clergy although himself a regular, and witnessing the Cardinal's writs and transactions some of which took place in the priory precincts. The administrator of the priory's affairs, Alexander Milne, was one of his vicars-general. The presence of the royal lodging virtually in the precincts brought the canons into continuous contact with secular and political activities.

Close relations were maintained with the orders of friars. Henry Adamson, prior of the Edinburgh Dominican house in which councils of the Scottish church were held, was the Cardinal's penitentiary south of Forth.[204] The archbishopric accounts record regular charitable payments to the St Andrews Dominicans and Franciscans and to the Dominican nunnery of St Catherine (Sciennes) near Edinburgh, as well as many occasional payments and gifts: half an ox to the St Andrews Franciscans at Easter, £20 to those of Edinburgh to buy a croft next to their garden, £11 to the Franciscan provincial when leaving for the chapter-general in Italy.[205] Before the Cardinal set out for France in July 1541 he gave £4 additional alms to the St Andrews Greyfriars and £20 to the Edinburgh Dominicans towards the repair of the high altar in their church, doubtless in return for their intercessions.[206] In spite of, or because of, the earlier reforms in the educational standards and spiritual commitment of the orders of friars there was much heartsearching leading to unorthodoxy among members of the two groups. It made the friars particularly sensitive to episcopal approval and authority without which they could not practise the itinerant preaching and public teaching which John Adamson had put at the heart of his reforming activity among the Dominicans. At the same time they could be used by the archbishop to impart to the church a more spiritual public face than his own personal priorities could give it.

The humble parish curates appear occasionally in the archbishop's accounts, supervising the collection of the rents and teinds at Kirkliston, or the repair of the manor at Monimail and attending the Cardinal's guest there, Dr Hilliard.[207] The condition of *mensal* kirks was not forgotten: repairs to the choir and glass windows at Kirkliston, which the suffragan visited in 1542, and the re-roofing of the choir at Stow, to which church the Cardinal presented a silk chasuble bearing his arms, in 1541.[208] In spite of his preoccupations it is possible to find the Cardinal-Archbishop actually in church: his recorded sermon at the trial of Sir John Borthwick in 1540 may not have been his only one, nor does the fact that a breviary was bought for his use in Edinburgh in 1540 imply that he had no other although it suggests he did not always carry one with him.[209] He officiated on several important public occasions, including the Queen's coronation on 22 February 1540 and the King's burial in December 1542. He lent his presence to the public observance of orthodox devotion: offering to the relics preserved in the burgh kirk of Dumfries, at the chapel of the Virgin of Loretto, the collegiate church of Restalrig and the abbey of Dunfermline and, on 12 April 1543, to the arm of St Andrew in the metropolitan cathedral.[210] He is found attending mass on the feasts of Epiphany and the Circumcision at St Andrews,[211] and on St Andrews Day in St Giles, Edinburgh,[212] and putting an offering in the alms box of St Andrews parish kirk on Trinity Sunday, the feast of its dedication.[213] He is recorded as having celebrated mass in St Andrews cathedral on several occasions, including Christmas Day 1540,[214] and made offerings at 'the first mass' of a number of priests in both St Andrews and Edinburgh.

More personal associations were reflected in the substantial offering of £13 15s at Crail collegiate church with which his maternal forbears had had a long connection,[215] where his nephews went to school[216] and where an obit, founded in October 1542 by sir David Bowman, one of the prebendaries, included the Cardinal among those for whom mass was to be said.[217] In the family's parish kirk of Markinch, where his mother founded a chaplainry towards the end of her life and the Cardinal himself paid the French carver, Andrew Mansioun, for a new brass for the family tomb,[218] he made regular payments to the chaplain who said mass there for the souls of his father and grandfather, in the same way as countless humbler inhabitants of his archdiocese did for the souls of their own forebears and families.

NOTES

1. S. Ollivant, *The Court of the Official in Pre-Reformation Scotland* (Stair Society), 24–5 (Ollivant, *The Official*)

2. *Letters of James V*, 323

3. G. Donaldson, *The St Andrews Formulare, 1514–46* (Stair Society), II, 94–7 (*Formulare*); *L.P. Henry VIII*, XIV, ii, 673

4. A.D.C.S., ix, fo 142

5. Vatican archives, Reg. Supp., 2543, fo 234, 2555, fo 135; *Orléans Records*, 84

6. *Rentale*, 126

7. Laing charters, 512; *R.M.S.*, V, 1191

8. Vatican archives, P.R.O. 31/9/Reel 1; R.M.S., V, 688

9. *Fasti*, 318–19

10. *Ibid*, 322
11. *Ibid*., 125–6, 317
12. *Ibid*., 320–1
13. *Ibid*., 316
14. *Statutes*, 96–7
15. *Rentale*, 118, 153
16. *Ibid*., 90, 118
17. *Ibid*., 173, 182
18. *Ibid*.
19. *Knox*, I, 53
20. C. Rogers, *Register of the Collegiate Church of Crail*, 47 (*Crail Register*); Crawford priory muniments (S.R.O.), GD 20/73
21. *Fasti*, 328
22. *Sheriff Court Book of Fife*, 91–2
23. *Arbroath Liber*, II, 588, 643, 746, 750, 836
24. *R.M.S.*, III, 897
25. *Ibid*., III, 2788
26. Register House charters, RH 6/1230
27. *Fasti*, 325
28. St Andrews charters, B 65/22/213 formerly in the Scottish Record Office, now in St Andrews University Library
29. *R.S.S.*, II, 1388
30. A.D.C.S., i, fos 119v–120; *R.M.S.*, III, 1017
31. Dick-Lauder Papers (S.R.O.), GD 41/375
32. *Rentale*, 184
33. Ollivant, *The Official*, 49–53, but see also 129–38
34. *Ibid*., 50; Dunlop, *Acta*, cliv–clv
35. St Andrews charters, B 65/22/285
36. St Andrews University muniments, SM 110 B.15.1
37. Ollivant, *The Official*, 61, 151–2
38. *Ibid*., 55–6
39. *Rentale*, 95, 107, 121, 197, 209
40. *Ibid*., 81, 96, 178–9, 201; witnesses a charter to Marion Ogilvy (1545), *R.M.S.*, III, 3095
41. Ollivant, *The Official*, 93
42. *Rentale*, 175; this may indicate punishment other than fines
43. *Formulare*, II, 448, 452
44. *Ibid*., II, 454
45. *Ibid*., II, 438
46. Erskine of Dun muniments (S.R.O.), GD 123 Box 12; *Formulare*, II, 405
47. Biographical notes on Milne in R. K. Hannay, *Rentale Dunkeldense* (S.H.S.), xiv–xvi
48. *Fasti*, 254
49. M. Mahoney, 'Notes on the Religious Orders', 193, 195
50. J. Leslie, *De Origine*, 538–9
51. J. Durkan, 'Education in the Century of the Reformation', in *Essays*, 160
52. *Formulare*, II, 448–9; *Rentale*, 137–8; Erskine of Dun muniments, GD 123/12
53. *Sadler*, I, 167; *L.P. Henry VIII*, XVIII, ii, 9
54. *Hamilton Papers*, II, 264
55. A.D.C.S., xvi, fo 42v; Crawford priory muniments, GD 20/106

56. A.D.C.S., xii, 131, XVII, 15

57. J. Burns, 'New Light on John Major', in *Innes Review*, V, 91–2

58. *L.P. Henry VIII*, XV, 640

59. *Formulare*, II, 439

60. *Ibid.*, II, 403a

61. *Ibid.*, II, 410, 435, 449

62. Biographical information on Lauder in *Formulare* II, Introduction

63. *Ibid.*, II, 406

64. *Rentale, passim*

65. *Formulare*, II, 467

66. *Rentale*, 120, 135; *Fasti*, 329

67. Vatican archives, Reg. Supp., 2493, fo 171v

68. See page 216, below

69. St Andrews Commissariot records, register of testaments (S.R.O.), CC 20/4/1, fo 162v

70. *Crail Register*, 43, 121; *R.M.S.*, III, 1017; Historical MSS Report VIII (Glasgow), 306, 14; Justiciary court minute book, JC 1/5, 6 May 1532; *Dunfermelyn*, 385

71. *Letters of James V*, 275

72. *Ibid.*, 364

73. St Andrews University muniments, SM 110 B1 P1 17

74. *Sadler*, I, 14

75. *Antiquities of Aberdeen and Banff* (Spalding Club), III, 249 (Fowlis–Easter, Angus); W. Fraser, *The Sutherland Book*, I, 110 (sub-dean of Trinity collegiate church, Edinburgh); R.M.S., V, 1050 (Ballantrae); R.S.S., V, 1402 (Carnbee); W. Rankin, *The Church of the Holy Trinity, St Andrews*, 98 (chaplainry of St Peter therein); Register of Presentations to Benefices (S.R.O.), CH 4/1/2, fo 79 (chaplainry of St Ninian, St Salvator's collegiate church, St Andrews)

76. Clerk of Penicuik muniments (S.R.O.), GD 18/459; Stair muniments (S.R.O.), GD 135/78; Dick-Lauder Papers (S.R.O.), GD 41/375

77. A. I. Cameron, *The Scottish Correspondence of Mary of Lorraine* (S.H.S.), 155 (*Scottish Correspondence*)

78. *Knox*, I, 18

79. *Sadler*, II, 239–40

80. *Peerage*, VIII, 432; Yester writs (S.R.O.), GD 28/653, 656, 657

81. *Rentale*, 94, 107

82. *R.S.S.*, II, 493; Vatican archives, Reg. Supp., 2485, fo 148v; A.D.C., xxxiii, fo 31

83. *Booke of the Universall Kirk* (Bannatyne Club), I, 131 (B.U.K.)

84. Yester writs, GD 28/541

85. *Rentale*, 77, 92, 209; Clerk of Penicuik muniments, GD 18/457; *Spalding Club Miscellany*, IV, 31–2; Protocol book of James Androsoun (S.R.O.), NP 1/5a, fo 23; *Charters of the Family of Burnet of Leyis*, (New Spalding Club), 171–5

86. Register of Deeds, Old Series, xi, fo 23v–4

87. Yester writs, GD 28/596

88. *Rentale*, 143

89. W. Angus, *Protocol Book of Gilbert Grote* (S.R.S.), 129

90. St Andrews charters, B65/22/227, 253, 261; *Rentale*, 81, 115

91. *Ibid.*, 155, 179

92. *Ibid.*, 92, 109, 200 (Hogg); St Andrews University muniments SM 110 B1 P1 9; *Register of Crail*, 121 (McMath)

93. Rankin, *Holy Trinity Church*, 87; *Register of Crail*, 72; *Rentale*, 83, 86, 92, 107, 121, 154; St Andrews charters, B 65/22/286, 295a, 299

94. *Rentale*, 101, 124, 138, 151; Herkless and Hannay, *Archbishops*, IV, 97

95. Abercairny muniments (S.R.O.), GD 24/5/1/58

96. Benholm writs (S.R.O.), GD 4/243

97. Airlie muniments, GD 16/25/81

98. *Rentale*, 147, 163, 175, 184, 185, 213

99. Forbes muniments (S.R.O.), GD 52/1695

100. Northesk muniments (S.R.O.), GD 130/15/C, 1545

101. *Formulare*, II, 426

102. Cowan, 'Patronage, Provision and Reservation', 82–3, 91–2

103. *Formulare*, II, 496

104. A.D.C., xvii, fo 144. xviii, fo 141; Vatican archives, Reg. Supp., 2515, fo 35; *Formulare*, II, 426

105. *Ibid.*, II, 423

106. Erskine of Dun muniments, Gd 123/12

107. R. K. Hannay, 'Papal Bulls among the Hamilton Papers', in *S.H.R.*, XXII, 37

108. Linlithgow burgh records (S.R.O.), B48/1/1, fo 92v

109. *Formulare*, II, 449

110. *Ibid.*, II, 393

111. D. McKay, 'Parish Life in Scotland', in *Essays*, 94; *Dowden*, 136

112. *Formulare*, II, 408

113. *Ibid.*, II, 435, 514

114. *Ibid.*, II, 467

115. *Ibid.*, II, 440

116. *Ibid.*, II, 444

117. *Ibid.*, II, 479

118. *Ibid.*, II, 433

119. *Ibid.*, II, 331

120. *Ibid.*, II, 420

121. *Ibid.*, II, 401

122. *Ibid.*, II, 367

123. *Ibid.*, II, 378

124. *Ibid.*, II, 370

125. *Ibid.*, II, 397

126. *Ibid.*, II, 394

127. *Ibid.*, II, 395

128. *Ibid.*, II, 427; *R.S.S.*, II, 2923

129. *Formulare*, II, 225–7

130. *Ibid.*, II, 416

131. *Ibid.*, II, 487

132. *Ibid.*, II, 431

133. *Ibid.*, II, 421

134. *Ibid.*, II, 417, 110

135. *Ibid.*, II, 399

136. *Ibid.*, II, 453

137. *Ibid.*, II, 403a

138. *Rentale*, xxxiv

139. *Statutes*, 284–5

140. *Fasti*, 217, 270
141. M. Mahoney, 'The Scottish Hierarchy', 49
142. *Ibid*; Cowan, 'Patronage, Provision and Reservation', 76–7
143. M. Mahoney, 'The Scottish Hierarchy', 49
144. *Ibid*., 50
145. *Ibid*., 50–1
146. Biographical information on Dunbar, D. E. Easson, *Gavin Dunbar*; *Fasti*, 149, 221
147. *Glasguensis*, No 502
148. *R.S.S.*, II, Appendix
149. Hannay, *College of Justice*, 70–1
150. Vatican archives, Reg. Resig., PRO 9/33/85
151. *Sadler*, I, 13
152. *Glasguensis*, II, 553–4
153. *Rentale*, 143
154. Grant of legateship, PRO, State Papers, 49/7
155. *Glasguensis*, II, 555–6
156. *Knox*, I, 72–4
157. *Statutes*, 252–9
158. Protocol book of Cuthbert Simon (S.R.O.), NP 1/195, fos 4v, 8v; Fraser, *Keir*, 318–19; *Glasguensis*, II, 541, 562
159. State Papers (S.R.O.), SP 1/2/107
160. A. F. Pollard, *Wolsey*, Chapter 5
161. R. K. Hannay, 'Letters of the Papal Legate in Scotland, 1543', in *S.H.R.*, XI
162. *Ibid*., 22
163. Swinton charters (S.R.O.), GD 12/118
164. St Andrews University muniments, SM 110 B16.6
165. *Rentale*, 179
166. *Scottish Correspondence*, 154–5
167. State Papers, SP 1/2/87; *L.P. Henry VIII*, XX, i, 516. 615; *R.S.S.*, III, 1397
168. Edinburgh Commissariot records, Register of Decreets (S.R.O.), CC8/2/3, fo 40
169. Abercairny muniments, GD 24/5/1/58; Morton muniments (S.R.O.), GD 150/309; S.R.O. Microfilm from original in Blairs College, RH 1/3/362/1
170. G. Chalmers, *Caledonia*, VI, 655
171. Protocol book of Edward Dickson (S.R.O.), NP 1/5b, fo 188–91
172. For the history of the University, R. G. Cant, *The University of St Andrews*; under the Cardinal's chancellorship, Dunlop, *Acta*, lvi–lxiii
173. J. Herkless and R. K. Hannay, *The College of St Leonard*, 39–40
174. Dunlop, *Acta*, lix
175. *Ibid.*
176. *Ibid*., lviii
177. Herkless and Hannay, *The College of St Leonard*, 220–3
178. Dunlop, *Acta*, xlviii–xlix and *note*
179. Herkless and Hannay, *The College of St Leonard*, 38–9
180. *Ibid*., 94–8
181. *Ibid*., 99–100
182. *Ibid*., 118–19
183. *Ibid*., 115
184. *Formulare*, II, 396
185. Dunlop, *Acta*, ccxxx

186. J. M. Anderson, *Early Records*, xviii–xix
187. Herkless and Hannay, *The College of St Leonard*, 177–85
188. Dunlop, *Acta*, lv
189. St Andrews University muniments, SM 110 B 15.1
190. Dunlop, *Acta*, liv
191. St Andrews University muniments, SM 110 B1.P1.17
192. *R.M.S.*, III, 1930
193. St Andrews University muniments, SM 110 B1.P.11
194. *Ibid.*, SM 110 B.13.67
195. See *D.N.B*; Durkan, 'The Cultural Background', 282
196. St Andrews University muniments, UY 305/1, fos 87, 104; UY 305/2, fo 30
197. *Rentale*, 141
198. St Andrews University muniments, B, fos 108r–v, 109r–v
199. *Ibid*. SS 600/2
200. J. H. Baxter, 'Dr Richard Hilliard in St Andrews', in *St Andrews Alumnus Chronicle*, XLIV, 2–10
201. *Rentale*, xxxvi, 95, 107, 121, 137
202. *Ibid.*, 107
203. *Ibid.*, 197
204. *Rentale*, 94, 121, 137
205. *Ibid.*, 94, 108, 109, 123, 155
206. *Ibid.*, 125
207. *Ibid.*, 85, 92, 101, 110, 115, 137
208. *Ibid.*, 93, 96, 123
209. *Ibid.*, 109
210. *Ibid.*, 96, 155, 179
211. *Ibid.*, 109
212. *Ibid.*
213. *Ibid.*, 200
214. *Ibid.*, 109
215. *Ibid.*
216. *Ibid.*, 95
217. *Register of Crail*, 12
218. *Rentale*, 125

8

A Great House

On the eve of his emergence as dominant public figure in Scotland the Cardinal's ecclesiastical pre-eminence was matched by his prestige as a great lord, head of a great household and personal following, eventually the possessor of six residences, superior of widespread estates, the secular merging with the ecclesiastical, in the Lothians, Fife, Angus, Kincardineshire and Aberdeenshire. His lavish way of life, which astounded observers even when public demands on his income were draining his financial resources, proclaimed his political power and social influence as he intended it should.

Because of the survival of accounts for the years 1538–46 we probably know more about his than about any other great household of the period, the royal household apart.[1] The Cardinal's, like the King's, moved with him, wholly or in part, from one residence to another: the castle towering above the sea at St Andrews, the manor at Monimail, the abbot's house in the precincts of Arbroath abbey, the episcopal lodging in Edinburgh, on the corner of the Blackfriars' Wynd and the Cowgate, and the more private houses of Ethie, about five miles north of Arbroath, belonging to him as commendator of the abbey, and Melgund, eight miles north-east of Forfar, acquired in 1542. Personal servants and trusted confidants attended him at the houses of others which he is known to have visited: the castle of the earl of Montrose at Kincardine-in-Menteith, the houses of Mr Adam Otterburn in Edinburgh, George Rollock in Dundee[2] or George Maxwell in Dumfries.[3] A great number of his household and even men-at-arms were with him when he was resident, as he was for long periods, in the royal palaces of Stirling, Falkland and Linlithgow.

The sight of his much-travelled retinue must have been a familiar one on the Forth and Tay ferry crossings and on the highways leading to Edinburgh, Stirling, St Andrews, Dundee and Arbroath: the personal servants, the master of the horse, chaplain, page and men-at-arms, the conspicuous figure of the Cardinal, armour under his red robes, riding his horse, White Bowis or, on occasion, a mule. Constantly on the move by well-used routes, he was a vulnerable target for opponents who were prepared to remove him by force; on at least one occasion his bodyguard had to ward off a hostile interception on one of his journeys across Fife. The known details of his itinerary show that he spent most of his time in Edinburgh or St Andrews, rather more in the former, constantly travelling between the two at all times of the year.

The many arrangements for a household of well over 100 recorded individuals were in the hands of numerous officials: the captain of St Andrews castle with his guards, men-at-arms, porters, engineers and gunners; the masters of works who supplied and paid the masons, smiths, wrights and workmen who were engaged during much of David Beaton's term of office in strengthening the castle's fortifications; the provisors of the garrison and of the household who bought food and fuel or received victual directly from the graniter; the master of the household, steward, cooks and kitchen staff, down to the keeper of the pewter and the scullions; the master of the horse, muleteer and stable servants; the Cardinal's personal attendants, pages, lackeys, barber, apothecary; the tailors, upholsterer, baker, brewers, gardeners and general servants.

The household had certain significant characteristics. As at Arbroath in the early years, the most trusted servants were either relatives or men who came from Fife families, or the Arbroath area, with whom the Cardinal had long been acquainted and whose loyalty had been tested. There was a tendency to replace clerics who had held posts under Archbishop James Beaton with laymen and among the ecclesiastics to choose them for their worldly wisdom rather than scholarly or spiritual qualities. The inner circle of personal attendants was largely French, recruited abroad, giving a foreign flavour to the impression made by the entourage. The changing group of noblemen's sons who were sustained in the household were there as much in the Cardinal's interests as to give them the experience of living in a great household. The Cardinal maintained remarkably close contact with his servants. His charitable payments, both regular and occasional, were on a lavish scale. He maintained, or at least gave regular financial and material support to, a circle of dependent relatives, a duty expected of successful ecclesiastics, and he planned carefully for the advancement of his own numerous children whom he intended to settle mainly in Angus, whence his own forebears had come, eventually acquiring a secular barony for his oldest son. In addition, he controlled the running of his landed estates from which came the income that was called upon to support his way of life.

Perhaps the most trusted servant was the captain of St Andrews castle, John Beaton, the Cardinal's nephew, who succeeded his father in the barony of Balfour about 1545. The hereditary office of constable of the castle belonged to the family of Wemyss of Lathockar but Bishop Kennedy had created a precedent for the appointment of an acting captain without prejudice to the hereditary constables. John Beaton appears as captain by the end of 1542. During the following years public events demanded a considerable strengthening of the castle's fortifications and an increase in the number of its defenders, as the Cardinal strove to achieve complete political control throughout 1543 after the King's death and, with the rest of south-east Scotland, faced the English invasions of the following two years. Thereafter, his increasing awareness of personal opposition was added to the fear of foreign hostilities. In this constantly changing situation, in which news was tardy and often conflicting, it was John Beaton's double responsibility to oversee the castle's defences and maintain the discipline of its garrison. With the advice of hired engineers, Christopher Grymmeschere, 'Master Wolf' and Robert Hector, the first of whom was a Frenchman, and the help of gunners whose fees ranged from £3 to £10 a month, the captain supervised the purchase and installation of guns, which included culverins, and powder, bullets and other ammunition. About the end of March 1543, when the Cardinal arrived in St Andrews after release from his 'imprisonment' and the castle guard had been increased to around 100 from about half that number, John Beaton received £300 for munitions. Forty-eight iron-headed spears for the guards were bought in Edinburgh, gunpowder was brought from as far away as Glasgow and, in the autumn of 1544, iron bullets from Dunbar.

John Beaton and the Cardinal may have been in roughly the same age-group since John's father was the oldest of a very large family. He was certainly one of his uncle's right-hand men, a witness to many of his writs and other business, an auditor of his accounts and the recipient of several charters, including one of the kirklands of Kilrenny from which he took his designation during his father's lifetime.[4] In May 1544 he was made one of the Cardinal's testamentary executors and was to stand by the interests of his uncle's sons after their father's death. Tied for much of the time to his vital post of captain, John and his wife, Agnes Anstruther, had living quarters in the castle.[5]

The man to whom most non-diocesan business was entrusted was also a layman, the Cardinal's cousin, Archibald Beaton of Capildrae, who had begun his career in the household of Archbishop James Beaton in the early 1530s when he was chamberlain of Dunfermline abbey.[6] Archibald became a close associate of his cousin, an auditor of the archbishopric accounts, graniter from 1540, chamberlain from 1541 to 1542, in an experiment which temporarily united both these offices in his hands, and bailie and steward of the regality from about 1541 to 1544. He was clearly a capable person who did not simply turn his offices into sinecures. The signature which he appended to documents, if somewhat unsophisticated, was less so than that of the Cardinal's brother, the laird of Balfour.[7] In 1541, with Mr Henry Lumsden, a cleric, Archibald was appointed commissioner and 'placeholder' in regality business for the Cardinal, then going abroad, and was also entrusted with a list of presentees to benefices in the Cardinal's patronage, to whom the secretary, Mr John Lauder, was empowered to grant collation.[8] Thus not only did the Cardinal often replace clerics with laymen in the running of his estates, Archibald Beaton replacing as graniter Mr Alan Lamont who had served Archbishop James Beaton since at least 1535,[9] but laymen are found handling a certain amount of ecclesiastical business. The laird of Capildrae was a curator of the son of Sir James Hamilton of Finnart,[10] in the affairs of whose family the Cardinal became involved after Hamilton's execution, and a tutor, with the Cardinal, of the son of the laird of Cranstonriddell.[11] He was made one of the Cardinal's testamentary executors in May 1544,[12] curator of his son, David Beaton of Melgund, and was one of the most regular witnesses of his writs.

The chamberlainry of the regality of St Andrews passed through the hands of five men in David Beaton's time, almost suggesting a deliberate policy of changing the holders of that office: Mr Henry Lumsden, who had been James Beaton's chamberlain, Archibald Beaton of Capildrae, Mr Alexander Kinmond, appointed regent in arts at the new college, who was chamberlain in 1543, Mr Bernard Bailie, one of David Beaton's closest friends since his Arbroath days, who held office in 1544, and Mr Alexander Crichton, a kinsman of Mr Abraham Crichton, official of Lothian,[13] who became chamberlain in 1545. Mr Henry Lumsden, James

Beaton's chamberlain since at least 1527, who as a chaplain in the abbey church of Dunfermline had been dispensed from making residence there in order to attend on the archbishop,[14] had been presented in 1534 to the vicarage of Tarves by David Beaton as abbot of Arbroath.[15] Although replaced as chamberlain by Archibald Beaton, Lumsden continued in the Cardinal's household, acted as his commissioner during his absences abroad, witnessed many charters and audited the accounts. He was a native of Fife, a relative of Lumsden of Pitello.[16]

As with the chamberlainry, the jointly-held offices of steward and bailie of the regality passed through several hands: those of Archibald Beaton (1542–4), George Winchester, another layman, during whose short term of office a tax-valuation of the regality was made (1544–5),[17] and Robert Beaton of Creich, the Cardinal's second cousin, who combined this office with that of steward of Fife for the King,[18] which had been in his family for three generations.

In making appointments to the important posts of provisors of the castle garrison and the household the Cardinal again replaced clerics who had served his uncle with laymen. Alan Coutts, from the Dunfermline district, took over the post of chief provisor of the household from sir Alexander Kerse (who had previously been assisted by sir James Auchmowty) in December 1540, holding office for the rest of the Cardinal's life. Coutts not only supervised the provisioning of the household in major residences like St Andrews and Edinburgh but also at such stopping places as Dysart, Kirkcaldy and Kinghorn. He also supplied the ship *Unicorn* in which the Cardinal sailed to France in 1541 and attended to a variety of other business. This included estate business, such as receiving the grain rents of Stow from the officer there, for the household's consumption, and riding as far as Argyll to deliver a letter from the Cardinal to the earl of Argyll, and ecclesiastical business such as accounting for the expenses of the consecration of the suffragan bishop, Mr William Gibson, in August 1541, and confirming testaments in 1545 'by the Cardinal's mandate', receiving quots to the amount of over £125. Coutts's considerable outlays as provisor can be judged from the fact that in presenting his accounts in February 1541 he produced evidence of expenditure, in the form of diet books and acquittances, to the amount of over £600 for the two winter months since his appointment. Coutts worked closely with the provisors of the garrison itself, Mr William Young, a chaplain in the private chapel in the castle, and then with William Paterson, a laymen, Young's successor. The great sums spent on provisioning the household included the cost of transporting the food, drink and fuel, whether rents or purchases, to whatever part of the country the household happened to be in: £245 for freight of part of a consignment of 110 casks of Bordeaux wine shipped from France in the summer of 1539, £42 for white wine and claret to be sent from Edinburgh to Arbroath in June 1541 when the Cardinal spent a week or two there before leaving on his longest embassy to France, £110 for several puncheons of wine bought from Archibald Campbell in Dundee and sent by sea to Edinburgh, wheat from the Fife rents shipped from St Andrews to Leith for the use of Walter Scott, baker in Edinburgh, who supplied the household there, £70 14s for seven boatloads of coal bought in Wester Wemyss and freighted to St Andrews, with a further £5 18s 6d for cartage from the harbour to the castle,

14 barrels of eels from the rents of the laird of Lochleven, and even the transport of lard from St Andrews for the kitchen in Edinburgh.

There was a succession of masters of work at the castle, the most important of whom was sir Walter Mar, a competent and busy man, who was also in charge at the new college and the parish church of the Holy Trinity.[19] At the castle payments to Mar cover the period beginning 2 May 1539 and ending 24 March 1543. His successor, sir James Bickarton, not only received help from thè captain but also from sir Henry Balfour, a servant of dubious reputation. It may be Balfour who appears in 1516 as procurator for the countess of Rothes in Fife sheriff court[20] and who, six years later, when he was said to be 'dwelling with the laird of Anstruther', was among those involved in the abduction of the 'lady Abercrombie'.[21] As a royal chaplain and almoner he petitioned at Rome for more lucrative livings, including a prebend in Elgin cathedral and the chancellorship of Aberdeen, apparently without success.[22] He wrote the controversial instrument alleged to have contained the 'will' of James V.[23] He appears to have entered the Cardinal's service soon after the King's death and is called one of the masters of work in 1544, when he paid for building materials, some of them from a Frenchman.

Constant travelling by the household meant much work for the master of the horse, muleteer and stable servants in marshalling the mounted retinue: maintaining the supply of fodder, arranging the frequent ferrying of the horses across the Forth and Tay and the stabling arrangements in Edinburgh, where the episcopal lodging did not provide sufficient stabling for all the horses, and the shipment of horses to France and back during the Cardinal's embassies. David Rutherford, master of the horse from 1539 to 1543, who had received a grant of land in Weddale from Archbishop James Beaton in 1535,[24] was probably a relative of Arbroath abbey's subprior, Thomas Rutherford, who in 1549 witnessed a charter to David and his wife of the lands of Murehouse, granted to them by the Cardinal's nephew, James Beaton, by then abbot of Arbroath, 'in return for his long service to the late Cardinal in Scotland and in France'.[25] David Rutherford witnessed a document in 'the inner chamber of the Cardinal' at St Andrews castle in 1544,[26] received royal letters of protection while his master was abroad[27] and was enough of a personal friend to be made curator of the Cardinal's second daughter, Elizabeth.[28] He was succeeded as master of the horse by Robert Lindsay, who may have set up as a stabler in Edinburgh after the Cardinal's death.[29]

A distinct group in the household were the French servants, some of whom were the Cardinal's personal attendants: Claud the barber, Baugé the lackey, another Claud, a page, who may be synonymous with a 'singing boy' of that name, Gabriel, the Cardinal's cook, who had his own servant, Stephen the tailor, who, having taken steady delivery of red cloth of all kinds, must have cut enthusiastically into the 'violet colored camelot' that cost £16 from an Edinburgh merchant, John the upholsterer, who was in charge of furnishing the Cardinal's private apartments, Francis, deputy master of the horse, and Michael the muleteer. Amand Guthrie, the Cardinal's chief page, listed among the French servants, may have belonged to an expatriate Scots family. He accompanied the Cardinal to France in 1541, receiving new clothes for the occasion costing over £10.

The apothecaries, who supplied both drugs and perfumes for the Cardinal's use, were Thomas Brown and Robert Deer. Walter Danestoun shared his tailoring with Stephen the Frenchman. Many other household servants are named in the accounts, including four cooks (apart from Gabriel) under the head cook, Alexander Jardine, one of them also having charge of 'the capon and poultry', another of the silver vessels and a third of 'the hall and pewter'. Jardine worked for twenty-three days at Seton castle in the spring of 1543 when the Cardinal was detained there. Ironically, when so much of the castle at St Andrews that knew David Beaton has disappeared, one perfectly preserved feature is a slop-sink out of which Troillus and Rutledge the scullions cast the kitchen refuse.[30] In the entourage were John Drummond, trumpeter, William Blair, 'player on the tabor' and John Lowis, the fool. The household had its baker, Thomas Morton, a citizen of St Andrews, and brewers, 'the Widow Fallisdale', who brewed in the castle, and others, unnamed, in the town. Robert Pate was tailor to the household: 'stuff' was delivered to him 'for the French lackeys' and pages' clothes' and linen bought for him to make shirts for the servants. There were separate gardeners at the different residences: John Mitchell at St Andrews, Andrew Strachan at Edinburgh and an unnamed colleague at Monimail. Capons were fattened and vegetables grown in the yard at St Andrews castle but the more formal garden at Edinburgh was planted with trees and hedges.

In addition to the regular household suppliers the Cardinal used the services of a large number of merchants, tradesmen and craftsmen in both St Andrews and Edinburgh. Notable were the 'by appointment' suppliers who also served the royal household: William Fraser, saddler to the Queen,[31] who carried out saddlery repairs on the orders of David Rutherford between September 1541 and January 1542 and in 1545, Adam Leyis, deacon of the Edinburgh goldsmiths as early as 1526,[32] who engraved the Cardinal's silver round seal in 1539, Walter Scott, baker to the Queen,[33] kirkmaster to the Edinburgh baxter craft from 1523,[34] to whom grain was delivered from the episcopal barony of Kirkliston to make bread for the household in Edinburgh, John Young, the royal tailor,[35] who made the Cardinal's white mourning mitre for the King's funeral in 1542 and an embroidered standard in 1545, and Arthur Littlejohn, cordiner to James V,[36] who made shoes for the Cardinal and his lackey in 1541. Cloth and wine were bought from eight different Edinburgh merchants, and money was borrowed from some of the wealthiest of them, who also lent to the government: William Fisher, Nicol Cairncross, Gilbert Lauder, Patrick Tennant and George Todrick who on one occasion conveyed £200 to his kinsman, William Todrick, citizen of Paris, for the Cardinal's use in France. The establishment at St Andrews also brought trade to prominent burgesses there: to William Mayne who supplied wood to build the house of Melgund in Angus in 1543, Alexander Napier, saddler, and Alexander Pate, baker. Robert Hall in Kinghorn supplied coal and Henry Miller in Dysart did smith's work. Money was borrowed on one occasion from William White, burgess of Aberdeen.

For much of the time the household would include those officials whose duties and the fact that they are regular witnesses of writs suggest that they were frequently with the Cardinal: his brother, Mr Walter Beaton, archdeacon of Lothian, his cousins, George Durie, abbot of Dunfermline and archdeacon of St Andrews, and Archibald Beaton of Capildrae, the graniter, Mr Bernard Bailie, Mr Henry Lumsden, Mr George Hay and the other secretaries, Mr John Lauder and Mr Andrew Oliphant. No doubt these officials had their own assistants and servants, adding to the number of residents in the household, and, like John Beaton of Balfour, may have had living accommodation in the castle or even in the commodious Edinburgh lodging.

Like the households of other great lords, that of David Beaton had its company of noblemen's and gentlemen's sons. Some may have been there to learn the art of living in a great household, others because the Cardinal had for one reason or another taken a hand in their affairs, and some were with him as pledges of their families' political support. Thomas Maule, son of the laird of Panmure,[37] had left home at the age of seven to be brought up in Edinburgh in the household of Robert Leslie of Innerpeffer, the Cardinal's lawyer in Arbroath business, 'quha wes ane famous man of lawe in that tyme, and also held the chief innes of the heale towne for noble men'. A childhood marriage contract to Elizabeth Lindsay, daughter of the earl of Crawford, having failed, Thomas joined the Cardinal's household in his early teens and was drawn into the latter's dynastic schemes. In 1533, when Thomas was twelve years old, his lands of Scryne in Angus were wadset, nominally to the Cardinal's daughter, Elizabeth, but really to himself, the 'reversion' of the land to take place on her marriage (or that of her elder sister, Margaret) to Thomas Maule.[38] King James V, probably in 1541, is said to have advised Thomas that he should ' "marie nevir ane preistis gett", quharupone that mariage did cese',[39] The Cardinal resented the slight and the Maules had to pay him 3,000 merks. Elizabeth Beaton, however, did not formally renounce her marriage contract until 28 September 1545, by which date she had completed her eighteenth year,[40] and in the meantime Thomas remained in the Cardinal's household, accompanying him to France in 1541. Maule's name does not appear in the archbishopric accounts so that he may have lived at his own expense.

The 'yong laird of Kellie in Angus', James Ochterlonie, was in the household in 1545, when clothes were bought for him. The mention of a lawsuit by the Cardinal against his father in 1541 suggests that James may have been in St Andrews as a result of a dispute which gave the Cardinal the opportunity to gain control over him and his affairs.[41] After David Beaton's death his youngest daughter, Agnes, became James Ochterlonie's wife, a match which may have been planned during the Cardinal's lifetime. The lands of Kellie, in the vicinity of Arbroath, were held from the abbey by the family. The Cardinal met the expenses of Andrew Kinnear, 'scholar' at Crail grammar school, and those of a handful of young men at St Andrews university, including George and John Nisbet, sons of Nisbet of Dalziel, and David Hume, 'son of Alexander Hume', a student at St Leonard's college. In the winter of 1542 he authorised a Paris banker to pay 100 crowns of the sum to the master of Erskine, then 'at the scholis in Paris', Lord Erskine binding himself to repay the loan.[42] The earl of Arran's oldest son, James Hamilton, joined the household after his father's capitulation to the Cardinal in the autumn of 1543, where he remained for the rest of the latter's life as a pledge of Arran's political alignment. The young Lord Gray lived in the household in terms of a bond of manrent between himself and the Cardinal, dated 1544.[43] Arrangements like these brought the uneasy political situation indoors.

Clearly, the revenues of the archbishopric alone, considerable though they might appear on paper, could not have maintained the Cardinal in the state in which he lived. For the upkeep of his household and for public purposes he drew on whatever income he could realise out of the bishopric of Mirepoix, the abbacy of Arbroath and the temporalities and diocesan jurisdictions of the see of St Andrews. There is not enough information on finance in the surviving accounts, detailed in character though these are, to enable us to determine the Cardinal's annual income or expenditure with anything like accuracy. Professor R. K. Hannay, in editing the accounts, pointed out that by 1543 the Cardinal faced a considerable deficit, although in 1539 he had inherited a comfortable balance from his careful uncle. Actually, it is for the accounting year 1542, for which the accounts were not rendered until May 1543 after the Cardinal's release from detention, that the deficit, of over £638, occurs. This deficit was certainly a sudden drop, from a clear balance of over £200 for 1541. There was to be a certain recovery in 1543–4 and a smaller deficit in 1545. There may have been reasons why 1542 was so bad. For one thing, the Cardinal had been in France for seven months of the year — indeed since July 1541 — on what was his most protracted embassy, in itself a considerable financial drain. It may be that the officers collecting the rents and dues were more dilatory in his absence. Certainly, it is remarkable that the 1542 accounts show an unusually high proportion of dues 'depending', £897 5s 8d, without which there would have been a clear balance of nearly £700.

However strained his finances became, from day to day David Beaton himself handled large sums of money: almost £5,000 from the archbishopric rents alone between 1539 and 1544, over £1,400 of this in March 1539 and £1,000, from the rents for 1541, handed to him on his return from France in August 1542. From the money and grain rents collected by his officers he authorised regular payments of maintenance, gifts and charities which were sometimes on a princely scale. The beneficiaries included a wide circle of relatives, representing three generations, who received gifts of money and victual, had their bills paid, expenses defrayed or waived, or received presents of clothing. The 4th Lord Lyle, husband of the Cardinal's aunt, Grizel Beaton of Creich, his son, the master of Lyle, and the Cardinal's brother-in-law, William Graham of Fintry, all had the expenses of new infeftments met. His second cousin, Margaret Beaton, lady of Reres, and his nieces, the 'lady of Barns', Christian Beaton, lady of Burleigh, and Elizabeth Graham, lady of Lathockar, received gifts of victual from time to time, worth considerable sums. The master of Lyle and young John Graham of Claverhouse, the latter being the son of the Cardinal's sister, Margaret, both received new jacks, while their sisters received clothes, both the materials and the cost of tailoring, in the spring of 1541. His sister Elizabeth, wife of John Wardlaw of Torry, who had gifts of victual and had her bill to an Edinburgh merchant paid for her, had needed the special support of her family since 1532 when her husband had been declared *non compos mentis.*

Other payments included those to the Cardinal's cousin, Janet, lady of Innermeath, and his 'kinswoman', the widow of Sir James Hamilton of Finnart. He paid the board and expenses of John Beaton of Balfour's two sons at Crail grammar school from 1539, and of his nephew, James Graham of Fintry at St Leonard's college. Elizabeth Monypenny, the Cardinal's mother, took seriously ill in the spring of 1541. In the midst of public business he crossed by the Queensferry, dining at Inverkeithing on his way to visit her in her last illness, having paid the prominent Edinburgh apothecary, Thomas Thomson, for medicines for her. On 25 May he gave Andrew Mansion, the French carver, £10 10s for a new brass for the family tomb in Markinch parish church and, about the same time, paid one Andrew Richardson for writing out the foundation of a chaplainry endowed by the lady of Balfour before her death. It was no doubt in order to see that all these arrangements had been carried out that he visited Balfour again on 3 July, with his French cook in attendance, about three weeks before he sailed for France. His visits to his early home must have caused a considerable stir locally: the accounts record the distribution of nine shillings 'to the poor at Balfour' on 9 February 1544, with another nine shillings in alms to the poor when he crossed at 'the Queen's ferry'.

The fees enjoyed by his officials and servants were paid in money, with an allowance of oats and meal for expenses and subsistence to those whose job meant travelling distances. The lesser servants also received livery and all residents in the household, great and small, their food and lodging. Wages, in the contemporary sense of extraordinary maintenance, were paid to the most responsible servants if they remained in Scotland when the Cardinal was overseas. The domestic servants were fairly well paid, in addition to food, lodging and livery: Alexander Jardine the head cook's fee of £6 13s 4d was the same as the money-part of the basic fee of Lord Forbes as bailie of the baronies of Keig and Monymusk, although for the latter there were doubtless other perquisites. The cooks, Thomas and William Murray, received £5 6s 8d each and the more menial of the kitchen staff from £3 6s 8d down to £1, comparable in scale with the fees of the serjeants of the various baronies comprising the archbishopric estates, which ranged from £3 6s 8d down to £1 6s 8d, depending on the extent of the territory for which they were responsible and its distance from St Andrews. The 'keeper of the great gate', Ambrose Stirling, whose responsibility was to cost him his life, and the watchman, David Smith, both of whom probably shared lodging and food with the men-at-arms, received £2 and £1 respectively, comparable with the fees paid to the much less responsible gardeners at Edinburgh and Monimail. Responsibility for others commanded higher fees: £13 6s 8d to the provisor of the household, Alan Coutts, £11 10s to Michael, the French muleteer, and over £30 to the master of the stable, Robert Lindsay. Regality and diocesan officials who may also have been in the household, at least for part of the time, received pensions charged on the accounts: £100 to Mr George Hay, parson of Rathven, £40, in addition to clothing, to Mr Adam Mure, one of the secretaries, £100 to Mr John Hay, the Cardinal's cousin.

The many occasional payments recorded in the accounts afford glimpses of the activity generated by the presence of a large household and the movements and contacts of the Cardinal himself: 10s to Francis, a French servant, with, presumably, a passable amount of the Scots tongue, to ride ahead on one occasion to hire a boat at Dundee for St Andrews, 44s to the sailors who rowed the Cardinal ashore on his return from France on 3 August 1542 and next day rowed him out to the ship to collect some papers personally, and ashore again, 44s to carpenters working at Burntisland, on 24 August following, when the Cardinal may have stayed at the castle which was then in the possession of his cousin, George Durie, as abbot of Dunfermline. There were expenses connected with the military operations that preceded the disaster of Solway Moss, such as 14s to an 'Englishman called Harry' when the Cardinal was in Haddington, presumably in return for military information, and a gift of 11s to 'a poor man called Beaton dwelling in Foulden'. There were parting gifts to the servants of the earl of Montrose after the Cardinal's stay at the castle of Kincardine-in-Menteith in May 1544, after he had fled from Edinburgh during Hertford's invasion: 44s each to 'the coverer of the tables' and 'William the gude guide' who had led the Cardinal's party there, 22s each to the earl's steward, janitor, cook and pantryman and to 'the priest celebrating mass there'. Twenty-two shillings in alms were distributed by Mr Andrew Oliphant in Stirling.

Disbursements to the poor, who gathered at all stopping places on the Cardinal's journeys, amounted to somewhere between £120–£130 a year. In addition, there were many charitable payments to individuals, or payments for services or to mark an occasion: to priests saying their first mass, to the nurses of the prince (£22), to the Queen's nurse at Linlithgow (£11), to the parson of Stobo's servant in Glasgow (22s), £4 in alms to 'Christian Lindsay, pauper', and 22s to 'a poor woman Ellen Bonar', both by mandate of the Cardinal, probably while travelling, 10s to 'old Byssate the Queen's messenger in alms', 14s to two Irish mendicant friars, £14 8s 4d to 'Elizabeth Dury, nun in Haddington', possibly a cousin, the expenses of 'eight poor Frenchmen from St Andrews to Linlithgow' to join the French envoy, de Lorges, alms on several occasions and a gift of 'russat cloth of Rouen' to one John Ainslie, meal to the widow of the gardener at Edinburgh. The liberal scale of these payments throws a welcome human light on the Cardinal, as does his readiness to add to the enjoyment of a special occasion: 14s to the officers and serjeants of the city of St Andrews at Christmas, half an ox to the St Andrews Greyfriars at Easter, 27s 'in particular sums', to the mock boy-bishop and his attendants on St Nicholas's Day, 1540, £3 6s to the frequently obstreperous 'Robert [Robin] Hude' and his companions in 1541, and the substantial sum of 44s to the upholsterer's young assistant 'to spend at his sister's wedding', perhaps the result of a personal encounter in the private rooms of the castle. All this largesse, of course, might have been aimed at balancing popular sympathy against political opposition.

People were astounded at the princely furnishings of St Andrews castle. The household certainly reflected the master's demand for high standards of comfort and impressive surroundings: the walls were hung with tapestries which he once took to France with him, when it took six pack-horses to carry them, minstrels played in the hall where diversions were created by Lowis the Fool, silver vessels were used at table where food and drink included bread and pastry baked with wheat flour, eels, salmon and wild fowl from the rents of vassals in Fife and Angus, lettuce and onions from the castle garden and artichokes presented by the gardener at the priory, with claret and Bordeaux wine. While he transacted business in his 'inner chamber' at St Andrews and Edinburgh, the Cardinal dined in public like other great lords and there were always guests at table. The accounts occasionally reveal the large sums spent on fine materials for his clothes: violet *camlet*, which had a watered appearance, tunics sent to the furrier to be fur-lined, red damask sandals for the Queen's coronation at which he officiated, black velvet, French black cloth, fustian and red taffeta. An envoy reported the Cardinal's appearance on 8 May 1544, just before the brief military action near Leith, wearing a yellow velvet cassock, slashed and 'pulled out' with white tinsel sarcenet.[44] He possessed two swords and in 1544, during the English invasion, had a new jack made, with silken ties, costing £4 15s. His personal and household expenses for the accounting year 1539–40 ran to something like two and a half thousand pounds, apart from public, ecclesiastical and political commitments, and not counting the expenses of the household when at Arbroath which would be charged on the abbey revenues, accounts for which have not survived for this period.

There was another household to be provided for, that of Marion Ogilvy and her family, firstly with land and gradually with provision for the sons' careers and the future marriages of the daughters. The Cardinal set about the provision for his children in the spirit of true sixteenth-century dynasticism. Indeed, his arrangements on their behalf were simply part of his own accumulation of landed property, interest and revenue, especially since most of them, including all his sons, were minors during his lifetime. With her considerable property in and around Arbroath and her liferent use of the house at Ethie Marion Ogilvy was well able to look after herself. She both borrowed and lent money. She was caught, however, between the freedom to stand up for herself in a court of law as an unmarried woman and the vulnerability that came from the resentment of those who had an eye on her goods and property, without a husband to protect her, and she is frequently found before the lords of council and session, sometimes in person, defending her rights.[45] She was extremely persistent in pursuing legal claims but in spite of the Cardinal's protection and the legal services at times of such a distinguished advocate as his friend, Mr Thomas Marjoribanks, she did not always win.

From 1538 onwards her sons were associated with her in grants of land.[46] In 1539 the Cardinal made an attempt to acquire for them a piece of secular property held from the crown. On 8 March that year, about three weeks after he had officially become archbishop of St Andrews, the King granted his son David a feu charter of the lands of Lundarteris, Murehouse and the Mains of Backy in Angus, forfeited from Lord Glamis, of which Marion Ogilvy had received a nineteen-year tack the previous year. The charter contained licence to rebuild the dwelling place on the Mains of Backy.[47] In May 1542, however, while the Cardinal was in France, the lords of session annulled the charter on the grounds that its terms had been 'in diminution of the rental', and the newly-acquired piece of heritable property slipped from the Beatons' grasp, although Marion Ogilvy herself maintained her right to her nineteen-year tack, defending it from time to time in court.[48]

In 1542 there came another change in the family's circumstances as the oldest sons, David, James and Alexander, took the first steps towards their future careers. On 20 July that year David and James, designated 'scholars', sailed from Kirkcaldy to France in the charge of sir David Christison who was given £55 for their travelling expenses and £3 12s for 'wraps and clothes for the voyage'.[49] The Cardinal, who was then about to leave France at the end of his longest diplomatic mission, may have met them before he left for Scotland, which he did not reach until 3 August. In 1544 books were being bought for Alexander by Mr Adam Mure, Paris graduate and former schoolmaster of Edinburgh grammar school, who from 1539 is described as the Cardinal's servant at a fee of £40 a year.[50] Alexander, who may have been one of a group of young men in the Cardinal's circle to be tutored by Mure, later studied in France in the 1550s.[51] In 1539 Adam Mure acted as pedagogue to the sons of John Beaton of Balfour, then going to Crail grammar school.[52] His copy of St Augustine, from Blairs college library, was given by him while schoolmaster at Edinburgh to Alexander Hume, notary public, perhaps the father of the David Hume whose upkeep at St Leonard's college was paid by the Cardinal.[53] Mure also witnessed a grant of church revenues by the Cardinal to his sons in 1543[54] and in the following year his feu charter to Lord Borthwick[55] who at that time held the *ward* of the oldest son, David, suggesting a connection between the tutor and the interests of the older sons, whom he may have taught at an earlier stage. In the autumn of 1544 Mure, as subdean of Trinity collegiate church, Edinburgh, petitioned at Rome to be allowed to defer major orders while retaining his benefices,[56] and in November his own son petitioned for half the fruits of the subdeanery of that church on his father's resignation.[57] In December of that year the Cardinal referred to Mure as his secretary in a letter to Cardinal S. Crucis[58] but he died before September 1545 when he is referred to as 'late' in the archbishopric accounts.

The prospect of academic careers made the acquisition of church benefices desirable for the Cardinal's sons. On 13 September 1542 David and James were dispensed by the Roman Court to hold clerical character, although suffering defect of illegitimate birth,[59] and about the same time David petitioned for the canonry of Govan when it should be resigned by his uncle, Mr Walter Beaton.[60] In the event, it was James who 'inherited' Govan, took his master's degree and followed an academic career.[61] In 1545 Alexander, as a clerk of St Andrews diocese, was granted the reservation of the 'fruits' of the churches of Monifieth and Abernethy belonging to Arbroath abbey which was then being resigned by the Cardinal in favour of his nephew, James Beaton.[62] Alexander held these revenues for the rest of his long life, in addition to the archdeaconry of Lothian which eventually came his way with the death of his uncle, Mr Walter Beaton, about 1551.[63]

Events at home were to turn the oldest son, David, into the laird of a secular barony, ultimately abandoning his clerical career. In the very month in which he and his brother James received their clerical dispensations, September 1542, Janet Annand, widow of the Cardinal's brother, James, sold the Cardinal her ancestral lands of North Melgund, a barony in Aberlemno parish, Angus, for an unspecified sum of money, with consent of her second husband, David Balfour of Balledmonth. The charter was dated at the latter's house of Kirktoun in Fife on 20 September 1542 and confirmed by the crown five days later.[64] On 23 January 1543, just four days before the Cardinal was arrested in council by the Governor's party, a crown precept was issued for a great seal charter to his son, David, conveying to him the barony of North Melgund on his father's resignation, a simple device by which David became heritable proprietor of land which as a natural son he could never have inherited.[65] The register of the privy seal in which the precept is recorded gives only brief details of the charter, as is usual in that register, but clearly the liferent of the barony was reserved to Marion Ogilvy who was designated 'lady of Melgund' shortly afterwards and for the rest of her life. In 1545 South Melgund was acquired in wadset from the neighbouring Cramonds of Auldbar.[66] The 'place of Melgund', the impressive ruins of which still stand, was built, or rebuilt, in the summer and autumn of 1543[67] soon after the Cardinal's release from detention and while he was working to gain control of the political situation and the Governor's desertion of the Anglophile party. It was, in effect, Marion Ogilvy's house, with her monogram at the foot of the staircase that gives access to the private apartments in the keep and the coats-of-arms of herself and the Cardinal over the west and south windows, respectively, of the great hall in the tower, like the arms of a laird and his wife on their newly-built house; Marion's arms are a lion *passant*, the Cardinal's those incorporated in his seal which he used as archbishop of St Andrews — they are not those of David Beaton of Melgund. The acquisition of this barony and the building of the house, designed to look like ancient keep and modern, domestic wing, as well as the re-establishment of the Beatons as crown vassals in Angus, must have seemed a satisfactory stroke to the Cardinal by 1543, a year in which his political fortunes ebbed and flowed.

NOTES

1. Factual information on the organisation and personnel of the Cardinal's household is culled from the *Rentale Sancti Andree* unless otherwise stated

2. Airlie muniments, GD 16/41/14

3. *Glasguensis*, II, 553

4. Crawford priory muniments, GD 20/108; *R.S.S.*, III, 749

5. *A.P.S.*, II, 474

6. *Exchequer rolls*, XVI, 232, XVII, 52

7. Morton muniments, GD 150/2187

8. *Formulare*, II, 406

9. Register House charters, RH 6/114a

10. Stirling burgh records (Central Regional archives, Stirling), former S.R.O. reference, B 66/1/3, fo 11

11. W. Fraser, *The Scotts of Buccleuch*, II, 179–80
12. *Formulare*, II, 624
13. *Rentale, passim*
14. *R.M.S.*, III, 482; *R.S.S.*, II, 796
15. *Arbroath Liber*, II, 798
16. Register of Deeds, Old Series, vi, fo 334
17. Miscellaneous collections (S.R.O.), GD 1/54/2
18. Clerk of Penicuik muniments, GD 18/461
19. Rankin, *Holy Trinity Church*, 87
20. *Sheriff Court Book of Fife*, 49
21. *Ibid.*, 244
22. Vatican archives, Reg. Supp., 2435, fo 8v
23. See page 155, below
24. A.D.C.S., vi, fo 53
25. Northesk muniments, GD 130, Box 19
26. Crawford priory muniments, GD 20/108
27. *R.S.S.*, II, 4117
28. Dalhousie muniments, GD 45/16/620
29. Edinburgh Testaments, CC8/8/1, fo 221
30. S. Cruden, *St Andrews castle* (H.M.S.O.)
31. *R.S.S.*, III, 74
32. Minute book of the Edinburgh goldsmiths (S.R.O.), GD1/482/1, 31 January 1526
33. *Extracts from the burgh records of Edinburgh, 1519–1666* (Scottish Burgh Record Society), 39–40
34. *Ibid.*, II, 214
35. *R.S.S.*, II, 1705
36. *Ibid.*, II, 2124
37. *Registrum de Panmure*, I, xxxi
38. Dalhousie muniments, GD 45/16/575
39. *Registrum de Panmure*, I, xxxi
40. Dalhousie muniments, GD 45/16/619
41. *Rentale*, 155
42. Register of Acts and Decreets, xvii, fo 240
43. *Spalding Club Miscellany*, V, 295–6
44. *L.P. Henry VIII*, XIX, i, 481
45. A.D.C., xxxv, fo 208v; A.D.C.S., i, fo 91v, ii, fo 177v, iii, fo 30r, x, fos 123r, 158v, xvii, fo 68v
46. *R.S.S.*, II, 2467
47. *Ibid.*, II, 2625
48. Register of Acts and Decreets, i, part ii, fo 310
49. *Rentale*, 139
50. *Extracts from the burgh records of Edinburgh*, II, 48; *Rentale*, 121; Bibliothèque Nationale, Paris, MS Lat., 9952, fo 125v
51. *Rentale*, 199
52. *Ibid.*, 95
53. *Early Scottish Libraries*, 132; *Rentale*, 198
54. *H.M.C. Report VIII* (Glasgow), 306
55. Stair muniments, Gd 135/78, temporary reference
56. Vatican archives, Reg. Supp., lv, 16 August 1544

57. *Ibid.*, 2528, fos 286r–v
58. *L.P. Henry VIII*, XIX, ii, 774
59. See Chapter 4, note 45
60. Vatican archives, Reg. Supp., 2486, fo 259v
61. *Muniments of the University of Glasgow*, II, 175
62. See Chapter 8, note 119
63. *Fasti*, 314
64. *R.M.S.*, III, 2788
65. *R.S.S.*, III, 50
66. *R.M.S.*, III, 3108
67. *Rentale*, 168–9

Part III

'Cairfull Cardinall'

'Of all Scotland I had the Governall;
But my awyse, concludit wes no thyng:
Abbot, Byschope, Archibyschope, Cardinall,
In to this Realme no hiear could I ryng,
Bot I had bene Pape, Emperour, or Kyng.
For schortnes of the tyme, I am nocht abyll
At lenth to schaw my actis honorabyll.'

Sir David Lindsay, *The Tragedie of the
Cardinall* (Scottish Text Society), lines 71–77

9

The Bid for Control

The fluctuation in relations which the Cardinal latterly experienced with the King was not unique to him. James, who has earned a posthumous reputation of 'the poor man's king' was 'ill-beloved' by many of his more substantious subjects. His avariciousness and vindictiveness, not to mention streak of cruelty, put the nobles in as much fear as the clergy. The reign was punctuated by fines, forfeitures and even the execution of members of prominent families, ostensibly on charges of communicating with the Douglases or plotting against the King, all of which greatly enriched the royal coffers. Prosecutions included those of Colville of East Wemyss, the comptroller, who paid £1,000 for his remission, and Adam Otterburn, the advocate. Relatives of the Douglases had to endure the King's vendetta long after Angus's banishment; Lady Glamis, Angus's sister, was burnt to death in 1537, the master of Forbes, his brother-in-law, was put to death in the same year (by the horrific English method of drawing, hanging and beheading) and Douglas of Parkhead was summoned on a charge of treason in 1540. Some felt that with the birth of his sons, in 1540 and 1541, the King became over-confident; the princes, however, died in infancy. The extant registers of the lords of council and session, admittedly relating more to judicial than administrative business, seem to substantiate the allegation made in 1540 that the nobles were excluded from his councils in favour of the clergy and lesser laymen, such as Henry Kemp of Thomastoun and David Wood of Craig, the latter becoming comptroller in 1538. It is significant that the Cardinal, himself an absentee from the council in 1540, gave large grants of church land to both of these officials — the archbishopric accounts recording a return gift from Kemp.[1]

In the summer of 1540, following Sir John Borthwick's condemnation, the King took the Cardinal, Huntly and Arran with him on a punitive voyage round the northern and western isles during which several chiefs were apprehended. David Beaton sailed in the *Mary Willoughby*, a captured English ship, and is said to have taken 500 men with him on his own expenses, feeing the mariners and provisioning those of his household who accompanied him.[2] His ability to command a following on this scale and his power to authorise any ecclesiastical sanctions that might be necessary probably explains why the King took him on the voyage. The followings mustered by Huntly and Arran must also have added to the impression made on the islesmen by the expedition — at no added cost to the King. By the autumn of 1540, however, it was rumoured that the Cardinal was less in the King's favour following the fall of Sir James Hamilton of Finnart, the royal master of works, who had been a friend of David Beaton and his tenant for land in the barony of Kirkliston.[3] Like other victims, Hamilton was accused of having plotted against the King and of being in touch with the Douglases, but it was widely believed that the King had mainly coveted his wealth, which turned out to include a hoard of gold. One reason for Hamilton's association with the Cardinal may have been Hamilton's responsibilities in connection with the prosecution of heretics, which are difficult to define but appear to have involved his appointment to a sheriffship.[4]

In late 1540 David Beaton spent much of his time away from the centre of politics at St Andrews.[5] Towards the end of the year, however, he returned to Edinburgh where he made his presence as archbishop felt by attending mass on St Andrew's Day at that saint's altar in St Giles' kirk, giving 22s to the choristers.[6] He was present in the parliament of early December but crossed to Fife to spend Christmas at St Andrews where he celebrated solemn mass in the cathedral on Christmas Day. He was one of the lords of the articles who met with the lords of session in February 1541 on five days before the opening of parliament.[7] Among the statutes which they framed, which were passed on 14 March, was a group of nine aimed at heresy and disregard of the church's authority.[8] The catalogue of punishable offences is a comment on the increase in the level of heretical activity since the act of 1525. The Pope's authority was to be upheld, the place of the Virgin Mary and the saints in doctrine and worship honoured, statues of the saints held in respect. In an attempt to deflect criticism and anti-clerical attacks a call was made both for the restoration of church buildings and for the reform of kirkmen in their 'habit and manners'. An effort was made to break up cells of Lutheranism and to stop the spread of shared beliefs by forbidding 'congregations or conventicles to commune or dispute of the holy scripture'. A social stigma and political ban was placed on even abjured heretics by denying them public office — a realistic admission of the unreliability of formal recantation. The friends and sympathisers of heretics who helped them to evade capture were to be made to feel the effects of the law while those who informed on them would be rewarded. The acts give a picture of attempts being made to contain a situation in which protestantism was more apparent than it had been in the 1520s, not only among academics and prominent figures at court and in certain burghs, but also where influential families were prepared to encourage its adherents in landward parts. The new legislation bore the stamp of the Cardinal's repressive policy, but unfortunately for him the pattern of events in public affairs postponed any attempt to mount an effective inquisition. It may have afforded the lay lawyers some satisfaction to see him charged, soon after parliament rose, with arrears of payment of over £700 towards the tax for the college of justice.[9]

A crisis in European politics in the summer of 1541 led to his last and longest visit to France as ambassador and, consequently, to a revival of the King's dependence on him. By July Charles V and Francis I were on the brink of war, a shift that always put bargaining power at the disposal of the English King and made James V apprehensive of losing his traditional ally. Knowing that the safety of vital trade routes would incline Henry towards an Imperial alliance, Francis felt it necessary to make the highest bid for English support. For some months in 1541 he held out a proposal for a marriage between Henry's daughter Mary and the duke of Orléans. At the same time Henry made another effort to win the co-operation of the King of Scots. After David Beaton had left Scotland at the end of July Henry sent Sadler once more to try to arrange a meeting with James, a meeting which at one point was put forward as a three-cornered conference between James, Henry and Francis.[10] James failed to keep an appointment planned for York, and Henry, having made the long journey north to no purpose, settled for more aggressive methods of consolidating the political front in the two kingdoms. Increased fortifications and outbreaks of hostility on the Anglo-Scottish border in the autumn of 1541 were a shadow of more warlike things to come.

For just over a year, from July 1541 to August 1542, the Scottish ambassador was away from home, keeping his finger on the diplomatic pulse, persuading the French King of James's loyal friendship and his unwillingness to co-operate in any way with his uncle of England, but pointing out that Scotland must have realistic French military help if she was to withstand the English forces already on her borders, which threatened not only her sovereignty as an ally but as a pocket of faithful Catholicism on the fringe of Christendom. Having failed to meet his uncle personally, James agreed to a conference of Anglo-Scottish commissioners to settle affairs on the border, but it is significant that the Scottish commissioners did not set out until they had received news of the international situation from the Cardinal in France. This uncertainty dragged on through the winter of 1541–2, requiring a close watch to be kept on developments. Letters passed between the King of Scots and his ambassador, the few that survive being chiefly concerned with inculcating patience in the King; 'I thank yor grace ryt humilie of yor gud and gracious writing send to me. I can do na forder for recompance bot I sall waire [spend] the body and guidis that god hes gevin me in yor gracis service with trew hert'.[11] At the end of November 1541 the Cardinal wrote to the King's secretary, Thomas Erskine of Brechin, with whom he had previously served as ambassador, that the French King had decided to send M. de Morvilliers to spy out the extent of the English fortifications on the border,[12] and in the spring of 1542 Paget informed Henry VIII that the admiral of France was ready to leave for Scotland after a conference with the Cardinal, a move which did not materialise.[13] It seems that David Beaton believed that whatever the moves at the time the traditional alliances would stand, and he worked hard to win a pledge of military support for Scotland, in vain as it turned out. He arrived home on 3 August from his longest and least effective embassy.

Everything was overshadowed that autumn by the rapid deterioration in Anglo-Scottish relations. Whatever the truth of the mutual accusations of aggression, a sharp turn was given to events in late August when a party under Sir Robert Bowes and including Angus and his brother, Sir George Douglas, was ambushed and overcome at Haddon Rigg while returning from a raid into Teviotdale.[14] The Douglases escaped but the important English captives were parcelled out among the bishops and their henchmen: Sir Robert Bowes and Sir Roger Lascelles were kept 'very straightly' in the Cardinal's castle at St Andrews, Richard Bowes and Thomas Slingsby were sent north to the bishop of Moray's castle at Spynie, Sir John Withrington was delivered to Oliver Sinclair of Pitcairns and Sir Cuthbert

Ratcliffe was sent to Archbishop Gavin Dunbar at Glasgow. Hertford, passing on this information to Henry VIII in mid-November, remarked that there would be peace were it not for the Scottish bishops.[15]

The prospect of war appealed to David Beaton inasmuch as it increased the distance between James V and his uncle and pushed further away the possibility of a meeting between them. In his correspondence with Rome he gave the hostilities the character of a holy war, telling the Pope that 'the only cause of the war is that the King will not revolt from the holy see and take part against the French King his father-in-law', an argument intended to put pressure on the Pope to encourage Francis I to support the King of Scots.[16] It must have been difficult, however, to remain sanguine in the face of France's clear reluctance to provide practical aid. Nevertheless, it was rumoured that the Cardinal hoped that the invasion of England would be sufficiently sustained to enable him to take over an English church in which to publish the seven-year-old papal bull against Henry.[17] Even although the collapse of the Pilgrimage of Grace nearly six years before had been a public triumph for Henry's administration and the Pope's later call for the bull to be implemented had come to nothing, the Cardinal must have hoped to cause sufficient disruption with his own proposed publication of it to give the council of the north something to think about other than Scottish harassment of the English border and the stalemate in negotiations for a meeting of the two monarchs. Ever since he had first offered to publish the bull, in 1536, at a time when he was in a position to know the attitude of English reactionaries, he had kept in mind the possibility of striking a public blow at the English administration, particularly in his prestigious, international role of Cardinal acquired at the end of 1538. He was never inclined to abandon an objective, as his chosen motto, 'Intentio, intentio', suggests, particularly if it might enhance his personal prestige.

Whatever he expected to happen, he joined the King's expedition to the borders which mobilised in November. Here, the English were already putting 'the enterprise' of Scotland into the first stages of operation as negotiations for the release of Bowes and the other detainees broke down.[18] The inhabitants of the borders, already harried by English raiding parties and now ordered by King James to supply horses to draw ordnance, 'exclaimed marvellously' against the King's requisition of sheep to feed his soldiers in the cold, wet autumn that followed by a bad harvest. Morale in the Scottish army itself was low and opinions were divided among the command as to the conduct of the campaign. A disturbing number of the King's vassals failed to muster, some of whom were known to be of Anglophile inclinations or at least in favour of peace between the two kingdoms.[19] Reports that the King had taunted his lords with faintheartedness hint at disagreements, even at altercations, between James and some of those who did accompany him.[20] Landholders on the marches, like Lord Maxwell, probably had misgivings about provoking wider English raids on the borders and Maxwell, in any case, who was openly known as 'a Lutheran' and was shortly to advocate the use of the English scriptures, was out of sympathy with the Cardinal's 'holy war'. Indeed, one of the main grievances of James's feudal captains was the prominence of ecclesiastics and confidants of the King in the planning of the campaign; when

King and Cardinal reached Selkirk Oliver Sinclair was dispatched to Home castle to confer with the men of the Merse.[21] The earl of Huntly, with whom the King was offended, was replaced as lieutenant by James's natural brother, the earl of Moray who, with the Cardinal, retired to Haddington to muster support in that quarter and await the King's decision as to the main route of the attack on England.[22]

Just as James's decision to raid the western marches was implemented, an international incident took place in the east as Somerset Herald, who had been sent north in mid-November to demand the release of Bowes and the other English prisoners but had been detained for over a week, was set upon and killed near Dunbar by three 'banished Englishmen', John Prestman, William Leitch and the latter's brother.[23] The attack was made in spite of the fact that the herald and his servant were accompanied by a Scottish pursuivant. The current association of the Cardinal's name with every anti-English activity gave rise to the allegation, which he later denied in council, that the murder of the herald had been 'with his sufferance'.[24] On 24 November a Scottish force reckoned at around 18,000 began to cross the Debateable Land in accordance with James's plan to invade the western marches and burn the country west of Carlisle. Incompetent leadership largely in the hands of the unpopular Oliver Sinclair and divided sympathies undermined the will of the army, and when confronted with an English force of probably a third their strength the Scots turned and began an ill-organised retreat which soon became a rout. Afterwards, some blamed Lord Maxwell for having deliberately created a panic during the retreat, making the Scottish flight irreversible.[25] Some Scots were drowned as they tried to cross the river Esk, others were set upon, robbed and slain by the opportunist inhabitants of Liddesdale. About 1200 were taken prisoner, including two earls, five barons and some 500 lairds and gentlemen.

The effect on the King of this humiliating end to the campaign was shattering. He left the borders for Edinburgh two days after Solway Moss, rode from the capital again on 30 November for Linlithgow where he spent about five days with the Queen who was awaiting the birth of their third child, and returned to Edinburgh on 5 December.[26] A week later he was at Falkland palace where he took to his bed, his health as well as his spirit broken. He did not rally when he learned that his child was a daughter, a marriageable commodity for the international market in which Scotland had not done very well of late. Reports filtering through to the English authorities during these weeks conveyed the atmosphere of shock and recrimination in the royal circle.[27] For the Cardinal, a leading advocate of the war, the débâcle brought discredit, jeopardising any ascendancy he might recently have gained. It was soon reported that the King had shown his displeasure with him and that in reply, possibly in desperation, he had offered to go again to France, to Rome if need be, to beg help for Scotland.[28] To those who cast aspersions on his Francophile policy, so recently a failure, he vowed that the King 'shall have party enough by the spring . . . as well forth of Denmark as other places'. Nevertheless, the thought of several hundred Scottish captives on English soil and the bargaining power that this could give Henry VIII must have preyed on his mind.

It was rumoured that some of the captives, including Lord Maxwell, 'would rather be Englishmen'. The Homes on the east march were said to be in touch with Angus. It looked as if some Scots were on the brink of making their own bargains with the English and, in fact, before long in the border area dozens of landholders, great and small, and many lesser men were 'assuring' themselves to facilitate the English hold on strategic points in southern Scotland in return for regular payment.[29] When King James died on 14 December, the tense situation was turned into a crisis and the country was plunged into the political toils of the second royal minority in thirty years.

The year 1543 saw David Beaton step to the front of the political stage. During the King's lifetime he had probably been more apprehensive about James's attitude towards him than his subsequent, prominent role might suggest or even his contemporaries may have guessed, although they were always quick to note his loss of royal favour. It was his value as a diplomat that saved his career at a time when friction with the King over resistance to the latter's fiscal demands and preference for Gavin Dunbar, the archbishop of Glasgow, might have jeopardised it. It was mainly in the diplomatic field that he had exercised a measure of independent action, although always in the King's interest. It was in Europe that he was referred to as 'the abbot whom one might call the king himself' and was later described as speaking 'more like a cardinal than as a partisan of Scotland or France'.[30] He acquired supremacy over the ecclesiastical estate in Scotland just after his greatest diplomatic successes but his relations with the King were less stable thereafter. The prosecution of heresy needed the King's concurrence, as demonstrated in the failure to take action against those on the list of heretics, and it has been argued that executions and the passing of penal legislation, although in the interest of the church, coincided with James's attempts to win concessions from the papacy. Even the often-requested grant of a legateship for the Cardinal was probably seen by the King as a way of increasing the Scottish church's ability to operate independently of Rome in financial terms. The demonstration of Scotland's vulnerability in international affairs, left to confront England single-handed in 1542, with its demoralising result, threatened David Beaton's continued influence with the King. James's unexpected death, however, left him free to make not only a personal impact on politics but a bid to control the direction taken by the ship of state, to steer her away from English waters and the new ideological argument for increased Anglo-Scottish amity that was to be found in the shoals of Lutheranism. Although at the first attempt his hand slipped on the tiller, he was to be in control again by the end of the year.

Unlike James IV before going off to battle in 1513, James V had made no formal arrangements for the government of the kingdom in the event of his own death in the campaign of 1542. There was debate at the time, as there has been doubt since, as to whether he even made his wishes clear at the last moment. In a state of nervous and physical collapse he was in no condition to give thought to matters of government but may have been able to indicate his approval or disapproval of proposals put to him. It was alleged afterwards, principally by the Cardinal, that he had in fact done so, but details are confusing and to some extent contradictory.

The man with best constitutional claim to be Governor on behalf of the week-old Queen was the 26-year old James Hamilton, second earl of Arran, heir-presumptive to the throne. Never had his family come so close to the crown since his grandfather had married the Princess Mary, daughter of King James II, in 1474. Unfortunately, never had the house of Hamilton produced a less suitable candidate in terms of initiative. Arran, in whom a certain self-preserving cunning served for gumption, not only found it impossible to make up his own mind about things but was notoriously prone to having it made up for him by other people, usually by whoever had spoken to him last. Like one of the characters in George Eliot's *Middlemarch*, the trouble with Arran was not that he could not be moulded but that he would not stay set. He was much given to voicing his opinions but it is doubtful whether his readiness to make them known was matched by the conviction with which he held them. He was clearly ideal as a figurehead, easily manipulated by a strong second-in-command who wanted his personal policies officially rubber-stamped, provided continuous pressure could be put upon him. At the same time he undoubtedly had considerable ambitions of his own.

The prospect of Arran as Governor must have given the Cardinal very mixed feelings if he thought about it during his vigil at the King's deathbed. Certainly, there were several reasons why he might hope to dominate him, quite apart from being nearly twice Arran's age and possessing all the resolution the other lacked. He knew Arran well as the son of his cousin, Janet Beaton of Creich, whom the first earl of Arran had married as his second wife. Moreover, he was in a position to remind Arran, if necessary, not only of the doubts cast on his legitimacy as the child of a second marriage which had followed on an annulment of doubtful validity but also that he himself, as primate and head of the ecclesiastical law courts in Scotland, had power to review and pronounce upon such matters. However dim or devious Arran might be, he at least knew which side his bread was buttered on. Another source of pressure, almost of blackmail if need be, was the fact that Arran's name is said to have headed the list of suspect heretics which, although the late King had declined to take action on it, was still a card in the Cardinal's hand. A public recantation would commit Arran to supporting the Cardinal's plans for the eradication of heresy. However, Arran's reputed unorthodoxy — he was quoted as saying that for the past five years he had considered the Pope to be no more than a bishop 'and that a very evil bishop' — was a double-edged weapon. There was the danger of his falling under the influence of the Anglophile party or worse still the influence of Henry VIII himself. It is doubtful if Arran had any real personal commitment to radical reform of the church but there were those whose reforming programme was more clear-cut than his own who might be prepared to use him as a figurehead. It must have seemed desirable to the Cardinal that Arran should not be given executive power.

On 18 December George Douglas was able to inform Lord Lisle that a meeting to choose governors was then taking place in Edinburgh.[31] It was believed that these would be Arran, Moray, Argyll and Huntly, with the Cardinal as 'governor of the princess and chief ruler of the council'. On 19 December a proclamation was read calling on the Queen's subjects to give obedience to these five.[32]

Characteristically, David Beaton personally attended the public reading of the proclamation in Edinburgh, no doubt to judge the mood in which it was received. If he had hoped to keep Arran out of the government altogether he had had to compromise, being astute enough to avoid antagonising a potential opposition at this stage.

It was not long before stories were circulating about the so-called 'will' of the late King in the matter of the regencies. Two days after the proclamation Lisle told the English council that he had heard that King James had not only willed that Arran, Moray, Argyll and Huntly should be governors, 'and the Cardinal to be of the council with them', but that he had also wished the Douglases to be brought home, a forgiving gesture that would scarcely have pleased the Cardinal.[33] By 22 or 23 December an English priest who had been sent to James by Lisle and had already received a written reply from the Scottish council was told by Arran in a private interview that the Cardinal, in whose arms the King had died, 'hath told the council many things in the King's name which he [Arran] thinketh is all lies and so will prove'.[34] Arran did not reveal what these 'things' were but objection to them was no doubt reflected in the growing resistance to David Beaton's authority in the council. By the end of December Arran and he had openly quarrelled; it may have been during a debate over the communication of the King's last wishes that Arran drew his sword on the primate, calling him 'false churl', so that others present had to separate them.[35] The force of Arran's outburst hints at frustration at being under Beaton's control. Shortly afterwards, in a second interview, Arran told the English priest to 'resort not to the Cardinal but to the chancellor, the bishop of Glasgow', Gavin Dunbar.[36]

On 3 January a meeting was held, the formal records of which have not survived, at which Arran was made sole Governor, superseding the joint regency proclaimed just over two weeks before.[37] The meeting, which is believed to have been a convention of the estates, must have been hurriedly arranged; Huntly, one of the regents thus deposed, was absent in the north when it took place. Writing long afterwards, George Buchanan stated that Arran was made Governor by 'a private party'.[38] If there is any truth in this assertion, the 'party' may have drawn its strength from various elements: resistance to the Cardinal's attempt to impose his authority on the council, a desire among some for the return of the Douglases and for co-operation with England in bringing about a settlement in relations between the two countries, to do which it was necessary to remove from the regency those who had supported the late King's war policy, with a certain impetus from those who were personally committed to protestantism and wished for a more radical reform of the church than had hitherto been contemplated by the prelates. John Knox asserts that the laird of Grange was one of those who encouraged Arran to call the assembly at which his 'just title' to be Governor was accepted.[39] The Cardinal and his party objected to the rule of one man and warned of the risk in vesting all power in the house of Hamilton, but they lost the debate. Arran's 'simple' demeanour in a speech asking for the opportunity to prove his intention of ruling justly, without favour to his kinsmen, created some euphoria among the radicals, among whom 'it was bruited that he favoured God's word'.[40]

If the Cardinal had had to compromise in accepting Arran in the joint regency, the latter's appointment as sole Governor was an even more serious setback. It has been suggested that his acquiescence — although if Arran's party was increasing its pressure he may have had little choice — was the result of a bargain between Arran and himself. Beaton's share was the office of chancellor and with it a reduction in the influence of his rival, Gavin Dunbar. If, however, the opposition was strong enough to achieve Arran's appointment as sole Governor, it is doubtful if the Cardinal could have had enough power to gain the chancellorship simply by asking for it, especially at the expense of Dunbar whom Arran at this time seems to have preferred as a mentor. Was there some source of extraordinary pressure at the Cardinal's disposal?[41] After all, something is needed to explain why Arran, having quarrelled with David Beaton at the end of December, advising the English agent to avoid him and accusing him of lying to the council, nevertheless had handed him the great seal by 10 January. When asked by Lisle how it had come about, Sir George Douglas simply said that the Cardinal had demanded it and Arran had complied;[42] whatever pressure was brought to bear was a secret between them. Could it have been evidence that the King had not willed Arran's appointment at all and that he was in office without warrant?

The only piece of documentation relating to the King's wishes is a notarial instrument, surviving in the Hamilton archives, which purports to have been taken in the King's presence before witnesses, in which the Cardinal, Moray, Huntly and Argyll are nominated governors — with no mention of Arran.[43] The document, dated 14 December, is under the hand of sir Henry Balfour who shortly afterwards joined the Cardinal's household, who 'wes nevir notar' according to an erroneous endorsement on the instrument. The fact that some of the eleven witnesses were not David Beaton's friends lends it an air of authenticity. The drawing up of instruments in the presence of the sick King is referred to by Knox who states that in James's extremity the Cardinal 'cries in his ear, "Take order, Sir, with your realm: who shall rule it during the minority of your daughter? Ye have known my service: what will ye have done? Shall there not be four Regents chosen? And shall I not be prinicpal of them?" Whatsoever the King answered, documents were taken that so should be as my lord Cardinal thought expedient'.[44] The episode is also mentioned in a report of Lisle on 5 January. Lisle had been told by one Archibald Douglas that when the King was no longer able to speak and 'had no perfect reason' the Cardinal asked him if he would choose Arran, Huntly, Argyll and Moray as governors, to which the King did not reply, 'but the Cardinal reported otherwise'.[45] Although the Lisle version of what the Cardinal asked the King differs from Knox's later account in that Lisle mentions Arran by name, the inference in both stories is that he included himself in interpreting the King's wishes. The Balfour document may be one of the instruments taken. If the witnesses had quibbled about the veracity of the instrument it would have been their word against that of the Cardinal as to what the King had actually indicated, and since David Beaton had supported the King in his extremity he could insist that he had been in the best position to interpret James's reply. Of the witnesses named in the instrument, two might have been as near to the King as the Cardinal, his physician, Dr Michael Durham, and his apothecary, Francis Aikman, both of whom were said to be Lutheran in sympathy. If they had felt inclined to dispute the truth of the instrument taken in their presence they were saved the trouble when Arran was proclaimed with the other regents within a week of the King's death. Thus it took the party to which they adhered only one week to achieve Arran's inclusion in the government, with the proclamation of 19 December, and another two weeks to put authority completely in his hands.

The 'lies' which the Cardinal was alleged to have told the council, which angered Arran so much, were presumably to the effect that the King had wished only four regents of whom Arran was not one. However, after the compromise of the joint regency in December and the more serious setback of Arran's personal appointment to the governorship early in January, David Beaton may have confronted Arran with *written* evidence, in the form of the Balfour instrument, of his earlier verbal assertion made in council.[46] However much he might deprecate the document, Arran could not afford to ignore it in case the Cardinal and his party regained the upper hand and used it to deprive him of office. David Beaton for his part, having lost ground through Arran's appointment and a certain loss of face before the Anglophile-reforming party, may have produced the document as a piece of blackmail in order to gain the long-coveted chancellorship and with it an increase of status in the secular administration to match his ecclesiastical pre-eminence. That the great seal and the Balfour instrument changed hands seems a plausible explanation of how the document came to survive in Arran's family papers. If it seems strange that the Governor, having got it, did not immediately burn it, we have only to recall the occasion when he publicly handed David Beaton, by mistake, a letter in which Lisle spelled out how the latter might be dealt with, to realise that the Governor did not always do the wisest thing with his papers.[47] Not until the following April did Arran put about the story that the Cardinal had forged a will in the King's name.[48] The charge was never formally levelled nor had the Cardinal ever produced in council written evidence of the King's wishes, only verbal statements. Arran's story that he had caused the dying King to sign a 'blank' which he then filled up to his own satisfaction can probably be discounted; the allegation is repeated by Knox who may have got it from someone in the Hamilton's circle. At any rate, the Balfour document is not signed but is in the standard form of a notarial instrument.

David Beaton's hope of achieving political ascendancy lay in keeping the Governor under his personal influence, however much this was resented. At first he was successful to the extent that in mid-January it was reported that 'the Cardinal is everything in Scotland'.[49] Since the end of the previous year he had been trying to buy the support of the Anglophile, religiously-suspect party, with charters and tacks of church property to Norman Leslie, son of the earl of Rothes,[50] to Melville of Raith[51] and to Mr Henry Balnaves.[52] Clearly, he was conscious of opposition. At the same time he strengthened the fortifications of St Andrews castle in the wake of the Solway Moss campaign. However strong his position might appear, time was not on his side. Arran's 'private party' and those who favoured amity with England and a Henrician-type 'reformation' of the church that would clip the wings of the clergy, with their legal immunities and Francophile politics, were considerably strengthened in morale when on 12 January Sir George Douglas slipped over the border to be followed shortly afterwards by his brother, the earl of Angus, and the Solway prisoners on parole, pledged to set forward the English King's plans for Scotland.[53]

It must have seemed to the Cardinal as if history was repeating itself. However, certain aspects of 'the Douglas factor' the second time round made the situation more dangerous than the first time. By now there was a growing idealogical basis for Anglo-Scottish co-operation in the desire for church reform as practised by Henry VIII and his agents in England. The Anglophiles were not simply the political and military leaders but a cross-section of the laity and clergy, some of whom had spent time in England in exile for reasons of religious dissent. Over and above this Sir George Douglas, who was about to take an active part in developments, was a far more astute politician than Angus had ever been. It is significant that David Beaton recognised his match in Sir George right from the start; during his first brief encounter with the younger Douglas the Cardinal was observed to sigh with exasperation as Sir George parried his question as to whether he was 'a good Christian' in spite of having lived in England.[54] Their intermittent attempts to catch each other off guard, under the guise of negotiations, shows that they had taken the measure of each other. It was Sir George Douglas who primed the Governor about the opposition's intended *coup*. If Scottish policy was to take a definite turn towards England in matters of church and state, the first thing to ensure was that Arran was taken out of the Cardinal's sphere of influence. On 27 January David Beaton was arrested in council, ostensibly for being too ready to invite French intervention in Scotland, and removed from the court.[55] In the contest for control since the King's death he had lost the first round.

NOTES

1. *Rentale*, 107

2. *Ibid.*, 102, 108; *L.P.Henry VIII*, XV, 634

3. *Hamilton Papers*, I, 57

4. M. Mahoney, 'The Scottish Hierarchy', 70; G Donaldson, *Scotland: James V to James VII*, 58–9

5. See Itinerary, Appendix 2

6. *Rentale*, 109

7. *A.P.S..*, II, 368; the accounts of the graniter of St Andrews were rendered at Edinburgh on 14 February, *Rentale*, 98

8. *A.P.S.*, II, 368

9. A.D.C.S., xv, fos 102r–v

10. *L.P. Henry VIII*, XVI, 990, 1130

11. *S.H.R.* 'Beaton letters', 158

12. *L.P. Henry VIII*, XVI, 1378

13. *Ibid.*, XVII, 232

14. Donaldson, *James V to James VII*

15. *L.P. Henry VIII*, XVII, 1100 (2), (4)

16. *Ibid.*, XVII, 1072

17. *Hamilton Papers*, I, 245

18. *L.P. Henry VIII*, XVII, 998, 1025; *Hamilton Papers*, I, 224, 226, 231

19. Donaldson, *All the Queen's Men*, 14

20. For details of the campaign, *L.P. Henry VIII*, XVII, 1039, 1100, 1105, 1117; Donaldson, *James V to James VII*, 59

21. *L.P. Henry VIII*, XVII, 1117; G. A. Sinclair, 'The Scots at Solway Moss', in *S.H.R.*, 11, 372–7

22. *L.P. Henry VIII*, XVII, 1124, 1136

23. *Ibid.*, XVII, 1140

24. *Hamilton Papers*, I, 257, 267

25. *L.P. Henry VIII*, XVII, 1207; Donaldson, *James V to James VII*, 60

26. *Calderwood*, I, 150–1

27. *L.P. Henry VIII*, XVII, 1199, 1221

28. *Ibid* XVII, 1193

29. M. Merriman, 'The Assured Scots', in *S.H.R.*, XLVII, 1–34

30. Herkless and Hannay, *Archbishops*, IV, 22, 62

31. *Hamilton Papers*, I, 260

32. *Ibid.*, I, 265; *L.P. Henry VIII*, XVII, 1233

33. *Hamilton Papers*, I, 263

34. *Ibid.*, I, 267

35. *Ibid.*

36. For a discussion of the power struggle at this time see A. Lang, 'The Cardinal and the King's will', in *S.H.R..*, III, 410 *et seq.*

37. *Hamilton Papers*, I, 273

38. Lang, 'The Cardinal and the King's will'.

39. *Knox*, I, 41

40. *Ibid.*

41. Lang, 'The Cardinal and the King's will'.

42. The Cardinal's appointment as chancellor, *R.S.S.*, III, 21

43. *H.M.C. Report XI*, vi (Hamilton), 219–20

44. *Knox*, I, 40

45. *Hamilton Papers*, I, 272

46. Lang, 'The Cardinal and the King's will'.

47. *Hamilton Papers*, I, 285

48. Lang, 'The Cardinal and the King's will'.

49. *L.P. Henry VIII*, XVIII, i, 44

50. Collection of Messrs Shepherd and Wedderburn (S.R.O.), GD 242/69/1

51. Leven and Melville muniments (S.R.O.) GD 26/3/900

52. *Rentale*, 118

53. Herkless and Hannay, *Archbishops*, IV, 85–8

54. *Ibid.*, 88

55. *Hamilton Papers*, I, 289; on 26 January Sir George Douglas wrote to Lisle that if Arran were sure of peace with England he would put hands on the Cardinal and reform the whole church as Henry had reformed that in England, *L.P. Henry VIII*, XVIII, i, 81

10

The Cardinal and the Governor

In a sense the ensuing struggle to control the situation in 1543 or even to gain advantage from it resolved itself into the need to control the Governor. Undoubtedly, Arran was easily manipulated and was of the type who finds it difficult to take decisions and stand by them. However, the problem was more complex than that for he did have his own considerable ambitions and his priority was to maintain his position as heir-presumptive and natural Governor for the Queen. Any threat to that right influenced his actions above all else. The atmosphere of uncertainty which surrounded him, successor to the tension that had surrounded James V, stemmed not only from his congenital hesitancy but from the fact that those around him could never be sure whether or not he was really committed to their plans. Aware that he was being used, he spent his time evading commitment to policies which in any way might threaten his interests. This was largely where his notorious 'inconstancy' lay.

Henry VIII's proposals, as agreed to by the freed Solway captives, could not have comforted the Governor when he heard of them for, if they were to be fully implemented, they would reduce him to a figurehead.[1] The real power would be Henry's: only persons of *his* choice would surround the Queen until she was removed to England to be married to Prince Edward. There was provision for an English military presence in Scotland, for the removal of Arran from the Scottish political scene if he would not co-operate and the prospect of Henry's direct rule in the event of Mary's death. At the same time Henry himself must have been uneasy about the possibility of Arran's succeeding to the throne of Scotland should the Queen die before the marriage arrangements were completed. The house of Hamilton had never been nearer to succession and Arran was in no mood to compromise the sovereignty of Scotland. The situation was the Governor's opportunity as well as Henry's.

The second unsettling element in 1543 was the historically unnatural alliance of Hamilton and Douglas. This was accepted by Arran because of Douglas support for the party that had got him the sole governorship. He may also have derived some moral support from the knowledge that tactically Sir George Douglas was a match for the Cardinal at a time when the latter was humiliating him. It is doubtful, however, whether the Governor, with his desire to keep the kingdom out of Henry VIII's clutches, could have entirely shared the feelings of the Douglases who out of self-interest were prepared to address the English King as 'sovereign lord', and who had pledged themselves to help Henry take over in the event of the Queen's death.

Thirdly, there was Arran's ambivalent attitude to those who wished to implement reform in the church. He probably would not have objected to a

160

Henrician reform of the church's property rights provided his own family got a lion's helping, which they were to do over the next decade through ecclesiastical offices, commendatorships and feu charters which ultimately extended their landed interests from Ayrshire to Angus.[2] No doubt he would be agreeable to a lessening of clerical influence in government and law courts and would be happy to see the fangs of canon law drawn, since the church took a critical view of his own legitimacy. However, it is questionable whether his reputed sympathy with protestantism was real enough to satisfy or assist the small but socially influential group of religious dissenters. He probably distrusted the subversive influence of heresy as much as did Henry VIII himself. Yet the reform party were glad of his outward co-operation with their programme, although time was to show that the 'reformation experiment' of 1543, dubbed 'the Governor's godly fit', which included the public appointment in some places of protestant preachers, had been their experiment rather than his. Its collapse in the autumn of that year, after Arran's *volte face*, was to leave them frustrated and their humbler followers vulnerable before the conservative backlash.

Clearly, in the month of February those who were apparently working together were not all of one mind. At the beginning of that month Lisle reported to Suffolk that 'the appearance of dissension is great'.[3] In spite of prodding from Henry VIII the Anglophile party could not find it in their power to arrange the transfer of strategic Scottish castles to English hands.[4] At the same time the Douglases' understandable haste in calling for a parliament at which their own rights would be restored was reprimanded by Henry who told them, through Lisle, that they ought to have consulted him in the first place. Henry was astute enough to suspect that having got themselves on the right side of the border and having gained Arran's ear, the Douglases' concern for their own rehabilitation was likely to take precedence over everything else; their independent tone comes over in the reassurances they sent him that they were well able to keep control of the Scottish castles without handing them over to the English.[5] Lisle in the meantime tried to frighten the Governor into sending David Beaton to Berwick *via* Tantallon by telling him that the Cardinal's party were putting their heads together to make trouble for him at the coming parliament.[6]

Although they included a commission to negotiate the marriage treaty with England, the proceedings of the parliament that met in mid-March were not entirely to Henry's liking.[7] Their tone was one of determination to safeguard Scotland's sovereignty, the rights of her native ruler and the position of Arran as 'secund persoun of this realme and narrest to succede to the crone of the samin falyeing of our sovirane lady and the barnis lauchfullie to be gottin . . . of hir body and nane utheris and be ressoun thairof tutour lauchfull to the quenis grace and governour of this realme'. The ratification of Arran's governorship was enacted. The earnestness of Angus's plea for clearer acknowledgement of Henry's claims over Scotland and the Queen was tempered by the grant of a reversal of his own attainder and the reinstatement of himself and his brother as Scottish subjects and landholders. The bill brought forward by Lord Maxwell, 'that it salbe lefull to all our sovirane ladyis leiges to have the haly write baith the new testament and the auld in the vulgar toung in Inglis or Scottis ... provyding alwayis that na man despute or hald [ie. openly] oppunyeonis under the panis contenit in the actis of parliament ... ', was formally accepted by the lords of the articles, although some of them must have felt less than enthusiastic about it, and enacted in spite of a divided assembly, to the satisfaction of the Anglophile lords but the outrage of the first estate on whose behalf Gavin Dunbar, archbishop of Glasgow, protested against it. The act was proclaimed publicly, in respect of the new testament only, by the clerk register on the Governor's instructions.[8]

The unfinished business of the Cardinal's detention was itself a cause of discord and mistrust and its handling suggested that Arran was drifting away from commitment to the Douglases' programme. At most, the arrest had been a move to get David Beaton out of the way while negotiations with England went ahead for, in spite of Arran's allegations in a private conversation, there never seemed any likelihood of the Cardinal's being formally charged with an offence, still less punished. He had too much support for the party in power to risk that; even Angus hesitated to send him to Henry. The fear of the party now in power, and of the English authorities, was that the Cardinal would make contact with Arran and reassert his influence over him, even before Anglo-Scottish negotiations could properly begin. In mid-February Lisle had sent a spy who had lived in France and knew David Beaton's servants by sight to keep a look-out for any coming and going between them and the Governor's household.[9] In fact, the conditions of the Cardinal's imprisonment became increasingly lax, as he was removed in February from the Douglas castle of Dalkeith to the house of his friend, Lord Seton, where he received an official communication from Arran,[10] some visitors who included the formerly disgraced earl of Bothwell,[11] and had the services of his personal staff[12] and transacted a certain amount of diocesan business.[13] In his own account of these weeks, the Cardinal attributed the transfer to Seton castle to the 400 crowns he gave to Sir George Douglas.[14] Lisle's request to Arran on 13 February that the Cardinal be sent to England was ignored, the Governor remarking with a laugh that 'the Cardinal would leifer go into hell',[15] and the suggestion that some learned man 'addict to the truth' be appointed commissary in the archdiocese of St Andrews 'with promise of succeeding' was not taken up, although the accompanying hint to 'let slip' the bible among the people, copies being supplied from England, was to be implemented by parliament a few weeks later.[16]

One reason for hesitancy in dealing with the Cardinal was fear of provoking a reaction among those who favoured him and resented the return of the Douglases; the latter had been particularly anxious to avoid trouble until their own reinstatement had been formally ratified by parliament. While the Governor and Angus were reassuring their English correspondents that the Cardinal would remain in ward, they were aware of a growing cohesion among those who were on his side at this time and were demanding his release – the bishops, understandably, and Argyll, Moray and Huntly who still resented their removal from power.[17] A close watch was kept on those drifting into the Cardinal's sphere of influence, like Bothwell, who was in need of rehabilitation himself, and some of the Scotts and

Kers, who were in a position to make trouble for the English in the vital area of the borders.[18] As the Cardinal's supporters retreated to their home bases, having failed to get a response to their demand for his release, it was feared that they might be organising more militant opposition.[19]

Contemporary sources hint at a wider support for the Cardinal and alienation from the ruling party. In the political heartland the antipathy of ordinary people towards England was exacerbated by the withdrawal of spiritual services by the clergy of St Andrews archdiocese in protest at the primate's arrest;[20] the clerical mood was probably one factor that made the appointment of a reform-minded commissary impossible. Who the 'commonalty' were who were said to resent the Cardinal's arrest it is hard to say, but they are unlikely to have been those entirely without influence or awareness of political moves; it was said that they 'grudgeth moche his keeping in pryson', saying that the Governor was a good man 'till he rounded with therle Anguishe and his broder'.[21] It is possible that someone as ubiquitous and frequently to be seen as David Beaton, whose strong hand conveyed a certain reassurance to vulnerable folk within his sphere of influence, may have attracted a measure of the popular support that authoritarian rulers often gain, who can charm the harmless while harming their own opponents.

During March he was transferred to the state prison at Blackness, but still under the guardianship of Lord Seton and still receiving occasional official communications from Arran as Governor.[22] Amid protests from English agents and threats from their master, King Henry, he was removed to his own castle of St Andrews at the end of the month.[23] The Governor maintained that this gave *him* power to take control of an important fortification, yet the castle was garrisoned with the Cardinal's men. Clearly, Arran's resolution to keep him prisoner in sure ward was crumbling, if it had not already done so. In effect, David Beaton was his own master in his own stronghold, able to establish open communication with others in the political game, including Sadler, the English ambassador, and Sir George Douglas.[24] At Easter, 11 April, he celebrated mass in the cathedral of St Andrews, proclaiming the return to normality in ecclesiastical affairs, and on the following day he made an offering of 22s to 'the arm of St Andrew' in a public, symbolic gesture of thanksgiving for his freedom.[25] A week later, on 18 April, he rewarded his ally and erstwhile 'gaoler', Lord Seton, with a feu charter of land in the episcopal barony of Kirkliston.[26] Whatever the state of his information on the progress of events and the fluctuations of personal alliances, he had had time to take stock and devise ways of breaking down the current English initiative in Scottish affairs. To this end full advantage would have to be taken of every vested interest in the situation: the concern of the French Queen Mother for the safety and rights of her daughter (it was said that she and Huntly had influenced Arran into transferring the Cardinal to Lord Seton's custody which had been the beginning of the end of his imprisonment), the dynasticism of the inconstant Governor, the solidarity which the threat to ecclesiastical authority gave to the hierarchy, the antipathy towards England of less influential folk, even the short-term advantages to be gained by a bribe or gift.

Throughout the late spring and summer the Cardinal gathered his forces and used every tactic in a war of nerves against Arran with two main objectives, to gain custody of the Queen and damage the negotiations with England. All parties temporised as the Scottish commissioners left for London and the Cardinal regained his initiative in public affairs. Sadler, the English ambassador, sent on to Henry VIII 'every man's tale in such sort as I hear them', without attempting to interpret motives or judge the reliability of his contacts.[27] The Governor himself, in response to Henry VIII's wishes, having complied with the recommendation to circulate the English scriptures, was hesitant over the more radical step of seizing monastic property, saying that while this might be justifiable on theological grounds, only a share of the spoils would bring the great 'papists and pharisees to agree to it' and, in any case, it would be best left until a final peace between the two realms had been established. He acknowledged the high honour Henry did him by offering his daughter, Elizabeth, as a wife for his son and admitted his 'mistake' in allowing Lord Seton to take charge of the Cardinal who was now at liberty.[28] He professed himself to be at a loss what to do next, which admission as well as revealing a characteristic state of mind implies Arran's reluctance to unquestioningly obey Henry's instructions.

Sir George Douglas told Sadler of his equally unsatisfactory interview with the Cardinal at St Andrews.[29] The latter had promised to be 'at the Governor's commandment' and to offer his body to trial if need be to prove his innocence of any charges against him. He maintained that although reputed 'a good Frenchman' he was a good Scotsman at heart and would not play France's game to the extent of neglecting 'the wealth and commodity of this realm'. It is remarkable how egotists, even at their most plausible, reveal glimpses of their real selves; David Beaton's protestations to Sir George Douglas hold a kernel of character, for after Arran's capitulation to him in the autumn he was always at pains to associate the Governor with himself in his public actions, thus imparting to them a visible constitutionality . At the same time, although France was a valuable ally in defying English infiltration, he was not prepared to put Scotland at French disposal unconditionally. In any case, both by temperament and experience he always guarded an area of freedom of movement around himself so long as he had the advantage and, when circumstances were less favourable, he was capable of withdrawing himself from the scene of action until matters sorted themselves out more to his liking. His reputation for being 'wily' stemmed from much the same source as the Governor's 'inconstancy': the common one of safeguarding freedom of action.

To Sadler personally he sent word that he hoped for peace between the two kingdoms, denying responsibility for having encouraged the late King to pursue war, and wished that an Anglo-Scottish union might be worked out to the benefit of both countries.[30] Mary of Guise, making her own contribution to the general deception of the English ambassador, had already told Sadler that had the Cardinal had the arranging of the marriage alliance he would have made a better job of it. She assured the disbelieving ambassador that the Cardinal 'was a wise man and could better consider the benefit of the realm than all the rest'.[31] Lord Fleming, who had joined Henry's party after Solway Moss, told Sadler realistically that if Henry did not soon get hold of the Queen, or sufficient pledges for performance of the Scottish part of the alliance, the marriage would never take place at all. He said he suspected that Arran was not genuinely in favour of the English match and remarked bitterly that if Henry was unable to implement his plans he, Fleming, would blame the Douglases for establishing the unsatisfactory Arran as Governor.[32] In a few weeks the disillusioned Lord Fleming was to change sides.

It was against this background of distrust and cross-purposes that the Scottish commissioners travelled to London to meet Henry VIII and his council in the second week of April.[33] Just as the first phase of English initiative, although gaining practical support at underground level, failed to achieve an official presence through the Governor's reluctance to hand over Scottish castles or remove the Cardinal from the political arena altogether, so now the negotiations themselves revealed the Scottish wariness in the face of Henry's demands. Not even the Douglases' apparent leadership of public policy could hide the reluctance of the estates, in the instructions to their commissioners, to come to terms with the English King without important safeguards. They stood firm on the points that the Queen should remain in Scotland until she was of marriageable age, that Arran should continue as Governor during her minority and that thereafter Scotland should have a native-born governor, retain her own laws and customs and keep control of Scottish castles, at least until the Queen and Prince Edward had children, in other words until Arran was no longer next in line to the Scottish throne. They refused to compromise the existing treaties with France, since these represented a second line of defence should Henry's involvement in Scottish affairs ever flare up into military aggression. Their determination to preserve Scotland's sovereignty in all decisions relating to the marriage infuriated Henry who demanded that the Queen should be sent to England within two years to be properly educated as the wife of a future king of England, that Arran's governorship should terminate with her minority, after which the election of a Scottish governor was to be at the discretion of Henry and his son and the Scottish castles were to be held by men of *their* choice. When word of these demands reached Scotland, Arran swore he would rather have war than agree to them — not surprisingly.[34] Amid the recriminations Sir Adam Otterburn, the Cardinal's friend, who changed his attitude to the future alignment of Scotland and England when he saw how far Henry threatened to go, told Sadler bluntly that had England had 'the lass' and Scotland 'the lad' Henry would not have been so anxious for the union.[35] While the haggling went on, which in itself demonstrated some weakness in the position of the Anglophile party, matters in Scotland were working in favour of the Cardinal, providing him with capital to invest in the 'patriotic', orthodox reaction to a possible English intervention.

During the spring of 1543 two people arrived in Scotland from France, to some extent with encouragement from the Cardinal, who each in his own way was able to put pressure on the Governor to reconsider his English policy. The first was Matthew, 4th earl of Lennox, then aged 26 and still unmarried, with whom there returned the spectre of Arran's doubtful legitimacy. If Arran was not legitimate, then Lennox, as a descendant on the female side of the Princess Mary, daughter of James II, and her husband, Lord Hamilton, was heir-presumptive to the crown of Scotland. The other arrival was Arran's natural brother, John Hamilton, then abbot of Paisley but aiming at higher things in his career. If the presence of Lennox was a publicly unnerving factor for the Governor, the advice of John Hamilton, who was in the Cardinal's confidence, became a private unsettling influence, one of the first signs of which was the Governor's dismissal of his recently-appointed protestant preachers.[36] Lennox made early contact with Mary of Guise who was by now emerging as a participant in the political manoeuvres in her own right and was trying to effect the removal of the Queen and herself from Linlithgow to her own more secure and strategic jointure-house of Stirling. The earl of Lennox had also been given the impression by the Cardinal that a dynastic marriage might be a possibility for him, either with the Queen Dowager or, although he was a quarter of a century her senior, with the Queen herself.[37]

Angus encouraged the Governor to try detaching Lennox from the Cardinal's party by allowing the earl to attend the June parliament while preventing the Cardinal from coming to Edinburgh, although David Beaton had no intention of doing so in any case. Lennox came to the parliament as the French ambassador, asking for a renewal of the treaties with France. He refused to acknowledge Arran's governorship, however, declining to sign the act which ratified his appointment, and instead went west to fortify Dumbarton castle.[38] This gave Arran a pretext for treating him as a traitor to his authority as Governor and for proceeding against him. While Angus worked on Lennox to give in, the Cardinal wrote to him advising him to adopt his own tactic of withdrawal in order to avoid prosecution or even arrest. Leaving Dumbarton well garrisoned, Lennox withdrew northwards. Once he was in a safety zone the Cardinal marshalled his own resources which had already included an appeal to France for military assistance should the Anglo-Scottish negotiations break down and war seem likely.[39] He also called a provincial council of the church in May, with the Governor's permission, at which the prelates promised to make a contribution of money and plate towards a war effort if necessary. Amid the clergy's relief at the Cardinal's release some of them professed themselves ready to fight if need be.[40] Even allowing for David Beaton's characteristically belligerent reaction to the situation, there was a good deal of tension in the air.

In June he himself rode into Angus to mobilise support and await the arrival of a promised French fleet, which appeared off Aberdeen and then Arbroath by the end of June and between Leith and St Abb's Head early in July.[41] The sight did not augur well for a peaceful conclusion of the Anglo-Scottish peace and marriage treaties the terms of which were completed in London on 1 July.[42] Publicly, Henry made grudging concessions to certain Scottish stipulations, including acknowledgement of the existing Franco-Scottish treaties and the postponment of the Queen's removal to England until her tenth year. Privately, however, he entered into certain 'devises' with the Douglases and Glencairn as to more direct methods of a takeover of Scottish affairs.[43] In July there was another council of the church of which little is known but at which the Governor's 'misguiding' of his office and liaison with heretics were deplored.[44] Ecclesiastical pressure had already caused Arran to prohibit the printing and circulation of the heretical and subversive literature which had accompanied the period of official approval of reform of the church.[45] By the middle of the month it was said that the Cardinal's party was numerically and in terms of prestige stronger than that of the Governor and the Douglases, although David Beaton, who was wise enough not to take support at its face value, was said to have received into his household, in effect as hostages, the sons or other kinsmen of the earls of Lennox, Huntly, Bothwell and Montrose.[46]

On 20 July he and members of his party met at Stirling, the uppermost consideration in his mind being the need to remove the Queen and her mother which if accomplished would be a serious loss of face for the Governor at the time of the ratification of the treaties with England.[47] Late the following night, with a force said to have numbered 6–7,000 men, the followers of himself and his associates, he came to Linlithgow only to find that the palace had been fortified by Arran, making it impossible to gain access to the Queens.[48] The Cardinal fell back on negotiation but not before he and his company had signed on 24 July a mutual bond to defend the realm and protect the Queen in the face of the English King's plans.[49] The Linlithgow bond was signed by eleven clergy, including the Cardinal himself but not the archbishop of Glasgow, six earls, eight lords and the sons of two lords, and twenty lairds. The extent of their commitment to the Cardinal and his conservative policy, however, must have varied. The clergy's support may be taken for granted but they had not all necessarily made a special effort to be with him at this time, for several of them were often in his circle and frequently witnessed his transactions: this applies to Bishop William Chisholm of Dunblane; Bishop Patrick Hepburn of Moray; the Cardinal's cousin Andrew Durie, bishop of Galloway; Bishop Robert Reid of Orkney; Andrew Hume, abbot of Jedburgh, the Cardinal's chaplain; and John Roull, prior of Pittenweem. The Erskine commendator of Dryburgh was doubtless there in the company of Lord Erskine, the Fleming prior of Whithorn in that of Lord Fleming, the Campbell abbot of Coupar Angus in that of the earl of Argyll, and the Dunbar prior to Pluscarden in that of Alexander Dunbar of Cumnock. It is possible, of course, that the Cardinal had taken the opportunity of the recent church council to rally clerical support for a political move of this kind.

The earl of Huntly no doubt accounted for his cousin, the earl of Sutherland, Gordon of Scheves, to whom the Cardinal had recently granted a substantial tack of teinds,[50] and possibly his fellow north-countryman Leslie of Boquhan. The earl of Argyll accounted for Campbell of Calder and Campbell of Lundy, the earl of Lennox for Buchanan of that ilk and, perhaps, Colquhoun of Luss, the earl of Bothwell for the signatory simply designated Patrick Hepburn. John, Lord Lyle was the husband of the Cardinal's cousin, Grizel Beaton of Creich, Robert Douglas of Lochleven was his tenant and Stirling of Keir was married to a daughter of the bishop of Dunblane. There were some whose support was significant, however, such as the disillusioned pensioner of Henry VIII, Lord

Fleming, and the keeper of the castles of Edinburgh and Stirling, Lord Erskine. The support of Huntly, from the north, and Argyll, from the west, was of longer standing, reinforced by their resentment at having been ousted from the government by Arran. The borders contingent was important. Lord Home representing the east marches had failed to keep a day of truce with his English counterpart towards the end of May[51] and his son had entered the Cardinal's household, while the latter had in turn lent masons to help repair the battered Home castle.[52] Sir Walter Ker of Cessford, warden of the middle marches, signed the Linlithgow bond with Mark Ker, who was probably his younger brother and the future commendator of Newbattle. 'Wicked Wat' Scott of Buccleuch, who was married to the Cardinal's redoubtable kinswoman, Janet Beaton, was a staunch ally. The support of these borderers helped to balance the activity of the Anglophile Lord Maxwell on the west marches.

There are some unexpected signatories of the Linlithgow bond, whose alignment may have been more with Lennox against the Hamiltons and Douglases than in support of the Cardinal himself: William, 2nd Lord Ruthven, who had supported the introduction of the English bible in March that year, William Murray of Tullibardine, Sir Alexander Dunbar of Cumnock, married to a daughter of the earl of Rothes, and two kinsmen of the Anglophile earls of Cassillis and Glencairn, Kennedy of Blairquhan and Cunningham of Caprington. John Ross of Craigie served both James V and Mary of Guise and had been used by the Cardinal, so it was claimed, to prejudice the late King against some of the nobility. Although he subscribed the Cardinal's bond at Linlithgow, Ross had been captured at Solway Moss and had been in English pay. He was to fall out with the Cardinal at one point the following year during the latter's attempt to interfere in the provostry of Perth.[53] In fact, of those who signed the Linlithgow bond, only a small nucleus were supporters of long standing in the political sense, most of the others were ecclesiastical colleagues, tenants and dependants who habitually formed part of the Cardinal's circle and others who were identified with him on this occasion because it suited them at the time. The bond was something less than a broadly-based demonstration of solidarity with his own standpoint of resistance both to ecclesiastical reform *and* alignment with England.

Arran's mood being what it was — it was reported that 'he begynneth a lytell to droupe'[54] — agreement was reached between the two parties at Linlithgow to the effect that the lords should have custody of the Queen by rota of four at a time, two to be chosen by the Governor and two by the Cardinal, and that the Governor should rule by advice of a council. An attempt by the Cardinal's party to have the Douglases excluded from the council failed.[55] During the negotiations David Beaton and Arran met for the first time in seven months and the agreements were concluded in an atmosphere of affability. In a few days the Queen and Queen Dowager travelled to Stirling with an armed escort. Arran began to put pressure on the Cardinal to attend the ratification of the English treaties, in reply to which David Beaton kept up a facade of conciliatory exchanges with the Governor's friends and the English ambassador. By the end of the month of July Sadler noted the buoyant mood of the Cardinal's party and guessed it was due to 'the hope of aid from France which is bruited to be coming in 19 or 20 great ships with ambassadors from the French King and Bishop of Rome'.[56]

Agreement having been reached on the removal and custody of the Queen, the next cause of dissension was the ratification of the Anglo-Scottish treaties. The Cardinal formally agreed that a convention should be held for the purpose but preferred Stirling as the venue while Arran and company favoured Edinburgh. While this was debated the Cardinal had another meeting with Arran, on whom their renewed personal contact was beginning to work a dissolution of will. It was rumoured that David Beaton had suggested to the Governor that if he broke with England his son might be married to the Queen.[57] At the same time Henry VIII worked to gain the Cardinal's agreement to the treaties, even offering him an English prelacy equal in value to that of Mirepoix.[58] David Beaton declined the English bishopric — one of few decisions he can be said to have taken in common with John Knox. With inevitable realism, however, Henry instructed his men to harass the Cardinal's friends on the borders and prepare to receive their castles.[59] He warned Sadler, in an eloquent metaphor, to beware of the Cardinal and his angels, since he had tricked the English twice already, in the matters of his own liberation and the custody of the Queen.[60] The Cardinal persistently refused to come to Edinburgh, even although Arran offered his own son as pledge for his safety, but instead retired to St Andrews and asked Sir George Douglas to come and speak with him there, Lord Seton this time acting as pledge for Douglas's safe conduct.[61] On 16 August, in writing back to the Cardinal after their interview saying that he had reported their discussion to the Governor, Douglas exhorted him to 'pacify all materis for your part and to have in your rememberance God and the common welth of this realme, nocht doubting bot your gud lord will.'[62] Nevertheless, when the treaties were signed in Edinburgh on 25 August, with due ceremony, during which the Governor and the English ambassador took the sacrament together, the Cardinal and most of his chief allies were absent.[63]

He bided his time in St Andrews and, when the Governor came over seeking an interview, refused to see him.[64] Once again, a turn of political fortune favoured the Cardinal, casting a creditable light on his uncooperative stance when the English seized two Scottish merchant ships, on the assertion that they were carrying victuals to France.[65] Anti-English feeling, which was never far from the surface, coupled with outrage among the merchants, exploded in Edinburgh, as a result of which Sadler's house was attacked by an angry crowd who threatened to set it on fire.[66] Indignation was also vented on the Governor who had just completed an alliance with the evidently treacherous 'auld enemy'. Arran's nerve was badly shaken and the impression spread among his contacts that he was planning to leave the capital.[67] He was not at all steadied on receiving a new set of instructions from Henry which in the circumstances were quite unreal: he must win over the Cardinal or prosecute him for treason, take Stirling castle, declare the earl of Bothwell and Lord Home traitors, place Glencairn and Cassillis over Dumbarton castle, making himself master of Scotland south of Forth. Help, in the form of councillors and money, was on its way from England.[68] How straightforward it seemed on paper. On 4 September the Governor rode out of Edinburgh, laying an

M

alibi about going to visit his sick wife at Blackness, which he did *en route*, and thereafter in accordance with a private arrangement met up with the Cardinal at Lord Livingston's house at Callander, halfway between Linlithgow and Stirling.[69]

The events of the next few days were a personal triumph for David Beaton who probably made the most of his conspicuous part in them. Reconciliation with Arran was followed by the latter's public recantation of his association with heresy and absolution at the Cardinal's hands.[70] Just as gratifying from the prelate's standpoint was the Governor's solemn oath, in the Grey Friars' kirk in Stirling, that he would support the profession of 'monks, friars and such other', a public assurance, for the benefit of Henry VIII among others, of a hands-off policy with regard to church property.[71] Arran piously remitted all his future actions to the advice of the Cardinal and the new council. On Sunday 9 September the nine-month-old Queen was crowned with, as Sadler disparagingly reported, 'such solemnity as they do use in the country, which is not very costly': the Governor carried the crown, Lennox the sceptre and Argyll the sword of state.[72] On 17 September the reconstituted government arrived in Edinburgh, none of them more determined to re-write the history of the last eight months than the Cardinal who, in Stirling, had been seen wearing armour and was overheard to remark that he and many of the clergy would rather die than let Henry VIII determine the country's future.[73] The autumn and winter of 1543-4 saw the high-water mark of his power.

The other figure to emerge from the recent contest with enhanced prestige was Mary of Guise, the Queen Dowager. With French support in the offing and the prospect of a political partnership with the Cardinal, with whom French interests and those of the Queen were entirely safe, she took an active role which was in contrast to that of Margaret Tudor during the previous royal minority. No longer beleaguered but free to act on her own initiative and at the centre of the royal court, Mary, with her entourage, gave a French emphasis to the character of court life which at this point, on its return to Edinburgh, seems to have flourished in a brief mood of relaxed optimism, 'for there was such dancing, singing, playing and merriness into the Court at that time that no man would have tired therein'.[74] Mary of Guise was later to prove that she could well survive without courtly pleasures when times were hard, but in the meantime the 'triumph, plays, farces and banqueting, and great dancing before the Queen with great lords and French ladies' that followed the coronation served the useful political purpose of projecting an acceptable image of the country whose interests she represented. Of all the Scots with whom she would have to work from then onwards, none had a closer affinity with France than David Beaton. That, together with the fact that she trusted him with her interests and probably conversed with him in her native tongue, was enough to arouse the resentment of those who were less sympathetic to the French alliance. The rumour that their mutual understanding and public co-operation involved a more personal association is almost certainly unfounded and arose from that resentment, but it is significant of the fact of their affinity of purpose in public affairs.[75] At the same time, it was a partnership between two self-reliant individuals neither of whom readily accepted restraints on their actions. It is not surprising that at one point attempts were made to sow distrust between them.

The Governor's reconciliation with the Cardinal, the incident of the merchant ships and the news that French envoys were on their way shook the foundations of the recent Anglo-Scottish agreements. This was made clear during Sadler's appearances before the council shortly after it returned to Edinburgh.[76] The English ambassador, still offended at his treatment by the Edinburgh folk who had attacked his house, and no doubt frayed by the lack of decisive action on the part of King Henry's 'assured Scots', must have regarded Arran with a jaundiced eye when he found himself before the council in a room in the Cardinal's lodging in the Blackfriars' Wynd, a symbolic venue. The Queen Dowager sat at the head of the table, with the Governor on her right, the earl of Moray on her left and the Cardinal next to the Governor. David Beaton acted as spokesman for the council in this diplomatic situation. He began by asking Sadler about his own grievances, his treatment by the Edinburgh rioters and the loss of his correspondence in the borders, questioning the seriousness of these incidents in such a way as to irritate his opponent into sounding like the more aggressive of the two and ultimately into being the first to mention the matter of the Anglo-Scottish treaties. What was it, the Cardinal asked, that had caused such 'sharp' letters to be sent by King Henry to the provost and citizens of Edinburgh? Surely the King had been misinformed. If Sadler had suffered injury they would do all they could to punish the offenders and provide for his safety. The council seemed sorry to hear of the 'ungodly violence of the townsmen' to him and their 'vile railing' against the English King. As to the missing correspondence, said to have been intercepted by the Homes, they asked him to put this down to the wildness of the borders.

Sadler replied that the English who suffered would have their revenge and if peace was not observed on the borders the fault would lie with the Scots. The Cardinal asked him 'to garr him understand how the default should be in them', to which Sadler answered with some asperity that the only cause of trouble on the borders was the non-performance by the Scots of their part of the treaties. As their verbal exchange slipped into high politics the Cardinal pointed out that since 'the greater part' of the Scottish nobility had not consented to the conclusion of the treaties these had the character of partial, 'private' agreements and said that he felt sure that Henry would prefer the solid foundation of full, public and 'honourable' conclusions to the treaties rather than a private deal 'which could not stand'. The present council, he assured the ambassador, wished equally to satisfy Henry as those who had privately treated with him, 'in all things reasonable standing with the honour and surety of their sovereign lady, and the honour, liberty and commonwealth of her realm'. If, however, on account of their reluctance to agree to a dishonourable arrangement, Henry persecuted his own kinswoman, an infant, it could not stand with his honour. Sadler, seeing plainly in this reply both an intimation that the treaties were under threat and a moral justification for any future hostilities, threw back an answer which was a personal challenge to the man who had worked the *volte face*, saying that the Cardinal should not be the judge of the King's honour and that as Henry had concluded things to 'the weal, honour and surety of his pronepte' he would regard the interrupters of his plans as *her* enemies. On a subsequent occasion, in rebuffing a superficial offer to negotiate peace on the borders put forward by the Cardinal to Sadler in a more private interview, Henry declared that he saw 'one man his enemy directing all things' and swore that unless the Governor and the Cardinal were imprisoned, removed from power and separated he would hardly be persuaded to make any agreement with Scotland on the present basis.[77] He wrote to Arran directly castigating him for failing to deny the Cardinal's allegation that the treaties had been a private deal, which 'the Cardinall your new recounted freende in the presence of our ambassador planely affirmed in your own hering ... '[78] To this Arran responded that the Cardinal had spoken the truth, especially in so far as he blamed Henry for the first violation of the treaties.[79] The warning shots had been exchanged.

Besides widening the break in Anglo-Scottish relations beyond repair the change in policy was soon to cause an upheaval in internal Scottish politics. The shifts began with the reaction of Lennox to the Governor's change of mind, for dynastic rivalry made it inevitable that they should take opposite sides. Lennox's first move was to go to the west after the coronation at Stirling in order to be the first to contact the French ambassadors, who it was hoped were bringing money and munitions with them, and the papal legate who was on his way to lend spiritual support to the Cardinal's efforts to reassert his authority, and supervise the collection of a tax conceded to James V before his death. Lennox evaded the Queen Dowager's attempts to elicit from him his intentions in leaving court but a correspondent, who was probably Lord Methven, warned her that Lennox probably had 'ane hey purpos as to be principall and to us all mone, artalyery and utheris thingis that com out of France to his own particular efecttis'.[80] He feared that Lennox's selfish behaviour could jeapordise Franco-Scottish relations as well as revive Henry VIII's opportunity in Scottish affairs.

Lennox forestalled Mary of Guise, the Governor and the Cardinal in meeting the envoys who arrived at Dumbarton on 5 October. He depressed the papal legate, Marco Grimani, who was bent on restoring peace among the political leaders, with his talk of removing Arran from power.[81] He prepared the ambassadors for the fact that they might see him in the company of the Anglophile lords by telling them that he was trying to persuade the latter to join the French party.[82] Grimani never grasped the divisions among the Scottish nobles, especially the dynastic rivalry between Hamilton and Lennox, or the mischief that had been wrought by the Douglases. The Frenchmen, Jacques de la Brosse and Jacques Ménage, although they handed over the money they had brought with them to Lennox for safekeeping in Dumbarton castle, distrusted him from the start. In fact, Lennox was already looking to England for backing against his rival, Arran, and was discussing the prospect of a marriage with Margaret Douglas, daughter of Angus and Margaret Tudor, who, next to Mary, Queen of Scots, and after Henry VIII's own family, was nearest in line to the throne of England.[83]

Discussion with Lennox and later with Mary of Guise, Arran and the Cardinal gave the ambassadors the distinct impression of a country divided against itself in which the antagonism among the rulers and their noble and other landed supporters affected all classes of society. 'The kingdom is so divided and in such confusion', wrote Grimani to Cardinal Farnese, 'that if God does not stretch forth his hand and inspire these lords to unite together, manifest ruin, both public and private, lies before it.'[84] 'Because of the aforesaid divisions', explained the French envoys, 'the realm of Scotland was and still is at the present time under arms; for all the friends of one faction mistrust all those of the other faction. So much so that not merely is the nobility in arms, but churchmen, friars and the country people only travel through the country-side in large companies all armed ... '[85] Mistrust and fear were intensified by the breakdown in Anglo-Scottish relations at government level.

It is remarkable that throughout the autumn and winter of 1543–4, in spite of the growing threat of hostilities and the apparent tactical victories of the new, reactionary régime, there was a much broader-based support for the party that centred on Angus and Lennox than had given its support to Arran's Anglophile policies in the spring of that year.[86] At that time, support had consisted mainly of the hard core of assured lords who were working for an accommodation with Henry VIII together with a small group of magnates and professional men who were committed to radical reform of the church, some of them even to protestantism. But now, those who were behind Lennox and his associates, many of whom were to be formally prosecuted or pardoned in the coming months for assisting him, included some who had previously been on the Francophile, conservative side. Some were the Cardinal's vassals and former allies, such as Lord Ogilvy whose temporary alignment with the Lennox party must have strained his relations with David Beaton for whom he was bailie of Arbroath abbey. Two of the Lennox-Angus faction, Murray of Tullibardine and Stirling of Keir, had actually signed the Linlithgow bond, presumably as allies of Lennox and not of the Cardinal himself. The so-called Anglophiles now included some who had never been compromised by Henry VIII. At the same time, Lennox's party did include a number of men with a consistent record of opposition to the conservative position, and included those lairds of Ayrshire, East Lothian, Fife and Angus who were to become open adherents of the protestant movement once it gathered momentum — Cunninghams and Campbells, Douglases and Lindsays, Leslies and even some Lanarkshire Hamiltons who were out of sympathy with Arran's changed attitude to reform. It was a broadly-based, territorially widespread party, incorporating a small but far from negligible ideological element. Considering that Anglophile attitudes could no longer be held without the imputation of treason, it must have drawn much of its strength from strongly-held convictions. Not least of these were an identification with Lennox against the Hamilton hegemony, chiefly in the west of Scotland, and resentment of the Cardinal's renewed initiative in public affairs, most marked among the magnates in the east of Scotland where his territorial and ecclesiastical influence lay.

Although he had apparently won the contest for power and in making his comeback had gained control of the Governor, the Cardinal had lost the support of those who had been with him in the early part of the year out of antipathy to Arran but who were now ranged against him because the Governor was identified with him. Awareness of this and of personal opposition, as well as a desire to consolidate his gains, caused him to take punitive action in the late autumn and winter of 1543–4 in an attempt to undermine the solidarity and resources of those who were identified with Angus and Lennox, to expose and punish those who had openly adhered to heretical beliefs in the lax situation that had existed since the March parliament, and officially to annul the treaties with England and renew those with France. He had also two personal goals in view in order to consolidate the basis of his power: the recovery of the office of chancellor of the realm and the papal grant of a legateship which would widen his authority over the church in Scotland.

The first lords to fall foul of his régime were Maxwell and Somerville who were captured while on their way to England as envoys for Angus and his party.[87] Their dispatches, assuring Henry VIII of his party's continued efforts on his behalf in Scotland, were confiscated and held up as evidence of their treason. A plea to the Queen Dowager on behalf of the captives, 'gif it ples hir grace to tak that pyn on hir', suggests that their treatment was looked upon as the Cardinal's personal doing rather than the policy of the government and points at the same time to attempts to detach her from the Cardinal and Arran.[88] With regard to the arrest of the earl of Rothes and his friends, the earl of Glencairn warned that these unconstitutional actions could 'mak impassemant bayth for the commoun weill of this realme and for the afferis of Franche'. [89] At one point it was even said that the earl of Moray, hitherto the Cardinal's staunch ally, was somewhat shaken in his loyalty by the detention without trial of these 'ancient barons'.[90]

There can be little doubt that David Beaton feared the effects of the ideological element in the attachment to England where the secular authority had interfered with church property. Rothes, who was arrested in November,[91] was one of a group of landholders, some of them holding from the Cardinal himself, who included in their number the new testament-owning treasurer, Sir James Kirkcaldy of Grange, and the lawyer, Mr Henry Balnaves, who had 'argued for the secularis' in the March parliament in favour of Lord Maxwell's motion to permit the reading of the vernacular bible and who was himself to write a treatise on *Justification by Faith* some three years later. Balnaves' earlier professional association with David Beaton as a procurator in the diocesan and civil courts and the fact that he had received a sizeable feu of archbishopric lands two years before probably added to the latter's rancour; he was said to have asked for the custody of Balnaves when the arrests were made. 'because he loved him worst of all'.[92] He hated Lord Gray, according to John Knox, 'because he used the company of such as professed godliness, and bare small favour to the Cardinal'.[93] He must also have been apprehensive about Gray's territorial influence as sheriff of Forfar among the vassals and tenants of Arbroath abbey and of the archbishopric itself. It may have been Gray who influenced Lord Ogilvy, his father-in-law, into a temporary identification with the Anglophile-reformists. Rothes and Balnaves were imprisoned for only a short time but Gray, who was held in Dalkeith castle, was not released until the following May. Seven or eight burgesses of Dundee were arrested on 21 November for having attacked the town's Dominican friary, one of several outbreaks of iconoclasm in Dundee, Perth and Edinburgh during the year.[94] There had even been an assault on the abbey of Arbroath where the bailie, Lord Ogilvy, whatever his flirtation with heresy amounted to, was able to prevent serious damage to the fabric. This incident on his own threshold only hardened David Beaton's resolution to take a firm line in maintaining respect for ecclesiastical authority. Information about his fact-finding tour of Angus, Perth and Dundee in November in company with the Governor, which resulted in the arrests of Rothes, Gray and Balnaves and, a few weeks later, in the Perth heresy trials, is given in the letters of Patrick Crichton of Brunston, a former servant of the Cardinal and envoy on behalf of the Governor, who had by now transferred his allegiance to the English authorities to whom he passed detailed information on the Cardinal's movements.[95] Brunston was one of those who were soon to commit themselves to a plot to murder the Cardinal and at the same time to lend their support to the preacher, George Wishart, when he appeared on the scene.

The meeting of the parliament early in December 1543 found the Cardinal in a determined mood, having shown his political opponents his hand and told the double-agent, Brunston, that Henry VIII would not have the honour to begin the war.[96] He was set to annul the Anglo-Scottish treaties and had been heard to swear that even if it cost him his life he would drive out the Douglases, whom he had failed to win over in spite of substantial material inducements. He must have judged that Angus and his brother were in a cleft stick, hounded by the Scottish government and, due to their lack of success on Henry's behalf, unwelcome in England. The English council warned them that when the Cardinal had brought his schemes to fruition they would 'surely go to the pot for it'.[97] Lennox, too, had resisted attempts to regain his co-operation and was assembling his party in the west of Scotland.

The chief business of the parliament was to turn the provisions and enactments of the March session upside down.[98] On 11 December it was stated that, due to the English attack on Scottish merchant shipping before the treaties were finally sealed, 'the said king of Ingland hes violate and brokin the said pece and tharfor, and becaus the said contract of marriage was grantit for the said peice to have bene had observit and keipit betuix the twa realmes, quhilk was nocht keipit bot brokin violet by the said king of Ingland ... ', therefore, the Governor and three estates declared 'the saidis contractis to be expirit in thame selfis and nocht to be keipit in tyme cuming ... ' It was less controversial to base the cancellation of the treaties on the patent English act of hostility against the merchant ships than on the politically debateable ground that the treaties had been agreed to by a 'private party', as the Cardinal had put it to Sadler before the council. A re-enactment of penal laws against heresy was a warning of a coming clampdown. The Governor, having been made aware that 'heretikis mair and mair risis and spredis within this realme, sawand dampnable opinionis incontrar the fayth and laws of haly kirk, actis and constitutionis of this realme', ordered all ecclesiastical authorities to proceed against suspects; significantly, the act added, 'My said Lord Governour salbe rady at all tymes to do therein that accordis him of his office' – the secular power was to be seen to lend its support to the action of the clergy against the unorthodox. An act of council of the previous June suggested that there had been an increase in that aspect of dissent which the authorities most feared and against which legislation had been specifically directed ever since 1525: debating the teaching of the church, especially on the doctrine of the sacrament, it having been 'hevelie murmorit ... that divers and sindrie personis, our soverane ladyis liegis, are sacramentaris', denying the real presence in the sacrament, and it was ordained that 'na man disput or hald opinionis of the sacramentis nor of the affect or assence thairof uther wayis nor is ellis ressavit be the haly kirk under the pane of tinsale [loss] of lif, landis and gudis'.[99] During the parliamentary session the great seal was handed back to the Cardinal who 'accepted the office of chancellor in and upon him at the desire of my lord Governour and the Lordis of the Articlis'. With the office came the means of patronage and prominence in council and civil court and the reopening of personal rivalry between him and the archbishop of Glasgow who was thus deprived of the chancellorship. The privy seal which David Beaton had held since 1529 was given to the Governor's half-brother, John Hamilton, abbot of Paisley, the Cardinal's confidant.

It could have been said at the end of the year 1543 that of all those who had suffered from the recent political upheavals the Cardinal was the one man who found himself where he wanted to be. The turnabout in diplomatic affairs, confirmed in the December parliament by the formal renewal of the treaties with France, the resumption of punitive measures against heresy which, although they were issued in the Governor's name, reflected the Cardinal's intentions, and the recovery of the office of chancellor – all suggested that he was firmly in control. There were other legacies of the last twelve months, however, which were far from resolved: the Douglases and Lennox were still in the field with considerable support, Henry VIII was preparing for war (the Cardinal, however belligerent he sounded, must have remembered that his last spell of warmongering had not enhanced his reputation), allies had to be constantly kept at heel (he was realistic enough to add the Governor's oldest son to his company of household hostages), he was in increasing financial difficulties, and relations with some of his influential vassals in Fife and Angus promised continued friction. His victory was perhaps more apparent than real.

NOTES

1. *L.P.Henry VIII*, XVII, i, 22
2. E. Finnie, 'The House of Hamilton: Patronage, Politics and the Church in the Reformation period', *Innes Review*, XXXVI, 3–28
3. *L.P. Henry VIII*, XVIII, i, 104
4. *Hamilton Papers*, I, 292–8, 301–3
5. *State Papers Henry VIII*, V, 250; *L.P. Henry VIII*, XVIII, i, 104
6. *Ibid.*, XVIII, i, 157
7. *A.P.S.*, II, 410–15, 424
8. *Ibid.*, 415, 425

9. *Hamilton Papers*, I, 299
10. *T.A.*, VIII, 172
11. *Hamilton Papers*, I, 301
12. *Rentale*, 138, 155
13. *Ibid.*,143
14. Herkless and Hannay, *Archbishops*, IV, 97
15. *Sadler*, I, 42–3
16. *L.P. Henry VIII*, XVIII, i, 156–7, 324
17. Fraser, *The Douglas Book*, IV, 146; *Hamilton Papers*, I, 292
18. *Ibid.*, I, 295
19. *Ibid.*, I, 303
20. *L.P. Henry VIII*, XVIII, i, 102
21. *Hamilton Papers*, I, 301
22. *T.A.*, VIII, 172
23. *Sadler*, I, 93–4
24. *Ibid.*, I, 131; *L.P. Henry VIII*, XVIII, i, 458
25. *Rentale*, 155
26. Clerk of Penicuik muniments, GD 18/459
27. *Sadler*, I, 127–35
28. Herkless and Hannay, *Archbishops*, IV, 101–2
29. *Sadler*, I, 131–5
30. *Ibid.*
31. *Ibid.*, I, 86
32. *Ibid.*, I, 135
33. Herkless and Hannay, *Archbishops*, IV, 108
34. *L.P. Henry VIII*, XVIII, 425, 458
35. J.A. Inglis, *Sir Adam Otterburn*, 74–5
36. *Hamilton Papers*, I, 362
37. *Ibid.*, I, 400
38. *Sadler*, I, 197
39. *L.P. Henry VIII*, XVIII, i, 572
40. *Sadler*, I, 189
41. *L.P. Henry VIII*, XVIII, i, 733; *Hamilton Papers*, I, 390, 392, 397
42. *Foedera*, XIV, 792–6
43. *L.P. Henry VIII*, XVIII, i, 834–5
44. Herkless and Hannay, *Archbishops*, IV, 117
45. *The Acts of the Lords of Council in Public Affairs*, 527–8 (*Public Affairs*)
46. *Hamilton Papers*, I, 414, 416, 418
47. *Ibid.*, I, 418
48. *Ibid.*, I, 419
49. *L.P. Henry VIII*, XVIII, i, 945
50. Register House charters, RH 6/1317
51. *L.P. Henry VIII*, XVIII, i, 580; *Hamilton Papers*, I, 400
52. *Ibid.*, I, 397
53, *Scottish Correspondence*, 58
54. *Hamilton Papers*, I, 419
55. *Ibid.*, I, 424
56. *Scottish Correspondence*, 20n
57. *Hamilton Papers*, I, 437

58. *L.P. Henry VIII*, XVIII, i, 479
59. *Hamilton Papers*, I, 458
60. *L.P. Henry VIII*, XVIII, ii, 9
61. *Ibid.*, XVIII, ii, 42
62. *Scottish Correspondence*, 22
63. *Foedera*, XV, 4–6; *Sadler*, I, 270
64. *Scottish Correspondence*, 26–7
65. *L.P. Henry VIII*, XVIII, ii, 111
66. *Hamilton Papers*, II, 20–2; *L.P. Henry VIII*, XVIII ii, 46
67. *Hamilton Papers*, i, 456
68. *Ibid.*, I, 439; *Sadler*, I, 246, *et seq.*
69. *Hamilton Papers*, II, 14, 18–19
70. *Ibid.*, II, 38–41
71. Herkless and Hannay, *Archbishops*, IV, 124
72. *Knox*, I, 50n; *L.P. Henry VIII*, XVIII, ii, 174
73. *Ibid.*, XVIII, ii, 174, 181, 188, 202
74. *Pitscottie*, II, 15–16
75. *Knox*, I, 40, 79
76. *Sadler*, I, 294, 300 *et seq; Hamilton Papers*, II, 56–62, 68–72
77. Herkless and Hannay, *Archbishops*, IV, 128
78. *Hamilton Papers*, II, 128
79. *Ibid.*, II, 153–4
80. *Scottish Correspondence*, 38–9
81. Hannay, 'Letters of the Papal Legate',
82. G. Dickinson, *Two Missions of Jacques de la Brosse . . . 1543* (S.H.S.) 37 (Dickinson, *Missions of de la Brosse*)
83. *Scottish Correspondence*, 81n
84. Hannay, 'Letters of the Papal Legate', 15
85. Dickinson, *Missions of de la Brosse*, 23
86. Donaldson, *All the Queen's Men*, 18
87. *L.P. Henry VIII*, XVIII, ii, 328
88. *Scottish Correspondence*, 50–3
89. *Ibid.*, 44
90. *Ibid.*, 50n
91. *L.P. Henry VIII*, XVIII, ii, 378
92. *Ibid.*, XVIII, ii, 425
93. *Knox*, I, 52
94. *L.P. Henry VIII*, XVIII, ii, 425
95. *Ibid.* and 428
96. *Hamilton Papers*, II, 161–2
97. Herkless and Hannay, *Archbishops*, IV, 135; *L.P. Henry VIII*, XVIII, ii, 450
98. *A.P.S.*, II, 431–2, 443
99. *Public Affairs*, 527–8

11

The Price of Victory

The political events of 1544 were the direct consequence of the Cardinal's success in re-establishing the Franco-Scottish alliance and weaning the Governor away from those who wished for some positive reform in the church which would take at least some of its pattern from England. The early weeks of the year saw attempts to bring about a formal agreement between the Cardinal and the Governor on the one hand and Angus and Lennox as leaders of the opposition on the other. There was little hope, however, of achieving either a genuine reconciliation or a workable compromise. It is clear from the tone of the Cardinal's letter to Mary of Guise written on 14 January[1] that to him 'agreement' simply meant an admission of their faults by the Angus-Lennox party to be followed by forgiveness by the government's representatives, almost a repeat of the reconciliation between himself and the Governor in the autumn. 'The Lordis beand met at Leith', he wrote, 'ar agreant with My Lord Governour and was contentit to summit thame to the ordinance and decrete of My lordis of Argile, Murray, Bischop of Orknay, My Lord of Sanct John, the Knycht of Caldour and Hew Campbell of Lowden ... Quha have devisit the mater and gevin in thair deliverance as followis: that is to say that all thir lordis of the Westland beand in Leith and thair followeris sall have fre remissioun of all faltis and crymes bygane: and all thingis quhair in at thai ar hurt or skaithit sall be dressit at the sycht of the Lordis forsaidis, and that thai ar to remane in tyme cuming faithfull to My Lord Governour and the authorite and to have na mair ado with Ingland.' Although sureties had been given, the opposition refused to commit themselves to the arbiters, three for each side as named above, without a personal meeting first with the Cardinal, Argyll, Moray and Bishop Reid, which duly took place at the chapel of the Greenside between Edinburgh and Leith, 'quhair we have ressonit with thame at length', the Cardinal went on to explain to the Queen Dowager in the same vein, 'and finally we agreit sa weill that thai ar contentit to fulfill all thingis at wes devisit be the saidis Lordis'.

The Governor received them all heartily in his lodging afterwards but the 'agreement' was superficial.[2] Sir George Douglas was soon promising Henry VIII his continued service in Scotland, received somewhat ungraciously by the jaundiced King, while Lennox broke the bargain by departing for the west where he gathered his forces for a show of strength against the Governor. The Cardinal got some satisfaction out of writing to Henry on the theme of the concord and unity now achieved among the Scottish lords, which was tantamount to telling the English King that his friends in Scotland had deserted him, at the same time drawing a picture of himself as architect of the prevailing unity and not the cause of division which Henry believed him to be.[3] At the same time he asked for a safeconduct for Scottish envoys who were to be sent to England to discuss the possibility of re-establishing peace between the two kingdoms. Henry's acid response was to accuse the Cardinal of double-dealing at every stage in the breakdown of Anglo-Scottish relations, administering a swipe at clerical politicians at the same time:[4] 'Wherefor we have thought good for an answer to your lettre ... to advise youe if youe entend to medle in thaffayres of the world and to leave the office of a ministre of Goddis worde, which youe professed when youe wer made a bishop, to have heraftre a better regard to the honour and weale of that realme then youe have had hertofore'. The Cardinal was told that if he wanted an answer to his request for a safeconduct for ambassadors, he could listen in council to the reply being sent back with Ross herald. Thus Henry verbally reduced the prime mover of the political *volte face* to the rank of an ordinary member of the Governor's council.

The political shift in favour of Lennox which had been apparent from at least late autumn, when the Governor at the Cardinal's instigation had laid hands on members of the Anglophile party, had increased by the spring to an impressive demonstration of support for the Angus-Lennox faction. Mainly drawn from the west of Scotland and including some of Lennox's vassals and neighbours, it also featured an unprecedented participation by Highland and Islands chiefs,[5] such as the Macleods of Dunvegan, the Captain of Clanranald, Cameron of Lochiel, MacNeil of Barra, the Macleans of Duart, Lochbuie, Coll and Ardgour, MacQuarrie of Ulva and others, whose willingness to take service on behalf of the King of England derived from the knowledge of Henry's plan for a separate administration on the western seaboard and was a legacy of the days when the semi-independent Lords of the Isles had provided the English King with a weapon against the King of Scots within his own boundaries. Towards the end of March 1544 it was rumoured that if the Governor's attempt to deal with Lennox's insurrection failed, the Cardinal might go again to France to beg for help, as other Scottish ambassadors were then doing in Flanders, France and Spain.[6] However, he was with the Governor in Glasgow early in April when the siege of the archbishop's castle, which was held by Lennox's men, was almost at an end. In that city, where Lennox's presence was said to have caused friction between the town and the bishop over the election of bailies,[7] there was also tension in ecclesiastical circles. On the morning of 5 April before the high altar in the cathedral the Cardinal repeated his undertaking to Archbishop Dunbar not to publicly elevate his cross in the archdiocese of Glasgow; among those in his company were Lords Seton, Livingston, Borthwick and Hay of Yester who acted as witnesses. Better relations with the friars are suggested by his gifts of £5 and £3 to the Dominicans and Franciscans of Glasgow respectively.[8] A payment of 22s to the servant of the parson of Stobo indicates contact with Mr John Colquhoun, canon of the cathedral, whose kinsman, Mr Adam Colquhoun, parish clerk of Paisley, was among those escheated for assisting Lennox.[9] During the fighting in the city one of Lennox's men assaulted the Cardinal's brother, Mr Walter Beaton, and a woman in his company.[10]

A sustained civil war was avoided when Angus, Cassillis and Lord Maxwell were captured, some said with their own connivance, about which Maxwell later made confession to Henry VIII.[11] The castle of Glasgow fell to the Governor's forces and the garrison was hanged. Lennox, placing Dumbarton castle under Glencairn's supervision, sailed for England where his envoys, Hugh Cunningham and Thomas Bishop, had already made contact on his behalf with the English warden in the hope of gaining English military support.[12] From being the likely leader of an effective party in Scotland Lennox, because of his personal opposition to the Hamilton Governor and the Cardinal's control of the malleable Arran, was pushed into the role of a traitor. When he returned in the autumn of 1544 to harry the lands of his dynastic rival in the Firth of Clyde it was with direct English backing.

A more serious confrontation than that with Lennox and Angus faced the Scottish government in the month of May in the form of Henry's military retribution for the breaking of the treaties. Since at least January he had been in close contact with his commanders in the north about 'the enterprise of Scotland', insisting on an early invasion in spite of Suffolk's advice that dearth of fodder and army supplies so early in the year would hamper operations and make the expedition more expensive than need be.[13] However, Henry was also planning his expedition to France and may have believed that a thrashing of the Scots would give him a psychological advantage over their French ally before the Anglo-French campaign properly began. In the event, the invasion of Scotland took place in May under the earl of Hertford, Suffolk's replacement. The intended damage was not entirely of a material nature, thorough though that was to be. Hertford was instructed to wage a simultaneous war of propaganda against the arch-enemy by posting in every devastated neighbourhood the jibe — 'You may thank your Cardinal for this'.[14]

The Scottish government did not have the resources to meet an English army in the field at that time. Battle was out of the question and even preparations for defence were taken at the eleventh hour. On 21 April all men liable for service were charged to make ready to meet the English, and a few days later the inhabitants of the south coast of the Firth of Forth were ordered to dig trenches with a view to impeding the advance of the enemy who was expected to arrive by sea. On 1 May the host was summoned from the sheriffdoms of Fife, Angus, Kincardine, Stirling, Clackmannan and Kinross to meet the Governor on the burgh muir of Edinburgh four days later, but this was too late. On this occasion as at other times during this period of invasion and revolt hundreds of Scots failed to turn up for the hosting.

On the borders the way was prepared for English operations by the large number of Scots, great and small, who had 'assured' themselves to the enemy.[15] Knowing that the government was unable to protect them, many borderers made shift to protect themselves by this means out of fear, intimidation and hope of gain. It was remarked by Shrewsbury in 1544 that the assured would soon appreciate the benefit of the protection and justice granted to them by the English wardens, a welcome reward for swearing to be 'full parte taykers with Englande'.[16] Most of the assured were paid for their services, like Henry VIII's noble Scots allies. By the summer of 1544 they had come to include some lairds from the Lothians, several of

whom were known to incline towards protestantism, such as Cockburn of
Ormiston and Crichton of Brunston, the latter having deserted the Cardinal's
service.[17] At the beginning of the war over the marriage of the young Queen the
government was fairly lenient with collaborators with the English: the register of
the privy seal contains many remissions, which represented government revenue.
Not until October 1545 were the laws of treason augmented by the Scottish
parliament to include collaboration with England.[18] Dissension among Scottish
landholders was aggravated as the assured harried the lands of those of their
neighbours who were Henry's 'adversaries'.

John Knox tells the story of how the Cardinal mocked the opinion of alarmists
that the fleet which appeared off Leith on 3 May was the English invading force
and of how he went on eating his dinner as if no danger threatened.[19] This can only
have been an attempt to avoid a panic because he must have been aware that the
English fleet was reported to be on its way. The English soldiers disembarked
between Leith and Newhaven the following morning without interference even
although the operation took some three hours to complete, long enough for a well-
organised opposing force to have inflicted some damage. A Scottish force
estimated by Hertford at about 6,000 waited for the invaders at the Water of Leith
but broke up and retreated towards Edinburgh after the exchange of a few shots.
The Cardinal and the Governor were present during the skirmish as were,
according to a newsletter report, the earls of Moray, Huntly and Bothwell. Knox
makes much of the fact that the Cardinal and the Governor 'fled as fast as horse
would carry them', and an English report announced that 'the first man that fled
was the holy Cardinal, like a valiant champion, and with him the Governor, the
earls of Huntly, Moray and Bothwell, with divers other great men of the realm'.[20]

The damage inflicted on the burgh of Edinburgh by Hertford's forces has
sometimes been exaggerated as far as the fabric of the buildings is concerned,
being mainly confined to houses and premises in the vicinity of the Cowgate and
Holyrood, but the loss of life and damage to certain properties such as the
merchants' stores at Leith was probably considerable.[21] Just as damaging was the
fuel which the attack added to the fires of recrimination within the burgh
community and council between those who favoured and those who opposed
closer alliance with England. The tensions which had accompanied the
Governor's brief 'reformation' in 1543 had even led to a demonstration by
conservative ruling families in the council chamber in August of that year, an
incident which provoked the privy council to intervene by bringing the rioters
before the supreme criminal court and, after Arran's change of policy, to reinforce
the conservative party by imposing Sir Adam Otterburn on the burgh as provost.[22]
In the invasion the loss of life and livelihood must have caused bitter feeling, and
even those who had deplored the Governor's protestant preachers and distrusted
the English alliance must have had cause to curse the Cardinal whose efforts to
remove both these elements from public policy had brought down the wrath of the
'auld enemy' on the community.

It is unlikely that the Cardinal and Arran contemplated a major offensive
against the invaders at this stage. They departed the scene of hostilities just as Sir

George Douglas arrived to make contact with Hertford.[23] The Cardinal made for Stirling, probably to warn Mary of Guise of the situation and possibly to take measures for the safety of the Queen. He abandoned the main route to Stirling at Corstorphine where a guide was hired to conduct him.[24] He was beginning to pay the price of his political *coup*, for ever since his altercation with Sadler in council in September 1543 English propaganda had laid the blame for the reversal in Henry's fortunes in Scotland squarely on his shoulders, giving the present invasion the character of a personal vendetta as well as providing a lesson for the Scots in general. Not only was it intended to draw popular odium upon the Cardinal but also to attack his property: Hertford was told to turn St Andrews, 'the Cardinal's town', upside down. His actions in the face of the invasion indicate a concern for his personal safety. On 8 May in the chapel royal at Stirling he drew up his will in which he nominated a handful of trusted kinsmen as his testamentary executors.[25] Towards mid-month he was on the border between Perthshire and Clackmannanshire, a journey which may have had something to do with plans, reported by the English, for removing the Queen to Dunkeld.[26] It may simply have been that the Cardinal was working his way back to St Andrews by a safer inland route which included Doune, Castle Campbell, the stronghold which Argyll held from the bishop of Dunkeld, Kincardine-in-Menteith, where he stayed for eleven days with the earl of Montrose, and Falkland. He was guided from Castle Campbell at Dollar to Kincardine near Auchterarder by a man of the barony of Muckhart, lands which he had feued to Argyll.[27] The son of the earl of Montrose was granted a feu of the barony of Torry in Aberdeenshire about two months after his father had given the Cardinal hospitality.[28] Fears of personal attack were not without foundation, for on 19 May his baggage train was seized at Dunning on its way from Kincardine-in-Menteith to St Andrews by Murray of Tullibardine who was by that time inclined towards active collaboration with Henry VIII.[29] Tullibardine's men carried off a large quantity of church and personal silverware, later valued at £2,800, including a mitre and processional cross. Even although the ambush missed David Beaton himself, the capture of items so symbolic of his pre-eminence must have been relished by his enemies. On 4 December that year Wharton told Shrewsbury that the laird of Tullibardine had told him at Carlisle that the Cardinal's cross and other 'necessaries' were at Cockpool ready to be brought to Carlisle, 'wherwith the larde is mery'.[30] Tullibardine was not arraigned in court for the theft for another ten months when he was ordered to refund the value of the goods which had never been returned. When he failed to obey, certain of his lands were apprised and granted to the Cardinal who promptly resigned them in favour of his sons.[31]

It is doubtful if he was fully aware of the extent to which plans had been laid to eliminate him from the scene. Proof of his ignorance seems to lie in the fact that in the summer of 1544, in connection with one of several attempts to impose his will on the burgh government of Perth, he used the services of two men who were already privy to a plot to kill him, John Charteris and Norman Leslie, master of Rothes, the second having at one time been a gentleman of his household but now sharing with others of his Leslie kinsmen a deterioration in relations with the

Cardinal. While at Newcastle in April 1544 the earl of Hertford had been handed a letter, destined for Henry VIII, in which the laird of Brunston conveyed an offer by a group of discontented Scots either to seize or kill David Beaton.[32] Since at that point the collapse of the Anglophile party in the west made it likely that the Cardinal's policies, endorsed by Arran, were set to continue, the plotters hoped that the English King might be inclined to take up their offer. Sir James Kirkcaldy of Grange, the former treasurer, Norman Leslie and John Charteris were prepared to waylay the Cardinal on his travels through Fife if Henry would protect them afterwards. They also offered to 'destroy' the abbey of Arbroath and other church property if Henry would give them enough money and supplies to enable them to hold together a force of 1,000 or 1,500 men for a month for that purpose. The attack on Arbroath was to be carried out by Leslie, Sandilands of Calder and other friends of Lord Gray assisted by the earl Marischal, all of whom were associated with protestantism. Their emergence as a group which was prepared, if all else failed, to remove the Cardinal by violent means marks a stage at which opposition to him became more intensely personal, not only reflecting political alignment but drawing some of its strength from shared family grievances and religious outlook. The group were proposing, in effect, to repeat the Governor's reformation-experiment of a year before, but this time eliminating the Cardinal altogether. The possibility of their being able to raise 1,000 men among them in Angus and Fife, provided money and supplies were forthcoming, is a comment on the Cardinal's failure to intimidate the magnates on his doorstep in spite of his campaigns against heresy and attempts to immobilise the ringleaders of Anglophile activity.

In reply to Brunston and his associates Henry cautiously let it be known that if they were prepared to deliver hostages, or if they joined the English army, their lands and goods would be preserved and that if they attempted their feat against the Cardinal and were compelled to flee to England, they would be relieved 'as shall appertain'. This was too short a notice, they were told, on which to assist them in burning the churchmen's lands, but if they would pledge hostages with Hertford to do what they had offered to do, Henry would would deliver them £1,000 'for their furniture'.[33] He thus made it appear that he was helping *them*, with substantial pledges on their part, rather than that they were in any way obliging *him*, which would have made him look like the instigator of the enterprise. It may be that Tullibardine's attack on the Cardinal's retinue a month or so later had something to do with these communications. It was the first personal assault that the Cardinal had sustained and it must have put him on his guard. It must be said that even after he did become aware of the threat to his life he continued to move around the country as before and cannot be accused of physical cowardice.

The Fife and Angus lairds were not alone in plotting a downfall at this time. According to communications between the English privy council and Hertford, the Cardinal and Argyll were said to be already 'covenanted' to depose the Governor.[34] If the protestant malcontents were trying to put the clock back to March 1543, the Cardinal was perhaps trying to put it back to the death of James V. If so, it is an indication of his confidence in his position on the eve of the English invasion, when this allegation was made. Others beside himself, however, were becoming tired of the Governor's performance. As the Cardinal had worked the change in public policy in 1543, Mary of Guise tried to make her mark the following year by attempting to take executive power into her hands.[35] This was a delicate operation. In the first place, she had no legal basis for her authority and her success depended on reliable support and decisive action at the right time, such as a vote of no confidence in the Governor taken in a public assembly. Besides, although she was prepared to plot the removal of Arran from the government, she probably had no wish to quarrel with the Cardinal with whose policies he was now identified. Above all, she had to trust her interests to men who had a variety of priorities, few of whom sympathised entirely with her personal, French-orientated standpoint: individuals who had suffered at Arran's hands, the Anglophiles and reformists whom he had deserted, the Lennox-Angus faction who were only encouraging her to take power into her own hands in order that they might get it out of those of the Cardinal and Arran. Although in the last analysis they all owed allegiance to the Queen and respect towards herself, making it easy for them to use loyal expressions about 'the weill of the realme' in their letters to her, Arran was the lawfully constituted Governor. Working mainly from her own jointure castle of Stirling, the Dowager's operations lacked the status afforded to those of the Edinburgh-based Governor and his council, while those officers of state who were sometimes in her company were susceptible to the pressure of his authority when he chose to recall them: the clerk register returned to Edinburgh in June at the Governor's command[36] and Sir George Douglas complained, as late as October, that although there had been talk of the Dowager's party's obtaining possession of the seals, 'naything is duyne'.[37] In Stirling she was nearer the west country whence some of the discontented drew their strength, but the border lords who vowed loyalty to her were distracted by the need to protect their homelands from the raiding English. Sir George Douglas, who posed as her adviser in planning the Governor's downfall, was playing a double game all the time, in touch with the English authorities and military personnel. Others who were in correspondence with her, such as Mr Adam Otterburn, knew the truth about Douglas's double-dealing. Equally damaging to the Queen Dowager's bid for independent power were, first, the capture of one of her agents, Bauldreul, whose dispatches showed that she had sought a truce with England and, second, the failure of effective help to come from France, although this circumstance could also be said to have qualified the Cardinal's credibility in his threat to bring English interference in Scottish affairs to an end.

The Cardinal, who ultimately shared Mary's concerns, must have watched with mixed feelings her efforts to form an independent party. Since her Francophile policy, even although it was somewhat more comprehensive than his, and conservative religious position suited his own purposes, he was probably prepared to work *with* but not *under* her.[38] Like Sir George Douglas, he probably never envisaged a woman ruler with real executive power and he would therefore expect to have a leading role in any government of which she was the head. However, he was determined to take action against the mixed group of malcontents and dissidents among whom she was seeking support, many of whom regarded him as

an enemy to their interests, which made it appear as if the Dowager and he were on
opposite sides. There is nevertheless evidence that they were in communication
with each other during those months in which she and her party were planning to
depose Arran. They were sometimes in touch through intermediaries, such as
Huntly and his brother, Alexander Gordon, who promised Mary 'I sall do my
detfull diligence to hald my lord cardinall at the best opinioun for your grace
affect'.[39] Cunningham of Glengarnock, in letting her know in April 1544 that
Lennox's messenger had returned from France, added 'Yowr grays pleses to lat
nayn wet [know] I send ther tayandes [tidings] exsap me lord cardnal for cawses as
I sal schaw yowr grays'.[40] On the other hand, in mid-May, Alexander Gordon told
her that he had had proclamations issued in her name at Perth and Dundee where
there was a strong antipathy to the Cardinal.[41] She herself sent letters directly to
the Cardinal at the end of June.[42]

To whatever extent he may have been prepared to accept an increase in Mary's
authority, the Cardinal must have been disconcerted at the distance which her
opposition to the Governor created, however temporarily, between himself and
some of his friends. This new cause of alienation compounded that which he had
already experienced when he regained Arran, and it occurred at about the same
time as the opposition of Anglophile-reforming magnates and lairds within his
archdiocese, notably in Fife, Angus and parts of the Lothians, took on the
character of a personal vendetta. Indeed, it is ironic that this period of his apparent
control of public policy, from late 1543 onwards, saw the growth of a broadly-
based opposition to him.

Throughout 1544, both before and after the June convention which formally
suspended Arran from the governorship, Mary of Guise received professions of
support from both the English party, led by Sir George Douglas, Glencairn, Lord
Maxwell and their friends, and some of the Cardinal's allies of long standing, such
as Sir Adam Otterburn, whom Arran had had removed from the provostry of
Edinburgh during the recriminations that followed the English attack, the border
lairds of Buccleuch, Cessford and Ferniehirst and Lord Home (although these
qualified their ability to attend her personally by reminding her that they had to
defend their territories — 'lat us nocht think to tyne sa noble ane realme to our
ennymeis that our foirbearis hes sa lang kepit and defendit', as Home put it), the
earl of Huntly who in November also explained his delay in coming south by the
need to settle the 'uproar' in his own country, and Bothwell who boasted of having
brought his neighbour, Lord Borthwick, the Cardinal's bailie in the lordship of
Stow, to her service.[43] Borthwick, however, had asked for security in land from
Bothwell before he would make a bond with the Dowager and was in any case
being offered 'grett proffittis' by the Governor and Cardinal to stay with them. Sir
George Douglas advised Mary to detach some of the Cardinal's remaining allies,
including Robert Douglas of Lochleven, whose father-in-law, Lord Erskine,
might be asked to work on him, 'and at he cum and speik with yow and se geif ye
maye haif hem to be yours, for he is bath throw and manle and well kyp that he
promisis'. On 25 June Lochleven received a feu charter of the lands of Bishopshire
from the Cardinal free of down–payment.[44]

On 10 June a convention held by the Queen Dowager at Stirling, which the dissaffected who had joined her party probably regarded as *their* convention convened in her name, formally suspended Arran from the government for having abandoned the English treaties on the Cardinal's advice.[45] On 22 June Angus told Wharton that he had caused the deposition to be proclaimed at Dumfries.[46] The bond by which the lords who met at Stirling promised to support the government of Mary of Guise was signed by four bishops — Glasgow, Moray, Dunblane and Orkney — each of whom may have had his own reasons for disagreeing with the primate's belligerent stance, seven earls who, in addition to the predictable Angus and Cassillis, included the Cardinal's associates, Moray, Argyll, Huntly and Bothwell, as well as Montrose who had recently given him lodging during the Hertford invasion, three lords — Maxwell, Somerville and Erskine — and Sir George Douglas himself. That some of his friends took action independently of the Cardinal at this time may reflect their greater concern for internal peace, whether in their own or the national interest. Meantime, he was reported to be keeping his distance from public affairs, usually a sign that he was playing for time.[47] Whatever the Stirling convention might determine, the Governor could only be lawfully deposed in parliament. The Cardinal's strategy was to try to win over the dissaffected before parliament met in November. In the long run the Queen Dowager's bid for power did not stand the test of time.

By October Sir George Douglas was telling her that 'the governour waxis proud and the cuntray fallis to hym mayr for feyr nor for luf', and that there were rumours that the earls of Huntly, Montrose and Argyll were returning to his obedience.[48] He warned her of the Cardinal's attempts to win over even Lord Gray who had great influence as sheriff of Forfar in the area of greatest opposition to him and who had assisted him in July over the provostry of Perth: 'it war ane greit weill to yow to haif tham [Gray and John Charteris]'. He added that it seemed as though the earl of Rothes 'will be the Cardenallis'. On 20 October the latter had granted Lord Gray a charter of the lands of Rescobie, and two days later they exchanged bonds of manrent and maintenance, Gray agreeing to enter the Cardinal's household at the latter's expense and where he could watch the sheriff of Forfar's movements.[49] The earl Marischal, whose religious attitudes were more than suspect, was chosen as one of the Governor's commissioners to treat with the Queen Dowager's remaining supporters towards the end of the year. Montrose, his fellow-envoy, had altered course since signing the bond at Stirling in June. On 25 October the Cardinal wrote to that uncaught heretic, Erskine of Dun, asking him to join the Governor and himself at St Andrews before setting out with them for Edinburgh where a 'diet' was to be held.[50] It was typical of David Beaton that he demanded the kind of alignment that had to be seen to be personal.

The Governor's parliament which met at Edinburgh on 7 November 1544 declared the parliament convoked by Mary of Guise for Stirling to be of no effect.[51] Angus, Bothwell and Sir George Douglas were pardoned for their treason and the Douglases entered on a period of co-operation with the government. There are conflicting accounts of how the reconciliation between Mary of Guise and the Governor was effected, but the fact that it was achieved on honourable terms suggests a concern on all sides for a degree of amity and concord. Some accounts credit the Cardinal with taking the Governor with him to Stirling for a reconciliation while others allege that Sir George Douglas took the initiative, apparently in his own interest since he is said to have made contact with the Governor and the Cardinal without Mary's knowledge.[52] While there was concord on the surface, the old divisions remained since all wanted agreement in their own interests and were acting for opportunist reasons. The Douglases, having lost the trust of Henry VIII, needed alternative acceptance and a base in Scotland. The lords who had been dissaffected towards Arran and the Cardinal for personal reasons welcomed the substantial material rewards of co-operation in the form of money and land. Mary of Guise herself, having made her political point, found herself chief of a council of sixteen who would from now on advise the Governor, a check on Arran's power which some of the prelates had long recommended. The Cardinal, having bought off some of his enemies, hoped to be able to call on greater resources for the continuing war effort for which he himself in council pledged the church's silver if necessary to turn kirk bells into cannon, at the same time boasting that come next summer Scotland should have such aid from France as to be 'able to beat Englishmen as dogs'.[53]

In the religious field where his personal authority was paramount he had also been waging war. The legislation of March the previous year, authorising the use of the English scriptures but not public discussion of them other than by the Governor's preachers, had encouraged those who inclined towards protestantism to put on a bolder front *vis-à-vis* the church authorities in the ensuing months. After all, the fact that the legislation had been carried through on a motion of and with a majority vote of the laity in defiance of ecclesiastical objections had been a public defeat for the first estate, the circumstances of which would be reported back home by parliamentary commissioners.[54] The debate in parliament as to whether the vernacular scriptures might be profitably read, or heard read to them, by the laity extended to some theological argument in which the laity were represented by Lord Ruthven and Mr Henry Balnaves. Their logic was that if Christ had commanded his word to be preached to all nations, then all should hear it in a tongue they could understand. The clergy's reply was the traditional objection of the medieval church that lay persons would be led astray by reading imperfect translations or in trying to understand difficult passages. In the end the burgh commissioners and part of the nobility demanded that it be permitted to 'everie man to use the benefite of the translatioune of the Old and New Testament, which then they had; together with the benefite of other treatises conteaning wholesome doctrine, till the prelats and kirkmen sett furth a translatioune more correct'. The kirkmen must have been as worried about the effects of the treatises of 'wholesome doctrine' which opened the door to Lutheran and other protestant literature, as about the use of Tyndale's new testament whose emphases they found suspect. Henry Balnaves and Lord Ruthven, by their prominent part in the proceedings, laid up trouble for themselves with the Cardinal later in the year.

Looking back on the ensuing euphoria, John Knox wrote with some distaste of those who had jumped on the bandwagon in the hope of winning the Governor's favour, parading copies of the new testament which some of them had scarcely read.[55] It would be unnecessarily cynical, however, not to admit that the atmosphere of apparent approval of vernacular bible-reading probably caused some genuine souls to share their views less guardedly than hitherto and that this brief period of reform resulted in a spread of protestant ideas among a variety of people. The year 1543 saw the circulation of heretical and strongly anticlerical literature which went further than the government intended reform should go, such as 'the new dialogue callit pascullus' and 'the ballait callit the bair' prohibited by the lords of council. The extent to which views were openly expressed is reflected in the lords' concern about the number of 'sacramentaris', who disputed the nature and effect of the mass, regarding this as a commemorative act as in the teaching of Zwingli, a belief which was probably strengthened as time went on by the teaching of Mr George Wishart.

There was a certain amount of iconoclasm, always an expression of dissatisfaction if not a guide to the depth of understanding of protestantism by those who indulged in it. It was simply a brutal way of making a point, as in the sacking of the friaries of Dundee, where Friars Guillaume and Rough had preached, advocating the use of the vernacular scriptures, and from which burgh two commissioners, David Rollock and Robert Mill, had attended the March 1543 parliament. Rollock and Mill stand for the many who must have been more disturbed than convinced by the new teaching. The former had received the escheat in 1538 of his more committed brother, James Rollock, who left Scotland and became involved in circulating controversial books coming from the press of the London printer and reformer, John Mailler. Mill, having suffered for his reformed opinions at an earlier stage, succumbed to pressure from the Cardinal and later served the latter's summons on George Wishart, with what heart-searchings we do not know.

Very little is known about the inquisition which took place in Angus and the Mearns late in 1543 after Arran's capitulation, which had connections with the punitive exercise against the Anglophile lords and gentlemen in that region, resulting in the arrests of Rothes, Gray and Balnaves and in an unrealised plan to take Lord Glamis as well. The Cardinal's relations with some families in the area were far from harmonious. Robert Maule of Panmure, one of whose sons is said to have taught him 'the cheif pointis of [the protestant] religione', and the widow of Peter Carmichael, a kinsman of the laird of Balmaddie who was later involved in the plot to kill the Cardinal, had their tacks annulled for arrears of rent.[56] Other local families must have been out of sympathy with their landlord: the Stratouns who had been associated with heresy since the 1530s, the Ochterlonies of Kellie, tenants of Arbroath abbey, one of whom took part in an attack on the kirk of St Vigeans and the Lady chapel of Arbroath, and, of course, Lords Gray and Glamis and the earl Marischal, the last of whom was soon to champion George Wishart.

There were some arrests as a result of the eastern inquisition: the laird of Brigton, near Forfar, who was in the circle of John Erskine of Dun, and two priests, David Lindsay and John Wigton.[57] The Dominican, John Roger, first appointed by the Governor to preach in Aberdeen in company with Friar Walter

Thomson, was apprehended for defiance of a monition against his preaching in Lord Glamis's parish kirk and was afterwards found dead on the rocks below St Andrews castle where he had been imprisoned.[58] The circumstances of his death were never explained, but the tragedy dates from a period when the Cardinal's attempts to staunch opposition showed signs of fury and a readiness to cut across the processes of justice. After the parliament of December 1543 had annulled the March legislation in favour of the English scriptures there was a cleaning-up operation in Aberdeen under the direction of the earl of Huntly as a result of which certain people were indicted: two burgesses, Thomas Branche and Thomas Cusing, were imprisoned for taking part in the public hanging of the image of St Francis,[59] evidence that the authorities took iconoclasm at this time seriously, while the lairds of Fyvie and Philorth and the earl Marischal paid for pardons for holding heretical opinions and reading forbidden books.[60]

The Cardinal's attack on heretics in Perth, where the strength of the protestant enclave encouraged them to be fairly open with their views, was two-pronged:[61] to make an example of a handful of heretics (Calderwood says that many were accused of heresy but only a few were put to death) and to let the ruling sector in the burgh know that he did not approve of their allowing heresy to breed in the burgh, by removing the provosts, first John Charteris and then Lord Ruthven. The Governor himself was concerned by the fact that a large contingent of men from Perth and its neighbourhood was supporting Lennox around the turn of the year, joining him at Leith, and on the back of a craft riot in Perth at Michaelmas this indicated a possible fusion of local and national disorder. In mid-January 1544 soon after the agreement with the Lennox-Angus party at Edinburgh the Governor and the Cardinal travelled to Perth to make an example of the burgh.[62] Expecting confrontation, they went as an armed force, taking artillery with them at considerable expense and trouble. The fact that the trial and execution of the heretics was accomplished with marked expedition indicates a previous gathering of evidence and preparation for the proceedings. In the atmosphere that prevailed in the burgh the judges saw the advantage of a quick demonstration of justice. The Governor and Cardinal were accompanied by the justiciar, the earl of Argyll, Sir John Campbell of Calder and Bishop Robert Reid, both experienced composers of quarrels, and William Chisholm, the bishop of Dunblane.

Those who were condemned under the re-enacted statutes which forbade the possession and reading of the vernacular scriptures and the discussion of central articles of faith such as the doctrine of the mass and the place of the Virgin Mary and the saints, included Robert Lamb, a merchant, three craftsmen, James Ranaldson, a skinner, James Hunter, a flesher, and William Anderson, a maltman, James Finlayson and Helen Stirk, Ranaldson's wife. Robert Lamb, who was arrested in the course of his business in the presence of his workmen, is said to have seen some of his fellow-protestants fleeing from the town.[63] Among those believed to have fled are Walter Piper, father-in-law of James Hunter and one of those who forced entry to the Black Friars' monastery at Perth in May 1543, whose family also used the surname Balnaves,[64] and sir Henry Elder, chaplain and burgh clerk of Perth, whose exile was short-lived since he was back in Perth towards the end of the year.[65] Those who were brought to trial were accused of having attended a discussion and bible-reading organised by Robert Lamb on the St Andrew's Day holiday in the chapel associated with the hospital of St Anne near St John's kirk.[66] James Hunter, 'a simple man', unable to read himself, had attended the gathering.[67] A month before, on All Hallows Day, Lamb is said to have interrupted the sermon in St John's kirk of Friar Spence, disputing with him the efficacy of prayers to the saints.[68] This personal confrontation split the congregation, and in the ensuing disturbance the women, for whom the saints were always a particular source of reassurance, were loudest in the denunciation of Lamb. One of the bailies, James Rhind, advised the preacher to remove himself and escorted him away from the crowd. Lamb's supporters and opponents carried the dispute out into the street where Lamb was only saved from physical attack, mostly at the women's hands, by his friends who heard him remark that 'the truth' had been hidden long enough. The meeting which he arranged four weeks later in St Anne's chapel was therefore an act of defiance, demonstrating his determination to give the whole debate an open character. Helen Stirk's reputed refusal to call on the Virgin Mary during childbirth was especially offensive to her female neighbours, some of whom doubtless testified to her attitude. Her husband and others were indicted for their insult to the image of St Francis, and she herself on her way to execution is said to have identified the Grey Friars as 'the caus of our death this day ... '[69] The Franciscans, who may have provided some of the evidence against the accused, were no doubt angered at the humiliation of Friar Spence during his public sermon.

The deaths of these people, especially of Helen Stirk whose children thus lost both parents, provoked a sense of outrage which spread further than their religious sympathisers, even outwith Scotland.[70] The chaplain of St Katherine's chapel, possibly thinking of a backlash of sympathy, is said to have publicly declared that the town would regret the events.[71] A last-minute appeal to Arran for more merciful treatment predictably failed. The justiciar's clerks and those of the privy seal issued escheats in return for payment immediately following the executions and banishments. John Stirk, burgess of Perth, received the escheats of his daughter and son-in-law free,[72] but the escheat of the banished Walter Piper cost his family £200. Robert Lamb's escheat and that of James Hunter went to Christian Piper, widow of Hunter and daughter of Walter Piper, and her daughter Violet.[73] Not only were these protestant families related to one another in Perth itself but they had contacts with a circle of landed families who shared their antipathy to the Cardinal and his actions. In 1530, for example, Walter Piper and his wife, Violet Hog, had received a charter from John Ross of Craigie,[74] who as keeper of the Spey Tower in which the heretics were lodged, fell foul of the Cardinal and Governor during the episode and had to hand over the keys of the tower. As early as 1516 John Balnaves, alias Piper, held land at Polkmill from the then Lord Gray.[75] Associations over more than one generation linked urban and landward families who were being drawn towards reforming ideas. John Charteris of Kinfauns, provost of Perth, was removed from office on the day following the executions and Mr Alexander McBreck, who had had considerable civic experience, was installed in his place by authority of the Governor. By the summer of 1544, however, when the Queen Dowager's party were extending their campaign for her support to Perth and Dundee, the Cardinal used the feud between the then provost of Perth, Lord Ruthven, whose religious leanings were suspect, and John Charteris to have Ruthven removed from his position of influence.[76] Charteris, backed by his friends Lord Gray and Norman Leslie and their men, tried to take possession of the provostry which the Cardinal had 'purchased' for him from the Governor. A brief battle between the two sides on the bridge which gave access to the burgh resulted in victory for Ruthven assisted by his son. As a result Charteris, Leslie and those who had acted with them reverted to their more usual attitude of animosity towards the Cardinal whose plot to gain control of the burgh, by using them for his own ends, had failed. 'For as manie of them entered in that action for his pleasure, so thought they to have had his assistance, wherof finding themselves frustrated, they beganne to looke more narrowlie to themselves, and so a new jealousie was kindled amongst them.'[77] In fact, Leslie and Charteris were already in the plot to kill the Cardinal during his travels and had only hoped to benefit personally from taking part in his Perth scheme.

A stronger current of heresy flowed from the presence in Scotland during 1544 of Mr George Wishart, kinsman of the laird of Pittarrow, who had come via England from Germany and Switzerland with an articulate theological message, put over in evangelical terms with the help of a charismatic personality. In a sense, his presence among the mixed bunch of Anglophiles, reform-minded laymen, convinced protestants and disturbed catholics, who until his arrival had lacked a spiritual focal point, was the counter-influence to much that the Cardinal had been able to achieve among them by force of his own character through fear or favour. Wishart's activities, his contacts with a circle of sympathisers, his apparent intention to speak his mind openly, must have reminded David Beaton of the phenomenon of Patrick Hamilton in the early years of his own career, although the two reformers were very different types of men.

The Wisharts of Pittarrow in Fordoun parish, Kincardineshire held some of their lands from Arbroath abbey; a precept dating from 1525, a year after David Beaton's appointment to the abbacy, was issued for the infeftment of John Wishart as heir to his father, Mr James Wishart of Pittarrow, clerk of the justiciary, who had died the year before.[78] The exact relationship between the laird of Pittarrow and the reformer is not clear. George Wishart was described as 'son of George Wishart of Dundee' when he matriculated as a poor scholar at the university of Louvain, although in another entry in the register he is referred to simply as 'of St Andrews', either archdiocese or university.[79] He was a brilliant student, graduating first in order of merit in the faculty of arts at Louvain in 1532. By 1535 he is said to have been teaching in the grammar school at Montrose under the patronage of Erskine of Dun but was among those who fled to England in 1538, the year before the Cardinal's first prosecutions when inquisitions may have been carried out.[80] Having received a preacher's licence from the suffragan of Bishop Latimer of Worcester, Wishart appeared in Bristol where his denunciatory style of preaching won many converts, it is said, in the city that had been an early centre of Lollardy and had later heard the preaching of Tyndale. The Scotsman's activities provoked a riot between rival parties and led to an accusation of heresy by the dean of Worcester, John Kerne, who passed Wishart on to Thomas Cromwell in January 1539. Notwithstanding, in the following May Wishart 'sett furth the moost blasphemous heresy that ever was heard'. He may have been something of an embarrassment to Latimer, and to Cromwell who had engineered Latimer's appointment to Worcester in 1535. He was championed by the Bristol craftsmen, chiefly pointmakers, who in defending him called him 'the faithful young man' and 'the honest reader'. He formally recanted in July 1539, without abandoning his beliefs, and Cromwell arranged his removal from the trouble area for a time during which he travelled in Germany and Switzerland.

For all his oratory it is said that Wishart's preaching was characterised by the fact that he made his hearers think for themselves and left questions in their minds. He himself had travelled some way along the paths of protestant thinking by the time he reached the crisis of his life in the mid-1540s.[81] It has been shown that his earliest ideas show signs of contact with Anabaptism, for example on baptism itself and on the idea of 'soul-sleepers', which he later abandoned. In Switzerland he adopted certain Zwinglian positions, especially on the doctrine of the Eucharist, as expressed in the first Helvetic Confession of 1536 which he translated: 'the Body and Blood of Our Lord are received verily of a faithful soul', not as a 'carnal' presence but 'tokens by which the very Communion or participation of the Lord's Body and Blood are exhibited of the Lord Himself to be the spiritual nourishment of the soul'.

Wishart's message, therefore, was thought-provoking not simply rabble-rousing. His character, too, was many-sided and he was a man of changing moods, vehement in his denunciations yet at other times withdrawn. He was both ascetic and benevolent: in Cambridge, like Thomas Bilney, he gave regularly to the poor and outcasts. By 1543 he was at Corpus Christi college, Cambridge, where the more stable academic background seems to have wrought another change in him. One of his students, Emery Tilney, remembered him as 'glad to teach, desirous to learn and well travelled', but that although 'he taught with great modesty and gravity ... some of his people thought him severe and would have slain him, but the Lord was his defence'.[82] Wishart returned to Scotland in the summer of 1543 in the company of those Scottish commissioners who had been to London to discuss the terms of the marriage and peace treaties. There has been much speculation as to how much Wishart may have known of the plot to kill the Cardinal which was first hatched in the spring of 1544. It seems impossible to prove or disprove his part in the business or to identify him with the 'Scotsman named Wishart' who carried Brunston's letter to Hertford in which the plotters intimated their intentions.[83] Apart from noting in passing that this messenger may have been George Wishart, a burgess of Dundee, who was among those accused of attacking the burgh friaries during the reformer's preaching there and who was known to be identified with radical reform, it does not seem profitable to pursue the possibility. Wishart was personally acquainted with the would-be assassins of

1543 and with some of the actual murderers of the Cardinal in 1546. He lived in days when vengeance was not always left to the Lord even in righteous causes, and there would be nothing alien in the possibility that he was told the content of the letter he carried to Hertford, if he did so. His movements in 1544 are difficult to date precisely but he seems to have moved around extensively in the east of Scotland, preaching in public in Dundee and elsewhere, and gaining a considerable amount of acceptability with his hearers for his contrasting gifts of denunciation and charity. The extent to which his presence tended to lend cohesion to the diverse groups of political and religious malcontents was not lost on the Cardinal, but he must have been aware that to trap Wishart would be a difficult business, hedged about as the preacher was with influential protectors many of whom harboured a growing resentment towards himself.

As the advocate of the French alliance the year 1544 had been a frustrating one for David Beaton, for little in the way of realistic French support had materialised. The many rumours, current since the end of 1543, that he might go to France, alone or in the company of other envoys, may be the echoes of his expressions of hope. His remark to the papal legate, Grimani, that although he had spent some 30,000 *scudi* besides all his own income on the affairs of the distracted realm, he would gladly pay 20,000 more to find himself with him in France sounds like a heartfelt wish to be out of the mess into a place which he much preferred.[84] Lennox's behaviour since his recall from France in the spring of 1543 had done little to give Francis I confidence in his Scottish allies, preoccupied with his own wars as he was, or to enhance the Cardinal's reputation as a diplomat, coming as the Lennox episode did on the heels of a long, unfruitful embassy in 1542. 'It is said heir', John Campbell told Lennox from Dieppe in March 1544, 'that ye ar all the caus of the hayll brek and devysoun that is in Scotland ... and daly spendis and waistis the kyng of Francys monye haldand ane gard of thevys and brokyn men about yow and wyll nocht answer the quenis grace not the ambassadoris of nane of the said mony'.[85] There were attempts to slight the Cardinal in the eyes of the French King, as when Sir George Douglas advised the Queen Dowager to ask Francis to send all material help directly to her and not to 'ony prevet persoun syk as the guvernur or the cardenell', since she had by her authority united all the lords for the Queen's service and the defence of the realm.[86] However, perhaps the fact that the five French ships that did arrive in mid-May 1544 put in at St Andrews indicates that he had not lost all his credit with the French government.[87]

De la Brosse and Ménage, whom James Stewart of Cardonald had described to the Cardinal on their arrival in October 1543 as 'na grett personages',[88] had been observers and foreign correspondents rather than military assisters, apart from the money and arms which they had injudiciously handed over to Lennox. David Beaton, with his lines of communication with Europe, such as news of the war in France which he received from David Paniter via a Leith merchant in April 1544,[89] must have known that although France was on Scotland's side in the long run, in the short term substantial military help was unlikely in spite of occasional rumours, and his own claims that it was on its way. During the summer of 1544 the French King was waging a war on two fronts, with the Emperor and with Henry

VIII, both on French soil. If the Cardinal was depressed by the news of the final fall of Boulogne to the English in September, he may have taken comfort from the fact that Francis had refused to abandon his Scottish allies, as the Scots had earlier refused to abandon the French alliance, even although this had contributed to the breakdown in Anglo-French peace talks and the continuation of the siege.[90]

In one respect he must have had a sense of satisfaction. He now possessed the long-awaited faculty of papal legate *a latere*, news of which had reached him in March 1544, although the actual document itself fell into English hands, giving him a powerful weapon in operating ecclesiastical patronage and enforcing his spiritual authority over the church in Scotland and, to some extent, over the lives of the laity. On Christmas eve he wrote to the Cardinal of S. Crucis relating his own efforts for the internal peace of Scotland and reassuring him of the country's continued loyalty to the holy see.[91] He asked for papal support in facing English aggression, considering 'our continued obedience to the Holy See and their [the English] disobedience', adding that the Patriarch of Aquilea, Grimani, and Adam Mure his own secretary would relate the afflictions of Scotland. After another long haul, throughout another year, through insurrection, invasion, political division and religious protest he had kept the ship of state on course — but only just. No one knew better than he how fragile the unity was or how much it was likely to be tried in the future.

NOTES

1. *Scottish Correspondence*, 446
2. *Ibid.*, 56–7
3. *Hamilton Papers*, II, 254
4. *Ibid.*, II, 273
5. Donaldson, *All the Queen's Men*, 19
6. *L.P. Henry VIII*, XIX, i, 235
7. Court book of the regality of Glasgow (S.R.O.), RH 11/32/1/1
8. *Glasguensis*, 555–6; *Rentale*, 181
9. *Ibid.*
10. *R.S.S.*, III, 962
11. *L.P. Henry VIII*, XX, i, 626
12. *Scottish Correspondence*, 72 and *note*
13. *Hamilton papers*, II, 256
14. *L.P. Henry VIII*, XIX, i, 188
15. M. Merriman, 'The Assured Scots'
16. *Ibid.*, 16
17. *Ibid.*, 23
18. *Ibid.*, 28
19. *Knox.*, I, 56
20. *Hamilton Papers*, II, 362–3; *L.P. Henry VIII*, XIX, i, 472, 481
21. M. Lynch, *Edinburgh and the Reformation*, 68–9

22. *Ibid.*

23. *L.P. Henry VIII*, XIX, i, 510

24. *Rentale*, 180

25. *Formulare*, II, 624

26. *L.P. Henry VIII*, XIX, i, 510

27. *Rentale*, 179

28. *Antiquities of Aberdeen and Banff*, III, 249–51

29. Register of Acts and Decreets, ii, fo 539

30. J. Stevenson, *Selections . . . illustrative of the reign of Mary, Queen of Scotland* (Maitland Club), 13–15

31. *R.M.S.*, III, 3105

32. *Hamilton Papers*, II, 344; *L.P. Henry VIII*, XIX, i, 350

33. *Hamilton Papers*, II, 351; *L.P. Henry VIII*, XIX, i, 404

34. *Ibid*, XIX, i, 389

35. *Scottish Correspondence*, 60–5

36. *Ibid.*, 64

37. *Ibid.*

38. *Ibid.*, 65

39. *Ibid.*, 104

40. *Ibid.*, 73

41. *Ibid.*, 82–3

42. *Ibid.*, 66–120, *passim*; *Rentale*, 180

43. *Scottish Correspondence*, 113

44. *R.M.S.*, V, 1145; Morton muniments, GD 150/962

45. *Hamilton Papers*, II, 264

46. *Ibid.*, II, 416

47. *L.P. Henry VIII*, XIX, i, 955

48. *Scottish Correspondence*, 110–13

49. *Spalding Club Miscellany*, V, 295–6

50. *H.M.C. Report*, IV (Erskine of Dun), 635

51. *A.P.S.*, II, 447

52. *Scottish Correspondence*, 65

53. *L.P. Henry VIII*, XIX, ii, 709

54. *Calderwood*, I, 156–7

55. *Knox*, I, 45

56. Sentence book of the official of St Andrews principal (S.R.O.), CH 5/2/1, fos 50v, 51v

57. Cowan, *The Scottish Reformation*, 101–2

58. *Knox*, I, 56; *Extracts from the council register of Aberdeen* (Spalding Club), 189

59. Cowan, *The Scottish Reformation*, 100

60. *Ibid.* and 109; Donaldson, *All the Queen's Men*, 24, 44

61. I am grateful to Dr Mary Verschuur for sharing with me in conversation her main findings contained in her unpublished thesis on Perth and the Reformation and for supplying me with biographical information on the Perth heretics for inclusion in Appendix 3. The interpretation of the Perth situation as expressed in this book is my own.

62. *T.A.* VIII, 252

63. *Calderwood*, 175

64. R.S.S., III, 113, 1437

65. *Calderwood*, I, 175; Charters of King James VI Hospital, Perth (S.R.O.), GD

79/4/119–20

66. *Calderwood*, I, 173–4

67. *Ibid.*, 172

68. *Ibid.*, 171–4

69. R.S. Fittis, *Ecclesiastical Annals of Perth*, 123

70 Durkan, 'Scottish "Evangelicals" ', 150

71. Fittis, *op. cit.*, 123

72. *R.S.S.* III, 609

73. *Ibid.*, III, 611

74. *R.M.S.* III, 1275

75. *R.S.S.*, I, 2495

76. *Knox*, I, 52–3

77. *Ibid.*, I, 53

78. Southesk charters, 4, Bundle 2. I am grateful to the Earl of Southesk for permission to examine a number of original charters.

79. Durkan, 'Scottish "Evangelicals" ', 143

80. *Ibid.*

81. *Ibid.*, 150

82. *Calderwood*, I, 185–6

83. *Hamilton Papers*, II, 344

84. Hannay, 'Letters of the Papal Legate in Scotland', 20

85. *Scottish Correspondence*, 68

86. *Ibid.*, 90

87. *L.P. Henry VIII*, XIX, i, 510; on 11 May the provost and bailies of St Andrews reached agreement with M. Liegur, provost-marshall of France, about two prizes taken by the French ships, Crawford priory muniments, GD 20/4/134

88. *Scottish Correspondence*, 34

89. *Ibid.*, 74–5

90. Knecht, *French Renaissance Monarchy*, 43

91. *L.P. Henry VIII*, XIX, ii, 774

12

The Best Frenchman

The fragile unity of the governing party and the opposing lords which had been achieved in the late autumn of 1544 was reinforced at first by the threat of further English invasion in the winter of 1544-5.[1] At one stage Henry's agent, Cassillis, advised him to withhold an attack as this would simply unite those who would otherwise be of different opinions. Outward signs of unity included the co-operation of Angus and Sir George Douglas, the latter being on particularly cordial terms with the Cardinal, possibly because Lennox, the alternative to Arran's régime, had meantime disappeared from the Scottish scene, although he carried out some destruction of the Hamilton lands in the autumn and around the turn of the year was sent by Henry to Carlisle to 'practice' with the Scots, especially with his father-in-law, Angus.[2] It was understandable that the lords should hold together for mutual defence, for the situation was demoralising: almost 200 towns, towers and settlements were burnt between July and November 1544, with over 400 slain and twice as many taken prisoners.[3] Certain border strongholds and the priory of Coldingham were in English hands. Attempts by both Angus in November and the Governor himself in December to retake the priory failed.[4] On the second occasion Arran fled after hearing of the English advance, leaving behind the valuable artillery which the exasperated Angus and his men managed to drag to the safety of Dunbar. In mid-February Sir Ralph Eure, the English warden of the middle marches, and Sir Brian Layton entered Scotland with 400 men, including a contingent of assured Scots, and burnt Jedburgh and Melrose abbeys and the surrounding country. At Melrose they sacked the burial place of the Douglases, a visitation on Angus and Sir George for their treachery which confirmed them in their adherence to the Scottish war campaign for the purpose of taking their revenge. Assisted by Buccleuch and the master of Rothes, Angus led the Scots to their only victory, at Ancrum Moor, on 27 February, in which both Eure and Layton were killed.[5] Angus had found it necessary before the action to exhort the Governor to join him in letting the world see what they could do to destroy their respective reputations of 'coward' and 'traitor'. He also anticipated Henry VIII's reaction by pointing out that he was fighting to avenge the invaders' insult to the tombs of his ancestors. In an access of relief as much as joy at their victory the Governor afterwards took Angus about the neck 'and kissed him twenty times, saying he repented having ever mistrusted him, who had that day done so much for Scotland. Whereunto Anguisshe answered that God knew his loyalty to his native country'.[6]

Beneath all the euphoria, however, the old divisions remained. After a mass at Holyrood during which Mary of Guise was accompanied by Arran, the Cardinal, Montrose, Argyll, Marischal, Bothwell and Glencairn, representing many shades of political and religious opinion, Glencairn whispered in the ear of a spy that he would keep every promise he had made to the King of England.[7] About the same time Angus swore he would work with Lennox, making him 'ruler of Scotland' if the latter would continue to negotiate.[8] When Arran gathered his force at Lauder in late February many refused to join so long as the Douglases were in the army, fearing some kind of treachery; later events were to prove that their fears were well-founded. When the devastation of the invasions failed to make the Scots sue for peace, Henry resorted to the services of his agent, Cassillis, whom he sent to Scotland at the end of March with the reminder that the safety of the Kennedy hostages in England depended on his support.[9]

It is hardly credible that the Cardinal really trusted the Douglases, but to gain their co-operation represented a victory over Henry VIII. He continued to purchase the support of those whom he must have known were playing a double game, such as the Fife and Angus lords and gentlemen to whom he granted charters and dispensations under his new legatine authority. It was said that he had procured a French pension for Sir George Douglas[10] and that he had offered Lord Maxwell great material inducements to come over the Francophile side.[11] From time to time he acquired the services of Englishmen. He tried unsuccessfully to get hold of Thomas Gower, who was held to ransom after Ancrum Moor, for whom Sir George Douglas was said to have offered £500 but who was bought by Home of Coldenknowes.[12] He had his agents abroad including an English priest who was said to be working for him at Rome in 1545 and the English-born Friar Elston, formerly of Greenwich but by then in Antwerp, who passed letters both to him and Cardinal Pole.[13] He even had contacts in England itself and in Ireland, about whom little is known, with whom his French correspondent de Moulins urged him, in April 1545, to 'work all things carefully' in passing the French King's letters, which had come into the Cardinal's hands via Zeeland, to French agents in Ireland.[14] More than once his foreign correspondence was seized from a captured ship. At the same time, the price of co-operation with the Douglases was that they knew what was going on along his lines of communication. On 14 April, for example, de Moulins, in reply to Sir George Douglas's request for help to release John Drummond, a Scottish detainee in England, told Douglas that attempts were also being made by the Cardinal's agent, Anthony Westputyus, a native of the diocese of Mirepoix.[15]

The constant interception of the Cardinal's post must often have delayed important news in both directions. In order to strengthen Franco-Scottish friendship he sent abroad accounts of Scotland's steadfastness towards the French alliance which 'made glad all France', as de Moulins told him.[16] After the failure to take Coldingham and before the Scottish victory of Ancrum had lifted morale the Cardinal was said to have promised the French ambassador that the French King should have the young Queen to marry where he wished and that she and her mother would go to France in the spring.[17] This was the first open suggestion of a French match for the Queen but may have been little more than a diplomatic move on the Cardinal's part in an effort to gain French intervention in the crisis, since there were later to be other marriage proposals for the Queen of Scots. It is significant that he had not suggested a French marriage at the time when he was intent on breaking the English marriage treaty but had rather suggested some Scottish alternatives which were calculated to retain the support of both Arran and Lennox. He was probably no more inclined to put Scotland, in the person of the Queen, into the hands of the Most Christian King of France, without political safeguards, than into those of the apostate King of England. Considering his own personal interests in France, it is interesting that he did not rush to sell Scotland out to the French. To do so would have upset the dynastically-minded Arran and caused him to look again to Henry VIII for advantage, which always brought with it the threat to Scottish church property. Besides, to keep the question of the royal marriage perennially open was one way of playing off England against France, so keeping Henry preoccupied. But he had to be careful, for there were signs that the state of Franco-Scottish relations and the Cardinal's French credit were not as good as they had been. In the long run, the French envoy, de Lorges, who came to Scotland in 1545, accused David Beaton of self-interest in the diplomatic game, blaming him, through his treatment of Lennox, for the latter's treachery towards France.

Two French ships with money and munition had arrived by the time Cassillis reached Scotland with a commission from Henry to wring some agreement out of the Scottish leaders. He discovered that the latter were in no mood to discuss peace terms, dominated as they were by Mary of Guise and the Cardinal who carried the Governor with them.[18] The victory at Ancrum and the arrival of the French doubtless strengthened their resolve, although Cassillis reported that there were among them 'dissensions which are too long to write'. After secret meetings with the pro-English lords he advised Henry to send a sufficiently strong force to reassure his supporters that he meant business in Scotland and at the same time to test their 'loyalty'. Relations among Sir George Douglas, the earl Marischal and the Cardinal were deteriorating.[19] A call-up of all men between the ages of 16 and 60 had gone out for an expedition against the English in the borders. His peace mission having failed, Cassillis hurriedly left Edinburgh, narrowly escaping arrest, and proceeded to revive the plot to kill the Cardinal. Meantime, on 12 April, de Moulins wrote to the Cardinal intimating that de Lorges and the main French force were about to sail for Scotland.[20] By whatever means word reached them, for the letter was intercepted, the Cardinal and the Governor made ready to go to the west to meet the Frenchmen. It was during this visit to Glasgow that the primate and the archbishop of Glasgow are believed to have had their confrontation in the cathedral over precedence, after which both the Cardinal and the Governor wrote to the Pope asking for his support on behalf of the former's ecclesiastical pre-eminence which they felt it to be particularly necessary to uphold in the present domestic and international situation.[21] The question was not simply one of personal rivalry. There are suggestions that the Cardinal could not always be sure of Dunbar's public support even with regard to the treatment of heresy. It was vital that he should be seen to be in command.

At the end of May the main part of the French forces arrived in the Clyde to reinforce the planned expedition to the borders. The next few months were to be a test of strength for the Cardinal's war policy. They were also to reveal the double-dealing of the Douglases whom Henry VIII had promised to forgive all their offences now that he was confronted with the French presence in Scotland. There are varying accounts of the strength of the French reinforcements, but they were probably fewer than 5,000 men, of whom about 500 were horsemen. They were commanded by Jacques de Montgomery, Seigneur de Lorges, of Scottish extraction, who was a captain of the King of France's Scots Guard, his force including a number of Scots guards themselves. Reports of their departure from France and even of their arrival in Scotland convey the extent to which the French King had attached safeguards to de Lorges's instructions, warning him not to trust anyone without due consideration, a lesson learned from Lennox's behaviour in 1534–4.[22] When they arrived the landing was held up while the captains made doubly sure of their contacts. A spy in Buccleuch's household, who heard a letter from the Cardinal to the laird read aloud, reported to Hertford that the Cardinal had told Buccleuch that de Lorges had brought 3,000 Frenchmen, including 500 horsemen, and 300,000 crowns in rewards for all 'good Scotsmen', as well as 100 men to wait on the Governor at the French King's expense. He had also mentioned a planned French invasion of the coast of England.[23] Before the ships sailed from France the Imperial ambassador, St Mauris, reported that de Lorges carried with him 150,000 crowns, forged from 10,000 crowns and copper, to pay his soldiers in Scotland.[24] However much money he brought, it was running out before the campaign ended.

At a hastily-called but well-attended convention in Stirling on 26 June, at which the lords heard de Lorges' commission from Francis, a formal statement in support of the French alliance and in favour of the pursuance of the war against England was drawn up and received 54 signatures. Angus, Huntly, Argyll, Bothwell, Rothes and Glencairn (their private allegiances evenly divided) were chosen to sit with the Queen Dowager, the Governor and the Cardinal to plan the conduct of the war.[25] Two days later, in implementation of an order already taken on a proposition of de Lorges, it was decided that there should be a nationwide muster at Roslin moor on 28 July.[26] From the first de Lorges acted like a commander rather than auxiliary captain, which may have caused friction with the Scottish leaders. It is clear that France regarded operations in Scotland simply as part of a wider military commitment, something which was reflected in the title, 'commissioner for payment of extraordinary expenses of the French King's wars', borne by the paymaster in Scotland, M. Jacques Veau, who on 2 July paid Lord Home 100 crowns for 'expenses in the castle of Home on the frontier with England'.[27] There were even more deep-seated sources of division in the ranks. On 4 July Hertford, Tunstall and Sadler, in reporting a secret meeting between Hertford's servant, Thomas Forster, and Sir George Douglas, quoted the latter as saying that he would do his best to wreck the muster at Roslin and the ensuing expedition in the hope that, as he put it, 'if they [the Scots army] stopped, after making such great brags, they would lose the commons' hearts for ever'. Douglas also gave details of Scottish military movements and remarked that the Cardinal, once again, was chiefly held responsible for the war and was 'smally beloved'.

Forster himself passed on information about the arrival of the French ordnance and mentioned the agreement by the merchant-shipmaster, John Barton, to victual the army, waxing eloquent about the Frenchmen's horses which he had sighted at Dalkeith, 'which be very fair pieces'.[28]

Meantime the Cardinal dispatched a piece of propaganda in the form of a letter to the Pope, telling him that things were better than they had been, that the quarrels of the nobles were appeased, that heretical opinions were almost extinguished and that an army was ready to repress English 'audacity' on the borders.[29] When the practicalities of war were discussed in council on 29 June he 'sperit at everie man present to declare thair mynd therintill'.[30] All he expected was their public acquiescence for, unlike the gullible Arran, he did not trust men's verbal protestations any more than he believed his own words to the Pope: he knew that political alliances were constantly shifting, that the Anglophile lords were not to be trusted and that the problem of heresy had not gone away. Whether he knew it or not, the threat to his own life was growing. In the month of July Sadler replied to a second offer from Brunston and his friends to take out of the way 'the worker of all your mischief'.[31] If I were you, Sadler said in effect, I would 'earnestly attempt it'. He asked them to name their price which would be paid 'immediately on the act executed'. But, they must understand, he was writing only as one giving advice. In fact, he was letting them know that Henry VIII had got their message. Sadler asked Brunston to pass on his reply to Sir George Douglas whom he understood to be of the same mind regarding the Cardinal and also to Cassillis whom he was beginning to fear had forgotten the proposal. The plotters thus gained an additional incentive to murder: not only the earlier promise of protection from justice following their deed but the hope of some blood-money as well. It is indicative of the grip that the Cardinal had on policy at this juncture, in association with Mary of Guise and Arran, of course, that for the Anglophiles and their allies there seemed no hope of changing the way things were going other than by getting rid of him altogether. They could see his hand in legislation against religious dissent and assurance with England and it was clear that he intended, in spite of setbacks, to pursue the war. On the eve of the military expedition he took steps to prevent the dissipation of vital crown revenues in the war conditions by stipulating that he must always be one of the compositors whose signatures the Governor required before he could make any gifts from the royal *casualty* or *property* and he himself headed the list of those who were to remain with the person of the Queen when the military leaders departed for the border.[32]

The offensive against the English was a failure and a humiliation for the Cardinal. The muster arranged for Roslin on 28 July was delayed and then poorly attended when it did take place. When the expedition set out, nominally under Arran but with the vanguard under the fateful command of Angus and containing the companies of the Anglophile Glencairn, Cassillis, Gray and Glamis, it accomplished little more than the burning of a few English towns near the border. The Cardinal's embroidered banner, newly made by the royal tailor, was unfurled at Wark castle but many of his vassals are said to have stayed away. 'Many had before promised', Knox wrote later, 'but at the point it was left so bare that with shame it was shut up in the pock again, and they after a show returned with more shame to the realm than scathe to their enemies'. On 14 August 1545 Hertford, Tunstall and Sadler could report that the wardens had sent word that the Scots and their French allies had retreated having done little damage. It was thought best to withhold the English follow-up until early September when 'the year being very forward, the Scots' corn will be ripe and shorn'.[33] Two days later the Douglases, Marischal and Cassillis sent an unofficial report to Hertford affirming their intention to serve Henry and further 'the peace and marriage', remarking that de Lorges had come to Scotland only to 'do battle for France not to defend the Scots'. They advised the English commanders to move into Scotland with as impressive a show of force as could be mustered and to make 'sure' all those who would co-operate in bringing about the union of the two realms. Their tone implied that instant action on England's part was needed to save the writers from reprisals in Scotland. They reckoned that they had earned their reward from Henry, pointing out that although this last expedition had been devised by the Queen Dowager, the Cardinal and de Lorges, supported by Huntly with considerable forces, 'yet all was stopped by us the King's friends'.[34]

Hertford reached Kelso on 9 September, and during the following week his soldiers worked terrible havoc on the border abbeys and their tenants, burning the newly-harvested corn, killing and pillaging as they went. Already some French soldiers were finding their way into the English camp, each one declaring that more of his companions were ready to desert. They were warily informed that in order to be received they must do something to show their 'honesty', such as trapping or killing some of the Scottish leaders.[35] Hertford did not trust the Douglases, nor the promise of Lord Maxwell, who had been imprisoned in England since May 1544, to hand over his castles: at any rate his son John refused to come to England as a hostage for his father. Men of the Merse, Teviotdale and parts of the Lothians, however, were seeking to assure with the English in large numbers, tired of the disruption of life in the south.[36] On 16 September the earl of Argyll, who had once before deserted the Cardinal, to sign the deposition of Arran the previous summer, entered a bond with Glencairn for their mutual defence, probably with reference to their lands in the west, 'the quenes grace hir authorite and hir graces derrest moder and thare kindnes to my lord Cardinal beand alanerly acceptit', which safeguarded Argyll's previous undertakings to David Beaton.[37] During that summer Argyll had had to handle the problem of the Lord of the Isles, thus depriving the governor of his services on the border. On 20 September Sir George Douglas advised Hertford that Lennox should be with the English army when it overran the west of Scotland where Lennox was loved and the Governor and Cardinal hated — not entirely true of Arran in his ancestral heartland but perhaps indicative of a certain shift away from him among some of his surname.[38]

The picture in the autumn of 1545 was one of distrust and hardship marching side by side through the lives of even the humblest people, some of whom were among those escheated for failing to join the Governor and the army. On top of everything else the plague took its toll that summer, autumn and winter and food was at famine prices. On 8 November the Cardinal authorised the distribution of two bolls of meal among the poor of the Ferrytoun of Portincraig (Tayport) who were suspected of having the plague, probably in order to deter them from begging in St Andrews and bringing the infection with them.[39] His graniter supplied victual and ale to French foot soldiers returning from the borders.[40] Tensions and recriminations were evident among the political leaders. If the French soldiers were disillusioned their commander, de Lorges, was said to be wishing himself in France. On 5 October the Cardinal wrote to Francis I to explain the military débâcle, not very convincingly, while the Scottish parliament met to repair the damage.[41] On the first day of the parliamentary session Lennox was found guilty of treason in taking part with the enemy in time of war and was forfeited. His condemnation provoked a quarrel between the Cardinal and de Lorges who regretted the loss of Lennox to the French cause and blamed David Beaton for alienating him.[42] Frayed tempers resulted in an exchange of blows between the two men in the presence of Mary of Guise. It was all a far cry from the respect the Cardinal had been accustomed to in France at the height of his diplomatic career, and it is indicative of the lack of deference shown him by the Scots lords that a foreigner could treat him in this way in the royal presence, calling him 'false priest', venting the fairly common resentment of clerical meddling in laymen's business (as laymen saw it), and cuffing him on the cheek, although, apparently, the Cardinal had been first to raise his hand.

Under his influence parliament pressed on with further war plans including the levying of a tax to raise 1,000 horsemen to guard the vulnerable eastern borders. The Kers and their dependants were required to give their public assent to the measures passed against assurance with the English, now made a treasonable offence, while the men of the Merse and Teviotdale, for whose defence the mounted men were to be raised, were made to grant a bond to maintain good order in that region. There were actions for recovery of arrears of the previous war tax, including an order to distrain the assets of the disaffected burgh of Perth for non-payment of its contribution to the collector, the laird of Buccleuch. There was a summons of treason against Murray of Tullibardine who had earlier robbed the Cardinal and had ignored subsequent royal letters. This was no time for legislation with a general application only but for pressure to be put on all those who resisted the official policy towards England.

One of the most significant moves on the Cardinal's part at this time was his attempt to gain personal custody of the Queen by taking her to St Andrews castle, a scheme which he failed to accomplish.[43] She would have been a prestigious addition to his household hostages who were a kind of conscripted 'court' of representatives of the nobility and gentry over whom he exercised close supervision, almost like the King of France over his nobles. Perhaps he meant to strengthen his hold over Arran by telling him that he was keeping the young Queen and the Hamilton heir safe until a marriage could be arranged between them. The idea grew sufficiently in Arran's mind at this time to encourage him to try to form a middle party of his own, concentrating his recruitment in the west country.[44] In August he even got the Douglases to grant him a bond of manrent for the duration of the Queen's minority, but the son of Lord Somerville was one of those who doubted their sincerity, for dynastic reasons. Arran also courted the earl of Eglinton and James V's natural son, James Stewart, commendator of Kelso. It was rumoured towards the end of the year that he and the Cardinal were going to France to put forward the desirability of the Hamilton match and to seek Francis's consent.[45] Brunston, in reporting the doings of the Scottish parliament of October, told Sadler on the authority of Sir George Douglas that some of the lords had signed an agreement in favour of the match.[46] It was said that 'great offers' had been made to the Douglases for their consent. As with Mary of Guise's attempt to form a party of her own, Arran's experiment did not last long. The fact that he pursued it at all may suggest that the Cardinal encouraged him for his own ends, for the Governor's son was his hostage against independent action on Arran's part which might endanger his policies.

As the year 1545 wore on, military plans continued to be foiled. In September a muster of about 10,000 men under the Governor at Greenlaw had 'skalit' and went home as a result, so it was said, of Angus's advice.[47] On 24 October Lord Maxwell's castle of Caerlaverock was handed over to the English.[48] In planning the castle's recovery a council of the Governor, Cardinal and eight bishops and abbots, at which 'nevir ane temporall man was', is said to have been held, a tactic which could only have added fuel to the lay resentment of the Cardinal's domination of affairs.[49] At the same time the laymen may have boycotted the meeting. The Scottish attack on Caerlaverock on 2 November was successful, but that and Ancrum Moor were the only victories for the Scots during the whole sorry year. The Cardinal's policy, however, to which he held the governor, was not so much one of fighting to gain a resounding victory over the auld enemy — even someone as aggressive as he could see that that was unrealistic — as of continuing to resist English inroads by recovering from setbacks and carrying out raids in order to convince Henry VIII that there was no likelihood of coming to terms, that the plan for a marriage alliance between the two countries and a declaration of peace on that basis was out of the question and a thing of the past. Only the arrival of a large French army on a scale that Francis I could not presently afford might have meant a defeat in the field for Henry's forces. But that would essentially have been an Anglo-French conflict in the successful outcome of which, for France, Scotland would have benefited. Francis did not choose to work that way at this time and so Scotland's only line was that of defence. With his experience of European politics the Cardinal knew that at best Scotland could only hope to benefit from the success of France's political and military exploits, that Scotland was never calling the tune, but had to wait until France decided it was in her own interest to take action involving her Scottish ally. His persistent calls for French assistance were attempts to convince Francis I that it *was* in his interest to confront Henry on Scottish or English soil. At the same time, from his experience at home over the past twenty years he had seen the unsatisfactory results of inadequate French military assistance on the one hand and reluctance on the part of Scotland's natural military leaders to invade England on the other. It is doubtful if he ever expected this pattern to be reversed, but it is certain that he entertained an unshakable antipathy towards England and all that it meant in terms of a threat to traditional ecclesiastical authority and the material basis of the church's power. His opponents, on the other hand, equally unable to visualise a major Anglo-French conflict on Scottish or English soil, could only sabotage Scotland's defences and facilitate the work of the English invaders, hoping that the Cardinal's party would be forced to reopen negotiations with the English government.

At the same time at least some of his opponents were increasingly attracted to the ideological reasons for regarding alliance with England as a natural partnership, and not a few of them were already in touch with a stream of thought from England and beyond which would have demanded a reform of the church beyond what even Henry VIII would have countenanced. These different aspects of the changing attitude towards England had fused in the experience of the years since the death of James V. The resulting politico-religious motives, which to a large extent still remain to be unravelled, were what now confronted the Cardinal in his attempt to direct Scottish affairs. In the spring of 1545, while corresponding with Mary of Guise about her potential supporters, Lord Methven warned that the attachment to reform among some of the lords and gentlemen, however misguided it might be, made it necessary to abandon coercion for conciliation: 'to recounsall in tendir maner all greit gentilmen that be innorance is of ill mynd towartis haly kirk, becaus it is now dowtsum to punes be law as the sammyn requiris'.[50] Mary of Guise was to implement this policy a decade later, but it was not of the kind to appeal to the Cardinal, even although he could see just how 'dowtsum' it was that he would be able to punish the real troublemakers among those of Anglophile-reformist opinions.

Whereas increased heretical activity during 1543 had been dealt with in inquisitions and prosecutions in the winter of 1543–4, the Cardinal's pre-occupation with war and political dislocation since then had prevented him from dealing effectively with the activities of George Wishart who during 1544 and the early part of 1545 gained a sympathetic hearing in Angus and his home country of the Mearns. He was clearly acceptable in Dundee where it took the ultimate authority of the Cardinal to silence him after he had ignored letters of cursing from the bishop of Brechin. The Cardinal's monition to cease preaching was served on him by the recanted heretic and parliamentary commissioner, Robert Mill, burgess of Dundee.[51] When Wishart defied the order by returning to the burgh in the autumn of 1545 to encourage the people during the plague, underhand methods were resorted to because the townspeople were largely on his side. This time the agent was a previously convicted heretic priest, John Wigton, who may have agreed to do the job in order to save his own life, lacking the conviction of the tragic Dominican John Roger. Wishart was aware of the possibility of violence, and one of his companions, ultimately John Knox, carried a sword for his protection. It hardly needed the gift of prophecy to sense danger. At any rate, Wishart himself foiled Wigton's attempt to stab him as he was leaving his improvised pulpit at the west port of Dundee by telling the priest that he knew what he was about and taking the weapon from him.[52]

His habit of preaching in public was reciprocated by open expressions of support for him from nobles and gentlemen in different parts of the country. Their protection enabled him to preach in churches, in the same way as Lord Glamis's sympathy for Friar John Roger had permitted him to preach in Glamis kirk. The earl Marischal and others who listened in Dundee kirk to Wishart's sermons on the epistle to the Romans offered to stand by him if he would defy the Cardinal's monition or move with them to safer locations.[53] However, Wishart did not allow them to use him as a means of defying ecclesiastical authority but instead withdrew to the west of Scotland. Having information on his movements, the Cardinal sent word to Archbishop Dunbar to forestall his taking possession of the pulpit in St John's kirk, Ayr. Once more Wishart's friends, led now by the earl of Glencairn and some gentlemen of Kyle, would have resorted to forcible entry in opposition to the archbishop, but Wishart chose the larger audience at the mercat cross where people would be less likely to incur censure for listening to him.[54]

Archbishop Dunbar, having complied with the Cardinal's specific request, did little thereafter to curtail Wishart's movements in Ayrshire. Under the protection of a local laird, Campbell of Cessnock, he preached in the parish kirk of Galston in the Irvine valley, a parish largely appropriated to the Trinitarian friary of Failford which was then in Cunningham hands and rapidly undergoing secularisation.[55] John Lockhart of Bar, who gave him frequent hospitality and liberty to preach in his house, soon afterwards followed up the preacher's more denunciatory sermons with a trail of iconoclastic activity in churches and chapels of the west for which he and some accomplices were later put to the horn.[56] When Wishart reached the outlying and extensive parish of Mauchline in the Ayr valley, in Melrose abbey's barony of Kylesmure, there was a difference of opinion as to whether he should be given access to the parish kirk. The building stood in the clachan of Mauchline itself, hard by the administrative headquarters of the abbey which included a tower that for over twenty years had been the property of Hugh Campbell of Loudoun who, as the abbey's bailie and sheriff of Ayr, had a double responsibility for public order and the safety of property. The church's furnishings included a valuable tabernacle, possibly presented by the abbey of Melrose to which the church was appropriated. The sheriff may have feared that as the tabernacle was so closely associated with the doctrine of the mass it might be the first victim in an iconoclastic attack. Ecclesiastical presence was minimal in Kylesmure, the scene of Lollard activity in the previous generation, the kirk of Mauchline being served by two successive curates from a local family, sir James and sir Andrew Mitchell.[57] The sheriff decided to ban the preacher's entry to the kirk, a step which was resented by some local gentlemen who took the view that they could not be denied access to their own parish kirk. Wishart again preached in the open air to a large congregation whose most vivid memory of this unusual proceeding may have been the dramatic conversion of a local well-known sinner, Laurence Rankin of Shiel. The sheriff was supported in his holding of the kirk door by his kinsmen, Campbell of Mongarswood and Campbell of Burnside and by George Reid of Daldilling from a family who were divided over the extent of their support for reform. Those who would have forced entry were led by Campbell of Kinzeancleuch who a decade later invited John Knox to Kyle.

Like Patrick Hamilton, George Wishart seems to have made a lasting impression on those who heard him. Unlike Hamilton, however, whose activities had taken place largely within academic circles and the households of his own social group, Wishart made wider contacts and preached to a general audience. His presence had an effect on morale, as at Dundee when he preached during an outbreak of the plague. Whether he was understood by all his hearers or not, his message had a wide and varied appeal: an encouragement to speak out in criticism of the ecclesiastical establishment (always popular), a symbol of peaceful contact with England and countries even further away, an opportunity for those with an interest in and capacity to understand theological truths to discuss the basic protestant propositions, most of which feature in the accusations against Wishart's teaching. Even the reference which he made in Dundee to 'the great hapinesse of those whome God taketh frome this vale of miserie, even in his owne gentle visitatioun, which the malice of men can neither eik nor pair',[58] tacitly denied purgatory and must have comforted the burgesses during the terror of the plague; it foreshadows the line to be taken by Victorian evangelicals in preaching to the poor.

In the late autumn and winter of 1545–6 while George Wishart was making an impact in the archdiocese of St Andrews and in the diocese of Brechin the Cardinal's affairs were at a depressingly low ebb. The Frenchmen prepared to go home, having made little difference to Anglo-Scottish relations. Both David Beaton and Mary of Guise were financially exhausted and there was the prospect of further taxation to maintain resistance to England, in connection with which the Cardinal planned to hold a provincial council of the church early in the new year.[59] At a meeting of the privy council at Linlithgow on 19 December he agreed to forward £300 from the arrears of tax due from his own archdiocese to Lord Home for the defence of Home castle.[60] It is worth noting that the winter meetings of the council were small and that laymen were conspicuous by their poor attendance. Only Lords Fleming, Erskine and Livingston were present at the morning session on 19 December. The Cardinal was still buying personal support. He had recently taken the Governor with him on a progress through Angus and Fife before they spent Christmas together at St Andrews 'with games and feasting'.[61] Their journey had been concerned, ostensibly, with the patching up of quarrels but was more likely to have been in order to judge the attitude of the Cardinal's vassals and others to the English question and, more immediately, to Wishart. Yet, fearing to make a public arrest and accusation of the preacher at this juncture, the Cardinal made a second attempt to trap him, but the ambush laid outside Montrose was discovered by Wishart in time.[62] The fact that the trap had consisted of a decoy letter which purported to come from Wishart's friend, John Kinnear of Kinnear, shows how fully the Cardinal was aware of the reformer's contacts.

On 21 December he dispatched the Italian secretary, Alessandro Thealdini, to Rome with a letter of credence to the Pope in order to explain the state of affairs in Scotland.[63] When Thealdini was captured for the second time by the English his alleged 'confession', reported by Henry VIII's agent in Antwerp, Vaughan, to Paget on 18 January, gave the English the impression that the intransigent Cardinal of Scotland had his back to the wall. Thealdini was reputed to have said that he was sent to tell the Pope and the King of France that Scotland was in such poverty that she must yield unless financial aid was obtained from somewhere and that the Cardinal was in such a predicament that 'if he feared not to lose all his dignities and livings' he would soon find himself capitulating to the King of England.[64] It is scarcely how the Cardinal himself would have put it, but it sounds like his ultimatum to France and the Pope in an attempt to get them to do something for Scotland. Yet he must have been aware that his long-running efforts to convince the European powers of the need to unite against the apostate King of England, by continually reminding them of their possible loss of Scotland as a card to be played against him, were at present having little effect. Although he was more likely to go down fighting than surrender, the situation was serious. Vaughan thought that 'if this Cardinal were spoken with and well handled with fair promises by some noble and wise man he would be won'. The English often misunderstood the Cardinal's attitude and underestimated his powers of resistance to pressure but they were right this time about the seriousness of his predicament. Historians, on the other hand, while generally appreciating the immutability of his attitude towards England and to serious reform of the church, have tended to underestimate the difficulties under which he laboured and the problems he faced in keeping control of affairs.

By the turn of the year he had decided to make an end of Wishart in order to show his authority, thus removing at least one rallying point of disaffection. Like the Cardinal, Wishart at this point found himself in more restricted circumstances than formerly and was a little depressed by the fact that the courage of some of his friends appeared to flag the nearer he drew to the centre of goverment.[65] It had been against the advice of Erskine of Dun that he left Montrose, where the earliest years of his career had been spent, and journeyed south by Innergowrie, Dundee, Perth and Fife to Leith where Cassillis and others from the west had arranged to meet him. In the midst of his successful preaching tour of Kyle they had discussed the possibility of a public debate with the prelates in Edinburgh, but now the men of the west country failed to turn up and this idea faded.[66] In any case, the Cardinal would never have agreed to allow the heretic the implied recognition which a public disputation would have afforded him, or have risked making him the focus of a sympathetic gathering of his friends. It did not accord with Wishart's temperament, however, to 'lurk as a man that were ashamed and durst not show himself before men', and he did preach in Leith, on the parable of the sower (Matthew 13) on Sunday 13 December.

Thereafter some of his Lothian friends rallied round and persuaded him to leave the vicinity of the capital. The following week he spent in the homes of Crichton of Brunston, Douglas of Longniddry and Cockburn of Ormiston, experiencing remarkable freedom to preach in the local kirks of Inveresk on 20 December and Tranent on 27 December and 3 January. Large numbers turned out to listen to him with no more official interference than that of two Grey Friars who stationed themselves at the doorway of the kirk at Inveresk in an effort to dissuade the people from going in. At one point the preacher lost his temper with them and with something of his old vehemence foretold a judgement upon them. The bold Sir

George Douglas, who attended the sermon, declared afterwards, 'I know my Lord Governor and my Lord Cardinal shall hear that I have been at this preaching. Say unto thame that I will avow it, and will nott onlye manteane the doctrin that I have hard, bot alsua the persone of the teachare to the uttermost of my power'.[67] Towards the end of the Christmas season the lairds suggested Haddington where it was hoped that the burgh would afford a good audience. It was here, however, that pressure from the authorities caught up with Wishart, and the local influence of the earl of Bothwell, commissioned by the Governor and Cardinal to arrest him, inhibited people from turning out to hear him. There was a marked difference in the number of those in the church even between the morning and afternoon of the same day, possibly 10 January.[68] Yet the fact that Wishart lodged not only with David Forrest, who was described by Knox as 'an old professor of the truth upon whom many depended at that time', but also at Lethington tower with the poet-laird, Sir Richard Maitland, who 'was ever civill albeit not persuaded in [the protestant] religioun', evokes the mood of both genuine interest and wary curiosity that surrounded Wishart's movements. However, the arrival of the Governor and Cardinal in the vicinity, the latter bent on making his personal role in the business clear for all to see, suddenly changed Wishart from talking-point into wanted man.

Leaving Haddington, the preacher spent the evening at Ormiston with the laird, young John Sandilands of Calder and Crichton of Brunston, having taken his leave of Hugh Douglas of Longniddry and dismissed his companion, John Knox, tutor of Douglas's sons. Just before midnight Bothwell and his men surrounded Ormiston and he was arrested. Being in his home territory, Bothwell was reluctant to appear as the Cardinal's servant and even promised Wishart at Ormiston to keep him in his own house at Hailes until he set him free, 'that neither the governour nor the cardinall sall obteane their intent of yow'.[69] Meantime he kept his promise to the Cardinal by handing Wishart over to him at Elphinstone tower nearby, after which he was sent back to Ormiston to arrest the others. He missed Brunston, who had escaped from the house, but Ormiston himself and young Sandilands were warded in Edinburgh castle in due course, the latter making his escape, the former remaining until he made a bond of manrent with the Cardinal. Wishart, after a brief detention in Edinburgh and Hailes, was taken across the Forth to the surer prison of St Andrews castle, not without another attempt by Bothwell at showing his personal authority by trying to hold on to the prisoner himself, and a show of reluctance on the part of Arran, representing the supreme secular power, to hand Wishart over to the church authorities at this juncture.[70] But David Beaton was carefully arranging matters to provide himself with a much needed public triumph, and so the Governor gave in.

There were repeated signs of friction in the early months of 1546 between the magnates and the Cardinal, leader of the first estate, whom they had recently seen humiliated in various ways. It was even inferred by some that he had had to bribe Bothwell to take on the matter of Wishart's arrest, not because Bothwell had any sympathy for the heretic but because he knew that the latter had lay support, including that of lairds in his own part of the country; Bothwell's obligation before the council on 19 January to hand Wishart over to the Governor or 'ony utheris in his behalff quham he will depute to ressave him' before the end of the month is the official version of Knox's allegation that Bothwell was 'made for money butcher to the Cardinal'.[71] At the beginning of February the latter had tried unsuccessfully to sue Sir James Campbell of Lundy, then master of the household to Mary of Guise, for £860 due to him as executor of his uncle the late Archbishop James Beaton.[72] On 15 February the Official of Lothian sentenced Lord Ogilvy, the bailie of Arbroath abbey, for 200 merksworth of arrears of teinds.[73] Both actions, had they been successful, would have brought the Cardinal some much-needed funds. About a week after Ogilvy's sentence in the official's court, the lords of session blocked an attempt in the Cardinal's name to bring Norman Leslie, master of Rothes and sheriff of Fife, to task for trying to arrest goods in the regality of St Andrews by saying that Leslie could only be summoned for this in full parliament.[74] There was further trouble with Lord Ruthven, as sheriff of Perth and provost of the burgh: on 5 February he had to grant a bond in council for payment of the arrears of the last two taxes for war from the sheriffdom, and on 15 March he wrote to the Queen Dowager about the imminent journey to Perth of the Cardinal and Governor in order to put him and his friends out of office, [75] one of their repeated attempts to remove his influence from the burgh.

In the court of session towards the end of March there seems to have been an argument requiring formal settlement as to 'quhat persounis ... spirituale of the seite [bench] suld remane heir for the administratioun of justice'.[76] On the 27th of the month the president, Abbot Alexander Milne of Cambuskenneth, asked for instruments to be taken that John Hamilton, abbot of Paisley, stated that the Governor had got letters from the Cardinal referring to Arran himself the decision as to which of the clerics ought to remain, 'quha [John Hamilton] declarit that all the spirituale persounis suld remane still and not depart, for the administratioun of justice to the quenis leigis. And my lord of Paisley tuk upoun hand to warrand thame in that behaff'. It is tempting to read between the lines and see some kind of dispute between the lay and ecclesiastical members of the court and to hear the Cardinal's mind expressed through the mouthpiece of the Governor. The churchmen, as represented by the president, appear to have felt threatened in some way, necessitating the taking of instruments and the assurance of warrandice. At that time the Governor and the Cardinal were on a progress, in the tense weeks after the death of Wishart, when the Cardinal associated the Governor with himself in a policy of repression.

It is against this backround of domestic and international frustration and failure and hint of lay-ecclesiastical friction that the trial of George Wishart has to be seen. The Cardinal did not preside over this episode in a mood of self-confidence but with an awareness of opposition, political, religious and personal, and in an attempt to restore his prestige. It may have been the need to counteract the more articulate heretical teaching, as exemplified in Wishart, that caused him to consider a measure of internal reform at this time.[77] Hitherto the meagre records of his church councils that survive suggest his preoccupation with raising clerical contributions to the war effort; it is significant that before the proper meeting of the council in St Andrews in 1545 he got a hastily-convened meeting of the clergy to agree to contribute the large sum of £13,000 by a tax on prelacies and benefices worth £40 a year. However, circumstances may have added weight to the arguments of those who envisaged a reform programme centred on the better instruction of the clergy, with a modern educational system such as that advocated to him as early as 1540 by his cousin Archibald Hay in connection with the new college. Early in 1546 the provincial council which he is believed to have convoked made arrangements to finance Scottish representatives at the Council of Trent, the Cardinal himself having excused himself three times from attendance. It may also have been on this occasion that he took measures for the appointment and material support of preachers, several months in advance of the Tridentine instruction on the same subject. As it turned out his new, constructive attitude made little headway in his remaining months.

NOTES

1. *L.P. Henry VIII*, XX, I, 203
2. *Scottish Correspondence*, 128
3. *L.P. Henry VIII*, XIX, ii, 625
4. *Ibid.*, XIX, ii, 657, 685, 692, 707
5. *Diurnal of Remarkable Occurrents* (Bannatyne Club), 36–41 (*Diurnal*)
6. *L.P. Henry VIII*, XX, i, 301
7. *Ibid.*, XX, i, 210
8. *Ibid.*
9. *Ibid.*, XX, i, 401, 477
10. *Ibid.*, XX, i, 174
11. *Ibid.*, XX, i, 626
12. *Ibid.*, XX, i, 395
13. *Ibid.*, XX, i, 696
14. *Ibid.*, XX, i, 508
15. *Ibid.*, XX, i, 509
16. *Ibid.*, XX, i, 508
17. *Ibid.*, XX, i, 5
18. *Ibid.*, XX, i, 547
19. *Ibid.*
20. *Ibid.*, XX, i, 508
21. *Ibid.*, XX, i, 781, 1127
22. *Ibid.*, XX, i, 457
23. *Ibid.*, XX, i, 909
24. *Ibid.*, XX, i, 1069
25. *Ibid.*, XX, i, 1027, 1049
26. *Ibid.*, XX, i, 1059
27. *Ibid.*, XX, i, 1091
28. *Ibid.*, XX, i, 1106
29. *Ibid.*, XX, i, 1126
30. *A.P.S.*, II, 595
31. *L.P. Henry VIII*, XX, i, 1106

32. *Ibid.*, XX, i, 1063

33. *Ibid.*, XX, ii, 130

34. *Ibid.*, XX, ii, 144

35. *Ibid.*, XX, ii, 308, 328

36. *Ibid.*, XX, ii, 524; M. Merriman, 'The Assured Scots', 25

37. Glencairn muniments (S.R.O.), GD 39/1/57

38. *L.P. Henry VIII*, XX, ii, 414

39. *Rentale*, 221

40. *Ibid.*, 197

41. *L.P. Henry VIII.*, XX, ii, 525

42. *Pitscottie*, ii, 47–8

43. *L.P. Henry VIII*, XX, ii, 535

44. *Scottish Correspondence*, 125, 147

45. *Ibid.*, 152n

46. *L.P. Henry VIII*, XX, ii, 622

47. *A Diurnal of Remarkable Occurrents in Scotland* (Bannatyne Club), 40

48. *Scottish Correspondence*, 151

49. *Diurnal*, 41

50. *Scottish Correspondence*, 133

51. *Knox*, I, 60

52. *Ibid.*, I, 63–4

53. *Ibid.*, I, 61

54. *Ibid.*

55. *Ibid.*

56. R. Pitcairn, *Ancient Criminal Trials*, I, 353

57. M. H. B. Sanderson, *The Mauchline Account Books of Melrose Abbey* (A.A.N.H.S.), 90; Register of Acts and Decreets, xxiv, 3 April 1562

58. *Knox*, I, 63

59. Herkless and Hannay, *Archbishops*, IV, 185

60. *R.P.C.*, I, 18

61. *Pitscottie*, II, 51

62. *Knox*, I, 64

63. *L.P. Henry VIII*, XX, ii, 1020

64. *Ibid.*, XXI, i, 82

65. *Knox*, I, 65–6

66. *Ibid.*, 1, 64

67. *Ibid.*, I, 66

68. *Ibid.*, I, 68

69. *Ibid.*, I, 69–70

70. *Ibid.*, I, 71

71. *Ibid.*, 68

72. A.D.C.S., xxviii, fo 30

73. Sentence Book of the official of St Andrews principal, CH 5/2/1, fo 136

74. A.D.C.S., xxviii, fo 33v

75. *Scottish Correspondence*, 159–60

76. A.D.C.S., xxviii, fo 92

77. A. R. McEwen, *A History of the Church in Scotland*, I, 470–1; T. Winning, 'Church Councils in Sixteenth Century Scotland', in *Essays*, 334–6

13

Careful Cardinal

The trial of George Wishart in St Andrews on 1 March 1546, over which the Cardinal presided, was conducted before a large convocation of the clergy, larger than was absolutely necessary for the purpose in order that their presence might lend the maximum ecclesiastical authority to the proceedings. The movement of judges to and from the cathedral, where the trial took place and sentence was pronounced, was accompanied by a show of force in the form of the Cardinal's own men-at-arms 'in their most warlike array' in order to intimidate the populace, many of whom crowded into the huge church to watch the proceedings, and to forestall any possible attempt at rescue of the prisoner. It was remembered that eighteen years before Sir James Hamilton of Kincavil had made plans to rescue his brother, Mr Patrick. Wishart was taken from the castle to the cathedral for trial under an armed escort of 100 soldiers commanded by John Beaton of Balfour, the captain of the castle, whose part in the events that followed betrays his mixed feelings in the circumstances.

Before the trial began an already tense atmosphere had received a charge of the acrimony between the Cardinal and the Governor. When the former had asked Arran, as law demanded, to supply a criminal judge to pronounce sentence after judgement had been passed on the accused, the Governor showed his customary hesitation, on this occasion due to the suggestion of David Hamilton of Preston, one of Wishart's friends from east Lothian, that the trial be postponed while Arran and the Cardinal had further discussion.[1] Beaton's predictable reply was to tell Arran that he had asked him merely for form's sake and that he judged his authority of no consequence. The incident sent him into an agressive mood which made some of his colleagues uneasy, but those who supported his repressive policy boasted about the way he had snubbed the Governor, saying that the church would have been in a much stronger position to demonstrate her authority if this line had been taken earlier.

Another source of annoyance to the Cardinal early in the actual proceedings may have been the tone of the sermon delivered at his request by Dr John Winram, subprior of St Andrews, who must have found the duty one of the most harrowing episodes in his life as he strove to be as honest with his own conscience as safety permitted while at the same time avoiding any possible accusation of unorthodoxy. He had spoken personally with the prisoner the day before when he was sent to serve the summons on him to compear, when Wishart had pointed out to him that the Cardinal had no need to stand on ceremony since he could compel him to obey. The text of Winram's sermon, the parable of the sower in St Matthew's gospel, was that on which Wishart himself had preached at Leith before Christmas. Perhaps there were some in the cathedral who were in a position to compare the two sermons. Winram's careful exposition, in which he made the work of God the touchstone in identifying heresy and placed firmly on the shoulders of the temporal power the unpleasant duty of destroying those who spread heretical ideas, did little to extol the authority of holy kirk. As a member of a regular order and a scholarly man Winram was probably none too impressed with the performance of many of the secular clergy. The cause of heresy within the realm, and all other realms, he maintained,

> is the ignorance of them which have the cure of men's souls, to whom it necessarily belongeth to have the true understanding of the word of God, that they may be able to win against the false doctors of heresy, with the sword of the Spirit which is the word of God.

To make no doubt of those who were qualified thus to teach the truth he reminded those present of St Paul's description of a bishop:

> ... faultless, as becometh the minister of God, not stubborn, not angry, no drunkard, no fighter, not given to filthy lucre; but harberous, one that loveth goodness, sober minded, righteous, holy, temperate, and such as cleaveth unto the true word of the doctrine, that he may be able to exhort with wholesome learning, and to improve [disprove] that which they say against him.

The prelates, not anticipating an exhortation, must have turned with some relief to the formal accusation of the heretic. Mr Wishart took Dr Winram's place in the pulpit and the Cardinal's redoubtable secretary, Mr John Lauder, armed with the case papers, stood up opposite him to make the most of his part in the drama. Wishart, with remarkable self-control for one of his temperament, listened while Lauder shouted the accusation at him, 'and hit him so spitefully with the pope's thunder that the ignorant people dreaded lest the earth then would have swallowed him up quick'. His 'What answerest thou to these sayings, thou runagate, traitor, thief, which we have duly proved by sufficient witness against thee?' came over as a defiance rather than a question and could not have added dignity to the official image. After kneeling briefly in prayer Wishart replied; his manner may have been controlled, but what he said must have bitten into the Cardinal's self-esteem.

He proposed to summarise the doctrine he had preached in Scotland, because, 'it is reasonable ... that ye hear me teaching truly the pure and sincere word of God ... , it were unrighteous if you should stop your ears from me teaching truly the word of God, ... that I perish not unjustly, to the great peril of your souls'. He maintained that he had taught only the ten commandments, the twelve articles of faith, the Lord's Prayer in the mother tongue and, at Dundee, the epistle of St Paul to the Romans. When he continued, 'I shall show your discretions faithfully what fashion and manner I used when I taught, without any human dread, so that [if] your discretions give me your ears benevolent and attent', Lauder suddenly interrupted him with 'It was not lawful of you to preach ... without any authority of the church ... ' The continuity of the proceedings was broken while a brief discussion took place among the bishops as to the advisability of letting Wishart launch forth into a sermon before the lay audience. In the pause Wishart nettled the Cardinal by asking for the Governor as an impartial judge. The loyal secretary jumped to his master's defence saying, 'Is not my Lord Cardinal the second person within this realm ... an equal judge apparently to thee?' 'I refuse not my lord Cardinal,' Wishart replied, 'but I desire the word of God to be my judge [here endorsing Dr Winram's opening sermon] and the temporal estate, with some of your lordships my auditors; because I am here my Lord Governor's prisoner.' The Cardinal's acute resentment at this slight to his supreme authority in religious matters would not be cooled even by his supporters' muttering, ' "Such man, such judge", speaking seditious and reproachful words against the Governor and other the Nobles, meaning them also to be heretics'.

At this point, in order to restore the authority of the court, the Cardinal apparently considered having the sentence pronounced but was advised to have the articles against Wishart read out to prevent its being said that he had been condemned unjustly. Naturally, he was reluctant to give Wishart the opportunity to defend himself at length or to give the trial anything of the character of a disputation. The call for delay which Arran had communicated to him beforehand had not only reminded him that a rescue might be contemplated by Wishart's friends but that matters had reached a stage at which there was a body of opinion that felt that the preacher's claims (and, for that matter, of those who supported him) should be thrashed out in public rather than be treated as a criminal offence. At least, there were some who may have hoped for a measure of public acceptability for religious dissent by using Wishart as the occasion for discussion. There were even some who agreed with Lord Methven's idea of conciliation. However, the trial of George Wishart was the first major opportunity afforded the Cardinal since the condemnation of Lord Borthwick in 1540 of demonstrating to the disaffected that heresy was a matter for punishment not debate, no matter how highly-connected the heretic might be socially or politically. He gave in to have the articles read out only after Wishart had been warned simply to answer 'Yes' or 'No' to the points of the indictment. John Lauder at first obeyed instructions to keep the accused to the point and, when Wishart showed signs of refuting an accusation at length, 'stopping his mouth with another Article'. But, in the long run, the secretary's abrasive manner militated against the smooth running of this central part of the trial. The Cardinal would have done well to have given the job on this occasion to the phlegmatic Andrew Oliphant.

Five articles against the teaching of Wishart involved the authority of the church and status of the clergy: that he had continued to preach in defiance of an inhibition from the Governor and letters of cursing from the bishop of Brechin, that he had in effect questioned the unconditional holy character of the priest at the altar, taught against the vows of chastity of monks and nuns and had said that priests should marry, had said that he would not obey the general or provincial councils of the church and that it was in vain to build costly churches to the honour of God. Another five articles concerned his alleged denial of the doctrine of the sacraments of auricular confession, infant baptism, the mass itself and extreme unction and had stated that there were not seven sacraments. Three articles involved his reputed attitude to certain practices, the use of holy water, fasting and the unlawfulness of eating flesh on Friday. Three were properly doctrinal, his teaching the doctrine of the priesthood of all believers, his attitude to the question of man's free will and to the anabaptist belief in the idea of soul-sleepers. Two articles concerned his attitude to the cults of purgatory and prayer to the saints. The articles are not arranged in these related groups, however, and, apart from those on the sacraments, change in character from one to the next, as they have come down to us. Wishart's replies to those questions affecting ecclesiastical authority provoked the greatest outrage among his judges, while the doctrinal points were most summarily dealt with. His reply to that about the priesthood of all believers raised some rather uncomprehending derision among the bishops, which in turn provoked audible resentment among sympathetic laymen in the audience.[2]

The most marked characteristic of Wishart's defence was his appeal to scripture as the highest and indeed only authority for his teaching. He claimed to have taught the people only positive truths found there and not to have spent time in refuting doctrines and practices for which he could find no biblical warrant. His preaching, he insisted, had been positive not negative. 'My lords, if it be your pleasure, I taught never of the number of the sacraments, whether they were seven or an eleven. So many as are instituted by Christ, and are shown to us by the Evangel, I profess openly. Except it be the word of God I dare affirm nothing.'[3] In reply to the charge of teaching that there was no purgatory he admitted, 'I have oft and divers times read over the Bible, and yet such a term found I never, nor yet any place of Scripture applicable thereunto. Therefore, I was ashamed ever to teach of that thing, which I could not find in Scripture'. He then embarrassed John Lauder by asking him if he could 'prove any such place'.[4]

His emphasis was on inward, personal holiness through faith, not on outward conformity through adherence to accepted practices. 'The moving of the body outward, without the inward moving of the heart, is nothing else but the playing of an ape, and not the true serving of God; ... '[5] 'Confession signifieth the secret knowledge of our sins before God: when I exhorted the people on this manner, I reproved no manner of Confession.'[6] Over the subject of baptism, a sociological sacrament which meant much to the ordinary layman, there was a slight altercation between accused and accuser after Wishart had used a homely metaphor to explain his teaching: 'there be none so unwise here, that will make merchandise with a Frenchman, or any other unknown stranger, except he know and understand first the condition or promise made by the Frenchman or stranger. So likewise I would that we understood the thing we promise in the name of the infant unto God in baptism'.[7] The implication of intelligent participation in the sacrament of baptism in place of complete dependence on the priest to bring the child into the Christian community provoked an outburst from Lauder who told Wishart that he had the devil in him to teach such error. Whereupon an obscure member of the crowd, possibly of the status of a serving man, shouted, 'the Devil can not speak such words as yonder man doth speak'.[8]

This sign that the company was really listening and not simply spectating disturbed the judges. If the articles have come down to us in historic order, it was from the point of this layman's interjection onwards that Wishart adopted more of the preacher's manner in his replies. As has already been mentioned, his defence of the doctrine of the priesthood of all believers, more particularly the bishops' reaction to it, aroused some sympathy for him among the audience. In the lesser matter of eating flesh on Friday, which Wishart openly set aside in favour of inward cleanliness of heart, the bishops were prepared to see outright denial of the outward practice as sufficient proof of his heresy. It was the old short-cut to conviction frequently taken with humbler heretics. However, the trial continued with Wishart giving a particularly extended reply to the accusation that he had said 'we should not pray to the saints, but to God only'. In this, he claimed, he had avoided a subject which was a matter of some doubt among many but had rather 'exhorted all men equally in my doctrine that they should leave the unsure [debateable] way and follow the way which was taught by our Master Christ: He is our only Mediator and maketh intercession for us to God his Father'.[9] 'These things', Knox recorded with some satisfaction at the impatient bishops' discomfiture, 'he rehearsed divers times.'

Their greatest annoyance was with his statement about obedience to the general councils of the church: 'If that they agree with the word of God I will not disagree'.[10] At this point it was suggested that the remaining articles be read out without giving him opportunity to reply, and Friar John Scott, standing behind Lauder, urged him to get on with it as quickly as possible. Yet, Wishart replied to the last three articles and at one point made the classic statement, 'Wheresoever is the true preaching of the word of God, and the lawful use of the sacraments, undoubtedly there is God himself'.[11] Although affirming that God was greater than the places built for him by men, he denied that he had encouraged the destruction of church buildings. He himself wound up this part of his trial with a prayer for those 'which do further Thy word in this world . . . that Thou conserve, defend and help Thy Congregation . . . '[12] His words may have been coloured by Knox in his later account but it is probably true that, even more than Patrick Hamilton whose testimony made many people think of these things for the first time, Wishart left behind him many who were already committed to reform, for whatever motives, and a body of sympathisers who, however beleaguered and confused believed that religious dissent had come to stay. Wishart's performance at his trial may have persuaded some of those who listened to him, for it had been a two-sided affair quite unlike the condemnation of the absent Sir John Borthwick six years before.

Such was the atmosphere of interest and even sympathy in the cathedral that it was thought advisable to clear the building of the populace before pronouncing sentence. This was duly delivered by the Cardinal, after which Gavin Dunbar, archbishop of Glasgow, who had sat beside him during the trial, was first to sign the sentence in assent to the verdict. The condemned man was then escorted back to the castle and lodged in the captain's own 'outer chamber' in the sea tower. His escort was shortly followed by that of the Cardinal, bishops and others who had taken part in the proceedings in an official capacity. Wishart was approached by Friar Scott and a fellow-Franciscan who asked him to make his confession to them before he died. He declined their services but asked, unexpectedly, 'Go fetch me yonder man that preached this day and I will make my confession to him'. After an emotional meeting at the end of which Winram asked Wishart if he wished to take the sacrament, which the prisoner requested, the subprior made his way back to the episcopal party. David Beaton took strong exception to Winram's having spoken with the prisoner and was riled by his suspicion of the reason for the apparent sympathy between them. When the subprior, with unwonted frankness, remarked that he thought Wishart did not deserve death, the Cardinal turned on him furiously, saying, 'Weill, weill, we knaw yow and quhat ye are sevin yeir syne'.[13] There was a short, tense silence before Winram asked if the prisoner was to be given the sacrament. After a brief consultation with his colleagues the Cardinal replied to the effect that it was not reasonable to give any spiritual benefit to an obstinate heretic condemned by the church. Winram must have expected this answer, which he then conveyed to the prisoner.

Meantime, John Beaton, the Cardinal's nephew and captain of the castle, was having his own personal trauma. He invited Wishart, whose conduct had clearly made an impression on him, to join him in taking some food.[14] Wishart answered, 'Very willingly, and so much the rather because I perceive you to be a good Christian and a man fearing God'. His knowledge of who the captain was doubtless made the humane gesture all the more welcome. John Beaton, however, had not bargained for the way in which the condemned heretic turned their meal into a protestant communion service, in place of the sacrament which his judges had denied him, asking the captain to allow him to 'make a short exhortation, and bless this bread which we are about to eat, so that I may bid you farewell'. According to Spottiswoode's account, he spoke for about half-an-hour at table 'about the institution of the Lord's Supper and of our Saviour's death and passion', then broke the bread, distributing to every man his portion, and did the same with the wine. While John Beaton broke bread with Wishart his uncle entertained his episcopal colleagues to dinner before the last part of the condemnation was carried out. After the executioners had prepared Wishart for the stake, dressed in a buckram coat into the pockets and sleeves of which they pushed pokes of gunpowder, as was customary, in order to shorten his agony in the fire, he told John Beaton while they awaited the completion of arrangements about the dream he had had of a fire at sea, portending disaster.

To the last moment the Cardinal took precautions against a possible intervention by Wishart's friends by arranging that the castle ordnance should be trained on the place of execution.[15] According to Knox's account Wishart was 'put upon the gibbet and hanged and then burnt to powder', but other accounts speak of his having endured the fire itself, at one point receiving encouragement from the captain of the castle who stood by in charge of the guard. Only some later accounts speak of the Cardinal and his colleagues having watched the execution. It would be entirely characteristic of the Cardinal that he should be there to see his orders carried out. Folk-history has made much of the fact that he gloated over the success of his attack on Wishart and his activities, partly because this lends drama and meaning to the backlash. But the sight of armed men and loaded cannon and, to those who were near him during the proceedings, his own edginess could hardly have conveyed the kind of self-satisfaction that found its way into later accounts of the event. He must certainly have hoped that the spectacle of Wishart's trial and death would impress his opponents with the strength of his determination and his ability to carry through his intentions. Ironically, it made his relations with some of them all the more difficult.

About mid-March the Governor and he made a progress to Perth, which resulted a month later in pledges given to the Governor by Lords Ruthven and Gray that they would keep good order in the burgh, and the deprivation of the provost for having shown himself a friend of Ruthven.[16] Apart from this demonstration of political intimidation it was business-as-usual in the archbishop's castle and chancery in the weeks following Wishart's death. The accounts of the chamberlain, Mr Alexander Crichton, were rendered at the castle on 8 April.[17] The Cardinal appointed as auditors his close associates Archibald Beaton of Capildrae, John Beaton of Balfour, Mr Bernard Bailie and Mr John Lauder, naming them 'by word of mouth', and may have sat with them at their labours for at least part of the time, 'admitting' personally many items of expenditure and the receipt of a number of payments. The long lists of enrolled expenses, the bundles of receipts, precepts and vouchers must in their own way have recalled the gains and losses of the past year: to John Young, tailor in Edinburgh, for the Cardinal's standard that had failed to rally his vassals at Wark, £11 18d, the expenses of messengers to the Governor and abbot of Paisley at Dunbar and Home, 30s, wages of the Cardinal's servants at Linlithgow, £106 9s 6d, letters to the Governor at Hamilton, 30s, the master of works at St Andrews castle, £62. Much of the deficit in the chamberlain's incomings was due to the fact that rents and feu-duties had been handed to the Cardinal directly at a time when he desperately needed the money: from Keig and Monymusk from the earl of Huntly, Tynninghame from the late King's natural son, James Stewart, Killeith kirklands from Oliver Sinclair, Bishopshire from Robert Douglas of Lochleven, Abthane-Kinghorn from Sir John Melville of Raith. On the other hand, there was the effect of remissions of rent and feu-duties granted to those whose support he was trying to hold on to: to Lord Gray, for example. There were arrears of feu-duty from those to whom he had alienated land for the same reason: Lord Borthwick, Ker of Cessford, Sir James Learmonth of Dairsie (provost of St Andrews) and the earl of Argyll. Concessions had been made to those whom he trusted or who deserved some reward: Lord Seton, John Beaton of Balfour, Robert Beaton of Creich. Other reminders of recent difficulties were the expenses of requisitioning horses from Angus to carry his baggage and that of his household 'towards the host against England' and the letters sent to the captain of Edinburgh castle and the provost of Edinburgh at 'the taking of Master George Wishart'.

The chamberlain's final account was a reflection of a year of war, political uncertainty, plague and dearth which in some respects compounded the losses of the previous, rather similar, year. Although an increase in arrears and payments 'depending' must have been disturbing, it is clear that a substantial part of the deficit was due to the Cardinal's manipulation of his temporal revenues for political purposes, and that much expenditure had arisen out of his determination to pursue a hostile policy towards England. It was unfortunate that his revenue had begun to slide down again after a recovery in 1543–4 from a previous deficit of over £600. The Cardinal was in considerable debt to some of his own officials, either through borrowing from them personally or by receiving sums of money or victual from their incomings, including £80 to Alan Coutts, provisor of the household, and over £1,000 to Mr Robert Auchmowty the graniter. In the midst of business he may have been aware of the rumours of vengeance for the death of Wishart that were drifting about. John Leslie of Parkhill, brother of the earl of Rothes, boasted openly 'in all companies' that he would kill the Cardinal.[18] There was also talk of 'something intended by the earl of Angus', possibly linked to the Anglo-Scottish plot to which Brunston and Cassillis were privy.

Since the treaty of Utrecht in January 1546 and the closer alliance of the Emperor and Henry VIII, the French were considering how to conciliate the English King into handing over Boulogne. One tactic was to appear to approve of an English marriage for the Queen of Scots, a possibility which would have put Scotland at risk without help from France. This made the Cardinal careful not only for his own safety but that of the Queen herself. His preoccupation with the defence of the castle of St Andrews at this time, laying in stores and even bringing extra victual from Arbroath, was done with his customary eye on the international situation as well as on the domestic scene.

To counteract opposition at home he put into operation his plans for a prestigious alliance in Angus, the marriage of his oldest daughter, Margaret, to David master of Crawford, heir of the earl. The 9th earl of Crawford had succeeded his cousin the 8th earl in 1542 on the disinheritance of the so-called 'Wicked Master' and in a short time had set about restoring the financial affairs of the family and their wide estates in the interest of his adopted heir, the Wicked Master's son.[19] The Cardinal saw the earl himself, head of the powerful Lindsay family, as a desirable ally: the 8th earl's three daughters had married Erskine of Dun, John Charteris of Kinfauns and Lord Borthwick, while the 9th earl himself had married a daughter of Patrick, then master and later Lord Gray. In 1546 the earl was a widower. It was also clear that the earldom lands in Angus might afford the Cardinal's daughter a comfortable jointure. Finavon castle, the earl's Angus stronghold, was for good measure reasonably near Melgund, the Cardinal's secular property. For several years he had been engaged in deals with the earl over the lands of Auchtermonsy and Cairnie in Fife which the earl held from the archbishopric and over which his predecessor had had a legal battle with Archbishop James Beaton. In 1543 the Cardinal made a gift of the casualties, due to him as superior of these lands, to three of his sons[20] but he soon afterwards got his hands on the lands themselves through a loan of 5,000 merks to the earl,[21] who then wadset them to David Beaton of Melgund.[22] At the same time the Cardinal bought out Lord Borthwick's interest in an earlier wadset arrangement by feuing to him his lands in the lordship of Stow of which Borthwick was already the archbishop's bailie.[23]

The contract for the marriage of Margaret Beaton and the master of Crawford was drawn up at St Andrews where it was witnessed on 10 April by Walter Lindsay, Lord of St John of Torphichen, and Sir Thomas Erskine of Brechin, David Beaton's early diplomatic associate, probably on the earl's behalf, and two civil lawyers for the Cardinal, his friend and legal representative of many years' standing, Mr Thomas Marjoribanks, and Herbert Gledstanes.[24] Perhaps one of these men had brought the Cardinal the letter which his friend and Marjoribanks' advocate-colleague, Sir Adam Otterburn, wrote to him on 8 April, in which he asked the Cardinal to help him wring some debts out of Oliver Sinclair, saying, 'I have na gude to pay my dettis and dochteris tocher quham I have marrit laitlie except that det'.[25] In the circumstances, the side-shaft was extremely pertinent. Margarets Beaton's tocher was the princely sum of 4,000 merks. The terms of the contract favoured the interests of the Crawford family whose lands had already been entailed due to the disinheritance of the master's father. There was no question of the young couple's receiving the lands in conjunct-fee, as often happened. The major part of the landholdings were resigned by the earl to the master and his heirs male, reserving to himself the liferent 'and reasonable terce to his wife and Lady for the time'; he was unmarried at this point. Margaret received as her provision the liferent use of some half-dozen territories. If both the earl and her husband should predecease her she was to relinquish her liferent of the Mains and castle of Finavon in exchange for the dowager's portion of the Mains of Downie. The Cardinal's gain was more prestigious than material, alliance with a powerful family and its dependants, at the same time increasing his own family's presence in Angus. On 17 April he granted the master of Crawford a feu charter of the kirklands of Kinnettles[26] in the barony of Rescobie, near to those of Aberlemno, next Melgund, which he had recently given to his sons.[27] It is remarkable how well the Cardinal's ecclesiastical estates of St Andrews and Arbroath almost fit into each other on the map and are filled out by those which he and his family held from the crown. The Kinnettles charter, dated at the cathedral of St Andrews, was witnessed by a small group of close relatives and associates who were nearest to him in his transactions at this time, Walter Beaton, George Durie, Archibald Beaton, John Beaton, Bernard Bailie, John Lauder and George Cook.

He moved out of St Andrews towards the end of April. His first journey was into Angus for his daughter's marriage which, according to contemporary allusions, was celebrated with the magnificence to be expected of princes.[28] The marriage contract had simply stated that it should take place 'in all possible diligence' without naming a limiting date. On 29 April the Cardinal was at Ethie,[29] his mansion as abbot of Arbroath, which in al probability had been Margaret's home and where the marriage may have taken place. The following day, in a document dated at Arbroath abbey, he assigned to Margaret's mother, Marion Ogilvy, his own right to a reversion which would ultimately bring here revenue.[30] While in Angus word reached him of the movements of the English fleet as a result of which he left for the south, anxious to inspect the fortifications of his own castle and take measures for the defence of his coastal territories. It is said that he called a meeting for the end of May of those Fife landholders whose possessions on his estates were most vulnerable to coastal attack. John Knox's allegation that he had a more sinister purpose in calling the gentlemen of Fife together cannot be entirely swept aside since Knox was in a position later not only to hear about but to see those incriminating papers relating to the plan which he says were found in St Andrews castle.[31] After all, there had been earlier attempts, not very successful it is true, to arrest the gentlemen of Angus. At any rate, the suspicion is suggestive of the bad relations between the Cardinal and some of the Fife families at this time.

He had recently quarrelled violently with Norman Leslie with whom he had a bond of manrent, reputedly over an obligation which, Leslie claimed, the Cardinal refused to honour. They parted with a bitter verbal exchange, the Cardinal insulted and Norman spoiling for revenge.[32] There had been many land transactions over the years between him and Rothes and his kin, some of which could have led to a breakdown in trust.[33] In 1540 the estates of Sir James Colville of East Wemyss, who had been outlawed by James V for collaborating with the Douglases, were forfeited on his death and granted to Rothes. In 1543, however, the Cardinal had used his influence to have the forfeiture annulled with the result that the Leslies lost the property.[34] It may have been the Cardinal's failure to keep a promise to compensate the family that caused Norman to quarrel with him. The Leslies were not the only Fife family to harbour a grudge. It was due to the Cardinal's influence that John Hamilton, abbot of Paisley, had replaced Sir James Kirkcaldy of Grange as treasurer of the realm, and that Kirkcaldy's friend, Mr Henry Balnaves, had been removed from the office of secretary. It may have been the impetus of a private quarrel that made Norman (in company with John Charteris who was himself in and out of the Cardinal's favour) offer to murder David Beaton in the spring of 1544 when their offer had been passed on to the English authorities by Crichton of Brunston, another of the Cardinal's estranged servants. Henry VIII was evidently prepared to use men with a private axe to grind in order to rid himself of his political enemy.

Nevertheless, there were wider motives behind the plot that was hatching than simply a private quarrel, even although that may have been the occasion in Norman Leslie's case. Revenge for the death of George Wishart was certainly another. Even men as rough and ready as John Leslie of Parkhill, who reacted violently to Wishart's execution, believed in some kind of church reform that would break the control of overbearing prelates and deprive them of the material sources of their power. James Kirkcaldy of Grange, reputed to have possessed an English new testament before this was permitted in 1543, who had been instrumental in quashing the Cardinal's attempt to bring the heretics on his blacklist to justice, had instilled reformed beliefs into his son, William, who was to adhere to them for the rest of his life whichever political side he took. Mr Henry Balnaves, who drew back from the violent means but supported the action of the conspirators, was a convinced protestant. The attachment of those two men to Lutheranism, as it was then called, was the main reason why the Cardinal had had them removed from public office. James Melville of Carnbee genuinely mourned Wishart as a friend and came to regard the removal of the Cardinal as 'this work and judgement of God'.[35] It is possible that a number of people had pinned their hopes on George Wishart as the sign of a wind of change and were now disappointed and bitter. Inclination towards alliance with England was also an element in the opposition. Norman Leslie, Cassillis and Brunston were prepared to act as English agents. John Leslie of Parkhill had been one of the Solway Moss assured Scots, released in 1543. Sir James Kirkcaldy's ascendancy under Arran's brief reformation-experiment had seen the progress of Anglo-Scottish negotiations and Henry Balnaves had been one of the envoys sent to London that year.

The conspirators were no artificial group merely thrown together by their grievances. They were a closely-related and allied circle who had had frequent contact with David Beaton over the years. Kirkcaldy of Grange was married to a daughter of Melville of Raith who had connections with the conspiracy. When Kirkcaldy was treasurer Balnaves was treasurer's clerk; in February 1541 both witnessed a charter by the earl of Rothes.[36] On 3 May 1540 Andrew Leslie, a son of Rothes, resigned his lands of Kilmany into the Cardinal's hands preparatory to receiving a new feu charter of them, when one of the witnesses was Alexander Crichton of Brunston.[37] A week later the earl of Rothes himself resigned some territory to the Cardinal 'in his inner chamber' in the castle.[38] Peter Carmichael of Balmaddie, one of the conspirators, came from a family who had at one time received letters of protection as dependants of David Beaton as abbot of Arbroath during one of his French embassies.[39] The long association of these families with the Cardinal had been more personal than the mere parchment connection between vassal and superior, if there was such a thing. He was no remote figure, however exalted he had become, but someone they knew only too well, who had never left that part of Scotland to which they and he belonged or the cirlces in which they were all familiar. This familiarity, and at the same time widening gap in sympathy, reduced any feelings of respect they might have had for him. It is possible that hard-pressed as he was financially, he was less able than formerly to put pressure on those who opposed him. It may be questioned whether he felt as confident as he appeared in these last months, or as he is portrayed by John Knox after the death of Wishart:

> And to write truth, the most part of the Nobility of Scotland had either given unto him their bands of manrent or else were in confederacy and promised amity with him ... And there [in his castle] he remained without all fear of death, promising unto himself no less pleasure nor did the rich man, of whom mention is made by our Master in the Evangel. For did he not only rejoice and say, 'Eat and be glad, my soul, for thou has great riches laid up in store for many days'; but also he said 'Tush, a fig for the feud, and a button for the bragging of all the heretics and their assistance in Scotland. Is not my lord Governor mine? Witness his eldest son there, pledge at my table? Have I not the Queen [Mary of Guise] at my own devotion? ... Is not France my friend, and I friend to France? What danger should I fear?'[40]

Knox was preaching a sermon with the Cardinal as object lesson; to accentuate his self-reliance made his fall all the more salutary. Perhaps there was beginning to be a gap between the form and the substance of his power, of which his recent experience of his French allies was a telling indication.

Personal danger or not, public affairs took the Cardinal to Edinburgh where the household was in residence by 8 May.[41] The master of Crawford with some younger relatives and friends and his curator, Lord Lindsay of the Byres, was also in the burgh, perhaps also his new wife. Their presence would enhance the prestige of the Cardinal's entourage. On 13 May the master subfeued his recently-acquired kirklands of Kinnettles to a relative, Patrick Lindsay of Monekie, and on 24 May the Cardinal confirmed this grant by his 'dearest kinsman'.[42] On the same day there was a meeting of the council at which the Governor and the Cardinal met for what may have been the first time since their journey to Perth in mid-March.[43] It was a small gathering of councillors, who included David Beaton's two cousins, Andrew and George Durie, two bishops who were often with him in later years, William Chisolm of Dunblane and Robert Reid of Orkney, and the Governor's brother, the abbot of Paisley, the Cardinal's firm ally. The only laymen present were the earl of Erroll, Lord Maxwell and Sir William Hamilton of Sanquhar. The only recorded piece of business was an order to the justice clerk to enforce the acts against those of the Merse and Teviotdale 'that sittis undir assurance of England'.

By the time the Cardinal and his household had returned to St Andrews on 28 May Norman Leslie and his associates had made their plans for an assault on the castle. The various accounts of the event put the number of those who took part at between twelve and eighteen, a small number on the face of it for such an enterprise. The attack must have been carefully planned during the weeks the Cardinal was in Edinburgh. It is inconceivable that the party could have contemplated the assault without the collusion of someone, or several people, inside. To begin with there was the matter of the garrison which at that time numbered about a hundred men. We can imagine that it would be easy for the intruders to evict unarmed workmen and the servants who had been turned out of their beds but hardly the soldiers whose job it was to guard against attack. The skilled men on the defences were gunners, about seven in number, with extras hired from time to time, and the engineers who erected and maintained the ordnance. It is significant that in his account of how the attackers took over the castle, Knox only mentions the removal of the workmen and servants but not what happened to the guards. Yet their evacuation must have been prearranged and, in fact, was the one act of collusion that made the *coup* possible. But for Knox to have admitted this would have detracted from the daring of Norman and his friends. John Poll, a gunner, who was among those later accused of complicity in the affair, may have been the key man here. A deal done with one member of the garrison would probably account for the co-operation of his mates if the assassins made it worth their while in material terms. If the guards, whose food and lodging is recorded in the archbishopric accounts, were local men from tenant families who were obliged to do guard duty at the castle it would be easier to gain their co-operation than if they had been professional soldiers. Collusion there must have been, but failure on the part of the government to undertake a thorough investigation has deprived us of the evidence.

It is also unlikely that the attack would have taken place had John Beaton of Balfour been personally in command at the time. It is unthinkable that he could have been bribed although the conspirators could simply have counted on overpowering him during the assault. John was at the castle as late as 18 May[44] but he had had a very long spell of duty before that, even remaining in charge while the Cardinal went to Angus for his daughter's marriage. It may be that the Cardinal had intended to give the laird of Balfour some leave once he himself was reinstalled in the castle and this may have been known in advance, since John Beaton would have to make arrangements in view of his departure and a deputy would be appointed. A few months later, in claiming compensation for the loss of his own and his wife's personal property which, as he explained, had been in their lodging in the castle at the time of the attack, he made no reference in his petition to his having been forcibly ejected from the place, which it seems likely he would have done had this happened to him. There is also the question of whether the Cardinal's administrative staff were away from the castle or were at least depleted in number at the time. The conspirators may have chosen a time when they knew the Cardinal had few of his usual associates with him. They knew that the castle was well provisioned and fortified, and at least Norman Leslie was familiar with the layout of the internal arrangements of the chambers, stairs and passages. The Cardinal's personal servants were known to the group who, in entering the gentlemen's quarters the next morning, were able to call on them by name.

On the evening of Friday 28 May Norman Leslie came to St Andrews where the laird of Grange's son, William Kirkcaldy, was waiting for him.[45] They were later joined by Norman Leslie's uncle, John Leslie of Parkhill, and others with whom they made plans to meet early in the morning in the cathedral burial ground, in groups as their respective parts in the operation required. Between 5 and 6 am on Saturday morning they moved towards the castle. This was not an early hour in sixteenth-century terms, especially in summer, and the masons and other workmen, to the number of over a hundred, were at work on the castle walls. Ambrose Stirling, the porter of the outer gate, who had had associations with the Beaton family since the early 1530s[46] and was therefore entrusted with this major responsibility, had already lowered the drawbridge to admit the loads of building materials. As they drew near, the group glimpsed Marion Ogilvy, who had spent the night with the Cardinal in the castle, slip out by the postern gate, unaware of what was happening. The level of activity about the castle entrance distracted attention from the conspirators, and under cover of one of the wagons, or perhaps a group of men and pack animals negotiating the entrance, William Kirkcaldy and six others stepped on to the drawbridge. Naturally halted by Stirling, they asked him if the Cardinal was awake, to which he replied 'No'. While Kirkcaldy held the porter in talk and his servants affected to watch the workmen, the penetrating, irregular noise of whose operations probably helped to disguise the first alien sounds in the courtyard, Norman Leslie and one or two companions reached the entrance. They had penetrated the inner close, Norman's familiar appearance having delayed suspicion, when the abrupt arrival of the aggressive laird of Parkhill and four others alerted the porter that things were not normal. As he reached for the mechanism of the drawbridge, Parkhill and his companions leapt to safety, broke Stirling's head and snatched his keys. They then toppled the unfortunate man's body into the ditch. The workmen, no doubt panicking at the sight of armed men, 'ran off the walls and were without hurt put forth at the wicket yett', along with the treacherous guards. William Kirkcaldy, being first inside, posted himself at the postern gate to prevent the escape of the Cardinal once he had been alerted. Norman Leslie, knowing the staff and gentlemen of the household by name, probably took charge of turning them out, to the number of about fifty people, and then locked the gate.

By then the Cardinal had been aroused by the shouting and sound of running feet and from a window of his chamber in the east blockhouse asked what the commotion was. Someone shouted unceremoniously that Norman Leslie had taken his castle. The absence of workmen and guards must have been a convincing shock. Investigation of a possible escape-route revealed the figure of Kirkcaldy at the postern gate. The last resort was to barricade himself and his personal servant into his chamber and try to bargain for his life. He had no sooner reached the room and got the servant to move heavy furniture such as kists against the door, and had himself hidden a quantity of gold under some coals, than John Leslie, James Meville and Peter Carmichael arrived in the passage outside and began to force the door. The Cardinal tried to wring a promise from them that if he let them in to talk with him they would not slay him, but he must have judged their mood and feared the worst. He asked to speak to Norman with whom he had made his bond but was told, 'Content yourself with such as are here, for other shall ye get none'. As the great door defied Leslie's attempt to force it he called for fire, at which it was opened, either by the Cardinal or his servant, and the three assassins crowded in. His appeal for their consideration of his priest's status, so uncharacteristic of him, was ignored. Norman Leslie did not come but his uncle, Parkhill, James Melville, the friend of George Wishart, and 'stout' Peter Carmichael did the work for which he and William Kirkcaldy were later paid by the English government.[47] John Leslie kept his vow of revenge by stabbing the Cardinal first, then Carmichael followed. James Melville, described as 'a man of nature most gentle and modest', seeing the other two act in anger, said ' "This work and judgement of God ... ought to be done with greater gravity"; and presenting unto him the point of the sword, said, "Repent thee of thy former wicked life, but especially of the shedding of the blood of that notable instrument of God, Master George Wishart, which albeit the flame of fire consumed before men, yet cries it in vengence upon thee ... I protest, that neither the hetterent of thy person, the love of thy riches, nor the fear of any trouble thou could have done to me ... moves me to strike thee; but only because thou hast been, and remain an obstinated enemy against Christ Jesus and his holy Evangel". And so he struck him twice or thrice through with a stog sword; and so he fell, never word heard out of his mouth but "I am a priest, I am a priest: fye, fye; all is gone" '.

The word spread quickly, the alarm sounded, but accounts of what had happened were confusing. Sir James Learmonth of Dairsie, provost of St Andrews and the archbishop's bailie, with a band of men, soon joined the crowds of clamorous, bewildered citizens at the edge of the fosse to ask of those in the castle what was going on. Norman Leslie, clearly in charge and elated with success, appeared on the wall-head and with almost schoolboy impertinence 'speerit what they desirit to see — ane deid man?'. The crowd would not disperse until they knew for certain that the Cardinal was dead. 'And so was he brought', relates John Knox, 'to the east blockhouse head and shown to the faithless multitude, which would not believe before it saw. How miserably lay David Beaton, careful Cardinal!'. Pitscottie adds that while his body lay on the wall-head 'ane callit Guthrie loussit doun his ballop poynt and pischit in his mouth that all the pepill might sie. Bot he wes ane knaif that did it', and apparently died a violent death soon afterwards.[48] Like Melville, Pitscottie felt there were limits to the way even hatred should be expressed. The Guthrie in question may have been the William Guthrie among those indicted two months later for art and part in the Cardinal's slaughter. It is just possible, however, that the 'chamber child', or body-servant, detained in the castle by the assassins presumably to help them dispose of the body in a salt-filled kist in the sea-tower, may have been Amand Guthrie, the Cardinal's half-French page; if so, his action was a tragic comment on their personal relations.

The Cardinal's death was not simply the outcome of a private feud. The reaction and comments of those who either passed on or received the news in Scotland, England and Europe reveal the wider context in which the deed was done, which was to be expected in the case of someone who for so long had occupied a key position in international politics. Most of them believed that it had been done in the interests of England, although carried out by a group of the Cardinal's 'familiar servants' who had had various grievances of their own. The names of Norman Leslie and William Kirkcaldy, being known to the English political underworld, are usually given as those of the murderers. The fact that they and Alexander Crichton of Brunston were later paid the blood-money, even although the latter had not taken any part in the actual assassination, suggests that this was the old plot, hatched in 1544, brought to fruition. The fact that the assassins planned not only to kill the Cardinal, after which they might have absconded, but to hold the castle in anticipation of English intervention shows that the *coup* was meant to turn the tables on the Scottish government. It was a more violent version of the turnabout of early 1543, but instead of the Cardinal's mere detention he was removed for good. Although the would-be revolutionaries did not control the Governor as their political figurehead, as they had done three years before, the fact that they held his son hostage in the castle had the same effect and was one reason why attempts to bring them to justice in the coming months were so half-hearted. Men like the Kirkcaldys of Grange and Henry Balnaves, the latter soon joining the assassins in the castle, were links with the earlier attempt to turn Scotland's face towards alliance with England and positive reform of the church. The Castilians were not long in sending for a protestant preacher in the person of Wishart's former companion, John Knox. Their protestant attitudes, albeit varying in maturity from that of Henry Balnaves who wrote a theological treatise to that of the two backsliding younger brothers of Norman Leslie, whom Knox reports became 'enemies to Christ Jesus and all virtue', were expressed during their captivity in France after the fall of the castle of St Andrews.[49]

Sir Anthony Browne remarked to Sir William Petre, on reading the news in a letter from Angus passed on by the captain of Berwick, that he was glad the King

[Henry] was rid of such a cankered enemy as the Cardinal.[50] 'I had almost forgotten', wrote Bishop Thirlby to Paget, whom David Beaton had known as the English ambassador in France, 'to tell my gladness of your tidings of the Cardinal of Scotland. It is half a wonder here [Ratisbon] that ye dare be so bold to kill a cardinal.'[51] In diplomatic circles, Englishmen were more reserved in their comments; when Van Der Delft asked at the English court about the rumour, so he told the Emperor Charles V, 'They said it was [true], and that the two men who committed the deed were of good family and now held the Cardinal's house. The crime, they said, was lamentable, and Scotland very low'.[52] 'The principal object of this letter is to report that the Cardinal of Scotland has been killed by two of his own servants, at the instigation of his Scottish enemies who are partisans of England', St Mauris explained to Prince Philip of Spain, adding, 'The French are certain that the King of England caused the murder, as he hated the Cardinal for opposing the marriage of the Princess of Scotland with the Prince of England. The worst of it is that the murderers are in a very strong fortress and may be aided by England, thus arousing a fresh conflict before the time for the restitution of Boulogne.'[53] When the Regent of the Netherlands heard of the Cardinal's death, at the point when she was rejoicing over the 'sincere amity between the King [Henry] and the Emperor', she said 'that we were despatched of a great enemy'.[54] 'The Cardinal of Scotland was killed by relatives of a man whom he had executed for heresy', Van der Delft reported again to the Emperor, 'But some people still assert that he is only wounded.'[55]

'Richt honourable', wrote a Scottish correspondent to Wharton, 'on Friday [*sic*] last the Master of Rothus has slain the cardinal of Scotland in his own castle of Sanct Androis, by treason, and has the Governor's son and heir with him there', adding that Lord Maxwell had got his own house of Caerlaverock from the Governor, but as soon as Arran had heard of the Cardinal's death he sent word to the captain not to give it to him.[56] David Maitland wrote in some excitement to Wharton on the day after the Cardinal's slaughter, 'Now there is such news as never was before. The Cardinal is slain in Sanctandros on Saturday afternoon [*sic*] 29th inst. by Normond Leslye and the laird of Grange; and all things change ... '[57] The writer explained that he was about to pass to the house of Lord Somerville, 'quha wyllbe blythe off the Cardenallis ded ... ' Writing to an anonymous correspondent 'in the toun [of St Andrews] this Satterday midnycht', after the excitement of the day had died down, James Lindsay related events and added, 'PS Sandy Drummond counsels you to come to my lord of Angus in Tantallon incontinent', for there would be 'great dipositioun of benefices at this time ... Sir, tarry not. I find few displeased at his death. Show yourself a wise man and you may profit.'[58]

It might have gratified the Cardinal to know that in spite of all the animosity and the rejoicing at his departure which is conveyed in the news bulletins, his passing did leave a vacuum. It was speedily filled, however, and in the realms of patronage and material wealth, to change the metaphor, the vultures were gathering. John Hamilton, the Governor's brother, was granted the temporalities of the archbishopric of St Andrews two days after the Cardinal's death. At a meeting of the council just four days after the assassination not only were his faithful colleagues, the bishops of Orkney and Galloway, present, with eight abbots and commendators, but the laymen had returned in force: seven earls including his opponents, Angus, Glencairn and Cassillis, and seven lords including Ruthven, Maxwell and Somerville.[59] No business is recorded in the register under this sederunt, but on 5 June at another meeting the earl of Huntly was made chancellor of the realm and accepted custody of the great seal. Apart from Angus's few months as chancellor in 1527–8, Huntly was the first lay chancellor for almost half a century, in fact since his great-grandfather had held the office at the end of the fifteenth century, soon after David Beaton was born. As David Maitland predicted, 'all things change'.

NOTES

1. *Knox*, II, 233–45 ; *Calderwood*, I, 199–219
2. *Knox*, II, 239–40; Knox reproduced the account of the trial from Foxe's *Actes and Monuments*(1563–64)
3. *Ibid.*, II, 237
4. *Ibid.*, II, 241
5. *Ibid.*, II, 236
6. *Ibid.*, II, 237
7. *Ibid.*, II, 237–8
8. *Ibid.*, II, 238, called 'child', the contemporary designation of a servant.
9. *Ibid.*, II, 240–1
10. *Ibid.*, II, 242
11. *Ibid.*, II, 242–3
12. *Ibid.*, II, 243–4
13. *Spottiswoode*, I, 159; *Pitscottie*, II, 77
14. *Spottiswoode*, I, 160
15. *Calderwood*, I, 217
16. *Scottish Correspondence*, 160
17. *Rentale*, 204
18. *Knox*, I, 74
19. *Peerage*, III, 25–9
20. Crawford priory muniments, GD 20/105
21. *Ibid.*, 113
22. *Ibid.*, 111
23. *Ibid.*
24. Dalhousie muniments, GD 45/17/9
25. *Scottish Correspondence*, 162
26. *R.M.S.*, V, 1191
27. Laing charters, 512
28. *Pitscottie*, II, 82
29. Crawford Papers in the John Rylands Library, Manchester University
30. A.D.C.S., xxviii, fo 85v
31. *Knox*, I, 76

32. *Pitscottie*, II, 83
33. Lord Herries, *Memoirs* (Abbotsford Club), 16; *Calderwood*, I, 220
34. Herkless, *Beaton*, 304–5
35. *Knox*, I, 77
36. A.D.C.S., xiv, fos 152–4
37. Protocol book of James Androsoun, NP 1/5a, fo 23
38. *Ibid.*
39. *R.S.S.*, II, 2166
40. *Knox*, I, 75
41. *Rentale*, 214
42. Lindsay muniments (S.R.O.), GD 203/5/5, 7
43. *R.P.S.*, I, 23
44. *R.M.S.*, III, 3257
45. *Knox*, I, 76
46. Justiciary Court Minute Book, JC 1/3, 13 January 1531
47. Herkless, *Beaton*, 313; L.P. Henry VIII, XXI, i, 1314; Dasent, *Acts of the Privy Council*, I, 527
48. *Pitscottie*, II, 83–4
49. *Knox*, I, 110
50. *L.P. Henry VIII*, XXI, i, 990
51. *Ibid.*, XXI, i, 1070
52. *Ibid.*, XXI, i, 1058
53. *Ibid.*, XXI, i, 1214
54. *Ibid.*, XXI, i, 1038
55. *Ibid.*, XXI, i, 1033
56. *Ibid.*, XXI, i, 959
57. *Ibid.*, XXI, i, 958
58. *Ibid.*, XXI, i, 948
59. *Ibid.*, XXI, i, 980, 1002

Epilogue

'That ever I brukit Benefice I rew,
Or to sic hycht so proudely did pretend.
I man depart: tharefor, my freinds, adew:
Quhare ever it plesith God, now man I wend.
I praye the tyll my freindis me Recommend,
And failze nocht at lenth to put in wryte
My Tragedie, as I have done Indyte.'

Sir David Lindsay, *The Tragedie of the
Cardinall* (Scottish Text Society), lines 428–434

It is eloquent of the effect that David Beaton's presence had on people that observers often conveyed the impression that his reactions were closely watched, so closely that one of them noticed that he was about to strike someone: 'the Cardinal laughed', 'the Cardinal shrugged', 'the Cardinal gave a great sigh', 'the Cardinal was something abashed'. They even thought it of interest to report what he wore, because this indicated his mood: clad in armour during the Lennox episode in the west of Scotland, resplendent in gold and silver when Hertford's soldiers disembarked at Newhaven. First-hand accounts of meetings with him evoked the effusive manner which was the most harmless aspect of his restless energy: taking Sadler by the arm, the elderly papal legate by the hand. They relived his outbursts of anger: shouting with 'furiositie' across the table at the prior of the Carmelites or taunting John Winram with his carefully-concealed unorthodoxy. People were so apprehensive of what he might do that when they were in his presence they read the signs. Yet his intentions and, for that matter, abilities were often greater than his opportunities, both in politics and in the prosecution of heresy. The fear and resentment that he inspired, which have gone down in the records, have disguised the difficulties he experienced in building his own career, maintaining Scotland's presence in European politics, controlling the political situation at home and intimidating religious dissenters. In this sense his reputation was, and perhaps still is, larger than life.

The measure of his ability is best seen in the political field where he was most at home and in which for two and a half years he was able to keep Scotland, in spite of opposition, to the lines of his chosen policy of non-co-operation with England whatever the cost. It could perhaps be alleged that he was enabled to dominate Scottish politics because he only had the irresolute Arran to deal with as acting head of state and that his triumph of the autumn of 1543, which was the high-water mark of his control, had in a sense made itself through the Governor's weakness of purpose and Henry VIII's overbearing tactics which provoked an anti-English reaction. Besides, the failure of the Hamiltons to build up a strong political hegemony under a forceful leader of their own, which might have given cohesion to the opposition, enabled the Cardinal to buy off one group against another in the fragmented state of Scottish political alliances. It also allowed him to use his personal skills, which were essentially those of a diplomat, to the full. Yet, his unquestionable ability showed itself when called upon: while he steadily wore the Governor down in the summer of 1543, he could at the same time remain in the background, temporising with all parties in the belief that time was on his side. Close observation of his career shows that it was more difficult for him to keep abreast of the shifting patterns of political alliances than used to be thought. The difficulties were real: it is significant that in the summer of 1544, when opposition to Arran was at its most solid, the Cardinal experienced a brief period of political isolation, deserted for a time even by some of his episcopal colleagues, with at one point the possibility that Mary of Guise herself might emerge as a rival. Even the Governor needed careful handling and respect for his own ambitions, otherwise he was liable to go off and listen to someone else's proposals.

In spite of his identification with France in the minds of his opponents — 'a French brag of the Cardinal's', one of them scoffed — the Franco-Scottish alliance appeared to give decreasing returns in the years of his personal ascendancy. Between the Cardinal and the rulers of France, where he had spent much of his early career and had personal assets, there was a divergence of ideas about what the alliance implied. To him it meant military and financial help against England without impairing the independence of Scotland. To Francis I, for whom a period of heavy military commitment was followed by a move towards conciliation with England, the alliance was simply a mechanism in the diplomatic machinery to be used when France was in difficulties. Even in the days of the Catholic League's plans for a confrontation with the King of England, the papal ambassador had been aware of the inequality of the Franco-Scottish alliance. Although the Cardinal knew the reasons for the French King's reluctance, and indeed inability, to become substantially involved in Scottish affairs in the mid-1540s, the sorry results of de Lorges' campaign, following as they did on the embarrassments during the visit of de la Brosse and Ménage, must have been a source of frustration and even humiliation, especially when accompanied by considerable English infiltration through the assured men of the eastern borders and Lothian. 'The Best Frenchman' must have found it difficult at times to refute the belief that he supported the French alliance mainly to strengthen his own credit in France. The unpopularity of the French in Scotland when they did come, as well as the association of the alliance with David Beaton's reactionary policies, built up an antipathy which in the later 1550s, when French intervention appeared to threaten the independence of Scotland, hastened the end of the 'auld alliance' altogether. David Beaton did not live to agonise over the necessary acceptance of French domination (as distinct from assistance) in the way that some of his Anglophile opponents must have had to search their hearts over how far to sacrifice Scotland to the King of England.

It is in relation to growing religious dissent, so often allied to amity with England, that the gap between the Cardinal's potential and his performance is

R

most clearly seen. His contemporary and posthumous reputation as a persecutor of heretics, and the hatred of him which that engendered, arose from awareness of his attitude and intentions rather than the fact that he burnt large numbers of them, which he did not. This does not mean that he exaggerated the problem, for it was there and it was growing. His very attitude encouraged reaction, not only his repressiveness but his lack of interest in serious, internal church reform. Even if he had been concerned about it he had little time to give to it because of his preoccupation with the maintenance of political control and the national defences, the latter necessitated by his chosen policy. His real fear was that concern for reform would encourage people to disregard ecclesiastical authority or threaten church property, a fear which he had experienced even during the reign of James V. It was the *kind* of thing that heresy was, although it lacked effective leadership, that caused him to take up a repressive attitude. Indeed, its scattered but persistent nature made it all the more difficult to deal with, but after 1543 he could see that what leadership it did have among articulate, socially-influential adherents was prepared to risk confrontation.

It was the potential spiritual leadership of George Wishart, which although he deplored it the Cardinal recognised, that decided him after an interval of two years to take punitive action in influential circles. Until then most, but by no means all, heretics who had been put to death were of comparatively modest standing. To remove Wishart must have seemed one way of striking a blow at those landed adherents of reform whom he had been unable to punish for fear of reprisals. The openness and acceptability of Wishart's preaching among them provoked the Cardinal into taking the risk. It has sometimes been said that his prosecutions held back the tide of Reformation, and certainly his repressive policy must have caused some people to remain underground. There was a sense, however, in which he had had to watch the tide rise slowly while unable to do anything to stem it; his warning to John Winram on the tense day of Wishart's trial betrayed his frustration. It is probable that those who were committed to theological reform were in a minority, although from varying social groups; it was the threat to the church's property and status, the Cromwellian pattern for 'the stay of the spirituality', that disturbed the Cardinal.

In the 1550s protestants benefited from both a bolder leadership and the conciliatory attitude, for their own purposes, of Mary of Guise and Archbishop John Hamilton. Besides, when the crisis came they were able to rely on the government of the protestant Queen Elizabeth of England. Yet, the beginnings of the situation in which they found themselves can be traced to those years when David Beaton influenced and eventually presided over the political and religious affairs of Scotland.

Appendix 1

Calendar of writs and other documents running in the name of David Beaton, Cardinal, Archbishop of St Andrews, Bishop of Mirepoix, Commendator of Arbroath and Legate *a latere*, 1539–46 and n.d.

Part 1   Dated documents
Part 2   Undated documents, approximate dates suggested
Part 3   Undated documents referred to in *Statutes of the Scottish Church*, ed. D. Patrick (S.H.S.)
Part 4   Undated documents contained in the *St Andrews Formulare*, ed. G. Donaldson and C. Macrae (Stair Society)

Part 1

1539
February
16   *Letters ordinary* to the dean of Haddington for presentation of Mr Thomas Hay to a prebend in Bothans collegiate church (Yester Writs, GD 28/541)
25   *Instrument of institution* in the parish kirk of Tynningham in favour of St Mary's college, St Andrews (St Andrews University muniments, SM 110.B1.P1.4)

March
7   *Charter* to Edward Sinclair of Driden of part of the lands of Lasswade (Clerk of Penicuik muniments, GD 18/457)
     Precept of sasine following on above (*Ibid.*, GD 18/458)
     Precept; payment for clothes for Lady Fleming (*Rentale*, 94)
     Precept; payment to Gilbert Lauder, merchant in Edinburgh, and wife (*Ibid.*)
8   *Precept*; payment to Mr Thomas Marjoribanks, advocate (*Ibid.*, 93)
     Precept; payment to Patrick Tennant, burgess of Edinburgh (*Ibid.*, 94)
     Precept; payment to the convent of St Catherine of Sienna, near Edinburgh (*Ibid.*)
     Precept; payment of pension to Mr George Hay (*Ibid.*)
     Letters of commission to Archibald Beaton of Capildrae and Mr Henry Lumsden to receive the resignation of the lands of Clatty from George Ramsay (Register House Charters, RH6/1188)
     Letters of regress to Ramsay of Clatty (*Ibid.*, 1189)
     Charter to Andrew Leslie of Kilmany (*Ibid.*, 1190)
     Precept of sasine following on above (*Ibid.* 1191)
9   *Charter* to David Wood of Craig, of the lands of Scotstoun (*R.M.S.* III, 2741)
23   *Precept* for payment to James Coutts, skipper, at Dieppe (*Rentale*, 93)

May
24   *Charter* in his name by Beaton of Capildrae and Mr Henry Lumsden to George Ramsay of Clatty, of half the lands of Kilmany (Register House Charters, RH6/1201)

June
9   *Charter* in his name by same to Andrew Leslie, son of the earl of Rothes, of half the lands of Kilmany (*Ibid.*, 1204)

July
28   *Supplication* to the Pope *re* annexation of the parish kirk of Inchbriock to St Mary's College (St Andrews University muniments, SM 110 B1.P1.11)

September
13   *Letters of provision and collation* by the abbots of Cambuskenneth and Kinloss, his vicars general, to Mr Robert Erskine as parson of Glenbervie (Erskine of Dun muniments, GD123/12)

October
6   *Charter* to Sir James Learmonth of Dairsie of lands of Kilmynnane (Register House Charters, RH 6/1210)
19   *Letters of absolution* to the earl of Bothwell, from a letter of cursing by the late archbishop of St Andrews (A.D.C.S., xviii, fos 64v–65)

November
8   *Charter* to Sir Thomas Erskine of Brechin, of lands of Logy (*R.M.S.* III, 2170)
16   *Letter* to Mr Andrew Oliphant, agent at Rome (*Sadler*, I, 3)

December
3   *Precept*; payment of pension to Mr George Hay (*Rentale*, 94)
4   *Precept*; payment to the French servant of the Constable of France (*Ibid.*)
7   *Precept*; payment to a priest saying his first mass (*Ibid*, 96)
10   *Letter* to Mr Andrew Oliphant, agent at Rome (*L.P. Henry VIII*, XV, 136)

1540
January
20   *Charter* to David Wood of Craig of the lands of Abbotstoun belonging to Arbroath abbey (*R.M.S.* III, 2741)

February
10   *Precept*; payment to the wife of Sir James Hamilton of Finnart (*Rentale*, 95)
20   *Charter* to James Ogilvy of Cukstoun of lands of Balfour, etc. (Dalhousie Muniments, GD 45/16/1131)
           Precept of sasine following on above (BL Add. Charters, 12, 776)

March
18   *Precept*; payment to George Philp, sent to France (*Rentale*, 102)

April
4   *Charter* in favour of the two chaplains of the principal altar in St Andrews parish church, of a quarter of the lands of Muircambus (Rankin, *Trinity Church*, 58)
6   *Mandate*; payment towards the bridge of the 'Northwater' (*Rentale*, 94)

8   *Tack*, as commendator of Arbroath, to John Pedye, of eighth of Kinclune (Misc. Collections, GD1/202/7)

9   *Precept* of sasine in favour of the chaplains of Trinity Church, St Andrews, in quarter of the lands of Muircambus (St Andrews Charters, in St Andrews University Library, formerly S.R.O., B65/22/285)

20   *Precept*; payment to the wife of Gilbert Lauder, merchant in Edinburgh (*Rentale*, 95)

21   *Charter* to Andrew Leslie, son of the earl of Rothes, of the lands of Balcaithlie (Protocol book of James Androsoun, NP1/5a, fo 22)

      Precept of sasine to above in these lands (Rothes Muniments, GD204/15) (another copy dated 1 May 1540, *Ibid,*)

26   *Precept*; payment to the convent of St Catherine of Sienna, Edinburgh (*Rentale*, 95)

      Acquittance for money received from the graniter of St Andrews (*Ibid.*, 102)

May

4   *Letter* to Cardinal Ghinucci (Caprington Letter Book, GD 149, 150)

      Letter to Pope Paul III (*Letters of James V*, 397)

8   *Charter* to Andrew Leslie of half of Kilmany, on resignation (Register House Charters, RH6/1230) (the resignation in the Cardinal's hands recorded same day in Protocol Book of James Androsoun, NP1/5a, fo 23)

      Precept of sasine on above charter (Register House Charters, RH6/1231)

11   *Precept* of sasine in favour of Andrew Leslie in lands of Wester Nydie (Protocol Book of James Androsoun, NP1/5a,fo23v)

      Acquittance for payment from graniter of St Andrews (*Rentale*, 102)

14   *Charter* to David Barclay of Mathers of lands of Aberluthnot (*R.M.S*, III, 2905)

28   *Sentence* against Sir John Borthwick, for heresy (*St Andrews Kirk Session Register*, 89–104)

29   *Precept*; payment to a chaplain in Markinch parish church to pray for members of the Beaton family (*Rentale*, 107)

June

8   *Precept*; payment of pension of Mr George Hay (*Ibid.*)

12   *Precept*; payment to Sir Walter Mar for work at St Mary's college (*Ibid.*)

13   *Precept*; payment to the Master of Lyle (*Ibid.*)

July

5   *Letter* to Cardinal of Carpi (State Papers: SP1/2/31 SRO)

August

2   *Precept*; remission to the Black Friars of St Monance for their part of the non-entry of the lands of Invery (*Rentale*, 108)

7   *Precept*; alms to the Grey Friars of Edinburgh (*Ibid.*)

15   *Precept*; payments to the apothecary for drugs (*Ibid.*)

24   *Precept*; payment to the widow of Sir James Hamilton of Finnart (*Ibid.*)

September

25   *Precept of sasine* for infeftment of Henry Kemp of Thomastoun in lands of Mondorno (Dalhousie Muniments, GD45/16/2333)

October

2   *Charter* to Andrew Leslie of Kilmany of lands of Balcaithlie (*R.M.S.* III, 2662) (see also under 21 April 1540)

4   *Precept*; payment for work done at St Mary's college (*Rentale*, 108)

      Charter to John Tennant, servant of James V, of lands of Bellilisk, etc. (*H.M.C. Report*, IV, 484)

20   *Precept* of sasine in favour of Alexander Whitelaw, of lands of Newgrange; as commendator of Arbroath (Eglinton Muniments: GD3)

29   *Disposition* to Thomas Richardson in Leith of the ward and marriage of a twelfth part of Innergellie (St Andrews University muniments, SM 110 B.16.9)

November

17   *Precept*; payment to the Master of Lyle (*Rentale*, 107)

22   *Precept*; payment to the sailors on the *Mary Willoughby*, after voyage with the king round the isles (*Ibid.*, 108)

29   *Precept*; payment to the upholsterer (*Ibid.*)

December

6   *Tack* to David Ramsay of Colluthie of the ferryboat of Tay for nineteen years (Fraser, *Southesk*, I, lxii)

27   *Precept*; payment to the minister of the Grey Friars, leaving for Italy (*Rentale*, 108)

28   *Precept*; payment to the prince's nurses (*Ibid.*)

30   *Precept*; payment to George Todrick in name of William Todrick, citizen of Paris (*Ibid.*)

1541

January

2   *Precept*; payment to the master of work at St Mary's college (*Ibid.*)

5   *Tack* to Sir Andrew Duncan, curate of Monimail, of the brewhouse of Monimail and its lands (Fraser, *The Melvilles*, III, 78)

      Tack to Janet Thomson of the smithland of Monimail (*Ibid.*)

      Tack to David Durie and his son, James, of the mill of Monimail (*Ibid.*)

      Tack to David Bontaveron of an eighth of Letham (Fraser, *Melvilles*, III, 79)

February

24   *Precept*; payment to Christina Lindsay, pauper (*Rentale*, 108)

      Precept; payment to the Edinburgh Grey Friars to enable them to buy a croft (*Ibid.*)

28   *Precept*; payment to Sir John Melville of Raith as remission of his fermes for Abthane Kinghorn (*Ibid.*)

March

7   *Charter* to Mr Henry Balnaves of the lands of Pitcuntie and Murefield (Leven and Melville muniments, GD26/3/1194)

26   *Tack*, as commendator of Arbroath, to Andrew Fraser of Stanewood, of the teinds in the barony of Farnes (Haddo House muniments, GD33/18/2a)

      Charter to same of the lands of Carnbrogie (*Ibid.*, GD33/18/2)

April

11   *Precept*; payment for clothes for John, the stable boy (*Rentale*, 125)
26   *Precept*; payment to the French muleteer (*Ibid.*)

May

14   *Precept*; payment to Gilbert Lauder, Edinburgh merchant, and his wife (*Ibid.*)
15   *Precept*; payment to Mr Thomas Marjoribanks (*Ibid.*)
25   *Precept*; payment to Andrew Mansioun for a brass for the Beaton family tomb in Markinch parish church (*Ibid.*)
28   *Aquittance* to the earl of Crawford (*Ibid.*)

June

12   *Precept*; payment to Lady Innermeath (*Ibid.*)
18   *Precept*; payment for clothes for the Cardinal's niece (*Ibid.*)
22   *Acquittance*; fee to Mr Adam Mure (*Ibid.*, 121)
23   *Precept*; clothes for Amand Guthrie, the Cardinal's page (*Ibid.*)
29   *Precept*; payment to the widow of Sir James Hamilton of Finnart, the Cardinal's 'kinswoman' (*Ibid.*, 122)
            Precept; part payment to Robert Gordon of Gordonshall (*Ibid.*, 125)

July

3   *Precept*; payment to the French cook (*Ibid.*, 126)
8   *Precept*; payment to William Scheves (*Ibid.*, 115)
12   *Precept*; part payment to the skipper of the *Mary Welshingham* (*Ibid.*, 123)
13   *Precept*; payment to the Black Friars to repair their high altar (*Ibid.*, 125)
            Precept; payment for material bought by the tailor (*Ibid.*)
            Letters of pension to the Cardinal's brother, Mr Walter Beaton (*Ibid.*, 126)
            Contract with William Graham of Fintry and his son, for a renewal of the infeftment of Easter Craigtoun (A.D.C.S., xvi, fo 42v)
14   *Precept*; payment to William Blackie in Leith for freight (*Rentale*, 123)
            Precept; on behalf of George Beaton, son of John Beaton of Balfour, at Crail Grammar school (*Ibid.*, 126)
15   *Appointment* of auditors of accounts in Cardinal's absence (*Ibid.*)
16   *Acquittance* to the chamberlain of St Andrews for money to play cards (*Ibid.*, 122)
17   *Appointment* of vicars-general to act in his absence abroad (*Formulare*, II, 405)
            Precept; payment to his servant, Alexander Morton (*Rentale*, 123)
21   *Precept*; payment on behalf of the sons of John Beaton of Balfour at Crail grammar school (*Rentale*, 126)

September

13   *Letter* to James V from Mascon (*L.P. Henry VIII*, XVI, 1178)
14   *Letter* to same from same (*Ibid.*, 1182)

October

25   *Letter* to same from Dijon (*Ibid*, 1288)

November

26   *Letter* to the Scottish secretary, Sir Thomas Erskine, from Paris (*Ibid.*, 1378)

December
12   *Letter* to Christian III of Denmark from Fontainebleau (*Ibid.*, 1446)

1542
May
28   *Appointment* of Robert Reid, bishop of Orkney, and Mr John Lauder as commissioners to confirm charters (Leven and Melville muniments, GD 26/3/436)

June
15   *Decreet* by suffragan confirming charter of prior of Pittenweem (Yester Writs, GD 28/596)

August
14   *Acquittance* for £1,000 from the fruits of the archbishopric on his return from France (*Rentale*, 143)
22   *Precept*; payment to Patrick Hume (*Ibid.*)
24   *Precept*; payment to carpenters working at Burntisland (*Ibid.*)
25   *Precept*; drinksilver to the masons working at St Mary's college (*Ibid.*)

September
5   *Contract*; Cardinal and James Rhynd of Carse (Graham of Fintry muniments, GD 151/Box 29)
18   *Precept*; payment of expenses of Mr Andrew Oliphant (*Rentale*, 143)
19   *Precept*; payment for gunpowder for St Andrews castle (*Ibid.*)

October
4   *Precept of clare constat* in favour of David Gardyne of Leyis, as heir of his father in lands held of Arbroath abbey (Bruce-Gardyne of Middleton muniments, NRA(S) Survey, 22, p.6)
7   *Acquittance* to Janet Beaton, lady Cranstounriddell (*Rentale*, 143)
14   *Tack* to John Melville of Raith of the kirklands of Abthane Kinghorn (Leven and Melville Muniments, GD 26/3/900)
21   *Precept*; payment to Alexander Sampson (*Rentale*, 143)

November
2   *Charter* to David Wemyss of lands of Methil, etc., (Fraser, *Wemyss*, II, 160–1)
3   *Precept of sasine* following on above (*Ibid.*, 284)
10   *Letter* to Pope Paul III on war with England (*Theiner*, no. 1061)
14   *Discharge*, with Archibald Beaton of Capildrae, as tutor testamentar of James Crichton of Cranstonriddell, to the latter's mother, Janet Beaton (Fraser, *Buccleuch*, II, 179–80)
22   *Precept*; payment to the widow and son of Evangelist Passer (*Rentale*, 143)
            Precept; payment to sir Thomas Knox for writing accounts (*Ibid.*)

1543
January
16   *Charter* to the earl of Argyll of lands of Balrudry, etc. (*HMC Report*, IV, 484)

26   *Confirmation* by his commissioners of a charter by Cardinal to Mr Henry Balnaves, of the lands of Pitcuntie and Murefield (Leven and Melville muniments, GD26/3/436)

February

12   *Precept*; payment to the Edinburgh Grey Friars (*Rentale*, 143)

17   *Precept*; payment to Robert Lindsay, marshall (*Ibid.*)

April

8   *Letters* repledging James Anderson, tenant of Arbroath abbey to the regality court (Airlie muniments, GD16/25/81)

18   *Charter* to Lord Seton of the kirklands of Kirkliston (Clerk of Penicuik muniments, GD18/459)

May

2   *Letter* to Pope Paul III in answer to call to attend the Council of Trent (*L.P. Henry VIII*, XVIII, ii, 494)

10   *Tack*, as commendator of Arbroath, to George Gordon of Scheves, of certain teinds (Register House Charters, RH6/1317)

June

17   *Precept*; payment to Christian Beaton, Lady Burleigh (*Rentale*, 193)

July

12   *Precept*; payment to workmen at St Andrews castle (*Ibid.*, 197)

24   *Band* by the Cardinal and others at Linlithgow (*Hamilton Papers*, i, 446)

August

17   *Letter* to the earl of Bothwell (*Scottish Correspondence of Mary of Lorraine*, 23)

      Charter to the earl of Argyll of lands in the barony of Muckhart (*HMC Report*, IV, 484)

      Precept of sasine following on above (*Ibid.*)

September

6   *Letter*, in conjunction with others, to the earl of Angus (*L.P. Henry VIII*, XVIII, ii, 139)

October

4   *Precept of clare constat*, as commendator of Arbroath, in favour of Lord Hay of Yester in lands of Auchcarmure, Lanarkshire (Yester Writs GD 28/615)

9   *Precept*; payment to Robert Hector, engineer at St Andrews castle (*Rentale*, 198)

November

12   *Precept*; payment to masons at St Andrews castle (*Ibid.*, 197)

14   *Charter* to Lord Borthwick of lands in lordship of Stow (*R.M.S.* III, 2985)

      Precept of sasine following on above (Stair muniments, GD 135/78)

15   *Precept*; payment to the canons of St Andrews priory for consenting to a charter to David Beaton of Melgund of the lands of Carsbank (*Rentale*, 197)

December
23   *Gift* of the casualties from the lands of Auchtermonsy to David Beaton of Melgund and his brothers (Crawford priory muniments, GD20/105)

1544

January
14   *Letter* to Mary of Guise (Register House transcripts, RH 1/2/361)
19   *Letter* to Henry VIII (*Hamilton Papers*, II, 254)

February
4   *Contract* between the Cardinal and the earl of Crawford over the lands of Auchtermonsy and Cairnie (Crawford priory muniments, GD 20/107)
     Indenture between the Cardinal and the earl about the same lands (*Ibid.*, 106)
5   *Charter* of confirmation to David, master of Crawford, of a charter by the earl of Crawford of Auchtermonsy and Cairnie (Register of acts and decreets, xiv, fo 114v)
7   *Charter* to the earl of Crawford of Auchtermonsy and Cairnie (Crawford priory muniments, GD 20/109)
     Precept; payment to the Grey Friars of St Andrews (*Rentale*, 197)
     Precept; payment of expenses of the sons of the baron of Dalziel at St Andrews university (*Ibid.*, 198)
9   *Precept*; payment to the masons of St Mary's college (*Ibid.*)

March
1   *Tack* to John Ogilvy of Cuckstoun of the wardmill of Arbroath (Airlie muniments, GD 16/196, fo 10v)
3   *Precept*; payment to sir James Wemyss, penitentiary (*Rentale*, 197)
6   *Acquittance* to John Beaton of Balfour for fermes of Kilrenny (*Ibid.*, 182)
8   *Acquittance* to chamberlain of St Andrews (*Ibid.*, 176)
21   *Charge*, in name of the official of St Andrews principal and Cardinal, to the curate of Panbride to denounce certain excommunicate persons for non-compearance in court (Dalhousie muniments, GD 45/13/189)

April
5   *Notarial instrument* recording the Cardinal's undertaking not to raise his processional cross in the archdiocese of Glasgow (*Glasguensis*, II, 555-6)
9   *Mandate*; payment to the Grey Friars of Glasgow (*Rentale*, 181)
22   *Precept*; payment to Henry Miller, smith in Dysart (*Ibid.*, 193)

May
1   *Precept*; payment to a mason (*Ibid.*, 197)
8   *Instrument* naming the Cardinal's testamentary executors (*Formulare*, II, 624)
27   *Letters* appointing John Wemyss executor dative to David Wemyss of that ilk (Fraser, *Wemyss*, II, 161-6)

June
9   *Precept*; payment to the wife of David Graham (*Rentale*, 193)
11   *Precept*; payment to sir Henry Sinclair, servant of Lord Seton (*Ibid.*)

25   *Charter* to Robert Douglas of Lochleven of the lands of Bishopshire (*R.M.S.* V, 1145)

27   *Letters* of remission to Douglas of Lochleven, of grassums due (Morton muniments, GD150/962)

July

13   *Precept*; payment to John Anstruther of that ilk (*Rentale*, 193)

21   *Charter* to John, Lord Innermeath, and Elizabeth Beaton, his wife, of the lands of Lunan (Misc. Collections, GD1/796/1)

      Precept; of sasine for infeftment of above in their lands (W. Blair, *A Record of Lunan*, 36–37)

23   *Precept*; payment for work at St Andrews castle (*Rentale*, 176)

August

2   *Precept*; payment to Margaret Anstruther, wife of Thomas Wood (*Ibid.*, 193)

12   *Charter*, as commendator of Arbroath, to Alexander Graham, son of the earl of Montrose, of the barony of Torry, Aberdeenshire. (*Antiquities of Aberdeen and Banff*, III, 249–51)

25   *Tack* to Robert Durie of that ilk of half of Cunzeoquhy (Register House Charters, RH6/1348)

September

1   *Precept*; payment to the widow of the gardener at Edinburgh (*Rentale*, 193)

16   *Precept*; payment to Andrew Anstruther of that ilk, younger (*Ibid.*)

17   *Tack* to Alexander Forbes of Colquhoun of the teindsheaves of Crosstoun belonging to Arbroath abbey (Forbes muniments, GD52/1695)

October

5   *Provision* as Legate *a latere* of James Hamilton to the deanery of Brechin (*S.H.R.* XXII, 37)

20   *Charter* to Patrick, Lord Gray, of lands in barony of Rescoby (*R.M.S.* IV, 3029)

22   *Bond of manrent and maintenance* to Lord Gray (*Spalding Club Misc.* V, 295–6)

25   *Letter* to John Erskine of Dun (*Spalding Club Misc* IV, 45–6)

November

1   *Letter* to the Cardinal of Carpi (State Papers, SP1/2/107)

      Letter to the Cardinal of Ancona (State Papers, SP 1/2/108)

19   *Letters* (2) to Pope Paul III (State Papers, SP 1/2/110,138)

      Acquittance to Alexander Forbes of Tolquhoun for £160 grassum for the teinds of Tarves (Forbes muniments, GD52/1696)

December

24   *Letter* to the Cardinal of S.Crucis (*L.P. Henry VIII*, XIX, ii, 774)

1545

February

10   *Charter* to Robert Arbuthnot of that ilk of the kirktoun of Arbuthnot (*RMS* III, 3065)

Letters to the Bishop of Dunblane, as Legate *a latere*, to grant dispensation for marriage of Andrew Toscheach and Janet Murray (Abercairney muniments, GD24/5/1/58)

April

12 *Letters* of dispensation as Legate *a latere* for the marriage of William Meldrum, son and heir of George Meldrum of Fyvie, and Elizabeth Abernethy, daughter of William, Lord Saltoun (Blairs College manuscripts (N.R.A.(S) Survey, 18)

14 *Charter* as commendator of Arbroath to Mr James Wishart, of lands of Balfeith (Southesk charters)

17 *Charter* to Alexander Burnet of Leyis, of the lands of Banchory-Ternan (*R.M.S*, III, 3116)

24 *Bond of manrent* with Norman Leslie, son of the earl of Rothes (Chalmers, *Caledonia*, II, 845)

May

1 *Faculty* as Legate *a latere* to the precentor and subdean of Glasgow to confirm a charter by the abbot of Kilwinning (Boyd Papers, GD8/130)

5 *Dispensation*, as Legate *a latere*, for the marriage of Patrick Lindsay and Euphemia Douglas (Morton muniments, GD 150/309)

12 *Precept of clare constat* for the infeftment of Adam Lindsay in the lands of Cavyll (Burnet Stuart papers, GD115/5)

17 *Dispensation*, as Legate *a latere*, for the marriage of William Meldrum and Elizabeth Abernethy (Register House transcripts, RH1/3/362/1)

25 *Commission*, as Legate *a latere*, to confirm his own charter to Alexander Burnet of Leyis (Burnet of Leyis muniments, NRA(S) Survey, 24, p. 8)

26 *Confirmation*, as Legate *a latere*, of his own charter to Alexander Burnet of Leyis (*New Spalding Club, Burnet of Leyis papers*, 176–181)

June

14 *Tack*, as commendator of Arbroath, to Jerome Ochterlony of the lands of Ethmithie (Northesk muniments, GD130/15c)
    Precept; payment to sir James Wemyss (*Rentale*, 197)

30 *Ratification* of a mortification by Robert, bishop of Orkney, of offices in the cathedral (Kinross House papers, GD29/156)

July

6 *Letter* to Pope Paul III (*Theiner*, No 1069)

25 *Charter* to John Guthrie of Collistoun (*R.M.S.* V, 1104; Original, Register House Charters, Supplementary, 25 July 1545)

August

28 *Precept*: payment to the Grey Friars at St Andrews (*Rentale*, 194)

September

1 *Precept*: payment to John Drummond, trumpeter (*Ibid.*, 209)

6 *Mandate:* payment to David Dog, mason (*Ibid.*)

October

5   *Letter* to Francis 1 of France (*L.P. Henry VIII*, XX, ii, 525)

8   *Precept*; part payment to William Fisher, burgess of Linlithgow (*Rentale*, 210)

16   *Charter* to John Moncur of the lands of Blacockmure (*R.M.S.* V, 1050)

November

8   *Mandate* for a grant of victual to the inhabitants of Ferryport suspect of the plague (*Rentale*, 221)

9   *Bond of maintenance* with John Wemyss of that ilk (Fraser, *Wemyss*, II, 170–2)

December

3   *Commission*, as Legate *a latere*, for confirmation of a charter to William Cunningham of Cunninghamhead of lands of Kilmaurs Collegiate Church (Register House Charters, RH6/2367b)
       Commission, as Legate *a latere*, for confirmation of a charter to same of lands belonging to the Trinitarian Friary at Failford (*Ibid.*, 1367c)

4   *Acquittance* for £500 received (*Rentale*, 223)
       Confirmation charter of the foundation of St Leonard's college (St Andrews university muniments, SL 110. Aq.)

15   *Precept*; payment for 4000 loaves for French soldiers (*Rentale*, 215)

21   *Letter* to Pope Paul III (*L.P. Henry VIII*, XX, ii, 1020)

31   *Letter* to the Cardinal of Carpi (State Papers, SP1/2/122)

1546
January

15   *Confirmation*, as Legate *a latere*, of a charter by James, abbot of Newbattle, to James Hamilton of Kirklee, of lands in the barony of Monklands (Curle Collection, GD111/2/3)

16   *Precept*; payment to the procurator fiscal at Edinburgh (*Rentale*, 209)

18   *Mandate*; payment to Mr Thomas Wemyss, dean of Fife (*Ibid.*, 223)
       Commission, as Legate *a latere*, for confirmation of feu charter by John, abbot of Lindores, to James Johnston of that ilk, of lands of Monkegy, Aberdeenshire (Collection of the Society of Antiquaries of Scotland, GD 103/1/38)

25   *Precept*; payment to Robert Lindsay, master of the stable (*Rentale*, 210)

February

3   *Commission*, as Legate *a latere*, for confirmation of a charter by the provost of Trinity collegiate church to John Wemyss of that ilk (Fraser, *Wemyss*, II, 284–5)

6   *Precept of clare constat* in favour of Nicholas Adamson in quarter of Lasswade (Clerk of Penicuik muniments, GD 18/460)
       Apostolic letter to abbot of Sweetheart, as Legate *a latere*, to confirm a charter to the son of Johnston of that ilk (Ailsa muniments, GD 25/1/462)

24   *Charge*, as Legate *a latere*, to subchantor of Moray and others to confirm a charter to Charles Cairncross (*H.M.C. Report*, V, 716, 5)

March

15   *Charter* to David Beaton of Melgund of the kirklands of Aberlemno (*Calendar of Laing charters*, 512)

17   *Letter* to Pope Paul III (State papers, SP 1/2/128)
      Letter to the Cardinal of Carpi (State papers, SP 1/2/129)
22   *Petition* to Pope Paul III to resign Arbroath abbey to James Beaton, his nephew, keeping the fruits and administration for his lifetime (Vatican archives, Reg. Supp., 2580, fos 214–5)
30   *Mandate*; purchase of coal for St Andrews castle (*Rentale*, 223)

April
4   *Ratification* of his own charter to Oliver Sinclair of the kirklands of Kildileith (Currie) (Dick-Lauder papers, GD 41/375)
6   *Confirmation* of a charter by John Wishart of Logywishart to his son of the lands of Kennymacartane (Airlie muniments, GD 16/14/16)
8   *Precept*; to pay £200 to Patrick Hume of Broomhouse, his 'kinsman' (*Rentale*, 225)
      Commission, as Legate *a latere*, to the prior of Pluscarden and others to confirm a charter by the bishop of Caithness of the lands of Skibo (Erskine of Dun muniments, GD 123 Box 6/23)
10   *Marriage contract* of his daughter, Margaret Beaton, and the master of Crawford (Dalhousie muniments, GD 45/17/9 – copy)
13   *Precept*; payment to Margaret Beaton, lady Reres (*Rentale*, 217)
17   *Letters of regress* to Edward Sinclair of Dryden, in a sixth of Lasswade (Clerk of Penicuik muniments, GD 18/462)
      Charter to David, master of Crawford, of the kirklands of Kinnettles (*R.M.S. V*, 1191)
      Precept of sasine on above (Lindsay muniments, GD 203/5/2)
30   *Letters of assignation* to Marion Ogilvy of a reversion granted to the Cardinal by Thomas Forrester on 18 May 1545, lands of Abthane Ketnes (A.D.C.S., xxviii, fo 85v)

May
24   *Charter* of confirmation of a charter by David, Master of Crawford, to Patrick Lindsay of the kirklands of Kinnettles (Lindsay muniments, GD 203/5/7)
29   *Charter*, as commendator of Arbroath, to John Irons of Baldovye (NRA(S) Survey 171, Rattray of Craighall-Rattray)

Part 2

UNDATED

Before 16 October 1539   *Letters of collation* under the round seal in favour of sir John Wilson, canon of Holyrood, as vicar of Kinneil (Linlithgow Burgh Records: B48/1/1, fo 92v)

Before 12 February 1540   *Charter* to Thomas Lichton of Ullishaven of lands of Heicham (*R.S.S.* II, 3346)

c. 1541   *Charter* to Oliver Sinclair of the lands of Kildileith (*Rentale*, 127)

c. 1541   *Charter* to James Learmonth of Dairsie of the lands of Pittendreich (*Ibid.*)

In or before 1541   *Charter* to Sir Thomas Erskine of Brechin of the lands of Logytarroch (*Ibid.*)

In or before	1541	*Charter* to David, earl of Crawford, of the kirklands of Inverarity (*Ibid.*, 124)
In or before	1543	*Charter* to James Stewart, elder, son of James V, and his brothers of the Mains of Tynninghame (*Ibid.*, 165)
In or before	1543	*Charter* to Henry Kemp of Thomastoun of the lands of Scotscraig (*Ibid.*)
	c. 1543	*Charter* to George, earl of Huntly, of lands in the baronies of Keig and Monymusk (*R.S.S.* IV, 1819)
	c. Nov. 1543	*Charter* to David Beaton of Melgund of the lands of Carsbank (*Rentale*, 197)
Before 3 May	1544	*Charter* to John Beaton, son of John Beaton of Balfour, of the kirklands of Kilrenny (R.S.S. III, 749)
In or before	1545	*Charter* to Sir John Campbell of Calder of the lands of Meikle Catpair (*Ibid.*, 267)
In or before	1545	*Charter* to Sir Walter Kerr of Cessford of the lands of Torsonce (*Ibid.*, 207)
	1545	Discharge to Lord Seton for the teind silver of Winchburgh and Humbie (Register House Series. RH 9/2/14)
Before 29 May	1546	*Charter* to Walter Ogilvy of Boyne of the lands of Ragald, Banffshire (Register of feu charters of kirklands, E14, ii, fo 75v)
Between 16 January and 29 May	1546	*Confirmation*, as Legate *a latere*, of charter by Malcolm, Lord Fleming, of the Collegiate church of Biggar (Chalmers, *Caledonia*, VI, 655)

Part 3

UNDATED DOCUMENTS referred to in D. Patrick, *Statutes of the Scottish Church*, (S.H.S.)

Monition — For convocation of suffragans and other clergy to discuss the defence of the realm and church (243–5)

Monition — To pay contribution or tax for the same purpose (245–8)

Monition and summary enforcement — for payment of contribution for military purposes (248–52)

Intimation and convocation — for a general provincial council, addressed to the archbishop of Glasgow (252–9)

Monition — for convoking by the bishops of inferior clergy, etc., to a general provincial council (260)

Monition — to a vicar, charging him to pay his curate's salary (284–5)

Monition — as to the payment of procurations and annual synod dues (285–8)

Part 4

UNDATED DOCUMENTS contained in *St Andrews Formulare, 1514–46*, 2 volumes, ed. Gordon Donaldson and C. Macrae (Stair Society) Volume II

110   *Summons* and inhibition by vicars-general during the Cardinal's absence abroad,

in a case raised by sir Robert D., presentee to a chaplainry in Aberdeen cathedral, *re* refusal by bishop of Aberdeen to give collation pertain to the archbishop by reason of non-entry (subscribed by Cardinal; round seal)

438   *Commission* for trial of three witches (c. 1542)

439   *Commission* to proceed in a case *re* a parish clerkship which had not been terminated by commissioners previously appointed

440   *Confirmation* of a parish clerkship to one of three claimants on renunciation of right by the two others. Written by a notary (subscribed by secretary; round seal)

441   *Assignation* of a tack of kirklands of Abthane Kinghorn to Sir John Melville of Raith who compeared personally in the Cardinal's presence

444   *Confirmation* of assignation of a pension or monk's portion from the priory of Coldingham

446   Preamble to the *appointment* of an Official Principal of St Andrews

448   *New commission* by Cardinal in an appeal to metropolitan see, which had been heard by suffragan vicar-general before his death. Addressed to the Official of Lothian

450   *Letters* by vicar general, conform to a sentence by the suffragan *re* sacristanry of Tain. Collation under the sign manual and subscription of the secretary

451   *Collation* to a vicarage granted to a canon of Holyrood by virtue of an apostolic indult given to the Cardinal. Dean of Fife to give institution

452   *Commission* in a case concerning provision by the Cardinal in virtue of apostolic indult

453   *Process* of testimony of purgation and declaration of innocence in favour of the dean of Restalrig, accused of tampering with text of a papal bull

454   Commission by Cardinal to receive resignation of two benefices

467   *Appointment* of John Lauder as a clerk of the court of the Official of St Andrews by the Cardinal

468   *Confirmation* by Cardinal of charter and sasine in favour of the Black Friars of St Monance

472   *Tack* for nineteen years (subscribed and sealed by archbishop and chapter)

477   *Grant* (?charter) of half the lands of Strickmartin to son of James Scrymgeour of Dudhope, on resignation of his mother, Isobel Gray, now wife of John Campbell of Lundy

479   *Confirmation* of a royal gift of a chaplainry

487   *Licence* by the Cardinal to proceed in a case *re* the parish clerkship of Kelso

494   Styles of *absolution*

495   *Commission* in a case *re* marriage previously committed to three commissioners one of whom had died

496   *Renunciation* by one of the claimants in a suit *re* patronage

510   *Indulgence* granted by Cardinal for the repair of a bridge across the river Earn near Perth (subscribed by secretary; round seal)

511   *Erection* of a new parish (subscribed by Cardinal; his own and chapter seals)

520   *Commission* by the Cardinal to extract instruments from a protocol book of a decreased notary (subscribed by him; round seal)

524   *Degree* of bachelor in decreets running in Cardinal's name. Published by his mandate (university seal appended)

525   *Degree* of licentiate in civil law, conferred by vice-chancellor in the Cardinal's name and published by mandate of the vice-chancellor

526   *Doctorate* in canon law; commission of the chancellor given orally

S

Appendix 2

Itinerary of David Beaton, 1524–1546

1524
April
17 Leith   *L.P. Henry VIII*, III, ii, 2182

September
15 France   *Ibid.*, IV, 665

December
22 Dunbar   *Ibid.*, IV, 935
25 St Andrews   *Ibid.*, IV, 1004

1525
February
22 Edinburgh   *A.P.S.*, II, 288

March
27 Edinburgh   A.D.C., xxxv, fo 12
30(?) St Andrews   *Ibid.*, xxxv, fos 20–20v

May
13 Edinburgh   *Ibid.*, xxxv, fo 27

July
 5 Edinburgh   *Ibid.*, xxxv, fo 75
 6 Edinburgh   *A.P.S.*, II, 291
 7 Edinburgh   A.D.C., xxxv, fo 79
10 Edinburgh   *A.P.S.*, II, 292
12 Edinburgh   A.D.C., xxxv, fo 81
13 Edinburgh   *Ibid.*, xxxv, fo 90v
14 Edinburgh   *Ibid.*, xxxv, fo 91
15 Edinburgh   *Ibid.*, xxxv, fo 94v
17 Edinburgh   *A.P.S.*, II, 294
19 Edinburgh   A.D.C., xxxv, fo 96v
20 Edinburgh   *Ibid.*, xxxv, fo 100
24 Edinburgh   *Ibid.*, xxxv, fo 104v
26 Edinburgh   *Ibid.*, xxxv, fo 108
27 Edinburgh   *Ibid.*, xxxv, fo 109v
28 Edinburgh   *Ibid.*, xxxv, fo 113

August
3   Edinburgh   *Ibid.*, xxxv, fo 121

September
30   Edinburgh   *Ibid.*, xxxv, fo 132v

October
4   Edinburgh   *Ibid.*, xxxv, fo 152
7   Edinburgh   *Ibid.*, xxxv, fo 152v
10   Edinburgh   *Ibid.*
23   Arbroath   *Arbroath Liber*, II, 633

November
13   Edinburgh   *A.D.C.*, xxxv, fo 155v
15   Edinburgh   *Ibid.*, xxxv, fo 156
17   Edinburgh   *Ibid.*, xxxv, fo 160
21   Edinburgh   *Ibid.*, xxxv, fo 161
                      (at house of Archbishop James Beaton)
22   Edinburgh   *Ibid.*, xxxv, fo 161v

December
1   Edinburgh   *Ibid.*, xxxv, fo 171
4   Edinburgh   *Ibid.*, xxxv, fo 176
11   Edinburgh   *Ibid.*, xxxv, fo 182v
20   Edinburgh   *Ibid.*, xxxv, fo 191

1526
January
2   Edinburgh   *Ibid.*, xxxv, fo 192
8   Edinburgh   *Ibid.*, xxxv, fo 194
22   Edinburgh   *Ibid.*, xxxv. fo 196v

February
6   Edinburgh   *Ibid.*, xxxv, fo 198v
8   Edinburgh   *Ibid.*, xxxv, fo 199v
19   Edinburgh   *Ibid.*, xxxv, fo 204
20   Edinburgh   *Ibid.*, xxxv, fo 218
23   Edinburgh   *Ibid.*, xxxv, fo 208

March
3   Edinburgh   *Ibid.*, xxxv, fo 218
7   Edinburgh   *Ibid.*, xxxv, fo 219v
14   Edinburgh   *Ibid.*, xxxvi, fo 8v

June
29   Dunfermline   Burnet Stuart collection, GD 115/4

December
| 14 | Edinburgh | A.D.C., xxxvi, fo 182 |
| 17 | Edinburgh | *Ibid.*, xxxvi, fo 188v |

1527
April
| 3 | Arbroath | *Arbroath Liber*, II, 641 |
| 18 | Edinburgh | A.D.C., xxxvii, fo 112v |

May
10	Edinburgh	*A.P.S.*, II, 318
11	Edinburgh	A.D.C., xxxvii, fo 117v
13	Edinburgh	*Ibid.*, xxxvii, fo 118v

August
| 6 | Edinburgh | *Ibid.*, xxxvii, fo 189 |

October
| 4 | Edinburgh | *Ibid.*, xxxvii, fo 240v |

November
21	Edinburgh	*Ibid.*, xxxviii, fo 24v
22	Edinburgh	*Ibid.*
23	Edinburgh	*Ibid.*, xxxviii, fo 29
26	Edinburgh	*Ibid.*, xxxviii, fo 29v
27	Edinburgh	*Ibid.*, xxxviii, fo 33v

December
2	Edinburgh	*Ibid.*, xxxviii, fo 40
5	Edinburgh	*Ibid.*, xxxviii, fo 45
7	Edinburgh	*Ibid.*, xxxviii, fo 48v
9	Edinburgh	*Ibid.*, xxxviii, fo 51
10	Edinburgh	*Ibid.*, xxxviii, fo 54
11	Edinburgh	*Ibid.*, xxxviii, fo 56v
12	Edinburgh	*Ibid.*, xxxviii, fo 59
13	Edinburgh	*Ibid.*, xxxviii, fo 62
16	Edinburgh	*Ibid.*, xxxviii, fo 66

1528
July
| 14 | Edinburgh | *Ibid.*, xxxviii, fo 131v (the King present) |

September
| 3 | Edinburgh | *A.P.S.*, II, 332 |
| 9 | Edinburgh | A.D.C., xxxviii, fo 165 |

December
6   Edinburgh   Hamilton muniments: Box 184–3/2

1529
January
21   Edinburgh   A.D.C., xxxix, fo 57

February
1   Edinburgh   *Ibid.*, xxxix, fo 66v
27   Edinburgh   Protocol book of Thomas Kene, NP 1/2a, fo 15v
                                         (in house of Archbishop of St Andrews)

March
2   Edinburgh   A.D.C., xxxix, fo 127
3   Edinburgh   Yester writs, GD 28/446
4   Edinburgh   A.D.C., xxxix, fo 135

April
10   Edinburgh   *Ibid.*, xl, fo 8v
12   Edinburgh   *Ibid.*, xl, fo 9

May
5   Edinburgh   *Ibid.*, xl, fo 16
7   Edinburgh   *Ibid.*, xl, fo 18
10   Edinburgh   *Ibid.*, xl, fo 21
11   Edinburgh   *Ibid.*, xl, fo 23
12   Edinburgh   *Ibid.*, xl, fo 24

June
1   Edinburgh   *Ibid.*, xl, fo 49
4   Edinburgh   *Ibid.*, xl, fo 52
8   Edinburgh   *Ibid.*, xl, fo 53v
15   Jedburgh   *Ibid.*, xl, fo 55
21   Edinburgh   *Ibid.*, xl, fo 56
25   Edinburgh   *Ibid.*, xl, fo 57

July
12(?)   Arbroath   *Liber Domicilii James V*, 22
13(?)   Arbroath   *Ibid.*
14(?)   Arbroath   *Ibid.*
15(?)   Arbroath   *Ibid.*
21   Edinburgh   A.D.C., xl, fo 63v
27   Edinburgh   *Ibid.*, xl, fo 70

October
8   Edinburgh   *Ibid.*, xl, fo 119
9   Edinburgh   *Ibid.*, xl, fo 119v
12   Edinburgh   *Ibid.*, xl, fo 122v
14   Edinburgh   *Ibid.*, xl, fo 123v

16	Edinburgh	*Ibid.*, xl, fo 125v
19	Edinburgh	*Ibid.*, xl, fo 127
20	Edinburgh	*Ibid.*, xl, fo 128v

1530
January

10	Edinburgh	*Ibid.*, xl, fo 155

March

7	Edinburgh	*Ibid.*, xli, fo 1
12	Edinburgh	*Ibid.*, xli, fo 4
14	Edinburgh	*Ibid.*, xli, fo 5v
15	Edinburgh	*Ibid.*, xli, fo 8v
16	Edinburgh	*Ibid.*, xli, fo 10
17	Edinburgh	*Ibid.*, xli, fo 13v
18	Edinburgh	*Ibid.*, xli, fo 18v
19	Edinburgh	*Ibid.*, xli, fo 22v
21	Edinburgh	*Ibid.*, xli, fo 25v
22	Edinburgh	*Ibid.*, xli, fo 30

May

23	Edinburgh	*Ibid.*, xli, fo 79v

June

2	Ethie (nr Arbroath)	Airlie muniments, GD 16/47/2

September

19	Aberdeen	B.L. Additional MSS 33245, fo 75v

October

8	Dundee	A.D.C., xli, fo 115
10	Dundee	*Ibid.*, xli, fo 116v
21	Dundee	*R.M.S.*, III, 972
31	Stirling	A.D.C., xli, fo 107

December

2	Edinburgh	*Ibid.*, xli, fo 134
3	Edinburgh	*Ibid.*, xli, fo 134v
4	Edinburgh	*Ibid.*, xli, fo 135v
14	Edinburgh	*Ibid.*, xli, fo 149
15	Edinburgh	*Ibid.*, xli, fo 151
16	Edinburgh	*Ibid.*, xli, fo 152

1531
January

14	Edinburgh	*Ibid.*, xli, fo 155
17	Edinburgh	*Ibid.*, xli, fo 156

19	Edinburgh	*Ibid.*, xli, fo 158
21	Edinburgh	*Ibid.*, xlii, fo 1
23	Edinburgh	*Ibid.*, xlii, fo 2v
24	Edinburgh	*Ibid.*, xlii, fo 5
26	Edinburgh	*Ibid.*, xlii, fo 8
27	Edinburgh	*Ibid.*, xlii, fo 11v

(left Edinburgh that day for Arbroath, *R.S.S.*, II, Appendix)

March
22	Edinburgh	A.D.C., xlii, fo 133v
25	Edinburgh	*Ibid.*, xlii, fo 144v
28	Edinburgh	*Ibid.*, xlii, fo 145
31	Edinburgh	*Ibid.*, xlii, fo 155v

April
| 5 | Edinburgh | *Ibid.*, xlii, fo 164 |
| 28 | Edinburgh | *Ibid.*, xlii, fo 169 |

May
| 2 | Edinburgh | *Ibid.*, xlii, fo 173v |

June
5	Stirling	*Ibid.*, xlii, fo 185
7	Stirling	*Ibid.*, xlii, fo 186
15(?)	Aberdeen	*R.S.S.* II, Appendix, 766 (Justice Ayre held)

July
| 8 | Aberdeen | *Antiquities of Aberdeen and Banff*, IV, 97 |

September
| 11 | Edinburgh | A.D.C., xliii, fo 46 |

October
| 9 | Edinburgh | *Ibid.*, xliii, fo 54v |

December
7	Edinburgh	*Ibid.*, xliii, fo 108v
13	Edinburgh	*Ibid.*, xliii, fo 118
15	Edinburgh	*Ibid.*, xliii, fo 124v
19	Edinburgh	*Ibid.*, xliii, fo 133

1532
February
5	Edinburgh	*Ibid.*, xliii, fo 145
17	Edinburgh	*Ibid.*, xliii, fo 157
19	Edinburgh	*Ibid.*, xliii, fo 159v
20	Edinburgh	*Ibid.*, xliii, fo 163v
25	Edinburgh	*Ibid.*, xliii, fo 166

| 27 | Edinburgh | *Ibid.*, xliii, fo 171 |
| 28 | Edinburgh | *Ibid.*, xliii, fo 175 |

May
2	Edinburgh	*Ibid.*, xliii, fo 185v
4	Edinburgh	*Ibid.*, xliii, fo 193v
10	Edinburgh	*Ibid.* and Register House Charters, RH6/1076
11	Edinburgh	A.D.C., xliii, fo 194v
17	Edinburgh	*A.P.S.* II, 334–5

July
| 18 | Edinburgh | Hamilton Muniments: Inventory, Box 7 |

August
12	Edinburgh	A.D.C.S., i, fo 104
15	Edinburgh	*Ibid.*, i, fo 105
22	Edinburgh	*Ibid.*, i, fo 107v

September
| 3 | Edinburgh | *Ibid.* i, fo 110v |
| 13(?) | Edinburgh | *Ibid.*, i, fo 124v |

December
| 16 | Edinburgh | *Ibid.*, ii, fo 27 |

1533
April
| 24 | France(?)Fontainebleau | *L.P. Henry VIII*, VI, 382 |
| 30 | France | *Ibid.*, vi, fo 408 |

May   [France]
June
| 23 | France | *Ibid.*, vo. 691 |

July
| 12 | France | *Ibid.*, vi, 929(35) |
| 27 | Dieppe | *Ibid.*, vi, 907 |

October
| 12 | Arbroath | Airlie Muniments: GD 16/47/2 |

November
| 11 | Edinburgh | A.D.C.S., iii, fo 90 |
| 26 | Edinburgh | *Acts of the Lords of Council in Public Affairs*, II, 410 |

1534
February
11   Edinburgh   *Antiquities of Aberdeen and Banff*, III, 349

April
10   France   *L.P. Henry VIII*, VII, 456
26   France   *Ibid.*, vii, 546

May
11   France   *Ibid.*, vii, 645
          (returned to Scotland towards the end of the year; *Letters of* James V, 280–1)

1535
January
5   Edinburgh   A.D.C.S., vi, fo 1

June
10   Edinburgh   *A.P.S*, II, 339
12   Edinburgh   *Ibid.*, ii, 341

July
13   Edinburgh   *Exchequer Rolls*, XVI, 402

November
21   Dumfries   *R.S.S.*, II, Appendix (Justice Ayre held)

1536
February
10   Stirling   *Treasurer's Accounts*, VI, 239

March
2   Arbroath   Airlie Muniments: GD 16/14/15
21   Edinburgh   *R.S.S.* II Appendix, 771
          (left Edinburgh that day, *Ibid.*)

April
21   Stirling   Hamilton muniments: Inventory Box 8/103/3

July
17   Edinburgh   *Exchequer Rolls*, XVI, 447

August
5   Stirling   Rothes muniments, GD 204/8
26   Stirling   Register House Charters, RH6/1136

September
1   Kirkcaldy

(sailed for France with the King)

10	Dieppe	Fraser, *Douglas*, IV, 145

November
21(?)	Chambord	*Correspondence des Nonces*, I, 210–11
28(?)	Cambuoy	*L.P. Henry VIII*, XI, 1172

December
15	Paris	*Ibid.*, XI, 1315
16	Paris	*Correspondence des Nonces*, I, 221
28	Paris	*L.P. Henry VIII*, XI, 1382

1537
January
1	Paris	

(marriage of James V and Princess Madeleine)
5(?)	Paris	*Letters of James V*, 327
12(?)	Paris	*Calendar of State Papers, Spanish*, V, 2, 8

(said to have gone to Paris by this date)
14	Paris	*Correspondence des Nonces*, I, 228
29(?)	St Germains	*Letters of James V*, 329

February
12(?)	Senlis	*L.P. Henry VIII*, XII, i, 414
18	Compiègne	*Ibid.*, XII, i, 463: *Correspondence des Nonces*, I, 238

March
5	Compiègne	*L.P. Henry VIII*, XII, i, 580
13	Amiens	*Correspondence des Nonces*, I, 242–3

April
12	Amiens	*Ibid.*, I, 251

(said to be leaving for Rouen in six days)
13	Amiens	*L.P. Henry VIII*, XII, i, 931
22	On way to Rouen	*Correspondence des Nonces*, I, 234

May
19(?)	Leith	*R.S.S.*, II Appendix

July
28	Dunbar	*L.P. Henry VIII*, XII, ii, 422
31	Berwick-upon-Tweed	*Ibid.*, XII, ii, 430

August
9	Stamford	*Ibid.*, XII, ii, 491
15	Grafton	*Ibid.*, XII, ii, 590
22	Dover	*Ibid.*, XII, ii, 566
23	Dover	*Ibid.*

| 24(?) | Boulogne | *Ibid.* |

October
| 22 | Lyons | *Ibid.*, XII, ii, 962 |

1538
January
| 30(?) | Lyons | *Ibid.*, XIII, i, 180 |

June
| 10 | Arrived in Scotland | |

July
| 15 | Edinburgh | *Exchequer Rolls*, XVII, 70 |
| 26 | France | |

August
| 13 | France (consecrated to Mirepoix by then) | Dowden, *Scottish Bishops*, 42 |

September
| 10 | Edinburgh | *Exchequer Rolls*, XVII, 155 |
| 24 | Edinburgh | *Treasurer's Accounts*, VI, 366 |

December
| 8(?) | Arbroath | *L.P. Henry VIII*, XIII, ii, 1129 |

1539
January
| 6 | Edinburgh | Register House Charters, RH 6/1180 |

March
7	Edinburgh	*Rentale*, 94
8	Edinburgh	*Ibid.*, 93
9	Edinburgh	*Ibid.*
23	Dieppe	*Ibid.*

June
| 3 x 9 | Paris | *Correspondence des Nonces*, I, 460–1 |

July
| 13 | Paris | *Ibid.*, I, 462 |
| 14 | Paris | *Ibid.* |

July
| 1 | Paris | *Ibid.*, I, 467 |
| 8 | Paris | *L.P. Henry VIII*, XIV, i, 1237 |

| 31 | Paris | *Correspondence des Nonces*, I, 472 |

August
| 27 | Crepye | *L.P. Henry VIII*, XIV, ii, 92 |

September
| 1 | Had sailed for | *Correspondence des Nonces*, I, 481, 501 |
| | Scotland by then | |

October
| 3 | St Andrews | *Rentale*, 94 |

November
| 16 | Kelso | *Sadler*, I, 13 |
| 24 | Dumfries | *Glasguensis*, No. 502 |

December
3	Edinburgh	*Rentale*, 94
4	Edinburgh	*Ibid.*, 95
7	Edinburgh	*Ibid.*, 96
10	Edinburgh	*Sadler* (Note: c. 10–11 said to be in
		Edinburgh when Dr Hilliard arrived), I, 3
c. 25	Dumfries	*Rentale*, 96

1540
January
| 8(?) | Arbroath | *Rentale*, 84 (Graniter's account rendered at) |

February
10	Edinburgh	*Rentale*, 95
23	Edinburgh	A.D.C.S., xii, fo 25v
29	Edinburgh	Fraser, *Chiefs of Grant*, I, lxiii

March
| 18 | St Andrews | *Rentale*, 102 |
| 21 | Edinburgh | *Ibid.*, 124 |

April
6	St Andrews	*Rentale*, 94
17	Restalrig	*Ibid.*, 96
20	Edinburgh	*Ibid.*, 95
26	Edinburgh	*Ibid.*, 102
27	Loretto Chapel	*Ibid.*, 96

May
3	St Andrews	Protocol Book of James Androsoun, NP1/5a, fo 23
8	St Andrews	*Ibid.*, fo 27
11	St Andrews	*Ibid.*, fo 23

| 28 | St Andrews | *HMC Report*, 631 |
| 29 | St Andrews | *Rentale*, 107: St Andrews Univ. muniments, 37490/24 |

June
8	Edinburgh	*Rentale*, 107
12	Edinburgh	*Ibid.*
13	Edinburgh	*Ibid.*

July
| 5 | Edinburgh | Register House Transcripts, RH 2/7/6/24 |

August
2	Edinburgh	*Rentale*, 108
7	Edinburgh	*Ibid.*
15	Edinburgh	*Ibid.*
24	St Andrews	*Ibid.*

September
| 29 | St Andrews (St Michael's pardon) | *Ibid.* |

October
| 4 | St Andrews | *Ibid.* |
| 17(?) | Brechin | *Reg. Honoris de Morton*, II, 263 |

November
17	Edinburgh	*Rentale*, 107
22	Edinburgh	*Ibid.*, 108
29	Edinburgh	*Ibid.*
30	Edinburgh	*Ibid.*

December
3	Edinburgh	*A.P.S.*, II, 354
10	Edinburgh	*Ibid.*, 355
25	St Andrews	*Rentale*, 109
27	St Andrews	*Ibid.*, 108
28	St Andrews	*Ibid.*
30	St Andrews	*Ibid.*

1541
January
| 2 | St Andrews | *Rentale*, 108 |

February
21	Edinburgh	A.D.C.S., xv, fo 2
24	Edinburgh	*Rentale*, 108
25	Edinburgh	*A.P.S.*, II, 368

March
14	Edinburgh	*Ibid.*
18	Edinburgh	A.D.C.S., xv, fo 103v
20	Edinburgh	*Rentale*, 119

April
11	St Andrews	*Ibid.*, 125
14	St Andrews	*Ibid.*, 119
26	St Andrews	*Ibid.*, 125

May
5	Edinburgh	*Edinburgh Burgh Records*, II, 106–7
14	Edinburgh	*Rentale*, 125
15	Edinburgh	*Ibid.*
18	St Andrews	*Ibid.*, 124
25	St Andrews	*Ibid.*, 125
28	Arbroath	*Ibid.*, 115

June
12	Arbroath	*Ibid.*, 125
18	St Andrews	*Ibid.*, 125
23	Edinburgh	*Ibid.*
29	Edinburgh	*Ibid.*, 122

July
2	Edinburgh	A.D.C.S., 2 July 1541
3	Balfour	*Rentale*, 126
8	St Andrews	*Ibid.*, 115
12	Edinburgh	*Ibid.*, 123
13	Edinburgh	*Ibid.*, 125; A.D.C.S., xvi, fos 42v–43
14	Leith	*Ibid.*, 123
15	Edinburgh	*Ibid.*
16	Edinburgh	*Ibid.*, 122
17	Leith	*Ibid.*, 123
21	Leith	*Ibid.*, 126
	(sails for France)	

August
| 6(?) | Moulins | *Correspondence des Nonces*, III, 71 |

September
1(?)	Moulins	*Ibid.*, III, 79–80
13	Mascon	*L.P. Henry VIII*, XVI, 1178
14	Mascon	*Ibid.*, XVI, 1182

October
| 25 | Dijon | *Ibid.*, XVI, 1288 |

November
21   French court   *Ibid.*, XVI, 1363
26   Paris   *Ibid.*, XVI, 1378

December
12   Fontainebleau   *Ibid.*, XVI, 1446

1542
January
23   Paris   *Correspondence des Nonces*, III, 112
30   Paris   *Ibid.*, III, 136

April
1   Paris   *L.P. Henry VIII*, XVII, 1542
2   Paris   *Ibid.*
3   Paris   *Ibid.*

July
9   French court   *Ibid.*, XVII, 479

August
3   Returns to Scotland *Rentale*, 138
14   Edinburgh   *Ibid.*, 143
16   Edinburgh   *Treasurer's Accounts*, VIII, 1
22   Edinburgh   *Rentale*, 143
24   Burntisland   *Ibid.*
25   St Andrews   *Ibid.*

September
5   Edinburgh   Graham of Fintry muniments, GD 151 Box 29
15   Edinburgh   *A.P.S.*, II, 385
18   Edinburgh   *Rentale*, 143
19   Edinburgh   *Ibid.*

October
7   Edinburgh   *Ibid.*
16   Edinburgh   *Rentale*, 143
21   Edinburgh   *Ibid.*

November
2   Kinghorn-Easter   Fraser, *Wemyss*, II, 160–1
3   Kinghorn-Easter   *Ibid.*, 284
14   Edinburgh   Fraser, *Buccleuch*, II, 179–80; *L.P. Henry VIII*,
                           XVII, 1140
22   Edinburgh   *Rentale*, 143
25(?) Haddington   *Hamilton Papers*, I, lxxxii
28   Haddington   *Ibid.*, I, xci

December

18	Edinburgh	*Ibid.*, I, 260
19	Edinburgh	*L.P. Henry VIII*, XVII, 1221
21	Edinburgh	Protocol book of Edward Dickson, NP1/5b, fo 155
24	Edinburgh	*Hamilton Papers*, I, 265
25	Edinburgh	*Rentale*, 141
30	Edinburgh	*Hamilton Papers*, I, 267

1543
January

16	Edinburgh	*L.P. Henry VIII*, XVIII, i, 59
27	Edinburgh (arrested)	*Rentale*, 142

February

12	Seton	*Ibid.*, 143
17	Seton	*Ibid.*

March

23	St Andrews	*Sadler*, I, 88
25	St Andrews	*Rentale*, 155

April

11	St Andrews	*Ibid.*

May

5	St Andrews	*Ibid.*
26	St Andrews	*Ibid.*, 168

June

9	Monimail	Morton muniments, GD 150/307
17	St Andrews	*Rentale*, 193
19	Gone to Arbroath	*L.P. Henry VIII*, XVIII, i, 733

July

2	Arbroath	*Hamilton Papers*, I, 392
8	St Andrews	*L.P. Henry VIII*, XVIII, i, 844
12	St Andrews	*Rentale*, 197
17	St Andrews	*Ibid.*, 193
24	Linlithgow	*Hamilton Papers*, I, 446
26	Linlithgow	*Ibid.*, I, 427
31	Stirling	*L.P. Henry VIII*, XVIII, i, 974

August

4	Stirling	*Rentale*, 166
29	St Andrews	*L.P. Henry VIII*, XVIII, ii, 94

September

5	Callander	*Hamilton Papers*, II, 18–19

T

6	Stirling	*Ibid.*, 21–2
9	Stirling	*L.P. Henry VIII*, XVIII, ii, 139
15	Stirling	*Sadler*, I, 290; *Rentale*, 167
27	Edinburgh	*Hamilton Papers*, II, 75

October
5	St Andrews	*Ibid.*, II, 90–2
8	St Andrews	*Rentale*, 167
9	St Andrews	*Ibid.*, 198
25	St Andrews	*Hamilton Papers*, II, 122–3

November
5	Edinburgh	*Sadler*, I, 331
6	Edinburgh	*Ibid.*
12	St Andrews	*Rentale*, 197
15	St Andrews	*Ibid.*
21(?)	Dundee	*Ibid.*, 167; *L.P. Henry VIII*, XVIII, ii, 425

(also in Perth about this time)

December
3	Edinburgh	Stevenson, *Selections*, 2–3
4	Edinburgh	*A.P.S.*, II, 427
9	Edinburgh	*Ibid.*, ii, 429
11	Edinburgh	*Ibid.*, ii, 432
13	Edinburgh	*Ibid.*, ii, 442
15	Edinburgh	*Ibid.*, ii, 443
23	Stirling	Crawford priory muniments, GD 20/105

1544
January
| 25 | Perth | *Knox*, i, 55 |
| 29(?) | Dundee | Adv. MSS.19.1.25.2 (N.L.S.) |

February
4	Dundee	Crawford priory muniments, GD 20/107
5	Dundee	Airlie muniments, GD 16/41/14
6	Dundee	Crawford priory muniments, GD 20/106
7	St Andrews	*Ibid.*, GD 20/108
9	Balfour	*Rentale*, 179
10	Dunfermline/South Queensferry	*Ibid.*

March
3	St Andrews	*Ibid.*, 197
6	St Andrews	*Ibid.*, 182
21	Edinburgh	A.D.C.S., xxviii, fo 43

April
5	Glasgow	*Glasguensis*, No. 504
6	Glasgow	*Ibid.*
9	Glasgow	*Rentale*, 181
22	St Andrews	*Ibid.*, 193
29	St Andrews	*Treasurer's Accounts*, VIII, 286

May
1	St Andrews	*Rentale*, 197
6	Edinburgh/Leith	*Hamilton Papers*, II, 362–3
8	Stirling	*Rentale*, xliv (later, Kincardine-in-Menteith)
21	Falkland	*Ibid.*, xliv

June
9	St Andrews	*Ibid.*, 193
11	St Andrews	*Ibid.*
24	St Andrews	*Ibid.*, 180
27	St Andrews	Morton muniments, GD 150/962

July
13	St Andrews	*Rentale*, 193
23	St Andrews	*Ibid.*, 176

August
2	St Andrews	Ibid., 193
8	Dunfermline	*L.P. Henry VIII*, XIX, ii, 52
12(?)	Arbroath	*Antiquities of Aberdeen and Banff*, III, 249
14	St Andrews	*Rentale*, 180
20	St Andrews	*Scottish Correspondence of Mary of Lorraine*, 104

September
1	St Andrews	*Rentale*, 193

October
22	St Andrews	*Spalding Club Miscellany*, V, 295
31	St Andrews	*Rentale*, 196

November
1(?)	St Andrews	State Papers, SP 1/2/108
7	Edinburgh	*A.P.S.*, II, 445
17	Stirling	*Treasurer's Accounts*, VIII, 332
20	Stirling	Forbes Muniments, GD 52/1696
30	Haddington	Stevenson, *Selections*, 11

December
12	Edinburgh	A.P.S., II, 449
19(?)	St Andrews	State Papers, SP 1/2/139

1545
January
18   St Andrews   *Rentale*, 223

February
15   Edinburgh   *L.P. Henry VIII*, XX, i, 203

March
21   Edinburgh   *Ibid.*, XX, i, 401
31   Edinburgh   *Ibid.*, XX, i, 477

April
1   St Andrews   State Papers, SP 1/2/129,130

May
1   Edinburgh   Boyd Papers, GD 8/130
18   St Andrews   A.D.C.S., xxviii, fo 85v

June
1   Stirling   State Papers, SP 1/2/122
7   Glasgow   *R.P.C.*, I, 2
11   Glasgow   *Ibid.*, I, 3
14   Glasgow   Northesk Muniments, GD 130/15/C(1545)
24   Stirling   *R.P.C.*, I, 5
25   Stirling   *Ibid.*, I, 6
26   Stirling   *A.P.S.*, II, 594
28   Stirling   *Ibid.*, II, 595
29   Stirling   *Ibid.*, II, 596

July
6   Linlithgow   *Theiner*, 616–7
7   Linlithgow   A.D.C.S., xxviii, fo 27
10   Linlithgow   *R.P.C.*, I, 10
25   Linlithgow   *Ibid.*, I, 12
26(?)   Linlithgow   Fraser, *Melvilles*, III. 85

August
5   Linlithgow   *Treasurer's Accounts*, VIII, 401
13   Linlithgow   *Ibid.*, VIII, 402
22   Linlithgow   *R.P.C.*, I, 14
28   St Andrews   *Rentale*, 188, 194

September
1   St Andrews   *Ibid.*, 209
3   St Andrews   *Ibid.*, 194
October
1   Linlithgow   *A.P.S.*, II, 455
5   Linlithgow   Eglinton Muniments: GD 3/1452
                                   (provisional number)

| 8 | Linlithgow | *Rentale*, 210 |
| 31(?) | Linlithgow | *R.P.C.*, I, 17 |

November
| 1 | Linlithgow | *Ibid.* |
| 9 | St Andrews | Fraser, *Wemyss*, II, 171 |

December
4	St Andrews	*Rentale*, 223
15	Stirling	*Ibid.*, 215
19	Linlithgow	*R.P.C.*, I, 18

1546
January
1	St Andrews	State Papers, SP 1/2/123
16	Edinburgh	*Rentale*, 209
19	Edinburgh	*R.P.C.*, I, 20
23	Edinburgh	*Ibid.*
25	Linlithgow	*Rentale*, 210

February
| 1 | St Andrews | A.D.C.S., xxviii, fo 30 |

March
| 1 | St Andrews* | Trial and death of Wishart |
| 30 | St Andrews | *Rentale*, 223 |

April
4	St Andrews	Dick-Lauder Papers, GD 41/375
6–8	St Andrews	*Rentale*, 204, 223
10	St Andrews	Dalhousie Muniments: GD 45/17/9
13	St Andrews	*Rentale*, 217
17	St Andrews	Clerk of Penicuik Muniments: GD 18/462
29	Ethie	Crawford Papers in the John Rylands Library, Manchester
30	Arbroath	A.D.C.S., xxviii, fo 85v

May
8	Edinburgh	*Rentale*, 214
23	Edinburgh	*R.P.C.*, 23; A.D.C.S., xxviii, fo 55
24	Edinburgh	Crawford Priory Muniments, GD 20/5/7
28	St Andrews	*Rentale*, 222
29	St Andrews	*Ibid.*

*In mid-March the Governor and Cardinal visited Perth

Appendix 3

List of persons accused of heresy or believed to have had protestant sympathies or associations, 1528–46. This is a provisional list which may be amended and added to and includes information which may yet be verified or otherwise. It seems advisable at the present stage of Scottish Reformation studies, when individuals and localities are being examined, to keep open as many avenues of investigation as possible. Full details of sources cited, which are usually the most accessible printed works, will be found in the Sources and Bibliography.

1   ADAMSON, William — Edinburgh merchant, became burgess in 1542 (*Lynch*, 276). 'Young William Adamson' favoured reformed ideas after the death of James V (*Knox*, I, 43).

2   AIKMAN, Francis — Edinburgh apothecary, appointed apothecary to the King 1532 (*R.S.S.*, II, 1162). Appointed apothecary to the Queen, 1543 (*Ibid.*, III, 34). Said to have favoured reformed ideas after the death of James V (*Knox*, I, 43). Witnessed document purporting to contain the King's will (*H.M.C. Report*, XI, vi (Hamilton), 219–20). Died 1549. (See, *Lynch*, 276). (?)Relative of William Aikman, burgess of Dieppe, 1552 (*Edinburgh Burgh Records*, II, 168).

3   ALLAN, Alexander — Augustinian canon, St Andrews, influenced by the teaching and death of Patrick Hamilton, 1528; imprisoned by prior of St Andrews, escaped, had an academic career in Europe, visiting England in 1535. Summary of his career (Durkan, 'Scottish "Evangelicals" in the Patronage of Thomas Cromwell',150–1, and *Protocol book of John Foular* (S.R.S.), xiv–xvi). Related to Robert Richardson (*q.v.*).

4   ALLAN, Thomas — relative of Alexander Allan, found in Copenhagen (Durkan, *Essays*, 280).

5   ALDJOY, George — Edinburgh merchant, one of the 'secret professors' in the 1530s (*Lynch*, 276; Durkan, *Protocol book of John Foular*).

6   ALEXANDER, Robert — advocate, tutor to the earl of Erroll whom he is said to have commended for his adherence to protestantism and knowledge of the new testament (*Lorimer*, 209).

7   ALEXANDERSON, Andrew — convicted of heresy before 23 August 1538 and 'justifeit to the deid for the samyn' (*R.S.S.*, II, 2686). See also, McCrie's *Knox* (1855), 314, 316.

8   ANDERSON, Mr Henry — 'Declared cursed', 28 August 1534 (*Diurnal*, 19).

9   ANDERSON, Robert — Burgess of Dundee, accused of heresy, abjured and bought his own escheat, 27 July 1538 (*R.S.S.*, II, 2648).

10   ANDERSON, William — maltman in Perth, tried before the Cardinal at Perth in January 1544 (*Knox*, I, 55). Executed for heresy and his escheat granted to his wife, 30 January 1544 (*R.S.S.*, III, 613).

11   ANNAND, George — burgess of Dundee, accused of heresy, abjured and bought his own escheat, 27 July 1538 (*R.S.S.*, II, 2648).

12   ANNAND, James — burgess of Dundee, accused of heresy, abjured and bought his own escheat, 27 July 1538 (*R.S.S.*, II, 2648).

13   BALCASKIE, Martin — Edinburgh merchant, arrested for refusing to hand

over his (?) English matin book to the official of Lothian; accused of having 'English books'; bought his own escheat, 12 March 1539 (*R.S.S.*, II, 2936). Imprisoned in England, 1541 (*L.P. Henry VIII*, xvi, 1163).

14 BALNAVES, Mr Henry — advocate, b.1509, probably in Kirkcaldy; studied at Cologne as a 'poor scholar' and later at St Andrews when Patrick Hamilton was there; became procurator in St Andrews commissary court but 'resorted often to Raith'; made treasurer's clerk by Sir James Kirkcaldy of Grange, Treasurer, whose wife, Janet Melville, was a daughter of the laird of Raith; ambassador to Henry VIII, honoured in the reign of James V but suspected by the clergy; practised as a lawyer in the consistorial court of St Andrews; procurator for David Beaton as abbot of Arbroath (*Arbroath Liber*, II, 758); witnessed charters by Archbishop James Beaton at Dunfermline in 1535 and 1537 (*Dunfermelyn*, 385, 386); witnessed a document in the dwelling house of the earl of Rothes in Edinburgh, 4 May 1538 (Rothes muniments, GD 204/15); advocate in the court of session, 1537, ordinary lord of session, 1538, commissioner to parliament for Kirkcaldy, 1538; feu charter of Fife lands from the Cardinal, 1541-2 (*Rentale*, 118); helped to influence Arran towards reform after the death of James V; favoured act introduced by Lord Maxwell for use of bible in English, for which he 'argued for the seculars' during the debate (*Knox*, I, 44); made secretary and keeper of all the seals, February 1543 but removed from the secretaryship and imprisoned in Blackness castle on the Cardinal's ascendancy in November 1543, but during the Cardinal's progress through Fife with the Governor he was liberated; witnessed the marriage contract between William Douglas, younger of Lochleven, and Agnes Leslie, daughter of the earl of Rothes, at Cupar, 19 August 1545 (Morton muniments, GD 150/311); probably knew of the Brunston plot to kill the Cardinal and may have been involved in the plot of 1546 although he did not take part in the assassination (Laing, *Knox*, III, 405 *et seq.*, which includes the text of Balnaves' treatise on Justification).

15 BELLENDEN, Mr Thomas, of Auchnoule — Lord of Session, 1535, and Justice Clerk, 1539, died 1549; at a meeting with English commissioners at Coldstream, in company of Balnaves, he impressed Eure with his desire to see a reform of the church and asked for copies of English acts concerning the suppression of the monasteries and the 'reformation of the misdemeanors of the clergy' (Lorimer, 215). Counsellor to Arran in the period of the treaty with England, 1543, until the Cardinal's ascendancy later that year (*Knox*, I, 48).

16 BEVERIDGE, John — Dominican friar, burnt for heresy on the Castlehill, Edinburgh, 28 February 1539 (*Knox*, I, 26).

17 BLACKAT, John — (?) Perth; in 1536 letters were dispatched to the provost and bailies of Perth and Dundee to search for John Blackat and George Lovell, suspected of hanging an image of St Francis (*Lorimer*, 217).

18 BORTHWICK, Mr David — advocate; studied at St Leonard's college in 1525, at the same time as William Johnston (*q.v.*); probably at St Andrews when Patrick Hamilton was there; one of Arran's counsellors in 1543 but later banished from the court on the Cardinal's return; his property at Addiston, Midlothian later said to have suffered at the hands of the French (*Knox*, I, 302); married into the Guthrie family who were prominent protestants in the 1560s (*Lynch*, 277).

19 BORTHWICK, Sir John — younger son of Lord Borthwick killed at Flodden; probably influenced by Nicholas Borthwick, a relative, who was at Wittenberg in 1528; knew Robert Richardson (*q.v.*), studying at the college of St Victor, Paris;

joined the guards of the French King's household in 1529; in 1536 in touch with Thomas Cromwell in London; with James V in France in 1536–7 when he objected, in a letter to Cromwell, to the papal gift of the cap and sword to James V; introduced Sadler to Edinburgh in 1540; in May of that year he was accused of heresy, escaped and burnt in effigy at St Andrews; wrote a defence of himself; advocated a 'Cromwellian' reformation of the church in Scotland, with the suppression of its property and privileges. His sentence revoked in 1561 (*St Andrews Kirk Session register*, I, 89, *et seq*; Durkan, 'Scottish "Evangelicals"').

20   BOTHWELL, David — Counsellor of Arran in 1543 but 'threatened by the papists' after the return of abbot (later, Archbishop) John Hamilton (*Knox*, I, 48).

21   BRANCHE, Thomas — burgess of Aberdeen; imprisoned at the instance of the earl of Huntly for hanging an image of St Francis, 1544 (Cowan, *Reformation*, 100).

22   BRIGTON, Laird of, near Forfar — may have been influenced by John Erskine of Dun; denounced with Friar John Roger in 1544 (Cowan, *Reformation*, 100).

23   BROWN, John — burgess of Edinburgh, convicted of heresy, his escheat granted to Mr James Foulis of Colinton, clerk register, 7 April 1547 (*R.S.S.*, II, 2946; *R.M.S.*, III, 1961; fled to England and still there in 1556 (*Lynch*, 277).

24   BROWN, Ninian (Ringean) — Canongate; favoured the reformed religion after the death of James V (*Knox*, I, 43).

25   BUCHANAN of Killearn — listed among the adherents of protestantism (*Lorimer*, 211); may have been the same as the brother of the laird of Arngibbon, burnt in 1539 at Edinburgh (Cowan, *Reformation*, 100).

26   BUCHANAN, Mr George — references to his identification with the protestants are numerous; studied at Paris and St Andrews; taught in France; tutor to the young earl of Cassillis (*q.v.*) and to the King's son; wrote *Franciscanus* against the Grey Friars; Cardinal is said to have tried to bribe the King to hand him over as a heretic but Buchanan escaped to France; later said to have left Paris when the Cardinal tried to seek him out there.

27   CAIRNS, Henry — skipper in Leith; set his ship to freight to Edinburgh merchants trading to France; summoned for heresy, 1534; probably recanted, gift of his escheat to his family four years later, fled into exile (*Lynch*, 277).

28   CAMERON, John — burgess of Perth; his escheat for heresy granted to John Henry, 26 May 1539 (*R.S.S.*, II, 3033).

29   CAMPBELL of Kinzeancleuch, Hugh — laird in Kyle, Ayrshire, wished to force the door of Mauchline kirk on behalf of George Wishart in 1545 (*Knox*, I, 62).

30   CANT, Robert — burgess of Edinburgh, grant to him of his own escheat after abjuring, 6 March 1539 (*R.S.S.*, II, 2915; *Lynch*, 277).

31   CARMICHAEL of Balmaddie, Peter — one of the Cardinal's assassins (*Knox*, I, 77).

32   CARMICHAEL, Richard — a singer in the chapel royal, accused of slandering the priests 'in his sleep' and compelled to 'burn his bill' (*Knox*, I, 19); his escheated goods remitted to him, 25 March 1539 (*R.S.S.*, II, 2976).

33   CASSILLIS, Gilbert, 3rd earl — educated at St Andrews, pupil of George Buchanan; taken prisoner at Solway Moss and became 'assured' to Henry VIII; offered to assassinate the Cardinal, whose French policy had aroused his 'envy' (*Sadler*, I, 191); met with the English party at Ayr, Christmas 1543 (*Knox*, I, 51); arranged with the gentlemen of Kyle and Cunninghame to meet Wishart at Edinburgh, 1545 (*Ibid.*, I, 65); resisted English aggression after Pinkie and went

to France with Queen Regent in 1550.

34   CHARTERIS, Andrew — Carthusian of Perth, went to England in 1538, then to Wittenberg, Zeeland and Italy; in touch with his brother in Dundee (*Calderwood*, I, 114).

35   CHRISTISON, William — lived in Bergen under protection of Bishop Geble Pedersen, one of the leaders of reform there; later minister of Dundee (Durkan, *Essays*, 280).

36   CLERK, William — burgess of Edinburgh; escheated c. 1539 (*Lorimer*, 218); may be same as William Clerk, clerk of the ship called the *Barge*, whose escheat was granted to Alexander Orrock of Sillebabe, 8 April 1539 (*R.S.S.*, II, 2989).

37   COCKBURN, John — according to Knox, 'a very honourable and religious gentleman, very diligent and zealous in the work of Reformation'; he married Alison Sandilands, daughter of Sir James Sandilands of Calder (*q.v.*); gift of his escheat to Alexander, master of Hume, William Scott, son and heir of Scott of Branxholm, and Andrew Kerr of Littledean, 25 October 1544 (*R.S.S.*, III, 930); sheltered Wishart who was arrested in his house in 1546 (*Knox*, I, 66).

38   COCKLAW, or Gibson, Thomas — Augustianian canon of Tullibody, in charge of the parish of Tullibody; had known Robert Logie (*q.v.*) and possibly Robert Richardson in Paris (Durkan, *Essays*, 299); others accused of heresy had attended his marriage to a widow, Margaret Jamieson; accused and condemned but escaped to England with the help of friends; escheat of his goods, 17 January 1539 (*R.S.S.*, II, 2858).

39   COUSLAND, Walter — burgess of Stirling; grant to him of his own escheat for heresy, 8 March 1539 (*R.S.S.*, II, 2923); it is probably he who is referred to in a commutation of penance, in *Formulare*, II, 427.

40   CRAIG, John — Dominican friar; imprisoned for heresy, released in 1536, went to England where he took refuge in the household of Lord Dacre; rector of the Dominican convent in Bologna but again imprisoned for heresy, condemned but escaped; in Vienna 1559; returned to Scotland in the same year to take part in the Reformation settlement; minister of the Canongate and later colleague of Knox at St Giles.

41   CRAWFORD of Leffnoris, George — laird in Kyle, Ayrshire; supported Wishart at Ayr in 1544 (*Knox*, I, 61).

42   CRICHTON of Brunston, Alexander — originally a servant of the Cardinal; later in plot to assassinate him; supported Wishart; forfeited but escaped; his forfeiture reduced at the instance of his eldest son, 1558.

43   CUNNINGHAM, Andrew — eldest son of William, master of Glencairn; summoned for heresy, escheated but recovered his goods by an act of grace of the King, 15 March 1539 (*R.S.S.*, II, 2952).

44   CUSING, Thomas — burgess of Aberdeen; imprisoned at the instance of the earl of Huntly, accused of hanging the image of St Francis, 1544 (Cowan, *Reformation*, 100).

45   DAYES, Adam — shipwright in Leith; called 'for the opinions of Martin Luther' with others before the bishop of Ross, by a commission from the archbishop of St Andrews, and 'burnt their faggots' (*Diurnal*, 18; *Knox*, I, 24).

46   DICK, Alexander — Observant Franciscan of Aberdeen; summons by the King's advocate against certain burgesses of Dundee for their failure to hand him over to the archbishop of St Andrews, although they had promised to do so if anyone accused him of heresy (Acts of the lords of council, xliii, fos 195r–v); said

to have laid aside the habit and accepted the new doctrines, moving to Dundee for safety (Cowan, *Reformation*, 100).

47 DOUGLAS of Drumlanrig, Sir James — met with the English party at Ayr at Christmas 1543; took an active part in the Reformation settlement, subscribing to the 'last band of Leith', at Edinburgh, 27 April 1560, and to the Book of Discipline (*Knox*, I, 51).

48 DOUGLAS of Longniddry, Hugh — East Lothian laird who supported George Wishart (*Knox*, I, 66); had been escheated, 25 October 1544 (*R.S.S.*, III, 930).

49 DUNCAN, John Andrew — laird of Airdrie, Fife; captured at Flodden in 1513, after which he is said to have lived for some time at Beverley, Yorkshire, with a relative of his mother's, Mr Alexander Burnet, a 'Wycliffite' (Lollard), whose daughter he is said to have married; knew Patrick Hamilton personally and is said to have taken part in his attempted rescue (*Lorimer*, 203, citing McCrie's *Melville*, based in turn on *Biographica Britannia*).

50 DUNCAN, John — burgess of Dundee; accused of heresy, abjured and bought his own escheat, 30 September 1538 (*R.S.S.*, II, 2733).

51 DUNCANSON, John — Augustinian canon; principal of St Leonard's college; said to have favoured reformed ideas after the death of Patrick Hamilton (*Lorimer*, 168); later became minister of Stirling.

52 DURIE, John — condemned for heresy 'to be shut up between two walls until he died', but was delivered by Arran (Hay Fleming, *Reformation*, 75, citing Spottiswoode, *History*, III, 83).

53 DURHAM, Michael — doctor of medicine, physician to James V; a counsellor to Arran in 1543 but 'threatened by the papists' (*Knox*, I, 48).

54 ELDER, Henry — chaplain and notary, burgh clerk of Perth for almost fifty years; probably relative of John Elder (*q.v.*); witnessed a charter to the St Andrews Dominicans as early as 1529 (B 65/22/246); said to have been banished Perth for heresy but a remission was granted to him having broken the acts of parliament anent heresy, 30 January 1544 (*R.S.S.*, III, 612); returned to Perth by November 1544 when he received a charter as chaplain of the altar of St Ninian in the parish kirk (Records of King James VI Hospital, GD 79/4/119,120); entered burgess and guildbrother in October 1559, married Barbara Chalmer (information from Dr Mary Verschuur).

55 ELDER, John — burgess of Perth, entered to the guild in 1530; married Christine Rhynd, in 1547 purchased property from the heirs of Robert Lamb (*q.v.*); bought a pardon from the Governor 30 January 1544 (*R.S.S.*, III, 612); treasurer of Perth in 1544, within a year of his alleged association with heresy (information from Dr Mary Verschuur).

56 ERROLL, William, 6th earl — said to have been commended by his tutor, Robert Alexander, in 1539, for his knowledge of the new testament (*Lorimer*, 209).

57 ERSKINE of Dun, John — laird in Angus; his career as a pre- and post-Reformation champion of protestantism is well known; as early as 1534 he was said to have been 'marvellously illuminated for the time'.

58 FLESHER, Alexander — burgess of Dundee; accused of heresy, abjured and bought his own escheat, 27 July 1538 (*R.S.S.*, II, 2648).

59 FLESHER, John — burgess of Dundee; accused of heresy, abjured and bought his own escheat, 27 July 1538 (*R.S.S.*, II, 2648).

60 FORMAN, William — Augustinian canon of Holyrood; 'careyed the name of the professioun and knawledge', c. 1543 (Cowan, *Reformation*, 103).

61   FORREST, David — General of the Mint; counsellor of Arran in 1543; supported Wishart in 1546; had 'long professed the truth and was depended on by many' (*Knox*, I, 67); a teacher in the Edinburgh privy kirk in 1558 but called a 'temporiser' by Knox, being one of those who tried to quell the riot on St Giles' Day (*Lynch*, 278).

62   FORREST, Henry — said to have been a student at St Leonard's in 1526; may have witnessed the death of Patrick Hamilton; accused of possessing the new testament in English; burnt for heresy c.1553; in minor orders (Hay Fleming, *Reformation*, 193; *Knox*, I, 21–2).

63   FORRET, Thomas — Augustinian canon of Inchcolm abbey, vicar of Dollar; son of Thomas Forret, master of the stable to James IV; educated at Cologne; served his parish of Dollar faithfully, built the 'vicar's bridge' near Dollar and taught the parishioners from the English new testament; brought before the bishop of Dunkeld but not prosecuted until the Cardinal came to power; burnt for heresy in February 1539 (*Knox*, I, 26; *Calderwood*, I, 126–7; Durkan, *Essays*, 280).

64   FORSTER, Robert — gentleman, burgess of Stirling; possibly related to the Forresters of Arngibbon who were said to have supported protestantism (*Lorimer*, 211); burnt for heresy in February 1539 (*Knox*, I, 26).

65   FORSTER, William — same family as Robert Forster, *above*; one of those prosecuted in 1539; all his goods forfeited and given to John Cowan and his wife, Janet Tennant (*R.S.S.*, II, 2975).

66   FORSYTH of Nydie, James — Fife laird; 'a man fervent and upright in religion' who, when he heard Knox preach at St Andrews, said that the 'papists had better look to themselves' (*Knox*, I, 86).

67   FRASER of Philorth, Alexander — Aberdeenshire laird; among those from Aberdeenshire pardoned in 1544 for holding heretical opinions and reading forbidden books (Cowan, *Reformation*, 100).

68   GAW, John — name occurs with that of David Beaton in the incorporations at St Andrews university in 1509; suspected of heresy and exiled to Sweden, where he published his book, *The Richt way to the kingdom of Hevine*, practically a translation of the Danish treatise of Christiern Pedersen.

69   GLENCAIRN, Alexander, 4th earl — succeeded his father, William, 3rd earl in 1548; influenced by his father's early adherence to protestantism; foremost leader of the reforming party in south-west Scotland; wrote a satirical rhyming epistle on 'The Holye Armite of Allarit' against Thomas Doughty, founder of the chapel of Our Lady of Loretto in 1553.

70   GLENCAIRN, William, 3rd earl — succeeded his father, Cuthbert, 2nd earl in 1541; supported George Wishart in Ayrshire in 1545; member of the pro-English party in the 1540s.

71   GOURLAY, Mr Norman — witnessed a charter by George, earl of Rothes, at the castle of Leslie, in 1520 (St Andrews University muniments, SS 'B', fo 84v); 'a man of reasonable erudition albeit jointed with weakness', John Knox described him; said to have married (Hay Fleming, *Reformation*, 74–5; *Pitscottie*, 1, 351); accused of heresy before the King and one of those burnt at the Greenside of Edinburgh, August 1534 (*Knox*, I, 24, *Diurnal*, 18).

72   GRAY, Patrick, 4th Lord — Knox says the Cardinal hated him because 'he used the company of such as professed godliness and bare small favour to the Cardinal'; latter tried to bribe him with grants of land; with Rothes and Balnaves at castle Huntly in July 1544, whence they were enticed to meet the Cardinal and

Governor near Dundee and go with them to Perth, where they were arrested and sent to Blackness castle; Gray was released on granting the Cardinal a bond of manrent and agreeing to live in his household (Spalding Club *Miscellany* IV, 295–6).

73   GUILLAUME, Thomas — Dominican Friar; may be same as prior of the Inverness priory in 1525 (*Exchequer* rolls, XV, 192); bore an east Lothian name, may have influenced John Knox (Durkan, *Essays*, 296, 300); preached for Arran and Angus in Edinburgh early in 1543, dismissed on the Cardinal's release; Sir James Balfour credited him with having translated the new testament into 'the vulgar tongue' (Hay Fleming, *Reformation*, 204).

74   HAMILTON of Kincavil, Sir James — sheriff of Linlithgow; brother of Mr Patrick Hamilton; delated for heresy in 1532, abjured and absolved; accused again in 1534, forfeited, but the King allowed his wife to administer his lands; contacted James V in France in 1537 who wrote to the pope on his behalf; attempts to raise sympathy for him in England largely failed and he did not return to Scotland until 1543 (Durkan, 'Scottish "Evangelicals"', 148).

75   HAMILTON, Mr Patrick — son of Sir Patrick Hamilton of Kincavil; the first Scot to be burnt for heresy, 1528; many notices of his career as academic and reformer, the most extended biography being by Peter Lorimer (1857); text of his thesis offered at Marburg university, known as 'Patrick's Places', printed in J. Knox, *History*, ed. W.C. Dickinson, 219–29).

76   HAMILTON, —, — nephew of Sir James Hamilton of Kincavil; among those summoned for heresy before the bishop of Ross in August 1534 and who 'burnt their bills' (*Diurnal*, 18).

77   HAY, James — burgess of Dundee; his escheat for heresy granted to David Wood of Craig, 27 July 1538 (*R.S.S.*, II, 2644).

78   HENDERSON, Mr Henry — graduate of St Salvator's, 1524; co-master of Edinburgh grammar school, summoned by Archbishop James Beaton for heresy, 1534, but fled to England where he died (*Knox*, I, 24; *Lynch*, 278).

79   HEWAT, James — Dominican Friar, first in Perth, where he was subprior, later in Dundee where he is said to have confirmed the Wedderburn brothers in protestantism (Durkan, *Essays*, 281 and 280n, citing *Calderwood*).

80   HOPE, Edward — Edinburgh merchant; burgess and guildbrother in 1540, a prominent member of the protestant party in the burgh in the 1560s (*Lynch*, 278); said to have favoured the reformed teaching after the death of James V (*Knox*, I, 43).

81   HUNTER, James — burgess of Perth; tried for heresy before the Cardinal and Governor, January 1544, at Perth; escheated for breaking the acts of parliament against disputing about the scriptures, dishonouring the Virgin Mary and questioning the communion of the saints in heaven; executed, his escheat granted to his widow, Christian Piper and their daughter, Violet Hunter (*R.S.S.*, III, 611); *see also, Calderwood*, I, 173–4.

82   HUTCHINSON, sir David — provost of Roslin collegiate church; escheated for heresy, 13 August 1540, his escheat granted to Oliver Sinclair (*R.S.S.*, II, 3612).

83   JAMIESON, Margaret — widow; married Thomas Cocklaw, or Gibson, (*q.v.*); escheat of Margaret Jamieson in Tullibody 'for non-fulfilling of certane penance ordained by her ordinar ... for certane crymes of heresy committit be hir ... ' granted to Thomas Murray, master of the King's ale cellar, 8 April 1539 (*R.S.S.*, II, 2987).

84 JOHNSTON, John — author of a tract entitled *Ane confortable exhortatioun of oure mooste holy Christen faith and her frutes writtin (unto the Christen bretherne in Scotlande) after the poore worde of God*, printed in Paris by Peter Congeth, 20 January 1536; described himself as 'an humble professor of holy divinitie' (Hay Fleming, *Reformation*, 178).

85 JOHNSTON, Neil — brother of Mr William Johnston, advocate, (*q.v.*); burnt for heresy in 1536 (Laing's *Knox*, I, 528).

86 JOHNSTON, Robert — accused of heresy but fled to England, c.1539, where he became a composer of music (Cowan, *Reformation*, 90).

87 JOHNSTON, Mr William — advocate; may have been a graduate of St Leonard's college, member of the faculty of advocates when founded in 1532; son of James Johnston, burgess of Edinburgh; had visited England in 1533 as part of an embassy under the bishop of Aberdeen, to whom his escheat was granted when he failed to compear before the archbishop of St Andrews on a charge of heresy in 1534 (*R.S.S.*, II, 1583); may have recanted but in April 1538 was again before the church courts and escheated for heresy; abjured in 1543 but relapsed again and escheated a third time, in 1550; this sentence revoked in 1563 (Durkan, 'Some local heretics', 72-3).

88 JOHNSTON, Mr Andrew — prebendary of St Andrew's altar in St Giles' church, Edinburgh; 'left the land for heresy' before 26 May 1535 (Durkan, 'Some local heretics', 72-3). Brother of Mr William Johnston, *above.*

89 KEILLOR, —, — Dominican Friar; the popular response to the message of a Passion Play which he had performed at Stirling before the King at Easter, 1538 is said by Knox to have contributed later to his accusation; burnt with others in February 1539 (*Knox*, I, 26); two men from Aberdeen were imprisoned for having helped him (Cowan, *Reformation*, 100).

90 KENNEDY, —, — a young man of Glasgow diocese, probably from Ayrshire, 'of excellent engine in Scottish poesy', was burnt for heresy after trial at Glasgow, 1539 (*Knox*, I, 27-8).

91 · KINNEAR of that Ilk, John — Fife laird; friend of George Wishart; Cardinal said to have laid a trap for the latter by sending him a letter purporting to have come from Kinnear (*Knox*, I, 64).

92 KIRK, sir William — chaplain in Leith; one of those who were called before the bishop of Ross 'for the opynionis of Martene Luther' and who 'burnt their bills', 26 August 1534 (*Diurnal*, 18; *Knox*, I, 24; *Lynch*, 279).

93 KIRKCALDY of Grange, Sir James — Treasurer of Scotland; clergy accused him to James V of 'always having a new testament in his pounch'; he is said to have advised the King to ignore the list of heretics drawn up by the clergy (Hay Fleming, 219, citing Sir James Melville's *Memoirs*).

94 KIRKCALDY of Grange, William, younger — son of Sir James Kirkcaldy; influenced by his father's identification with the reform party; implicated in the plot to assassinate the Cardinal; staunch protestant in the 1560s but loyal to Queen Mary for whom he held Edinburgh castle during the civil war; executed when the castle surrendered, 1573.

95 KYD, Thomas — burgess of Dundee; accused of heresy, abjured and bought his own escheat, 30 September 1538 (*R.S.S.*, II, 2733).

96 LAMB, Robert — merchant in Perth; convicted of breaking the acts of parliament anent heresy and put to death, January 1544; his escheat with that of James Hunter was granted to Christian Piper and her daughter, Violet Hunter,

although he had surviving heirs, who appear to have remained crypto-protestants and to have emerged in the 1560s to help in the establishment of the reformed church (information from Dr Mary Verschuur); escheat (*R.S.S.*, III, 611).

97   (?)LAMBERT, sir John — prebendary of Ayr in the chapel royal, Stirling; presentation of Alexander Scott to the prebend, Lambert having been degraded, possibly for heresy (*R.S.S.*, II, 2899).

98   LESLIE of Parkhill, John — second son of William, 3rd earl of Rothes; prisoner after Solway Moss, released in 1543; vowed vengeance on the Cardinal after the death of George Wishart and took part in the assassination; uncle of Norman Leslie (*q.v.*).

99   LESLIE, Norman — eldest son of George, 4th earl of Rothes; leader of the party that took over St Andrews castle after the assassination of the Cardinal, in which Leslie took part; taken prisoner to France on fall of the castle; entered the French King's service and died of his wounds after the battle of Renti, 1554.

100   LINDSAY, Alexander — friar; one of the 'secret professors' in Edinburgh of the 1530s; brother of Patrick Lindsay (*q.v.*) (*Lynch*, 279; Durkan, *Protocol Book of John Foular*, xv).

101   LINDSAY, Patrick — Edinburgh goldsmith; respite to him for assisting Angus, 8 June 1529 (*R.S.S.*, II, 147); favoured reformed ideas after the death of James V (*Knox*, I, 43).

102   LINDSAY, Sibilla — one of those who favoured reformed beliefs after the death of James V; wife of John Foular, burgess of Edinburgh (*Knox*, I, 43; *Lynch*, 279; Durkan, *Protocol Book of John Foular*, xv).

103   LOCKHART of Bar, John — laird of the Kyle district of Ayrshire; George Wishart was at his home in 1545, and he himself invited Knox to Ayrshire in 1556; accused of breaking into churches in Ayrshire between 1545 and 1548 (*Knox*, I, 61, 121; Pitcairn, *Criminal Trials*, I, 353).

104   LOGIE, Mr Gavin — principal of St Leonard's college, 1523–34; said to have secretly encouraged reformed opinions at the college after the death of Patrick Hamilton; brother of Robert Logie (*q.v.*) (*Knox*, I, 15).

105   LOGIE, Robert — Augustinian canon of Cambuskenneth; said to have taught the novices there and to have encouraged reformed ideas among them; friend of Thomas Forret (*q.v.*); Forret and Cocklaw (*q.v.*) helped Logie to escape arrest when suspected of heresy (*Calderwood*, I, 123–4); may have been at Paris with Cocklaw and Robert Richardson (*q.v.*).

106   LOVELL, George — burgess of Dundee; letters dispatched to the provosts of Perth and Dundee for search to be made for Lovell and John Blackat (*q.v.*), suspected of hanging an image of St Francis (*Lorimer*, 217).

107   LYN, John — Franciscan Friar; said to have 'left his hypocritical habit' c.1539–40 (*Knox*, I, 26); may have studied at Cologne; knew Melanchthon at Wittenberg, who later recommended him to John Fidelis, a Scot, at Frankfurt (Durkan, *Essays*, 297).

108   McALPINE, John — Dominican friar of Perth; suspected of Lutheranism in 1534, summoned to appear before a tribunal but fled to England where he remained till 1540; made doctor of theology at Wittenberg, February 1542, Luther himself presiding at the ceremony; professor of theology at Copenhagen and translated the bible into Danish (Durkan, 'Scottish "Evangelicals"', 151–2).

109   McBRAIR, John — Cistercian monk of Glenluce abbey; incorporated in St Salvator's 1531, determined in the same year; may have been at St Andrews at the

time of Patrick Hamilton's death; may also have known Robert Richardson (*q.v.*), with whom he was later associated in London; witnessed testament of William Nisbet, burgess of Ayr, who died at Pinkie in 1547; Nisbet's family had had Lollard associations; associated with John Lockhart of Bar (*q.v.*); taken from Lockhart's house and imprisoned in Hamilton castle but rescued by Lockhart; left about this time for England where he received a preaching licence from Cranmer (Durkan, 'Some local heretics', 74).

110 McCARTNAY, Donald — monk of Glenluce; accused before the inquisitor of the diocese of Glasgow, 4 February 1539, abjured and absolved (Durkan, *op.cit.*, 71–2); recantation recorded in protocol book of Cuthbert Simon (NP 1/195).

111 McDOWELL, John — Dominican friar; subprior of the Glasgow house, 1530, in which year he was incorporated into Glasgow university; prior of Wigtown, 1533–34; went to England, 1534, and later to Germany; bachelor of theology of Cologne (Durkan, 'Some local heretics', 67–71).

112 MacKAW, John — burgess of the Canongate; favoured reformed ideas after the death of James V; possibly in Arran's household (*Knox*, I, 43; *T.A.*, VIII, 100, 248; *Lynch*, 279).

113 MAIN, John — merchant in Edinburgh, one of the 'secret professors' in the 1530s (*Lynch*, 279; Durkan, *Protocol book of John Foular*, xv–xvi).

114 MARISCHAL, William, 4th earl — among those pardoned for holding heretical opinions and reading forbidden books, 1544 (Cowan, *Reformation*, 100, 109); befriended George Wishart, 1546 (*Knox*, I, 61); said to have remarked at the Reformation parliament that the hesitant attitude towards the Confession of Faith on the part of the bishops reinforced his acceptance of it (Donaldson, *All the Queen's Men*, 44).

115 MARSHALL, John — rector of the grammar school of Aberdeen; summoned before the provost and council in 1521 to answer charges of his contempt of the church; in his reply he repudiated the authority of Rome, but two years later recanted (Cowan, *Reformation*, 215).

116 MELDRUM of Fyvie, Sir George — Aberdeenshire laird; among those pardoned in 1544 for reading heretical books (Cowan, *Reformation*, 100; Donaldson, *All the Queen's Men*, 24).

117 MELVILLE (or Melvin), James — Observant Franciscan Friar; refused to compear in the court of the archbishop of St Andrews in 1526 and left Scotland; had returned by April 1527 when the pope revoked a letter he had written in Melville's favour and asked that he be imprisoned or banished until licensed to return (*L.P. Henry VIII*, IV, ii, 3019, 3020, 3021); in March 1535 James V, at the request of the Observants, begged the Pope not to restore him to the Order as he had returned from Germany infected with Lutheranism which he was attempting to spread among 'the ignorant people' (*Ibid.*, VIII, 469; Durkan, 'Scottish "Evangelicals"', 131–2).

118 MELVILLE of Raith, Sir John — member of a circle of Anglophile reformist families; Fife laird and favourite with James V; captain of Dunbar; involved in the plot to assassinate the Cardinal; executed for treason in 1548 (*Knox*, I, 106).

119 MILL, Robert — burgess of Dundee; Knox says that at an earlier stage he professed the reformed doctrine and had 'suffered for it' but was won over by the Cardinal; served writs on Wishart to inhibit him from preaching (*Knox*, I, 60).

120 MILL, Walter — parish priest of Lunan, Angus; said to have embraced the reformed faith and left his cure; eventually burnt for heresy, when over 80 years of

age, in 1558 (*Knox*, I, 153, 190).

121 MONYPENNY of Pitmilly, David — Cardinal's cousin on his mother's side; involved in the assassination plot and one of those who held St Andrews castle; taken to France where he was one of the Castilians who resisted attempts to make them attend mass (*Knox*, I, 107).

122 OCHTERLONIE, John — brother of Ochterlonie of Kelly, near Arbroath; broke into the Lady chapel of St Vigeans kirk; his escheat granted to Richard Baillie, the Cardinal's servant, 17 February 1544 (*R.S.S.*, III, 636).

123 PATERSON, Robert — burgess of Dundee; accused of heresy, abjured and bought his own escheat, 30 September 1538 (*R.S.S.*, II, 2733).

124 PIERSON, Andrew — left for England prior to 1532 when he was dwelling in Redcross Street, London; an organmaker and said to be an Anabaptist (*L.P. Henry VIII*, Add. I., i, 809).

125 PIPER, Walter — burgess of Perth; married to Violet Hog before January 1531 (*R.S.S.*, III, 1275); craftsman councillor of Perth, 1545 (Burgh records, B 59/12/2, fo 7v); and craftsman bailie in 1547 (*Ibid.*, fo 9v); father of Christian Piper whose husband, James Hunter, was hanged in January 1544 (*q.v.*); his granddaughter, Violet Hunter, was with her second husband, John Maxton, a declared supporter of the Congregation in 1560 (Court of Session records, CS7/20, fo 257); he died in December 1554 (information supplied by Dr Mary Verschuur).

126 PIPER, Walter, younger — son of John Piper; burgess and guildbrother of Perth 1550 (Guildry book, 266); member of the flesher craft; he is identified by Knox as one of those who was banished or fled from Perth in January 1544; he was also one of those who forced entry into the Black Friars' monastery at Perth in May 1543 (Milne, *Blackfriars*, 229). NB: the Piper family of Perth are also designated in legal documents as 'alias Balnaves', but no formal explanation is given for this in the records (information supplied by Dr Mary Verschuur).

127 PULLER, Laurence — burgess of Perth; said to have been banished for heresy in 1544 (*Knox*, I, 55).

128 RANKIN of Shiel, James — laird in the Kyle district of Ayrshire; converted during the preaching of Wishart at Mauchline, 1545 (*Knox*, I, 62).

129 RICHARDSON, Robert — Augustinian canon of Cambuskenneth; wrote a *Commentary on the Rule of St Augustine*; may have been at Paris with Thomas Cocklaw (*q.v.*), and Robert Logie (*q.v.*); came within the patronage of Thomas Cromwell, Henry VIII's minister, and settled in England (Durkan, 'Scottish "Evangelicals"').

130 ROGER, John — Dominican Friar; ignored a monition against his preaching in the parish church of Glamis, Angus, imprisoned in the sea tower of the castle of St Andrews where he died in suspicious circumstances, 1544; had 'fruitfully preached Christ Jesus to the comfort of many in Angus and Mearns' (*Knox*, I, 56); Aberdeen council agreed at Arran's request to give Friars John Roger and William Thomson (*q.v.*) a chamber and 3s a day for 'preching and teching the true word of God', May 1543 (*Extracts from the council register of Aberdeen*, 189).

131 ROLLOCK, James — burgess of Dundee; accused of heresy, abjured and bought his own escheat, 13 October 1538 (*R.S.S.*, II, 2742).

132 ROLLOCK, James — Dundee merchant; convicted of heresy and his escheat granted to his brother, David, 22 March 1539 (*R.S.S.*, II, 2962); went abroad and set up as a merchant in Campvere where he bought and probably imported to

Scotland books from the press of the protestant printer, John Mayler, the White Boar, Botolph's Lane, Billingsgate, London (A. Maxwell, *Dundee before the Reformation*).

133   ROLLOCK, Richard — burgess of Dundee; accused of heresy, abjured (Cowan, *Reformation*, 96).

134   RONALDSON (Ranaldson), James — Perth skinner; with his wife Helen Stirk (*q.v.*) among those put to death for heresy at Perth in January 1544; Ronaldson said to have personally provoked the Cardinal with an anti-clerical gesture (*Knox*, I, 55); his father-in-law, John Stirk, a skinner, received his escheat; Ronaldson and his wife had held land in feu from the abbey of Inchaffray on the north side of the Northgate, Perth, the property being said to be delapidated by 1551 when Ronaldson's three daughters had a rent out of it; it eventually passed into the possession of Barbara Logie, mistress of the commendator of Inchaffray, Alexander Gordon, after Ronaldson's son, Robert, had been forced to resign his interest in it to the superior in lieu of arrears of rent; the Ronaldson children become lost in the record in the 1550s although the name persisted in the burgh (information supplied by Dr Mary Verschuur). *See also,* STIRK, Helen.

135   ROUGH, John — Dominican Friar of Stirling; educated at St Leonard's college; one of Arran's preachers in 1543; when the preachers were dismissed on the Cardinal's return to power Rough went to Kyle (*Knox*, I, 42, 48); eventually he went to England where he was burnt as a protestant at Smithfield in 1557.

136   RUSSELL, Jerome — Cordelier Friar; 'a young man of meek nature, quick spirit and good letters'; apprehended in Dumfries, 1538, and condemned at Glasgow with the young man named Kennedy (*q.v.*) in 1539 (*Knox*, I, 27–8).

137   SANDILANDS of Calder, Sir James — Midlothian laird; probably sympathetic to protestantism in the 1540s; his daughter, Alison, married John Cockburn of Ormiston (*q.v.*) at whose house Wishart was apprehended in 1546; Knox preached and dispensed the Lord's Supper at Calder 1555–56 (*Knox*, I, 121).

138   SANDILANDS of Calder, John, younger — supporter of Wishart; had studied at Paris; after the arrest of Wishart at his brother-in-law's house Sandilands was imprisoned in Edinburgh castle and was released on granting a bond of manrent to the Cardinal (*Knox*, I, 71).

139   SCRYMGEOUR of Dudhope, Sir James — provost of Dundee and constable of the castle; told Prior Hepburn that he would have helped Alexander Allan (*q.v.*) to escape had he known of his plight; he accompanied to St Andrews a Dundee man accused of helping Allan to escape (*Lorimer*, 199); his sympathy with the accused need not imply any commitment on his own part to reformed ideas.

140   SCRYMGEOUR of Glaswell, Walter — granted his own escheat for heresy, 28 March 1539 (*R.S.S.*, II, 2981).

141   SETON, Alexander — Dominican Friar; son of Sir Alexander Seton of Touch and Tullibody; educated at St Salvator's; prior of the St Andrews Dominicans, 1531; the King's confessor; accused of heresy after preaching in St Andrews and Dundee; fled to England, 1537; became a chaplain to the duke of Suffolk, died 1542 (*Knox*, I, 19 *et seq*; Durkan, *Essays*, 306–7).

142   SIMPSON, sir Duncan — chaplain; burnt for heresy with others, 28 February 1539; escheat of his goods granted to James Menteith, 1 March 1539 (*R.S.S.*, II, 2903).

143   SPALDING, Walter — friend of the Spanish reformer, Enzinas; sent by

Melanchthon to Cranmer and after a period in Oxford was active in Ireland, where he died in 1551 (Durkan, *Essays*, 297).

144   SPALDING, William — frequented the house of James Watson (*q.v.*) in Innergowrie, near Dundee where he met Wishart (*Knox*, I, 64).

145   SPOTTISWOODE, John — incorporated in Glasgow university, 1534; joined the reformers in England but returned to Scotland in 1543; many notices of his career in printed sources; took part in the Reformation settlement of 1560 and became Superintendent of Lothian.

146   STEWART, John — indweller in Leith; summoned for heresy in 1534, left Scotland and died in exile, having 'burnt his bill' (*Diurnal*, 18; *Calderwood*, I, 108).

147   STEWART, John — son of Lord Methven; said to have been 'a fervant professor of the truth and made many ballads against the corruption of the times after the death of the vicar of Dollar' (Thomas Forret, *q.v.*); convicted of heresy, presumably abjured, and rehabilitated (*Lorimer*, 209; *R.S.S.*, II, 3396).

148   STEWART, Walter — son of Andrew Stewart, Lord Ochiltree; in March 1533 was summoned for breaking an image on the Observantine Friary, Ayr; his father first given his escheat, 29 December 1537 (*R.S.S.*, II, 2420); granted a second time, to Mr John Porterfield, 13 December 1538 (*R.S.S.* II, 2797).

149   STIRK, Helen — wife of James Ronaldson, executed with him for heresy at Perth, January 1544 (*q.v.*); said to have refused to call on the Virgin Mary during childbirth (*Calderwood*, I, 171–4).

150   STRATOUN of Lauriston, Andrew — laird in the Mearns; said to have read the scriptures to his kinsman David Stratoun (*q.v.*).

151   STRATOUN, David — kinsman of Andrew Stratoun of Lauriston; came to accept protestant beliefs through the influence of the laird; had a confrontation with the factors of the priory of St Andrews for non-payment of teinds; summoned to trial with Norman Gourlay and others, accused of heresy, refused to recant and was burnt at Greenside, Edinburgh, August 1534 (*Knox*, I, 24–5).

152   THOMSON, Walter — Dominican friar; appointed to preach at Aberdeen in 1543 with John Roger (*q.v.*) (Ross, *Essays*, 205).

153   VANNAND, Alexander — burgess of Dundee; accused of heresy, abjured and bought his escheat, 30 September 1538 (*R.S.S.* II, 2733).

154   WATSON, James, in Innergowrie, near Dundee, — 'a faithful brother' at whose house Wishart stayed on his way south in 1545 (*Knox*, I, 64); a James Watson was escheated as a Lutheran, 16 June 1532 (*R.S.S.* II, 1302).

155   WATSON, John — probably relative of *above*, gave Knox first-hand account of Wishart's visit to the house of James Watson (*Knox*, I, 64).

156   WEDDERBURN, David — burgess of Dundee; had in his possession the so-called 'Matthews bible', which was actally sponsored by John Roger, a colleague of John McAlpine (*q.v.*) at Wittenberg (Durkan, *Essays*, 299).

157   WEDDERBURN, James — son of a Dundee merchant; wrote a tragedy, *The beheading of John the Baptist*, and a comedy, *Dionisius the Tyrant*, in both of which 'he nipped the abuses and superstition of the time'; the plays were acted in Dundee, the first at the West Port and the second in the playfield; in 1540 he was forced to flee to Dieppe (Brother Kenneth, *Essays*, 173–4; *Calderwood*, I, 141–3).

158   WEDDERBURN, John — priest in Dundee; fled to Germany on suspicion of heretical beliefs; wrote the collection known as *The Gude and Godly Ballattis*; returned to Scotland after the death of James V and was pursued by the Cardinal's

agents and fled to England (Brother Kenneth, *Essays*, 174).

159   WIGTON, sir John — priest who was one of those tried as a result of the inquisition in Angus and Mearns in 1544; released on submitting to the Cardinal on whose instructions, it was claimed, he tried to kill Wishart (Cowan, *Reformation*, 101–2).

160   WILKIE, James — Augustinian canon of St Andrews; said to have been one of those who accepted reformed beliefs after the death of Patrick Hamilton (*Lorimer*, 168).

161   WILLOCK, John — Dominican friar of Ayr; fled from Scotland either in 1533–34 or 1538–9; preacher in London, 1541; later in Europe; returned to Scotland and took part in the Reformation settlement, 1559–60 (Durkan, 'Scottish "Evangelicals"').

162   WINRAM, Gilbert — student at St Leonard's college; joined the reformers c.1527 and went with Patrick Hamilton to Marburg where he died c. 1530; probably a relative of John Winram, *below* (*Early Scottish Libraries*, 160; Durkan, *Essays*, 282).

163   WINRAM, John — Augustinian canon of St Andrews, subprior; secretly in sympathy with reformed ideas for some time before the Reformation, but took part in heresy trials; after the Reformation became superintendent of Fife.

164   WISHART, Mr George — details of his career are well-covered in printed sources and an account of his trial is printed in *Knox*, Volume II; for recent notes, see Durkan, 'Scottish "Evangelicals"'.

ADDENDA

165   DOUGLAS, Sir George, of Pittendreich — brother of Archibald, 6th earl of Angus; evaded answering the Cardinal's question as to whether he was a 'good Christian' in spite of having lived so long in England, on his return to Scotland early in 1543, but spoke out in support of George Wishart and his teaching towards the end of 1545; died 1552 (*Scots Peerage; Knox*, I, 66).

166   MAXWELL, Robert, 5th Lord — taken prisoner at Solway Moss; supported the English alliance and reform; brought forward the bill for permitting the use of the vernacular scriptures, in the March 1543 parliament; never on good terms with the Cardinal (*Scots Peerage*; Donaldson, *All the Queen's Men*, 15–17).

167   MELVILLE of Carnbee, James — Fife laird; friend of Mr George Wishart; took part in the Cardinal's assassination, 1546 (*Knox*, I, 77).

168   TAIT, sir John — chaplain in Haddington; on 20 May 1537 one of the chaplains in Haddington collegiate church, sir Mungo Millar, was required to publicly ask Tait's forgiveness, at command of the bishop's letters, for having accused him of saying that the Virgin Mary had no more power than any other woman to do anything for man (Protocol book of A. Symson, quoted in *Transactions of the East Lothian Field Naturalists' and Antiquarian Society*, X, 57).

ANONYMOUS

1   *Ayrshire* In 1537 there were payments made for searching for 'the heretics in the westland'; probably relating to those cited to appear in the case of Walter Stewart (*q.v.*) (Cowan, *Reformation*, 92).

2   *Aberdeenshire* In 1525 it was reported that 'syndry strangearis and otheris … has bukis of that heretik Luther, and favoris his arrorys and fals opinionys' (Cowan, *Reformation*, 93).

3   Reference in 1539 to 'two menne of Abirdene' who were imprisoned for helping Friar Keillor (*q.v.*) (Cowan, *Reformation*, 93).

4   *Fife* Reference in May 1539 to an unnamed man at Cupar convicted of heresy and burnt (*Pitcairn*, I, 297).

5   *Renfrewshire* In 1539 three Paisley monks were charged with heresy and recanted, one of the novices having been involved in witnessing against them (Durkan, 'Paisley abbey in the sixteenth century', 121–2).

6   In 1532 there was said to have been 'ane greit abjuration of the favouraries of Mertene Luther', at Holyrood abbey (Cowan, *Reformation*, 96).

Appendix 4

Genealogical Tables

Note

These genealogical Tables do not contain all known members of the families concerned but only those of social, political and dynastic significance and those immediately descended from them, in order to illustrate the social network surrounding the Cardinal in his public life.

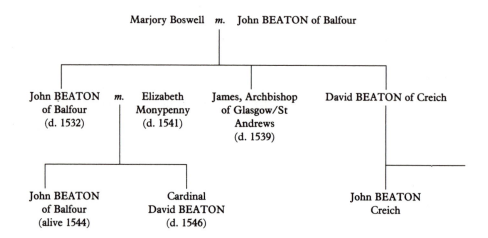

GENEALOGICAL TABLE I

The Stewarts, Hamiltons and Beatons

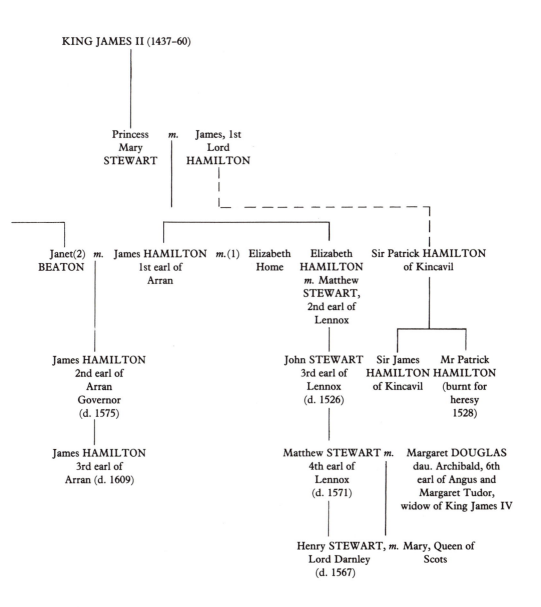

KING JAMES II (1437–60)

Princess   *m.*   James, 1st
Mary   Lord
STEWART   HAMILTON

Janet(2) *m.* James HAMILTON *m.*(1) Elizabeth   Elizabeth   Sir Patrick HAMILTON
BEATON   1st earl of   Home   HAMILTON   of Kincavil
               Arran   *m.* Matthew
                                             STEWART,
                                             2nd earl of
                                             Lennox

James HAMILTON   John STEWART   Sir James   Mr Patrick
2nd earl of   3rd earl of   HAMILTON   HAMILTON
Arran   Lennox   of Kincavil   (burnt for
Governor   (d. 1526)   heresy
(d. 1575)   1528)

James HAMILTON   Matthew STEWART *m.*   Margaret DOUGLAS
3rd earl of   4th earl of   dau. Archibald, 6th
Arran (d. 1609)   Lennox   earl of Angus and
                                     (d. 1571)   Margaret Tudor,
                                             widow of King James IV

Henry STEWART, *m.* Mary, Queen of
Lord Darnley   Scots
(d. 1567)

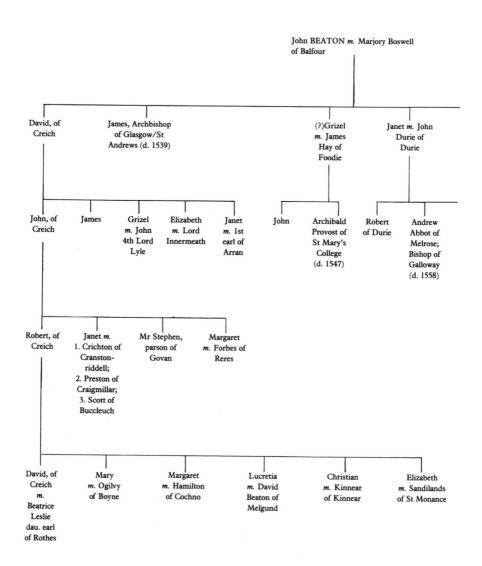

GENEALOGICAL TABLE II

The Beatons of Balfour and their connections

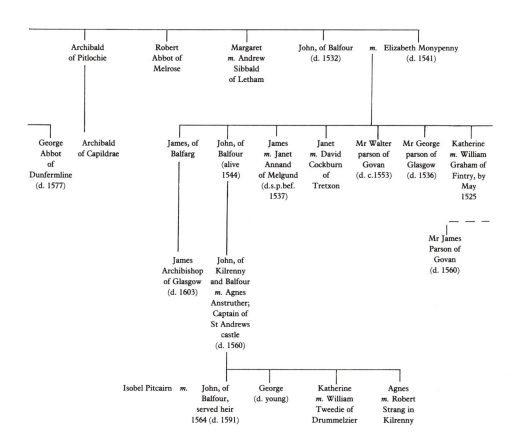

Archibald
of Pitlochie

Robert
Abbot of
Melrose

Margaret
m. Andrew
Sibbald
of Letham

John, of Balfour   *m.*   Elizabeth Monypenny
(d. 1532)   (d. 1541)

George   Archibald
Abbot   of Capildrae
of
Dunfermline
(d. 1577)

James, of
Balfarg

John, of
Balfour
(alive
1544)

James
m. Janet
Annand
of Melgund
(d.s.p.bef.
1537)

Janet
m. David
Cockburn
of
Tretxon

Mr Walter
parson of
Govan
(d. c.1553)

Mr George
parson of
Glasgow
(d. 1536)

Katherine
m. William
Graham of
Fintry, by
May
1525

James
Archibishop
of Glasgow
(d. 1603)

John, of
Kilrenny
and Balfour
m. Agnes
Anstruther;
Captain of
St Andrews
castle
(d. 1560)

Mr James
Parson of
Govan
(d. 1560)

Isobel Pitcairn   *m.*

John, of
Balfour,
served heir
1564 (d. 1591)

George
(d. young)

Katherine
m. William
Tweedie of
Drummelzier

Agnes
m. Robert
Strang in
Kilrenny

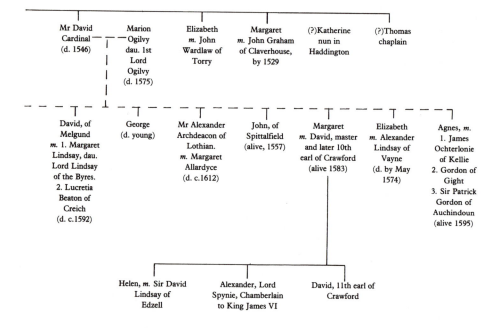

Appendix 5

Table of Events

Year	Scotland and England	Europe
1492	Renewal of Franco-Scottish alliance	
1494	?David Beaton born	Charles V of France invades Italy and enters Rome
1495	Aberdeen university founded	
1498		Savonarola burnt to death
1499	Tripartite treaty; Scotland, Denmark and France	
1502	Treaty of perpetual peace; England and Scotland, with papal approval	
1503	Marriage of James IV and Margaret Tudor	
1508	?David Beaton incorporated in St Andrews university	
1509	Accession of Henry VIII	League of Cambrai
1511	David Beaton incorporated in Glasgow university	
1512		Holy League of papacy, Aragon, Venice and England against France; Scotland under pressure to join
1513	Battle of Flodden; death of James IV, accession of James V	Death of Pope Julius II and election of Pope Leo X
1515		Accession of Francis I of France
1516		Concordat of Bologna, increased power of French crown over church appointments Erasmus publishes his Greek New Testament
1517		Treaty of Rouen, contains provision for marriage of James V and a French princess Luther's theses against indulgences
1518		Zwingli appointed people's priest at Zürich
1519	David Beaton admitted to Orléans university	Death of Emperor Maximillian, election of Charles V
1520	Fight of 'Cleanse the Causeway' in Edinburgh	Meeting of Francis I and Henry VIII at Guisnes Luther excommunicated by the Pope The reformer Lefèvre goes to diocese of Meaux to continue his programme

Year	*Scotland and England*	*Europe*
1521		Alliance of Charles V, Henry VIII and the papacy
		Luther at the Diet of Worms
		The Sorbonne condemns Luther's *Works*
1522	David Beaton on diplomatic business to England	
1524	David Beaton's first diplomatic mission to France	
	David Beaton appointed abbot of Arbroath	
1525	Anti-Lutheran legislation by the Scottish parliament	Defeat and capture of Francis I at Pavia
1526	Battle at Linlithgow; 3rd earl of Lennox killed	Francis I released
	Publication of Tyndale's New Testament	
1527	Amplification of 1525 heresy act (Scotland)	Constable of France killed at sack of Rome by Imperial army
	Beginnings of Henry VIII's divorce case in England	Reformation formally established by Swedish law
1528	Patrick Hamilton burnt for heresy	
	James V escapes from the Douglases and assumes the government	
1529		Execution of French reformer Louis de Berquin
		Peace of Cambrai; Francis I retains Burgundy but abandons claims in Italy
		Zwingli and Luther debate the Eucharist at Marburg
1530		Diet of Augsburg; definition of protestantism
1531	English clergy recognise Henry VIII as head of the church in England	
1532	Endowment of the College of Justice by James V	Alliance of France and England
1533–4	Legislation in England severs the English church from the papacy	
1534	Act of Supremacy; Henry VIII declared head of the church in England	Death of Pope Clement VII and election of Pope Paul III
		Calvin leaves France
		Affair of the Placards, in France; radical protest against the mass
		Publication of Luther's complete bible in German

Year	Scotland and England	Europe
1535	Ratification of the Scottish heresy act of 1525–7; provincial council of church Henry VIII excommunicated by the pope	First edition of Calvin's *Institutes* published
1536	Last session of the 'reformation parliament' in England Act for dissolving the lesser English monasteries The pilgrimage of Grace	
1536–7	James V in France for his marriage	
1537	David Beaton made coadjutor of the see of St Andrews David Beaton made bishop of Mirepoix; Suppression of greater English monasteries begins	
1538	Marriage of James V and Mary of Guise; David Beaton made a cardinal	Meeting of Francis I and Charles V at Aigues-Mortes
1539	David Beaton becomes archbishop of St Andrews The Six Articles drawn up in England	
1540	Trial of Sir John Borthwick for heresy, in St Andrews	
1542	Scottish defeat at Solway Moss; death of James V	Renewal of war between Charles V and Francis I
1543	Arran made Regent of Scotland Act of Scottish parliament permitting the reading of the vernacular New Testament Treaty of Greenwich, for marriage of Mary, Queen of Scots and Prince Edward of England; negotiations break down and the treaty is cancelled; renewal of Franco-Scottish Alliance	Alliance of Charles V and Henry VIII; Henry invades Picardy, Charles Champagne Copernicus publishes his work on the solar system
1544	Hertford's first invasion of Scotland David Beaton made legate *a latere*	Peace of Crépy; France loses rights over Flanders
1545	Scottish victory at Ancrum Moor Hertford's second invasion of Scotland	Opening of the Council of Trent
1546	George Wishart burnt for heresy Assassination of Cardinal Beaton	Death of Luther

Appendix 6

Glossary

Note: the following definitions apply only to the period and context of this book and are explained in such a way as to be of most use to the general reader.

Abjuration	a renunciation in the presence of witnesses of an idea or association previously held, most frequently demanded from heretics.
Admission	the bishop's approval of a presentee, that he was fit to serve in the church.
Anathema	sentence of excommunication.
Archdeacon	originally appointed to assist the bishop with clerical discipline, finance and preaching, throughout the diocese, he carried out visitations and became referred to as 'the bishop's eye'; latterly his business devolved on the rural deans (*q.v.*).
Auditor (of accounts)	originally one who literally 'heard' the accounts rendered; attested that the completed accounts were in order.
Bailie	chief executive officer of the barony or regality, often presiding over its court.
Barony	basic unit of local government in landward parts of medieval and early-modern Scotland.
Benefice	an ecclesiastical living, drawing revenue from the temporalities (i.e. lands) and teinds assigned to it.
Celibacy (clerical)	the rule of non-marriage of the clergy, first applied to the monastic orders and then extended to all secular clergy in holy orders.
Chamberlain	the chief financial officer of an estate, barony or regality.
Coadjutor	one appointed to assist a bishop, sometimes having right of succession on next vacancy.
Collation	institution in a benefice of which the ordinary (*q.v.*) himself is the patron.
Commendator	the holder of the revenues of a monastery, appointed by the Pope with lay recommendation, not the internally-elected head of the community; the term *in commendam* usually indicates that the monastery was held in addition to another prelacy (*q.v.*).
Commissary	holder of an episcopal commission for a particular purpose, e.g. commissary of the 'greater excesses'; the judicial deputy of the bishop's official (*q.v.*).
Commissioners	deputies appointed by the bishop to attend to matters which were within his personal jurisdiction, e.g. in matters relating to benefices.
Corsepresent	customary due normally paid to the vicar or his deputy on the death of a parishioner, e.g. a young animal.
Curate	one charged with the cure (i.e. care) of souls of a parish; the term is

sometimes applied to the benefice-holder (i.e. parson or vicar, *q.v.*) but frequently to the working parish priest, who may have been unbeneficed and was simply paid to deputise.

Cursing   excommunication; letters of cursing might be issued by the court of the official or commissary for offences such as debt to the church as well as for more serious offences.

Determination   the stage at which a student in the faculty of arts in a medieval university took the preliminary qualification of Bachelorship, in the course of his third year of study.

Ferme   originally, land let as a fixed rent; the rent itself; that part of the rents paid in kind, usually in grain.

Formulare   style-book.

Freeholder   proprietor.

Fruits   rents or emoluments attached to a benefice.

Incorporation   matriculation at a medieval university, which was essentially a corporation of masters or teachers.

Induction   the final stage in the appointment of a presentee to a benefice by which he was placed in legal possession of the temporalities (i.e. lands and other revenue).

Indult   a dispensation from the Pope, conferring powers or liberties in particular circumstances, e.g. to the King of Scots, in 1487, to appoint to prelacies within eight months of the vacancy's occurring, or to Cardinal Beaton to appoint to benefices otherwise reserved to the Pope.

Infeftment   legal instatement in heritable property.

Institution   act of admission of a new incumbent into a benefice or parochial cure, followed by induction to the temporalities.

Justice ayre   the supreme criminal court on circuit.

Justiciar   the chief officer in criminal matters on behalf of the crown or important landholder.

Lawborrows   a legal undertaking not to harm a person in life or property.

Lollard   may originally have meant 'mumbler of prayers'; the term was applied to the followers of John Wycliffe and continued to be associated with radical reformers long after his death.

Lords of council   members of the sovereign's council (later known as the privy council); the lords of council and session were the lords sitting in the court of session, or college of justice as it was originally called, the supreme civil court.

Lutheran   follower of the reformer, Martin Luther; the term used generally of heretics and protestants during Cardinal Beaton's lifetime, even in parliamentary legislation.

Maill   rent, commonly money rent.

Mensal   parishes whose teinds and revenues were set aside for the specific upkeep of the bishop and his household, literally, his table; the Scots rendering of the term was 'buird kirks'.

Metropolitan   archbishop, with provincial as well as diocesan powers.

Monition   command to do something or a warning to abstain from an ecclesiastical offence.

Nations   groups into which all those incorporated into a university were

	divided for voting purposes. For discussion of how this applied at St Andrews university, *see* R.G. Cant, *The University of St Andrews* (1970), 7–8.
Official	chief judicial officer of the diocese.
Orders (holy)	sacrament of the church by which men were admitted to the priesthood; major orders are those of bishop, priest, deacon and subdeacon; minor orders are those of acolyte, exorcist, lector (reader) and porter (doorkeeper).
Ordinary	ecclesiastic who has jurisdiction attached to his office – ordinary jurisdiction.
Pallium (Pall)	The circular band of white woollen material with two hanging strips bearing crosses, granted by the pope to archbishops and certain bishops, to be worn by them.
Parson	the benefice-holder with legal right to the teinds and other parochial revenues, which when appropriated were divided between parson and vicar (*q.v.*).
Pluralism (plurality)	the holding of two or more benefices by the same incumbent.
Portion	monk's share of the monastic revenue, the usual means of support of members of the convent by the sixteenth century, although they did continue to hold certain revenues in common.
Prebend	canon's or prebendary's share of the revenues of a cathedral or collegiate church.
Prelacy	commonly used to describe a major Scottish benefice, such as a bishopric or abbacy.
Primate	archbishop with authority over other archbishops and bishops.
Procurations	contributions paid by clergy of the diocese to the bishop in visitations, the equivalent of hospitality to him and his household.
Procurator	an advocate in a court of law, lay or ecclesiastical.
Procurator fiscal	the bishop's procurator charged with the collection of fines and other matters relating to the bishop's revenue, in both civil and criminal causes.
Protestant	term applied to reformers which derived from the Protestatio of the reforming members of the Diet of Speyer (1529).
Province	area of jurisdiction of an archbishop consisting of several dioceses.
Purgation	legal process by which an accused person was required to make a declaration of innocence before an ecclesiastical court, supported by the oaths of compurgators.
Provincial council	council of the church in Scotland as a province of the catholic church.
Provision	papal right to appoint to benefices; for discussion of appointments to benefices, see I.B. Cowan, 'Patronage, Provision and Reservation ... ', in *The Renaissance and Reformation in Scotland*, ed. I.B. Cowan and D. Shaw (1983).
Regality	unit of local government in which the lord enjoyed certain exemptions from royal authority.
Repledge	to recall an accused person to his lord's court from the jurisdiction of another.
Reservation	the Pope's power to reserve to his own disposal benefices which might otherwise have been in the patronage of laymen or ecclesiastical institutions.

Rural deans	also called deans of Christianity, deputies of the archdeacon in supervising the clergy of the diocese.
See	bishopric.
Suffragan(s)	assistant-bishop, often appointed to undertake the bishop's work in his absence; the bishops of those dioceses which comprised an archbishop's province.
Synod	meeting of the clergy of the diocese.
Synodals	payments to the bishop by the diocesan clergy when he held a synod.
Tabernacle	receptacle in which the pyx or vessel containing the reserved sacrament was kept until required to be taken to the sick or dying; it might be an ornate piece of church furniture.
Tack	a lease.
Teind(s)	tenth part of the produce of a parish, set aside for the support of the parish service but by the sixteenth century very often appropriated to a religious institution or major benefice.
Temporalities	land and revenue attached to a benefice.
Tocher	dowry.
Tonsure	shaving of the hair on the crown of the head, indicating monastic and clerical status.
Vassal	one who held land from a superior.
Vicar	deputy of the parson; according to the details of division of teinds at the time when these were appropriated the vicar might be a vicar-perpetual or vicar-pensioner. *See* I.B. Cowan, *Parishes of medieval Scotland* (S.R.S.), 1967.
Vicar-choral	deputy of a canon or prebendary in a cathedral. Each canon had his own vicar-choral but the vicars-choral as a body were usually assigned certain revenues.
Vicar-general	deputy of the bishop for administrative acts for which episcopal rank was not necessary; duties would end on the bishop's return.
Zwinglian	follower of Ulrich Zwingli, the Swiss reformer (1484–1531); usually referring to his emphasis on the purely commemorative and symbolic nature of the Eucharist.

Sources and bibliography

1. *Manuscript*

Acts of the lords of council (S.R.O.)

Acts of the lords of council and session (S.R.O.)

Register of acts and decreets (S.R.O.)

Register of deeds (S.R.O.)

Minute book of the high court of justiciary (S.R.O.) JC 1

Minute book of Fife sheriff court (S.R.O.) SC20

Edinburgh commissariot records (S.R.O.), register of testaments, CC 8/8; register of decreets, CC 8/2

St Andrews commissariot records (S.R.O.), register of testaments, CC 20/4

Diligence records, Forfar (S.R.O.) DI 57

State Papers (S.R.O.) SP

Exchequer records, register of abbreviates of feu charters of kirklands, (S.R.O.) E 14

Sentence book of the official of Lothian (S.R.O.) CH 5/2/1

Register of presentations to benefices (S.R.O.) CH 4

Notarial records (S.R.O.), protocol book of James Androsoun, NP 1/5a; protocol book of Edward Dickson, NP 1/5b; protocol book of Cuthbert Simon, NP 1/195; register of admission of notaries, NP 2/1

Register House charters (S.R.O.) RH 6

Court book of the regality of Glasgow (S.R.O.) RH 11/32/1/1

Protocol book of William Pettilock (S.R.O. microfilm) RH4/96

Linlithgow burgh records (S.R.O.) B 48

Abercairny muniments (S.R.O.) GD 24

Ailsa muniments (S.R.O.) GD 25

Airlie muniments (S.R.O.) GD 16

Benholm writs (S.R.O.) GD 4

Boyd papers (S.R.O.) GD 8

Burnet Stuart collection (S.R.O.) GD 115

Clerk of Penicuik muniments (S.R.O.) GD 18

Crawford priory muniments (S.R.O.) GD 20

Cunningham of Caprington muniments (S.R.O.) GD 149

Curle collection (S.R.O.) GD 111

Dalhousie muniments (S.R.O.) GD 45

Dick-Lauder papers (S.R.O.) GD 41

Eglinton muniments (S.R.O.) GD 3

Erskine of Dun muniments (S.R.O.) GD 123

Forbes muniments (S.R.O.) GD 52

Glencairn muniments (S.R.O.) GD 39

Graham of Fintry muniments (S.R.O.) GD 151

Hamilton muniments (S.R.O. Survey, under revision)

Charters of King James VI Hospital, Perth (S.R.O.) GD 79

Kinross House papers (S.R.O.) GD 29

Leven and Melville muniments (S.R.O.) GD 26
Lindsay muniments (S.R.O.) GD 203
Morton muniments (S.R.O.) GD 150
Northesk muniments (S.R.O.) GD 130
Rothes muniments (S.R.O.) GD 204
Collection of Messrs Shepherd and Wedderburn (S.R.O.) GD 242
Collection of the Society of Antiquaries of Scotland (S.R.O.) GD 103
Stair muniments (S.R.O.) GD 135
Swinton charters (S.R.O.) GD 12
Yester writs (S.R.O.) GD 28
Minute book of the Edinburgh goldsmiths (S.R.O.) GD 1/482/1
Southesk charters (Kinnaird castle)
Vatican archives (Ross Fund microfilms held in the Department of Scottish History, University of Glasgow)
St Andrews University Muniments (St Andrews University Library, Department of Manuscripts)
St Andrews charters (formerly S.R.O., B65, now in St Andrews University Library, Department of Manuscripts)
David Hay Fleming papers (Hay Fleming Reference Library, St Andrews)
Stirling burgh records (formerly S.R.O., B66, now in Central Regional Archives Department)
Crawford papers in the John Rylands Library, University of Manchester; catalogue in S.R.O.
British Library, Additional Manuscripts

2. Printed primary sources, including narrative and literary works

Acts of the parliaments of Scotland, ed. T. Thomson, vol 11 (1814)
Acts of the Lords of Council in Public Affairs, 1501–54, ed. R. K. Hannay (1932)
Accounts of the Lord High Treasurer of Scotland, vols I–VIII (1877–1908)
The Exchequer rolls of Scotland, vols XIV–XVII (1893–98)
Register of the great seal of Scotland, vols III–V (1883–88)
Register of the privy seal of Scotland, vols I–III (1908–36)
Register of the privy council of Scotland, vol I, ed. J. H. Burton (1877)
Liber Domicilii James V (Bannatyne Club), 1836
The Hamilton Papers, 2 vols (1890–2)
Letters and papers, foreign and domestic, of the reign of Henry VIII (1862–1910)
State papers of King Henry VIII (1830–52)
State papers of Sir Ralph Sadler, ed. A. Clifford, 2 vols (1809)
Scottish Correspondence of Mary of Lorraine, 1543–60, ed. A. Cameron (S.H.S.), 1927
Two Missions of Jacques de la Brosse ... 1543, ed. G. Dickinson (S.H.S.), 1942
Balcarres Papers, ed. M. Wood (S.H.S.), vol 1 (1923)
Letters of James V, ed. R. K. Hannay and D. Hay (1954)
Selections ... illustrative of the reign of Mary, Queen of Scots, ed. J. Stevenson (Maitland Club), 1837
Correspondence des Nonces en France, ed. J. Lestocquoy, 3 vols (1961)
Papiers d'état ... relatifs a l'Histoire de L'Ecosse du XVIème siècle, ed. A. Teulet (Bannatyne Club), 3 vols (1841)

Vetera Monumenta Hibernorum et Scotorum historiam illustrata, ed. A. Theiner (1864)

Foedera, ed. T. Rymer, vols XIV–XV

Liber S. Thome de Aberbrothoc, ed. C. Innes (Bannatyne Club), vol II (1855)

Rentale Sancti Andree, 1538–46, ed. R. K. Hannay (S.H.S.), 1913

The St Andrews Forumulare, ed. G. Donaldson and C. Macrae (Stair Society), vol 11 (1944)

Statutes of the Scottish Church, ed. D. Patrick (S.H.S.), 1907

Early records of the university of St Andrews, ed. J. M. Anderson (S.H.S.), 1926

Acta Facultatis Artium Universitatis Sanctiandree, ed. A. I. Dunlop (S.H.S.), 2 vols, 1964

Records of the Scottish Nation at Orleans, ed. J. Kirkpatrick, in *Miscellany 11* (S.H.S.), 1903

Registrum Episcopatus Glasguensis, ed. C. Innes (Bannatyne Club), 2 vols, (1843)

Munimenta Universitatis Glasguensis, ed. C. Innes (Maitland Club), 2 vols (1844)

St Andrews Kirk Session register, 1559–1600, ed. D. Hay Fleming (S.H.S.), 2 vols, (1889–90)

The Sheriff Court Book of Fife, 1515–22, ed. W. C. Dickinson (S.H.S.), 1928

Register of the Collegiate Church of Crail, ed. C. Rogers (Grampian Club), 1877

Registrum de Dunfermelyn, ed. C. Innes (Bannatyne Club), 1842

Rentale Dunkeldense, ed. R. K. Hannay (S.H.S.), 1915

Accounts of the Collectors of Thirds of Benefices, 1561–72, ed. G. Donaldson (S.H.S.), 1949

Registrum de Panmure, ed. J. Stuart (1874)

Calendar of Laing charters, ed. J. Anderson (1899)

Historical Manuscripts Commission, Report V (Allardyce); VIII (Glasgow); XI (Hamilton); IV (Erskine of Dun)

William Hay's Lectures on the Law of Marriage, ed. J. C. Barry (Stair Society), 1967

Ollivant, S., *The Court of the Official in Pre-Reformation Scotland* (Stair Society), 1982

Criminal Trials in Scotland from 1488 to 1624, ed. R. Pitcairn (1833)

The Booke of the Universall Kirk of Scotland (Bannatyne and Maitland Clubs), 1839–45

Protocol Book of Gavin Grote, ed. W. Angus (S.R.S.), 1914

Extracts from the burgh records of Edinburgh (S.B.R.S.), 1869–92

Extracts from the council registers of Aberdeen (Spalding Club), 1844–8

Antiquities of Aberdeen and Banff (Spalding Club), 1847–69

Records of Aboyne (New Spalding Club), 1894

Charters of the family of Burnet of Leys (New Spalding Club), 1893

Notices of the local records of Dysart (Maitland Club), 1853

Lang, A., Letters of Cardinal Beaton, 1537–41, in *S.H.R.*, vol VI; transcripts of originals in British Library Additional MSS 19401

Diurnal of Remarkable Occurrents . . . within Scotland (Bannatyne and Maitland Clubs), 1833

Knox, J., *History of the Reformation in Scotland*, ed. W. C. Dickinson, 2 vols (1949)

Buchanan, G., *Rerum Scoticarum Historia*, ed. J. Aikman (1827)

Herries, Lord, *Historical Memoirs of the reign of Mary, Queen of Scots* (Abbotsford Club), 1836

Spottiswoode, J., *History of the Church of Scotland* (Spottiswoode Society), 1851

Calderwood, D., *History of the Kirk of Scotland* (Wodrow Society), Vol 1 (1842)

Leslie, J., *De Origine, moribus et rebus gestis Scotorum* (S.T.S.), 2 vols (1888, 1895)

Keith, R., *History of Church and State in Scotland* (Spottiswoode Society), 1844

Laing, D., ed., *The Works of John Knox* (Bannatyne Club), Vol 1 (1844)

Hay, A., *Ad D. Davidem Betoun . . . Gratulatorius Panegyricus*, 1540 (N.L.S.)

Lindsay of the Mount, Sir David, *Ane Satyre of the Thrie Estaitis* (S.T.S.), 1931

Lindsay of the Mount, Sir David, *The Tragedie of the Cardinall* (S.T.S.), 1865

Lindsay of Pitscottie, R., *Historie and Cronicles of Scotland* (S.T.S.), Vol 2 (1899)
Law, T. G., ed., *The New Testament in Scots, Purvey's Revision of Wycliffe's Version turned into Scots by Murdoch Nisbet, c.1520* (S.T.S.), 1901

3. Reference works

Watt, D. E. R., *Fasti Ecclesiae Scoticanae Medii Aevi ad annum* 1638 (S.R.S.), 1969
Cowan, I. B., *The parishes of medieval Scotland* (S.R.S.), 1967
Haws, C. H., *Scottish parish clergy at the Reformation, 1540–74* (S.R.S.), 1972
Durkan, J., and Ross, A., *Early Scottish Libraries, Innes Review* (1958)
Paul, J. B., *The Scots Peerage*, 9 vols (1904–14)
Chambers, R., *Biographical Dictionary of Eminent Scotsmen*, 5 vols (1864)
Dictionary of National Biography
Report of the Royal Commission on the Ancient and Historical Monuments of Scotland, Fife, Kinross and Clackmannan (1933)

4. Secondary works

Aston, M., *Lollards and Reformers, images and literacy in late medieval religion* (1984)
Bainton, R., *Erasmus of Christendom* (1969)
Baxter, J. H., 'Dr Richard Hilliard at St Andrews', in *St Andrews Alumnus Chronicle*, XLIV
Bossy, J., *Christianity in the West, 1400–1700* (1985)
Brown, P. H., *History of Scotland*, vol II (1911)
Burns, J. H., 'New light on John Major', in *Innes Review*, V
Burns, J. H., 'The political background to the Reformation', in *Essays on the Scottish Reformation*, ed. D. McRoberts (1962); cited as *Essays* hereafter.
Burton, J. H., *History of Scotland*, Vol III (1905)
Cameron, J. K., 'Aspects of the Lutheran contribution to the Scottish Reformation', in *R.S.C.H.S.*, XXII, i; ' "Catholic Reform" in Germany and in the Pre-1560 Church in Scotland', in *R.S.C.H.S.*, xx, ii
Cant, R. G., *The University of St Andrews* (1970 edition)
Chalmers, *Caledonia* (1887–1902)
Clark, J. T., *MacFarlane's Genealogical Collections* (S.H.S.), 1899
Cowan, I. B., 'Patronage, Provision and Reservation: Pre-reformation appointments to Scottish Benefices', in *The Renaissance and Reformation in Scotland, Essays in honour of Gordon Donaldson*, ed. I. B. Cowan and D. Shaw (1983)
Cowan, I. B., *The Scottish Reformation* (1982)
Cross, C., *Church and People, 1450–1660* (1976)
Cruden, S., *St Andrews castle; official guide* (n.d.)
Dickens, A. G., *The Counter Reformation* (1968)
Dickens, A. G., *The English Reformation* (1964, 1983)
Dickens, A. G., *Reformation and Society in Sixteenth-Century Europe* (1966)
Dickinson, W. C., Donaldson, G. and Milne, I. A., *A Source Book of Scottish History*, vol II (1953)
Donaldson, G., *All the Queen's Men* (1983)
Donaldson, G., *Scotland: James V to James VII* (1965)
Donaldson, G., *The Scottish Reformation* (1960)
Dowden, J., *The Bishops of Scotland* (1912)

Dowden, J., *The Medieval Church in Scotland* (1910)

Durkan, J., 'The Cultural Background in Sixteenth-century Scotland', in *Essays* (1962)

Durkan, J., 'Education in the century of the Reformation', in *Essays* (1962)

Durkan, J., 'Paisley abbey in the sixteenth century', in *Innes Review*, XXVII

Durkan, J., 'Scottish Evangelicals in the Patronage of Thomas Cromwell', in *Records of the Scottish Church History Society*, XXI

Durkan, J., 'Some Local Heretics', in *Transactions of the Dumfries and Galloway Natural History and Antiquarian Society*, XXXVI

Easson, D. E., *Gavin Dunbar, Chancellor of Scotland, archbishop of Glasgow* (1947)

Elton, G. R., *England under the Tudors* (1955)

Elton, G. R., *Reformation Europe* (1963)

Finnie, E., 'The House of Hamilton: Patronage, Politics and the Church in the Reformation period', in *Innes Review*, XXXVI

Fittis, R. S., *Ecclesiastical Annals of Perth to the period of the Reformation* (1885)

Fleming, D. H., *The Reformation in Scotland* (1910)

Fraser, W., *The Douglas Book* (1885); contains original documents

Fraser, W., *The Melvilles Earls of Melville and the Leslies Earls of Leven* (1890); contains original documents

Fraser, W., *The Scotts of Buccleuch* (1878); contains original documents

Fraser, W., *The Stirlings of Keir* (1858); contains original documents

Fraser, W., *The Sutherland Book* (1892); contains original documents

Fraser, W., *Memorials of the family of Wemyss of Wemyss* (1888); contains original documents

Gundersheimer, W. L., ed., *French Humanism, 1470–1600* (1969)

Hale, J. R., *Renaissance Europe, 1480–1520* (1971)

Hannay, R. K., *The College of Justice* (1933)

Hannay, R. K., 'The Letters of the papal legate in Scotland, 1543', in *S.H.R.*, XI

Hay, G., *History of Arbroath* (1876)

Head, D. M., 'Henry VIII's Scottish policy, a reassessment', in *S.H.R.*, LXI

Herkless, J., *Cardinal Beaton, Priest and Politician* (1891)

Herkless, J., and Hannay, R. K., *The Archbishops of St Andrews*, vol. IV (1913)

Herkless, J., and Hannay, R. K., *The College of St Leonard* (1905); contains original documents

Huizinga, J., *Erasmus and the age of Reformation* (1957)

Inglis, J. A., *Sir Adam Otterburn* (1935)

Brother Kenneth, 'The Popular Literature of the Scottish Reformation', in *Essays* (1962)

Knecht, R. J., *Francis I and Absolute Monarchy* (1969)

Knecht, R. J., *French Renaissance Monarchy: Francis I and Henry II* (1984)

Lang, A., 'The Cardinal and the King's will', in *S.H.R.*, III

Lorimer, P., *Patrick Hamilton* (1857)

Lynch, M., *Edinburgh and the Reformation* (1981)

MacDougall, N., ed., *Church, Politics and Society, 1408–1929* (1983)

McEwen, A. R., *History of the Church in Scotland*, Vol. I (1913)

MacKay, D., 'Parish Life in Scotland, 1500–1560', in *Essays* (1962)

Mahoney, M., 'The Scottish Hierarchy, 1513–1625', in *Essays* (1962)

Marshall, R. K., *Mary of Guise* (1977)

Mattingly, G., *Renaissance diplomacy* (1955)

Merriman, M., 'The Assured Scots', in *S.H.R.*, XLVII

Ozment, S., *The Reformation in the Cities, the appeal of protestantism to Sixteenth-century*

Germany and Switzerland (1975)

Pollard, A. F., *Wolsey* (1929, 1970)

Pryde, G, S., *The Burghs of Scotland* (1965)

Rankin, W., *The parish church of the Holy Trinity of St Andrews* (1955)

Ross, A., 'Some Notes on the Religious Orders in Pre-Reformation Scotland', in *Essays* (1962)

Salmon, J. H. M., *Society in Crisis, France in the Sixteenth Century* (1975)

Sanderson, M. H. B., 'The Mauchline account books of Melrose abbey' (A.A.N.H.S.), XL

Sanderson, M. H. B., *Scottish Rural Society in the Sixteenth Century* (1982)

Sanderson, M. H. B., 'Some aspects of the church in society in the era of the Reformation', in *R.S.C.H.S.*, XVII

Scarisbrick, J. J., *The Reformation and the English People* (1984)

Sinclair, G. A., 'The Scots at Solway Moss', in *S.H.R.*, II

Taylor, M., 'The conflicting doctrines of the Scottish Reformation', in *Essays* (1962)

Todd, J., *Martin Luther* (1964)

Wiedermann, G., 'Martin Luther versus John Fisher; some ideas concerning the debate on Lutheran theology at the University of St Andrews, 1525–30', in *R.S.C.H.S.*, XXII, i

Wilson, W., *The House of Airlie*, 2 vols (1924)

Woodward, G. W. O., *The Dissolution of the Monasteries* (1966)

Wormald, J., *Court, Kirk and Community* (1981)

Wormald, J., *Lords and Men in Scotland: Bonds of Manrent, 1442–1603* (1985)

Youings, J., *Sixteenth-Century England* (1984)

Index

Note: the material in the Appendices has not been indexed.
D.B. = David Beaton